Making Majesty

The Throne Room at Dublin Castle

A Cultural History

IRISH ACADEMIC PRESS

Making Majesty

The Throne Room at Dublin Castle

A Cultural History

Edited by **Myles Campbell** & **William Derham**

Foreword by **HRH The Prince of Wales**

First published in 2017 by
Irish Academic Press
10 George's Street
Newbridge
Co. Kildare
Ireland
www.iap.ie

9781911024729 (Paper)
9781911024736 (Cloth)
9781788550079 (Kindle)
9781788550086 (Epub)
9781911024743 (PDF)

British Library Cataloguing in Publication Data
An entry can be found on request.
Library of Congress Cataloging in Publication Data
An entry can be found on request.

Front cover/jacket image: The Throne Room, Dublin Castle.
Photograph by Davison & Associates, courtesy of the Office of Public Works, Dublin Castle.

Back cover/jacket image: 'St Patrick's Day in Ireland – Trooping the Colours before the Lord Lieutenant at
Dublin Castle'. *The Graphic*, 20 April 1880. Courtesy of the National Library of Ireland.

Front flap image (PB): Gaetano Gandolfi, *Mars with his Sacred Animals, the Wolf and the Woodpecker*,
c. 1767. Photograph by Davison & Associates, courtesy of the Office of Public Works, Dublin Castle.

Back flap image: Gaetano Gandolfi, *Minerva with her Sacred Bird, the Owl, c.* 1767.
Photograph by Davison & Associates, courtesy of the Office of Public Works, Dublin Castle.

Design by edit+ www.stuartcoughlan.com
Set in Sabon 10/14

Printed and bound by Gráficas Castuera, Spain

Dublin Castle

OPW
Oifig na nOibreacha Poiblí
The Office of Public Works

Contents

One

The Presence Chamber at Dublin Castle in the Seventeenth Century

Jane Fenlon

2

Two

'Trophys and Festoons'

The Lost Presence Chamber, 1684–1788

Patricia McCarthy

22

Three

'Sketches of their Boundless Mind'

The Marquess of Buckingham and the Presence Chamber

at Dublin Castle, 1788–1838

Myles Campbell

46

One of the photographs in this fascinating book shows a banner erected in the streets of Dublin during the visit of my great-grandparents in 1897. The banner reads 'Frequent Acquaintance Promotes True Friendship'. This sentiment seems just as relevant in the context of the modern, quite different relationship between our countries and between the British Royal Family and the people of Ireland, capturing so well the spirit that could be sensed during Her Majesty The Queen's visit in 2011 and, indeed, during the recent visits which my wife and I have paid to the Irish Republic.

In this atmosphere, this scholarly book on the history of the Throne Room at Dublin Castle is particularly welcome since it describes such an important part of the common architectural heritage of Great Britain and Ireland. Just as from a previous volume, on the Chapel Royal (2015), one came to realise that when George IV's adviser Sir Charles Long advocated the doubling of the height of the keep at Windsor Castle he had already performed this trick at Dublin, so this book reveals many more connections between architects, craftsmen and patrons on both sides of the Irish Sea during the eighteenth and early nineteenth centuries. In this way its several chapters can be seen as the 'missing' chapter of a much bigger story.

The Office of Public Works is to be congratulated for its stewardship of the Throne Room and its furnishings, and for the promotion of scholarly research and re-interpretation represented by this book. I am so pleased that one of the most recent loans by Her Majesty The Queen from the Royal Collection to museums and galleries in Ireland has involved the temporary return of the Irish Sword of State, for the first time since 1922, for exhibition in the setting of the Throne Room where it has spent most of its life.

I hope very much that this book, and the continuing care and interpretation of Dublin Castle in ways which acknowledge the differences of the past as well as the common heritage of Great Britain and Ireland, will allow us even more fully to enjoy and exploit our modern friendship. I wish the book every success.

Preface

On behalf of the Chairman and Commissioners of Public Works in Ireland, the Director of National Historic Properties, and of Irish Academic Press, I am honoured to congratulate the authors and editors of *Making Majesty* on their remarkable achievement of shining considerable light on this erstwhile overlooked cultural history of Ireland's Throne Room at Dublin Castle, over a period of more than 300 years.

In this book ten writers of distinction successfully draw us in to the story of the power and potency of this unique room in Ireland and the art of using it to wield authority, for personal advancement, to foster national industry and to emphasize the changeover to national independence. The writers draw on a spectacularly rich network of previously untapped sources and the book is illustrated magnificently. The heart of the book lies in the richly intimate and nuanced portraits of the many *dramatis personae* carefully portrayed, from Wentworth and Ormond to Buckingham, Owen, Drummond, Gandolfi, Lady Aberdeen and de Valera amongst others. Attributions for the supply and manufacture of substantial elements of the fabric of the Throne Room are also revealed here for the first time.

In 2014, an in-house research unit was established at Dublin Castle led by Dr Myles Campbell and William Derham. Their tireless work on the history of Dublin Castle has already resulted in *The Chapel Royal, Dublin Castle: An Architectural History*. This new book on the Throne Room is again testament to their drive, talent, scholarship and commitment to ensure that OPW can lead in

our understanding of Dublin Castle resulting in great social benefits, for everyone from international visitors to Government, from school children to conservators. The opportunity to glean so much information from the OPW papers held at the National Archives has been of particular importance for this project. As a team, we wish to be able to stand over all of our work in the public domain and to enrich society by adding to our understanding of the past.

It is particularly welcome that in reaching our goals, our colleagues at Historic Royal Palaces, at Hillsborough Castle, have enthusiastically come on board with this cultural work and we intend to pursue future collaborative projects that will continue to strengthen ties between our two organizations. Another fortuitous outcome has been the agreement of the Royal Collection to loan the Irish Sword of State to Dublin Castle for the duration of the exhibition that launches in conjunction with this book, also entitled *Making Majesty*.

This book goes a long way to restore a loss of cultural memory. We are filled with admiration for everyone involved in putting this work on the public record.

Mary Heffernan
General Manager
Dublin Castle
National Historic Properties
Office of Public Works

Contributors and Editors

Dr Myles Campbell works in Collections, Research and Interpretation for the Office of Public Works at Dublin Castle. He received his doctorate in architectural history from Trinity College Dublin in 2014, where he served for several years on the teaching staff of the Department of History of Art and Architecture. Recent publications include contributions to volumes 2 and 3 of *Art and Architecture of Ireland* (Yale University Press, 2014) and a chapter on the country houses of his native Co. Monaghan in *Monaghan: History and Society* (Geography publications, 2017). He is a serving member of the Council of the Royal Society of Antiquaries of Ireland and is the current holder of the George B. Clarke Prize (2016–18).

William Derham works in Collections, Research and Interpretation for the Office of Public Works at Dublin Castle. He is an architectural graduate of the Dublin Institute of Technology and holds a postgraduate diploma in Applied Building Repair and Conservation from Trinity College Dublin. He is the author of *Lost Ireland: 1860–1960* (Hyde Park Editions, 2016). His primary interest is in the architectural evolution of Dublin Castle, in particular the use and evolution of the campus in the twentieth century.

Dr Jane Fenlon obtained her doctorate from Trinity College Dublin in 1993 and completed a Paul Mellon Post-Doctorate at the Yale Center for British Art in 1999. Jane has worked as an advisor and consultant to the Office of Public Works since the 1980s. Her work there has been diverse, with research projects on the Royal Hospital, Kilmainham, Kilkenny Castle, the Ormonde Picture Collection, Portumna Castle, Co. Galway, and Dublin Castle resulting in several publications. Recently she has contributed several entries to *Art and Architecture of Ireland: Painting 1600–1900* (RIA & Yale University Press, 2014) and was co-editor and contributor to *Irish Fine Art in the Early Modern Period* (Irish Academic Press, 2016). She has also contributed a chapter on early modern Irish art and architecture to volume 2 of *The New Cambridge History of Ireland* (Jane Ohlmeyer, ed., forthcoming 2017), and an essay to *The Colonial World of Richard Boyle, 1st Earl of Cork* (David Edwards & Colin Rynne, eds, forthcoming 2017).

Graham Hickey is Conservation Director at Dublin Civic Trust. He is a media and broadcasting graduate of Dublin Institute of Technology and a postgraduate, in Applied Building Repair and Conservation, of Trinity College Dublin, where his thesis focused on the reconstruction of the State Apartments at Dublin Castle in the period 1941–68. More recent study has focused on the architectural and design evolution of the state rooms in Dublin Castle during the eighteenth and nineteenth centuries. His primary interests involve the identification and regeneration of the historic urban environment with an emphasis on the mercantile street architecture of Dublin. He is a regular media writer on architectural heritage and the development of Dublin city.

Dr Sylvie Kleinman is an eighteenth-century historian and translator, and Visiting Research Fellow at the Department of History, Trinity College Dublin, where she held an Irish Research Council postdoctoral fellowship, 2007–9. From 2011 to 2014, she taught the *Ireland in the Age of O'Connell 1775–1847* module, and has also taught European history in UCD. Her research interests include nationalism, visual history, and political cartoons. Sylvie has also worked for the *Dictionary of Irish Biography* and as a Guide and Information Officer at Dublin Castle, where she researched the Red Cross Hospital, 1915–19.

Dr Patricia McCarthy is an architectural historian who has published widely on eighteenth- and early-nineteenth-century subjects in a number of books and in publications such as the *Irish Arts Review*, *Country Life* and *Irish Architectural and Decorative Studies*. She is the author of '*A favourite study': building the King's Inns*, co-author of *Farmleigh* – a history of the government guesthouse, and has contributed to two volumes of the Royal Irish Academy's *Art and Architecture of Ireland* (RIA & Yale University Press, 2014). Her latest book, *Life in the Country House in Georgian Ireland*, was published by Yale University Press in 2016.

Dr Kathryn Milligan is the inaugural ESB Fellow at the ESB Centre for the Study of Irish Art, National Gallery of Ireland. She received her doctorate from Trinity College Dublin in 2015, where her thesis examined the depiction of Dublin in visual art in the period 1850–1950. This is currently being prepared for publication. Additional research interests include art historiography, the painting of modern life, and artistic networks between Ireland and Britain in the late nineteenth and early twentieth centuries.

Ludovica Neglie was born and raised in Rome. She holds a BA in Art History from Sapienza University of Rome (2012), with a specific focus on European and American contemporary art. She obtained a master's degree in Economics and Management of the Arts and Cultural Activities from Ca' Foscari University of Venice (2014). She also holds an M.Phil in Public History and Cultural Heritage from Trinity College Dublin (2016), where her dissertation focused on the six Italian Baroque paintings in the Throne Room at Dublin Castle. She is currently working as a Tour Guide and Cathedral Assistant in St Patrick's Cathedral, Dublin.

Dr Éimear O'Connor is an art historian, curator, lecturer and arts consultant. She has published books, chapters, articles and reviews on Irish art for publications in Ireland, England, America and France, and has lectured on Irish art in cultural institutions and universities at home and abroad. The predominant concerns in her work are the complex national and international contexts pertaining to the construction of Irish visual identity in the late nineteenth and twentieth centuries. Her next book, *Art, Ireland, and Irish America 1893-1939: Culture, Connections and Controversies* is forthcoming with Irish Academic Press. O'Connor is an honarary member of the Royal Hibernian Academy.

Dr Christopher Warleigh-Lack is the Curator for Historic Royal Palaces (HRP) at Hillsborough Castle, the official residence of HM The Queen in Northern Ireland. Dr Warleigh-Lack has worked with HRP since 2009, and prior to this worked with the National Trust in England and Northern Ireland, and with Shannon Heritage and the Limerick Civic Trust in the Republic of Ireland. His interests include architectural histories and, in particular, understanding the use of historic space; this draws on his PhD thesis, awarded by the Art and Design Research Institute through Middlesex University, which explored the hidden histories of architect John Carr of York.

Editors' Acknowledgements

The seeds of this book were sown over two years ago when we commenced a programme of ongoing original research into the cultural history of the State Apartments at Dublin Castle. As one of the first fruits of that research, this book has involved the dedication of many individuals who helped bring it, and its associated exhibition, educational and conservation projects, to ripeness. Together, these elements form part of the 'Making Majesty' module of this research programme, which has focused on the Castle's Throne Room.

Our first and foremost thanks are due to our employer, the Office of Public Works (OPW), and in particular to its Chairman, Maurice Buckley, its Commissioner for Heritage, John McMahon and its Director of National Historic Properties, Rosemary Collier. They provide a vision for the preservation and interpretation of some of the nation's most important heritage sites, ensuring that places such as Dublin Castle are accessible to the widest possible public. Their support for this project demonstrates the commitment of the OPW not only to opening doors but also to opening minds.

While expressive of so many thoughts, ideas and interpretations, books can only ever articulate in a limited way the hard work of those who make them. Behind each line, image and endnote is a long and complex process of thought, archival research, reading, discussion, planning, writing and editing. At each stage in this process, we saw at first hand the exceptional amount of effort that each of our contributors invested in this project. While they are far too modest to speak of their own achievements, we would like to voice our most heartfelt thanks to each of them for all their hard work, dedication and passion. Their individual voices are what make this volume what it is.

The efforts of our contributors have been aided and complemented by the many individuals and institutions that have given so freely of their time and expertise. We would like to express our thanks and gratitude to the Royal

Collection Trust, in particular to HRH The Prince of Wales, Jonathan Marsden, Rufus Bird, Caroline de Guitaut, Sally Goodsir and Karen Lawson. We also wish to thank Caroline Clarke, Brendan Rooney, Anne Hodge, Marie McFeely and Victoria Sanchez at the National Gallery of Ireland; Mary Broderick, Berni Metcalf, Sandra McDermott and Glen Dunne at the National Library of Ireland; Gavan Woods and the Very Revd Dr William Morton at St Patrick's Cathedral; Louise Cooling, Jessica Freeman and Anna Sheppard at the Victoria and Albert Museum; David McNeff at the National Portrait Gallery in London; Lucy Porten, Ben Dale and Jenny Liddle at the National Trust; Anna McEvoy, Roger Potter, Annabel Westman and Deborah Clarke of the Hall Bequest Trust and Stowe House; Rachel McGarry, Tanya Morrison, Thomas E. Rassieur and Heidi Raatz of the Minneapolis Institute of Art; Michela Bonardi at the British Museum; Valentina Bandelloni and David Galley at Scala Archives; Morex Arai at the Huntington Library; Paul Ferguson, Paul Mulligan and Christine Casey at Trinity College Dublin; Fanchea Gibson, Patricia Wrafter and Mary Clark of Dublin City Council; Eamonn McEneaney and the staff at Waterford Treasures and Waterford City Council; Melanie Bryan at the Country Life Picture Library; Colum O'Riordan and the staff of the Irish Architectural Archive; Aaron Binchy and Marysia Wieckiewicz-Carroll at the Royal Society of Antiquaries of Ireland; Chris Rawlings at the British Library; Matthew Slack and Iain Whyte at Whyte's Auctioneers; Christine Watts at the Northern Ireland Assembly; Alexander, 7th Marquess of Aberdeen and Temair, and Marge Pocknell at Haddo House; Anna Moran of the National College of Art and Design; William Laffan; Lady Juliet Tadgell and Jackie Dale; Donatella Biagi Maino; J.B. Maguire; Marie Harpur; the National Archives of the United Kingdom; the Public Record Office of Northern Ireland; and the staff at the National Archives of Ireland, where so much of the research for this book was carried out.

For conserving and photographing several of the objects illustrated in this volume, we are grateful to Pat McBride, Ciara Brennan, Cresten Doherty, Siobhan Conyngham, Susan Mulhall, Mark Reddy, David Davison, Edwin Davison and Brian Byrne and the staff at Church Art Metals.

We are very fortunate to share our workplace with so many dedicated and supportive colleagues who, through their good cheer and hard work, have lightened our workload along the way. In particular, our thanks are due to Joanne Bannon, Fergal Martin, Nuala Canny, Hugh Bonar, Angela Cassidy, Dorothea Depner, Niamh Guihen, Jenny Papassotiriou, Cormac Molloy, Jennifer Laverty,

Dervilia Roche, and all our colleagues within National Historic Properties, as well as the great teams of guides, events staff, maintenance staff and constables at Dublin Castle.

Dublin Castle is but one of many sites in the wider OPW family. We would like to thank Jacquie Moore, Louise Kelly, Avril Percival, Davey Moor and all the staff of the OPW's Art Management division; Noel Collins and Emma Stevens at the OPW Library; Aisling Ní Bhríain, Aoife Hurley and John Cahill, architects with the OPW's Heritage Services division; Robert Guihen of the OPW's Furniture division; Dolores Gaffney at Kilkenny Castle and Jurga Rakauskaite at Farmleigh House.

We reserve a special mention for Ludovica Neglie who completed her internship with us and whose diligence, good humour and unrelenting enthusiasm for the 'Making Majesty' project filled the lives of its editors with much appreciated manuscript material and Mediterranean sunshine.

Although not actively working on this project, those around us – our families, partners and friends – have been a constant source of support and cooked food, for which we are both equally grateful. Our warmest thanks are reserved for them.

It has been a joy and a pleasure to work with the team at Irish Academic Press. Conor Graham, Fiona Dunne, Myles McCionnaith and Stuart Coughlan deserve the utmost credit for their stewardship of this publication. To our raw materials, they applied skill, precision and patience to make a book that is as majestic as its subject.

Finally, our most enduring thanks are due to Mary Heffernan, General Manager of Dublin Castle. What you will read on the following pages and experience when you visit this special place would not be possible without her vision, engagement and extraordinary work ethic.

Myles Campbell and William Derham
Dublin Castle, July 2017

Editors' Note

The chief governor of Ireland was variously styled lord lieutenant, deputy, justiciar, lord justice, lord deputy or viceroy. In the interests of clarity, the term viceroy is used predominantly throughout this volume, except with reference to the early modern period or where an alternative appears in an original quotation.

The terms Presence Chamber and Throne Room have each been used at different times over the centuries, sometimes simultaneously, to refer to the space in which the viceroy or monarch received people. They are used throughout this volume as appropriate to the period under discussion.

Irregularities and inconsistencies in spelling, grammar and punctuation, where they appear in direct quotations, have been allowed to remain in their original form.

Every effort has been made to credit the photographers and sources of all illustrations in this volume; if there are any errors or omissions please contact the Office of Public Works so that corrections can be made to any subsequent edition.

Editors' Introduction

Myles Campbell and William Derham

'The average person, dependent on his senses and unable to reason, is incapable of comprehending the majesty of the king. But through the things that meet the eye and in turn activate the other senses, he receives a clear, if imprecise, idea of this majesty, or power and authority. We see, then, that an impressive court with its ceremonies is not something superfluous, much less reprehensible.'[1]

Christian Wolff, 1721.

Majesty, a somewhat abstract and fugitive idea of power and authority, is not something that is easily made. Its physical manifestation is perhaps most readily associated with the expression of *royal* authority and, as such, it has taken many forms, from coins minted with the royal image to public displays of pageantry. As far back as 1721, Christian Wolff recognized the importance of these forms, or 'things that meet the eye', in giving tangible shape to this somewhat intangible idea. Among the forms he referred to, an 'impressive court', which served as an architectural backdrop to ceremonial and pageantry, gave it, perhaps, one of the clearest and most tangible shapes of all. Where music, costume, procession, and even coinage were, in a sense, fleeting and ephemeral, architecture was comparatively permanent and enduring. At the heart of an impressive court, the throne room, or presence chamber was, as Anna Keay has observed, 'the most important ceremonial room in the state apartments'.[2] Designed around the royal presence, furnished with a throne, canopy and regal insignia, and accommodating the choreography that reinforced the social and political hierarchy, its creation was perhaps the ultimate architectural demonstration of how majesty was made.

In Ireland, this architectural demonstration was rooted at the core of Dublin Castle, seat of the English, and later British, administration in the country for just over seven centuries, until 1922. For much of that period, the Throne Room's chief incumbent was not typically the monarch but their representative in Ireland, known variously as the justiciar, lord deputy, lord lieutenant or, more generally, the viceroy. Derided by many, most notably W.M. Thackeray, as 'a sham court' with a 'sham sovereign', the viceregal court was, at least insofar as it met the eye, a royal court nonetheless, with a throne room at its centre.[3] For Queen Victoria, who first saw Dublin Castle in 1849, it was, above all, the Throne Room and the grand approach to it that gave the Castle its majestic quality, making it 'quite like a palace'.[4] Unlike in Britain, where the royal court had several homes, each equipped with its own throne room, or in some cases, two, Ireland only ever had one – where in Britain this type of space was relatively commonplace, in Ireland it was unique. The Irish room's singularity extended beyond its form to its location, both physically and in the public consciousness. As James Loughlin has observed, where similar sites in Britain 'acted to reinforce a developing British nationality, in Ireland they represented an *assertion* of authority'.[5] This assertion was compounded by the physical location of the Dublin Castle Throne Room:

> While the great royal palaces in Britain could be seen increasingly as symbolic of the separation between the constitutionally representative and the politically functional (Westminster) in the nineteenth century, as the monarchy lost its direct political influence, this was not the case in Ireland. Dublin Castle housed both the Throne Room and offices dealing with the suppression of rebellion, agrarian crime and popular agitation.[6]

Its unique form, function and situation make the Irish Throne Room the inevitable and perhaps ultimate touchstone for examining the ways in which the viceregal court sought to shape its image in Ireland across the centuries.

Despite the assertion that the importance of Dublin Castle in historical terms 'cannot be over estimated', its most formal ceremonial space, and the significance of that space in the affairs of the Irish people, has remained relatively overlooked.[7] This is, of course, understandable. The Castle, once described by Michael Collins as 'that dread Bastille of Ireland', represented little that was reflective of the aspirations of the new Irish state after 1922.[8] It suffered from a perception that had dogged it, and its principal ceremonial chamber, even before independence, when it was viewed by many as something alien or superfluous. Nonetheless, tacit acknowledgement by the new Irish state of the Throne Room's historical and artistic importance can be gleaned from the attitude of Éamon de Valera, who, as Taoiseach, saw the value of preserving its royal emblems and symbols in the 1950s. As this book demonstrates, that importance has yet to be fully appreciated. The room is significant not only as a unique embodiment of a vanished court, but also as a testimony to the social order it sustained, supported, challenged and left behind. Though comparatively few Irish people passed through its portals, fewer still were unaffected by its wider influence. This volume of essays explores its significance in unprecedented detail, in the context of the broader political, economic, social and cultural context of Ireland across the centuries. In doing so, it attempts to take account not only of those who were defined by it, but also those who defined themselves against it.

Some measure of the room's political import can be gauged from an amusing incident that took place in the 1840s. On 24 March 1842, *The Freeman's Journal* reported on the discovery of a letter that had been 'picked up beneath the balcony of the Presence Chamber' at Dublin Castle on St Patrick's Day.[9] Addressed to the Prime Minister of the day, Sir Robert Peel, and containing a satirical verse, it targeted the viceroy, the 2nd Earl de Grey, as well as Queen Victoria:

> … She hates us, and detests our cause;
> But what of that? – the Chandos clause
> Secures our rule – keeps Her at bay,
> And makes her swallow even De G—y![10]

Satire aside, the letter had a serious purpose, linking the Throne Room and its occupants with the political imperatives of the day. In this way, the space was seen a leitmotif for the political administration, headed by the Chief Secretary for Ireland on the other side of the Upper Castle Yard; an administration it was nominally distinct from. Despite its nominal political detachment, various figures have utilized the Throne Room in a markedly political manner. This was particularly the case following the abolition of the Irish Parliament in 1800, which deprived the viceroy of a political platform in the Parliament House on College Green.

For Viscount Ebrington, viceroy in 1840, the inauguration of the Lord Mayor of Dublin in the Throne Room appears to have represented an opportunity to reflect his own staunchly Unionist politics. Through a divisive speech delivered from the throne, expressing a preference for civil war in Ireland over the repeal of the Union, he politicized the space in a way that was exceptional for the time, as Graham Hickey relates in his essay. It echoed the approach taken by an earlier viceroy, the 1st Marquess of Anglesey, whose use of the room to announce the application of a new coercion bill to Co. Kilkenny, in 1833, added weight to his words. This sweeping and controversial move effectively limited public assembly of any kind in Kilkenny after dark and was greeted with dismay in Ireland as a 'curfew law'.[11]

Conversely, the substitution of the Throne Room's traditional royal portraits with a series of six comparatively apolitical, allegorical paintings in this period may indicate the influence of a more moderate political ideology. Sanctioned by the Under-Secretary for Ireland, Thomas Drummond, their installation may, as Ludovica Neglie explores, be representative of his own, more conciliatory brand of politics. Later that century, a similar brand of politics found its expression in the mode of dress adopted by the vicereine, the Countess of Aberdeen, as explored by Éimear O'Connor. Through her support for native Irish industries and her use of traditional Celtic motifs, Lady Aberdeen incorporated visual signifiers of her support for Home Rule in Ireland into the very fabric of what she wore in the Throne Room. Her introduction of recognizably Irish nationalistic symbols into the space is unexpectedly at odds with the attitude demonstrated by Éamon de Valera, in the decades following Irish independence. In addition to expressing a private view that the Throne Room's emblems of British rule were worth preserving, he used the space in a way that suggested a greater willingness to acknowledge Ireland's royal past than might have been expected, as William Derham describes.

The nationalistic ardour that characterized the patronage of Lady Aberdeen had deeper roots than might readily be imagined. Certainly as early as 1831, the 1st Marquess of Anglesey, as viceroy, was stipulating that every item commissioned for Dublin Castle, including for the Throne Room, was to be of Irish manufacture. This contrasts with the practices of the seventeenth century, which, as Jane Fenlon records, involved the procurement of the Throne Room's furnishings from London. Both before and after the English Civil War, viceroys such as the 1st Earl of Strafford and the 1st Duke of Ormond, respectively, took delivery of large quantities of furnishings for the room. These included wall hangings, canopies and chairs of state, footstools, royal portraits and, most significantly, the Irish

Sword of State. These trappings of sovereignty were commissioned for Ireland through the Royal Wardrobe in London, to the inevitable disadvantage of the local economy. It was only in the eighteenth century that this culture of external provision and procurement began to decline. With the rise of a more artistically fluent class of Irish artisans, the viceregal court gradually began to look more to Dublin, and to Ireland in general, for the fulfilment of its material requirements. As Patricia McCarthy reveals, the quality and range of furnishings ordered for the remodelled Throne Room of 1749 is testament to the ability of the local economy to satisfy the demands of viceroys such as the 1st Earl of Harrington. Suppliers and craftsmen such as Richard Harford, Mark Forward and John Houghton, all of whom were based in Dublin, provided a wide range of fixtures, furnishings and decorative items for the room. Among their commissions were crimson window curtains trimmed with silk lace, a velvet canopy replete with the arms of King George II, embroidered in gold, and a large carved and gilt chandelier.

By the late eighteenth century, with the development of the popular press in Ireland, the viceregal court had begun to recognize the value of supporting the local economy not only out of convenience, but also for social and political gain. As Myles Campbell demonstrates, the press coverage surrounding the creation of the new Throne Room of 1788–9 was a crucial barometer of the socio-political import of such patronage. The viceroy responsible for that room's creation, the 1st Marquess of Buckingham, was only too aware of the social and political advantage to be gained from being seen to 'buy Irish'. Reports of his commissions for the room from artisans such as the glassmakers Chebsey and Co. and the painter Peter de Gree are illustrative of his concern for making the right impression. By visiting the workplaces of Irish artisans in the company of the Irish aristocracy, and thereby being seen to encourage members of the ascendancy to follow his patriotic example, he ultimately enhanced not only the reputation of the court, but also, and crucially, that of himself. Each of these acts of patronage, as expressed in the fabric and furnishing of the Throne Room, was also of real and tangible economic benefit to the ordinary people who carved out a living just beyond the Castle gates. A mark of how highly evolved this symbiotic relationship had become by the 1780s was the reversal of the trends of consumption witnessed in Ireland only a century earlier. Through Buckingham, as viceroy, orders of Irish linen and silk hangings were by now being supplied to some of the premier households of England, among them that of King George III at Windsor Castle. Imports had given way to exports.

The Throne Room could also be of considerable benefit to the status and position of those at the apex of the social order, as well as to those who aspired to reach it. Attendance at one of the drawing-rooms, levees or receptions held in the space throughout the social season, which typically lasted from early January to St Patrick's Day, 17 March, was, for many, a hallmark of social distinction. For young debutantes, in particular, the room was associated with the hugely symbolic and formative presentation ceremony that marked their entrance to and acceptance by 'society'. From a contemporary vantage point, this formal ceremony appears contrived, trivial and archaic but to those who organized it, and to the young women who experienced it, it was nonetheless a very real gateway to adulthood and social advancement. A sense of the solemnity and nervous excitement associated with this rite of passage was conveyed by Elizabeth, Countess of Fingall, in her memoir, *Seventy Years Young*:

> That waiting was agony ... Supposing one's hair collapsed? How could it stand the weight of the feathers and long tulle lappets? And how should one ever manage one's train? ... In ten minutes perhaps it would be over, and one would be still alive. (Would one be?) And one's curtsey? Could one be sure of it? Supposing one wobbled and fell at Their Excellencies' feet! Well. One could not practise it now! An A.D.C. in the doorway. A name that sounded like one's own. The Throne Room was picturesque on such an occasion. I saw it clearly later. Not then, when it swam before my frightened eyes.[12]

George Moore evoked a similar impression of the semi-sacred character of such scenes in his 1886 novel, *A Drama in Muslin*:

> The girls continued to advance, experiencing the while the nerve atrophy, the systolic emotion of communicants, who when the bell rings, approach the altar rails to receive God within their mouths. The massive, the low-hanging, the opulently twisted gold candelabra, the smooth lustre of the ... columns are evocative of the persuasive grandeur of a cathedral; and ... a vast congregation of peeresses and judges watch the ceremony in devout collectiveness.[13]

The theme of religion was not only a useful metaphor through which to evoke the gravity of a debutante's experience, but was also at the forefront of social developments that took place in the Throne Room in the late eighteenth and nineteenth centuries. As Sylvie Kleinman explores, the admission of Roman Catholics and Dissenters into the space, and the publication of a visual representation of one of these events, tested the prevailing social order of the 1790s. The reception of such 'outsiders' in the Throne Room, at such an early date, challenges the perception of the viceregal court as a somewhat closed and insular entity that served only the social needs of the Protestant elite. By the 1840s, groups that would once have been considered outsiders were slowly becoming insiders. This is perhaps best exemplified by Daniel O'Connell's attendance at a levee in the Throne Room in 1841, as the first Roman Catholic Lord Mayor of Dublin since the reign of King James II. The gradual loosening of the old social order and the rise of the Catholic middle class posed an even greater threat to the relative exclusivity of the Throne Room, and by extension to Irish social norms. It exposed the court to ever more stinging recriminations of artifice and insignificance, as a *Belfast Newsletter* report from 1865 makes clear:

> It is a mock Court to this extent, that scores of people are admitted into the Presence Chamber in Dublin Castle who would be shown to a different door if they attempted to enter the Queen's palace … People with a couple of hundred a-year, instead of embarking in trade or opening shops like many of their wealthier neighbours, aspire to be "Castle folk," and scorn the drudgeries of commerce. They eat Sunday's mutton cold on Monday, but they do it with a frigid gentility that is a caution to all beholders … When the Levee and the Drawing-room come round, a month's income is spent on millinery and hired horse-flesh. Children are reared up with notions of a character wholly unwarranted by their position or their prospects; and, instead of becoming useful members of society, degenerate into mere waiters on Providence.[14]

Towards the end of the nineteenth century, select admission to the Throne Room was gradually losing its cachet. The democratization of majesty through the dissemination of images of the space, as well as of the events staged within it and the grand processions to it, made it cheaply and widely accessible to new audiences and social classes. As Kathryn Milligan shows, the rise of illustrated reportage demystified this once hallowed space. Where once the wider population could only catch a glimpse of the monarch or viceroy processing past them as they lined the streets of Dublin, they were now guaranteed regular, intimate views of events such as Queen Victoria's levee, through the ever-expanding medium of print. This process of demystification was accelerated when the room was appropriated for use as a Red Cross Hospital ward during the First World War. It was consolidated when wounded rebel soldiers, who had aimed at overthrowing the British administration in Ireland in 1916, were later nursed in the space, possibly beneath the once quasi-sacred canopy of state, where the throne had lately stood. In tandem with the handover of Dublin Castle to the independent Irish state on 16 January 1922, the decommissioning of the Throne Room and the return of the Irish Sword of State to London signified the end of the old order. However, as Christopher Warleigh-Lack demonstrates, the Throne Room's social functions did survive, albeit in a different location on the island of Ireland. They were transferred to the new state of Northern Ireland and to a new throne room at Hillsborough Castle, Co. Down. For the rest of Ireland, majesty, once so cannily and carefully made, had been swiftly and resolutely dismantled.

Notwithstanding this book's exploration of the political, economic and social context that shaped and was shaped by the Throne Room at Dublin Castle, it is also the first comprehensive record of the space in its different locations, forms and iterations. From the Presence Chamber of the 1st Earl of Strafford with its imported London furnishings, and the light-blue Neoclassical chamber of the 1st Marquess of Buckingham, to the Union-inspired room of 1839 that remains largely intact today, it is an architectural history of a space that is unique in Ireland. Drawn together, these political, economic, social and aesthetic strands offer insight into a wider cultural history that transcends the idea of the viceregal court as a self-reflexive institution dependent on British skill and example. This book of essays locates the room not only within the traditional British sphere of influence but also within a more diverse cultural context that encompasses the immediately local and Irish, as well as the broadly European. Names associated with the room, such as Gandolfi, Callaghan and de Groot; Harford, Mytens and Maguire; and Lagraviere, Stapleton and Sims, and many more besides, speak of this confluence of European cultures. Among the other names to conjure with is that of Charles Dickens. Observing the Throne Room during one of its ritual displays in the 1860s, he offered his own contribution to the room's rich story:

> How then does a city, without trade, or manufactures, or law, look as gay and
> busy as if it were fattening on trade, and manufactures, and wealthy citizens?
> We may set all this down to the presence of a Court – a Court which has been
> called "Brummagem," "a sham," and a hundred such contemptuous names

(who does not remember Mr. Thackeray's epigram ...) ... For a "sham," and a thing we are taught is Brummagem, the materiel for a "sermony" is very complete. Peeping into this Throne-room, which is all a-blaze with gold, with a coved ceiling, which has rich amber hangings and furniture to match, and which recalls a state-room in the palace of St. Cloud, we can see a throne with a handsome canopy, and for a matter of spectacle, a very glittering pageant indeed.[15]

As Dickens's contribution suggests, the viceregal court at Dublin Castle was perhaps more than a mere pale imitation of its British counterparts, not least as a result of the social and economic life it sustained in Ireland. How much more, remains to be fully explored. Viewed in this light, the Throne Room at Dublin Castle and through it the making of majesty was, as Christian Wolff might equally have contended, 'not something superfluous, much less reprehensible'.[16]

Endnotes

1   S.J. Klingensmith, *The Utility of Splendor: Ceremony, Social Life, and Architecture at the Court of Bavaria, 1600–1800* (Chicago: University of Chicago Press, 1993), p. xvi.

2   A. Keay, *The Magnificent Monarch: Charles II and the Ceremonies of Power* (London: Continuum, 2008), p. 90.

3   W.M. Thackeray, *The Irish Sketch Book of 1842* (New York: Charles Scribner's Sons, 1911), pp. 469–70.

4   Queen Victoria with Arthur Helps (ed.), *Leaves from the Journal of our Life in the Highlands, from 1848 to 1861* (New York: Harper & Brothers, 1868), p. 238.

5   J. Loughlin, *The British Monarchy and Ireland: 1800 to the Present* (Cambridge: Cambridge University Press, 2007), p. 9.

6   Ibid., p. 11.

7   C. Casey, *Dublin: The City within the Grand and Royal Canals and the Circular Road with the Phoenix Park* (New Haven and London: Yale University Press, 2005), p. 348.

8   A. Jackson, *Buildings of Empire* (Oxford: Oxford University Press, 2013), p. 33.

9   *Freeman's Journal*, 23 March 1842.

10 Ibid.

11 *Freeman's Journal*, 8 April 1833.

12 The Countess of Fingall and T. West, *Seventy Years Young: Memories of Elizabeth, Countess of Fingall* (Dublin: The Lilliput Press, 1991), p. 62.

13 G. Moore, *A Drama in Muslin* (Buckinghamshire: Colin Smythe Limited, 2010), pp. 174–5.

14 *Belfast Newsletter*, 12 January 1865.

15 C. Dickens, 'The Castle of Dublin', *All the Year Round*, 15, 370 (26 May 1866), pp. 462–3.

16 See Klingensmith, *Utility of Splendor*, p. xvi.

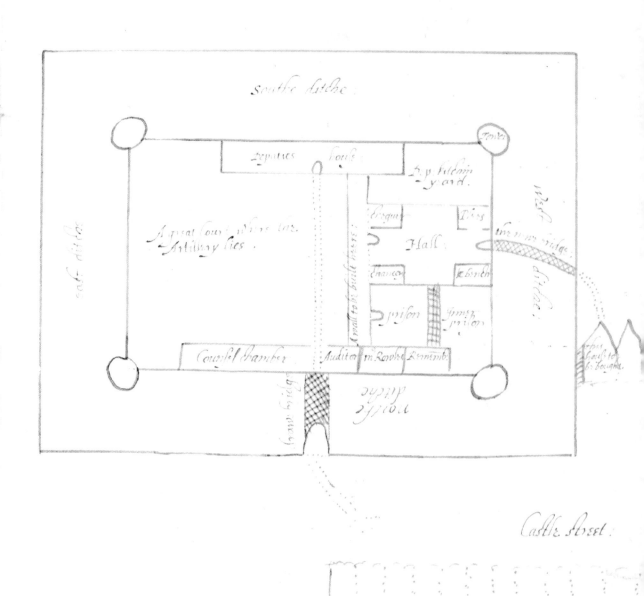

Fig. 01.01.
Thomas Watson, plan of Dublin Castle, 1606.
Courtesy of the National Library of Ireland.

One

The Presence Chamber at Dublin Castle in the Seventeenth Century

Jane Fenlon

'Ceremony though it is nothing in itself yet it doth eveyething – for what is a king more than a subject but for ceremony and order'.[1]

William Cavendish,
1st Duke of Newcastle (1593–1676) to King Charles II

The presence chamber was the principal ceremonial room in palaces and great houses during the early modern period. Fragmentary information has been gathered about the form and function of the early Presence Chamber in Dublin Castle, which was destroyed by fire in 1684. Meanwhile, an exploration of architectural and organizational changes put in place at court and within English royal palaces during this period has shown how these had impacted on several aspects of the Presence Chamber and adjoining rooms in Dublin. Documentary evidence confirms that the ceremonial usage and furnishings of the chamber usually conformed to changes introduced in the Household Regulations that were current in royal palaces.[2] Some of these regulations were ponderously slow to change, with those governing the Presence Chamber remaining the same for centuries. Probably the most fruitful source consulted on this subject has been the correspondence of Thomas Wentworth, 1st Earl of Strafford (1593–1641) who was Lord Deputy of Ireland from 1632 to 1641. In his letters, Wentworth provided information concerning the protocols, ceremonial aspects and furnishing of the early Presence Chamber in Dublin Castle. Inventories taken at Dublin Castle during the period in question have also thrown some light on the functioning of the Presence Chamber there under the regimes of the various lords deputy, mainly during the period of the Stuart monarchy.

Changes to the planning and usage of rooms within English royal palaces, especially Hampton Court and Whitehall (York Place), took place during the period of King Henry VIII's remodelling and rebuilding of those houses that had previously been occupied by Cardinal Thomas Wolsey (*c.* 1473–1530). At this time, 'the process of withdrawal and subdivision entered a new phase'.[3] From 1530 onwards the King commenced his retreat from the public rooms (outward rooms) and his more frequent use of the new Privy Chamber within the Privy Lodgings (inward rooms). This retreat to more private spaces was a change that would influence the planning of rooms within royal buildings for the next 200 years. When Dublin Castle was designated the residence of the Chief Governor of Ireland by Queen Elizabeth I, we may assume that protocols for the ceremonial use of its Presence Chamber would have been based on the English model and were put in place at that time. As well as the architectural layout of various palaces that was changed during the Henrician period, the royal household was also reorganized in a way that would ensure continuity into the later centuries. This did not mean that household organization and planning remained static, or that successive monarchs changed nothing; far from it. For instance, King Charles I introduced severely formal protocols and even further separation of public and private domains. His son King Charles II, following his restoration, proceeded to have Whitehall Palace remodelled with architectural innovations, such as the relocation of the royal bedchamber and its adaptation of French style and usage as 'the king's most intimate reception room'.[4] During his short reign, King James II made changes to the Palace of Whitehall, but according to Simon Thurley, until that time 'Wolsey's … guard chamber, presence chamber and privy chamber had a remarkable 150-year history of continuous use as the principal rooms of the palace'.[5] When King William III and Queen Mary II succeeded James II, the importance of the Presence Chamber was already in decline. As a result of two fires during their reign, the first in 1691 and a later conflagration in 1698, Whitehall Palace lost its position as the principal royal palace and administrative centre of the monarchy.[6] The disaster also freed William and Mary to establish their new palace at Hampton Court, where they launched into an extensive building campaign in the last decade of the seventeenth century.

The presence chamber, also known as the great chamber or dining chamber in the sixteenth century, or sometimes as the chamber of estate, formed part of the outward or public rooms and, as stated, was the principal ceremonial room within the palace. As an outward room within the hierarchy of royal household organization, the presence chamber came under the control of the Lord Chamberlain. At that time the outward rooms comprised the great hall, the guard or great chamber and the presence chamber.[7] The private/inward rooms encompassed the King's with-drawing room or privy chamber and bedchamber – or in the case of Dublin Castle, those of his deputy. Within royal residences, the arrangement of outward rooms provided a waiting area and a processional route that gave access to the inward (private) rooms. King Henry VIII had often dined in the presence chamber and had also used it for entertaining ambassadors, but later in his reign this practice was superseded by his preference for holding such receptions in the privy chamber. In the case of Dublin Castle, by the 1630s the presence chamber was where courtiers would assemble to partake in elaborate rituals that acknowledged the royal presence in the form of its principal feature: the cloth of state and accompanying canopied chair.

Prior to the reign of Queen Elizabeth I, those holding the post of Lord Deputy/ Lieutenant (viceroy) of Ireland had often resided in accommodation outside of Dublin Castle. Before the arrival of Sir Henry Sidney (1529–1586) who was lord deputy from 1565 to 1571 and again from 1575 to 1578, the buildings of the Castle had been described as 'ruinous, foule, filthie and greatlie decaied'.[8] Sidney had seen previous service in Ireland as vice-treasurer when he accompanied his brother-in-law, Thomas Radcliffe, 3rd Earl of Sussex (*c.* 1526/7–1583) and lord deputy, to Ireland some years earlier. At that time, Radcliffe and Sidney, with their wives and families, occupied a number of residences in Dublin in preference to the Castle. A house at Kilmainham, described as 'well suited to be the residence of the king's deputy in Ireland', was located on Kilmainham Priory lands; St Thomas Court, another house on church lands, and the Archbishop of Dublin's episcopal palace of St Sepulchre, were two other properties occupied by their party.[9] These same residences had also housed the previous lord deputy, Anthony St Leger (*c.* 1496–1559), who served from 1553 to 1556. During his two terms in office, Sidney applied himself to rebuilding and repairing several of the structures at the Castle, spending large sums of money on the work. Among the buildings named in accounts were the South Hall (the Gale), the South-East Tower (Wardrobe Tower), buttresses to the Great Hall, the Chapel and 'a Stately

Drawing Room' above it.[10] He also had a new Deputy's House built on the south side of the Castle enclosure and had the Council Chamber rebuilt in 1570.[11]

Locating the Presence Chamber in Dublin Castle in the Sixteenth Century

A presence chamber was not named in the accounts of Sidney's expenditure on the rebuilding and so we cannot with any certainty locate that chamber within the sixteenth-century Castle. No documentary evidence for the existence of such a chamber has been found, and no presence chamber was indicated on the rough plan of the Castle made by Watson in 1606 (Fig. 01.01). However, based on protocols followed in royal palaces, it seems safe to assume that one existed in Dublin Castle during the latter part of Elizabeth I's reign.[12] If so, it was probably located in the range of Sidney's buildings called the 'Deputies house', which contained the Drawing Room, on the south side of the enclosure. The

Fig. 01.02. Turlough Luineach O'Neill submits to Sir Henry Sidney. John Derrick, *The Image of Irelande, with a discoverie of Woodkarne*, 1581, pl. xii. Courtesy of the National Library of Ireland.

contemporary illustration of Sidney seated under an elaborate canopy on a chair of state receiving homage from Turlough Luineach O'Neill (*c.* 1530–1595) in an outdoor setting would seem to add weight to this assumption (Fig. 01.02).

Locating the Presence Chamber in Dublin Castle during Wentworth's Lord Deputyship (1632–1641)

The only other relevant reference to this subject prior to the 1630s has been found in a contemporary description of Sir Arthur Chichester, later 1st Baron Chichester of Belfast (1563–1625), lord deputy from 1604 to 1616, seated on a chair of estate in the Hall of Dublin Castle in 1613, during the first Stuart parliament.[13] In the 1620s Henry Carey, 1st Viscount Falkland (1575–1633) and lord deputy from 1622 to 1629, added a long gallery that crossed the Castle Yard from north to south, which would have facilitated ceremonial processions within that area and enhanced the approach to the Presence Chamber. In Sir William Brereton's 1635 account of Dublin Castle, a presence chamber was named. It formed one of a sequence of rooms leading off a hall on the south side of the Castle enclosure, where it was preceded by a dining chamber (great chamber), forming the 'outward rooms', and was followed by a with-drawing chamber that in turn adjoined the Long Gallery or 'the inward rooms'.[14]

The arrival in 1633 of Thomas Strafford, Viscount Wentworth, later 1st Earl of Strafford, first as lord deputy, elevated to lord lieutenant in 1640, ushered in a radical new regime at the Castle in Dublin (Fig. 01.03). This was a lord deputy who, 'ever conscious of his own honour and the dignity of his office, also sought from the outset to transform his own entourage in Dublin into a quasi-royal court'.[15] Without delay, he set about improving the buildings within the Castle enclosure and, perhaps more importantly, introduced major changes to ceremonial rituals and stricter protocols for courtiers and their followers attending the viceregal court. Wentworth's instructions for these changes were detailed in his correspondence and include paragraphs containing information relevant to the Presence Chamber at Dublin Castle. These instructions were based on and adapted from the Household Regulations then in use for King Charles I. In a letter written in January 1633, Wentworth stated: 'The Rooms of this House are almost become common, every ordinary Gentleman thinking it a Disparagement to stay any where but in the Drawing-Chamber, which indeed is occasioned in part, by suffering the Presence to be so familiar, that for the most Part it is filled with their Servants, whilst their Masters are within'.[16]

Wentworth also decreed that in the future: '… none but Noblemen come further than the Drawing-Chamber; the Gallery only free for those that be of the Council, and that all their Servants stay in the great Chamber, where they and all others are to be bare[headed], as well as in the Presence'.[17] These paragraphs confirm Brereton's description of the position of the Presence Chamber as located before the (With-)Drawing Chamber.

In a further set of instructions, based on those intended for the conduct of the English Privy Council and with regard to ceremonies within these rooms, Wentworth wrote that both the chancellor and treasurer of Ireland should process through the rooms with their gentlemen ushers, and that the ushers should be required to depart at the door of the Presence. The chancellor would then carry 'the purse' (containing the great seal) into the inward rooms. Wentworth's introduction of these more formal rituals in the Castle reflected the influence of the rigid etiquette of the Spanish court as witnessed by King Charles I during his visit to that country in 1623. Acknowledgement that this influence was widely recognized comes in the form of a letter that the Spanish ambassador wrote to Wentworth congratulating him on hearing that the lord deputy had '… become already like a *Spanish* Vice-Roy in what is befitting the Greatness of the Lieutenant of his Majesty, and the Honour of so eminent a Dignity …'[18]

Furnishings in Wentworth's Presence Chamber

A document issued from the Master of the Great Wardrobe and dated March 1632 provides evidence that three suites of hangings (tapestries) were to be delivered to Wentworth 'for furnishing the presence, drawing chamber and Councell chamber in the said kingdom of Ireland'.[19] Two portraits were also sent – one of King Charles I, the other of Queen Henrietta Maria – probably versions of the official state portraits by Daniel Mytens (*c.* 1590–1647/48), as they were in place by 1633. It seems likely that these were the same royal portraits seen by Walsingham Gresley, steward to John Digby, 1st Earl of Bristol (1580–1653), during the elaborate inauguration ceremony devised for Wentworth that took place in the Presence Chamber at Dublin Castle.[20] The most prominent feature in that chamber would have been the chair of state with the cloth of state (estate), set up on a dais and with a canopy over it. Gresley's description places the portraits in question on either side of the chair. The tapestries sent on the instructions of the Master of the Great Wardrobe would have been hanging on the walls. Other ceremonial objects in the chamber would have been the Sword of State and the mace.

Facing page; Fig. 01.03. Sir Anthony van Dyck, *Thomas, Viscount Wentworth, later 1st Earl of Strafford, c.* 1635–6. © The Trustees of the Rt Hon. Olive, Countess Fitzwilliam's Chattels Settlement, by permission of Lady Juliet Tadgell.

O Sydney worthy of tryple re-
nowne,
For plaguyng the traytours that
troubled the crowne. 1581.

Rituals Associated with the Presence Chamber at Wentworth's Inauguration as Lord Deputy

Fig. 01.04.
Sir Henry Sidney's
return to Dublin.
John Derrick, *The
Image of Irelande,
with a discoverie of
Woodkarne*, 1581,
pl. x. Courtesy
of the National
Library of Ireland.

Wentworth's inauguration as lord deputy broke with the earlier tradition of presenting the new incumbent with the Sword of State in St Patrick's Cathedral following his entrance to the city, as was the case with Henry Sidney (Fig. 01.04). Instead, Wentworth decided that he would receive the Sword of State in the Council Chamber of the Castle. During the ceremony, the regalia of sword and mace were processed through the streets, carried by the then lord justices Richard Boyle, 1st Earl of Cork (1566–1643) and Adam Loftus, 1st Viscount Ely (*c.* 1568–1643). Inside the Castle, the privy councillors who had assembled in the Presence Chamber, joined the lord justices as they processed on through the Gallery and made their way to the Council Chamber. Once there, the oath of office was administered and the sword was presented to the new lord deputy. The party then returned to the Presence Chamber, where Wentworth bowed before the portraits of the King and Queen. His actions have been seen as 'Wentworth cleverly harnessing the royal portraits ... to conjure up the "memory" of the monarchs back in London in both his own mind and those of the assembled spectators', a process which 'enhanced the viceroy's prestige and the mystique surrounding his office'.[21] It is also interesting to note that Wentworth's introduction of stricter regulations for access to the Presence Chamber in Dublin Castle meant that his audience was confined to the 'oligarchs of the Dublin administration' rather than the general populace.[22] As a result it was more exclusive than the same chamber in Whitehall Palace, where those who were fashionably dressed might enter at will. What was seen as Wentworth's high-handedness in his management of overall policies in Ireland did not enamour him to either the oligarchy or the populace, nor did his devotion to his King save him when the monarchical crisis occurred in 1640. His subsequent execution following the political and religious crisis of 1641 in Scotland and in Ireland would lead to a period of upheaval and changing fortunes in these islands.

The Presence Chamber in the Interregnum, 1649–1660

The dramatic circumstance of King Charles I's execution in January 1649, when his 'kingly office' was also abolished, saw Oliver Cromwell (1599–1658) appointed Lord Lieutenant of Ireland for a year in 1649/50. It seems that he did not reside in Dublin Castle. Later, as the Protectorate was drawing to a close, his son Henry Cromwell (1628–1674) was appointed Chief Governor of Ireland from 1657 to 1659 and lived in nearby Cork House. However, we should not assume that all ceremonial aspects of Dublin Castle life were abandoned during the Commonwealth period. For example, Cromwell's usage of royal palaces in England led to suites of state rooms being appointed for his accommodation and use as Lord Protector. His actions have been understood to demonstrate that 'as the Commonwealth became more established it started to need more of the apparatus of a normal European monarchical court'.[23]

The 1643 appointment of James Butler, Marquess of Ormond, later 1st Duke of Ormond (1610–1688) as lord deputy to Charles I marked the beginning of an extended and final period when Irish-born magnates would occupy the post of viceroy in Dublin Castle (Fig. 01.05). Ormond served two further terms as lord lieutenant to King Charles II, from 1662 to 1668 and again from 1677 to 1684, with his sons Thomas Butler, 6th Earl of Ossory (1634–1680) and Richard Butler, 1st Earl of Arran (1639–1686) serving as his deputies. Richard Talbot, 1st Earl (later Jacobite Duke) of Tyrconnell (1630–1691) was lord deputy to

Iames Duke of Ormond

King James II from 1687 to 1690 and, finally, Ormond's grandson, James Butler, 2nd Duke of Ormonde (1665–1745) was lord lieutenant to Queen Anne from 1703 to 1707 and again from 1710 to 1713. During that time the post was also occupied by English-born viceroys and by New English administrators usually resident in Ireland, who served as lord justices.

The Restoration Period and Ormond Viceroyalty

During the Interregnum, Charles II had been in exile in Europe, where he endeavoured to recreate royal apartments wherever he lodged, and so the Presence Chamber at Dublin Castle would not have had a royal function. With the restoration of the monarchy in 1660, Charles returned to Britain and appointed Ormond as his Lord Lieutenant of Ireland, also raising him to a dukedom. Once again the Presence Chamber would accommodate ceremonial functions within Dublin Castle, but this time on fewer occasions and in a reduced manner. To mark this return to royal authority, a warrant was issued on 7 August 1660 to the Master of the Great Wardrobe for the creation of 'three Canopyes of State with Chaires and Footstools, one for the Chamber of Presence, one for the Dyninge Roome, and one for the upper house of Parliament, two suites of hangings, one for the Chamber of Presence, and the other for the Dyninge Roome'.[24] The warrant also extended to the making of a new Irish Sword of State, which had been ordered by King Charles II, as well as 'two guilte Maces'.[25] The sword was created by George Bowers in late 1660 (or possibly early 1661) and had 'a scabbard of silver plate with ... Armes and devices and a rich hilt' (Figs 01.06 & 01.07).[26] It remained in use, as an integral part of state ceremonial in the Dublin Castle Presence Chamber, until its return to Britain in 1922. It seems that Charles II, probably due to his peripatetic experience around Europe, changed protocols for the reception of the many visitors who clamoured to see him in the early years of his reign. Instead of receptions in the Presence Chamber or any of the outward rooms at Whitehall Palace, important visitors were now being invited into the privy lodgings, and in many instances into the King's own bedchamber.[27] Following the Restoration, Charles had the Royal Bedchamber at Whitehall reconfigured in the French manner, where the bed was located behind a carved wooden rail and set within an alcove. This was to accommodate the ceremony of 'the levee' derived from the French *le lever* and *coucher*, or formal rising and retiring of the king, as favoured by King Louis XIV. Even though procedures for the reception of visitors had become in some ways less formal, state dining continued to take

Facing page:
Fig. 01.05.
Sir Peter Lely,
*James Butler, 1st
Duke of Ormond,*
1662. Courtesy of
the Office of Public
Works, Kilkenny
Castle.

Fig. 01.06. George Bowers, the Irish Sword of State, 1660–1. Royal Collection Trust/© Her Majesty Queen Elizabeth II 2017.

Fig. 01.07. George Bowers, the Irish Sword of State, 1660–1, detail. Royal Collection Trust/© Her Majesty Queen Elizabeth II 2017.

place in the Presence Chamber – or, if more splendid circumstance were required, in the Banqueting House at Whitehall. Based on these new arrangements put in place by the King in London, it is not surprising to find that in Kilkenny Castle the Ormonds had also adopted this new fashion for a grand bed alcove.[28] Later, a council chamber would be installed in the White Tower at Kilkenny Castle, probably by the 2nd Duke.

As Ireland's only duke and duchess, the Ormonds would have been obliged, on account of their newly elevated status, to have grand displays of magnificence both in their own properties and as viceroy and vicereine of the King. No documentary evidence has yet been found that describes the appearance of the ducal apartments within Dublin Castle during the period from 1662 to 1668. However, at the time of the Ormonds' later occupation in the 1670s, inventories taken there provide a record of their property within their apartments. These rooms were now located on the north side of the Upper Castle Yard enclosure, in a renovated building where the Council Chamber had been until 1656, when it was moved to Essex Quay.[29] The documents provide some information about the furnishings of the Castle during that period and in particular the fittings of the Presence Chamber. Inventories listing the sparse contents of that room were also taken during the viceroyalty of Arthur Capel, 1st Earl of Essex (1631–1683), lord lieutenant from 1672 to 1677, who preceded Ormond. The location of the Presence Chamber during both of their tenancies was in the same sequence of rooms as had existed when Wentworth was lord lieutenant and that chamber was situated on the south side of the enclosure between the Dining Room and the King's With-Drawing Room (Fig. 01.08).[30] The inventories list some rudimentary items and fittings in the Castle that were purchased for Ormond following Essex's departure, as well as descriptions of Ormond's own property. In the Presence Chamber in 1677, the items left by Essex consisted of 'Old Red Baise about the Windowes' and a 'Chymney Pèece'.[31] In the 1678 inventory of Ormond's property, the only items listed in the same room were 'Six guilt Sconces'.[32] Obviously, these were fittings in the room; however, the apparent sparseness of the space may be explained by the custom of furnishing the Presence Chamber with little more than its usual chair of estate, dais and canopy. All of those items would have been supplied by the Royal Wardrobe department and would remain the property of the Crown, and so were not mentioned in either of the previously quoted inventories. A reference to two chairs of state that were standing in the Presence Chamber during Ormond's tenure gives some measure of the lavish fabrics that went into the construction of this furniture: 56 yards of branched velvet and 525 oz. of gold and silver fringe.[33] The chairs with their 'several estates' (canopies), stools, and cushions cost a total of £427.1.10.[34]

These richly upholstered chairs were the only exceptions to the quite sparse furnishings in the Presence Chamber. In some of the other outward or more public rooms, the furnishings listed were mainly upholstered or carpeted in hardwearing Turkey-work, as in 'a large Turkie [Turkey] worke Carpet' or '21 Turkie [Turkey] worke Chaires' in the Dining Room and the King's With-Drawing Room respectively.[35] This was in sharp contrast to the magnificence of the rooms where Ormond's own furniture was in place. For instance, the opulent furnishings of the Duke's Drawing Room included a suite of the famous Lambeth tapestries known as 'The Horses', sixteen elbow chairs (with arms) of crimson velvet, silver sconces and silver andirons.[36] This room was clearly differentiated in

Fig. 01.08.
Ground plan of
Dublin Castle,
1673. Reproduced
by permission
of Staffordshire
Record Office,
D(W)1778/III/85.

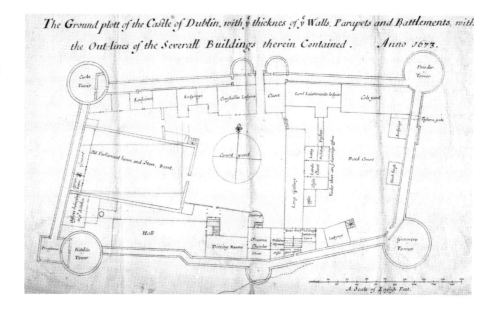

The Ground plott of the Castle of Dublin, with y thicknes of y Walls, Parapets and Battlements, with the Out-lines of the Severall Buildings therein Contained. Anno 1673.

A Scale of English Feet.

the inventories from 'The King's with Drawing Roome'.[37] Another of Ormond's magnificently furnished inward rooms was his dressing room, hung with 'new guilt leather hangings', with nine matching 'guilt Leather Chayres' and a table carpet.[38] This would strongly suggest that he had adopted the King's new custom of receiving visitors in this more personal room or in his bedchamber, which also contained several chairs.[39] Such a proliferation of chairs in these inward rooms would surely indicate that they were used for seating an audience for some form of ceremony, such as the levee as practised at the English court of Charles II.

The contrast highlighted in these accounts between the Presence Chamber and Ormond's inward rooms may explain his decision, evidence of which has recently come to light, to rebuild the Presence Chamber in 1679. In a memorandum headed 'Concerning ye building of ye Presence chamber in ye Castle of Dublin' made in August of that year, he records the circumstances of this scheme:

Eight Hundred One Pounds Two Shillings Threepence ... was by his Majesty ... granted to mee to apply to such publick uses as I should thinke fit ... to bee issued as it comes in to Mr Robinson who has also direction to supply ye same for ye rebuilding of ye Presence chamber according to a draught agreed upon wch remains in Mr Robinson's hands.[40]

The 'Mr Robinson' referred to by Ormond was Sir William Robinson (*fl. c.* 1643–1712), the Irish surveyor general.[41] The year 1679 was a particularly busy one for Robinson. On the second of two visits to London, at the end of March, he is known to have shown drawings to King Charles II.[42] The fact that a drawing of the proposed Presence Chamber at Dublin Castle is now known to have existed just a matter of months after Robinson met Charles II, suggests that it might have been among those shown to the King, who later that year granted the funds to Ormond. No detailed account of this new Presence Chamber is known to survive, but Ormond's intention to allocate substantial funds for its reconstruction suggests his desire for an improved, and perhaps more majestic, space. This work and some of the Castle apartments described above were destroyed in the great fire of 1684 that engulfed, among several other buildings, the old 'Deputies House' of Sidney's time with its later additions. Later that same year Ormond departed for England; following the death of Charles II, he was succeeded as lord lieutenant by Henry Hyde, 2nd Earl of Clarendon (1638–1709), who had been appointed by King James II and served from 1685 to 1687, with lord justices appointed briefly during the interim. In Clarendon's time, following the fire, plans were drawn up and new buildings swiftly constructed. These were situated along the south wall of the Castle, on the site of the previous apartments, and were described as 'the Great New Building on piers and arches, that runs along the south wall of the Castle ...'[43] On a number of floor plans of the Castle dating from the 1680s, the named rooms do not include a Presence Chamber (see Fig. 02.02). Later information gleaned from other documents provides an alternative naming for this room during the 1690s; this would change again during the early eighteenth century.

James II, and William and Mary

The influential Richard Talbot, Earl of Tyrconnell and commander of King James II's armies in Ireland, had quickly superseded Clarendon. When James arrived in Dublin in 1689, Tyrconnell carried the Irish Sword of State before him as he rode to Dublin Castle.[44] The dramatic events of the early 1690s that led to the defeat of James and his army at the Battle of the Boyne and the victorious King William III's arrival in Dublin must have caused many upheavals at Dublin Castle, with one king succeeding the other and lord justices and lord deputies alternating at brief intervals. Just a year after William's departure from Ireland, an inventory taken in May 1693 and bearing the title '... of the Kings Goods in the Castle of Dublin', records the arrangements and furnishings of the state rooms of the Castle during the short period when Henry Sidney, 1st Earl of Romney (1641–1704), lord deputy from 1692 to 1693, was in residence. No presence chamber was listed among the rooms; however, there were a number of rooms described as rooms of 'State'. One of these was simply referred to as the 'State roome'. This room was situated between 'The Bed Chamber of State' and 'Ye Dineing Roome' and was well furnished with 'Two pieces of fine Tapestry hangings' and also contained a canopy of state and one state chair, footstool and cushions of red serge, with cases (these were annotated in the margin as 'brought over', presumably from England).[45] The presence of the canopy of state and state chair – prerequisites for a presence chamber – would confirm that this was the function of the room, but under a new title. There was also a room designated as the 'Old Dineing roome' and it contained 'Five pieces of Fine Tapestry Hangings Landskip ... One State [canopy] & State Chayre Footstool, & [document torn and illegible]'.[46] The roguish London bookseller John Dunton visited Dublin Castle in 1698 and described seeing 'several stately rooms one of which is called the Presence Chamber and has a chair of state with a canopy over it'.[47] Presumably this is the same room as that named 'The State Room' in the 1693 inventory.

The context for the lack of a named presence chamber in Dublin at this date is intriguing; perhaps it was simply an anomaly, although the fact that it was not named in three different inventories taken at different dates is perplexing. Such a change of name does not seem to have come from royal palaces. At the rapidly growing, newly built palace for William and Mary at Hampton Court, the couple displayed the same enthusiasm as their uncle, Charles II, for French custom and design, and had their new apartments modelled along those lines. However, the demands of English court etiquette would have required that, however French-inspired their ideas might have been, they would have had to conform to regulations inherited from the court of Charles II.[48] Even though they adopted the French style of *apartement* rather than what had previously been called lodgings for their own accommodation and for entertaining, both a Presence and a Privy Chamber, so named, were installed in the new building scheme. According to Thurley, 'In the English Tradition, since the early Stuart Period, the Privy chamber had become the principal reception room in the palace'.[49]

The eighteenth century at Dublin Castle saw James Butler, 2nd Duke of Ormonde and grandson of the 1st Duke, serve his two terms in office as lord lieutenant to Queen Anne. Ormonde would divide his time between Dublin Castle and his ancestral seat at Kilkenny. Inventories were taken in Dublin Castle during his viceroyalty, the first in 1705 and others in 1707. The 1705 inventory lists rooms and descriptions of their splendid furnishings, such as the bed with crimson damask furniture fringed with gold lace.[50] Large numbers of Butler family portraits and other paintings from their various houses in Ireland and England were carefully recorded and distributed throughout the state rooms. The sequence of state rooms listed in these documents differs from that in the 1693 inventory quoted above. Again, the term 'Presence Chamber' was not recorded in the 1705 inventory, nor in 1707 when the second Duke was departing Ireland for London. It lists the contents of rooms with household furniture left by him for the use of the Queen, and 'was appraised by two upholsters for the use of her Majesty'.[51] In this 1707 inventory, a sequence of eleven rooms was recorded; some of these were described as 'State' rooms, as in: 'Two State Closets', a Dining Room and Bedchamber, an Ante Chamber, and a 'Second State Room' with 'A Drawing Room, Bedchamber, Dressing Room and Closet' also listed.[52] No canopy or chair of state was listed in any of the rooms designated 'State' in that inventory. A separate inventory of pictures belonging to Ormonde also listed various rooms, including a 'State Room', but no furnishings were described.[53] Like those of his grandfather, Ormonde's own rooms within the Castle were extravagantly furnished and it would appear that he too followed the earlier arrangement of receiving important visitors in his own rooms.[54] Barnard remarks that, 'To a bewildering extent the Ormondes regularly swopped their own props between their mansions and the castle. Furthermore, by holding court frequently at their own Kilkenny … they irretrievably confused the private and public'.[55]

Wentworth's term as Lord Deputy/Lieutenant of Ireland for King Charles I probably marked the zenith of importance and usage for the early Presence Chamber in Dublin Castle, when it was still the chosen place for the most formal of occasions. These included receptions for ambassadors and the inauguration of the lord deputy. In the following decades, its ceremonial role diminished somewhat, yet the Presence Chamber maintained its position within the hierarchy of rooms until, after being remodelled in 1749, it was eventually superseded by the new Presence Chamber installed in the Castle in the 1780s, and known as the Throne Room today.

Endnotes

1 A. Keay, *The Magnificent Monarch: Charles II and the Ceremonies of Power* (London and New York: Continuum, 2008), p. 209.

2 M. Girouard, *Life in the English Country House* (New Haven and London: Yale University Press, 1984), pp. 82–3, 319–320.

3 Ibid., p. 110.

4 S. Thurley, *Whitehall Palace: An Architectural History of the Royal Apartments, 1240–1690* (New Haven and London: Yale University Press, 1999), p. 106.

5 Ibid., p. 135.

6 S. Thurley, *Whitehall Palace: The Official Illustrated History* (London and New York: Historic Royal Palaces and Merrell Publishers, 2008), pp. 107–9.

7 S. Thurley, *Hampton Court: A Social and Architectural History* (New Haven and London: Yale University Press, 2003), pp. 52–3.

8 J. Hooker (alias Vowell), 'The Supplie of this Irish Chronicle, continued from the death of king Henrie the eight, 1546, until this present yeare 1586…', in R. Holinshed, *The First and Second Volumes of Chronicles Comprising 1 The Description and Historie of England, 2 The Description and Historie of Ireland, 3 The Description and Historie of Scotland* (London: 1586), vol. 2, p. 152.

9 K. Holland, 'The Sidney Women in Ireland, c. 1556–94', *Sidney Journal*, 29, 1–2 (2011), pp. 52–3.

10 S. Kinsella, 'Colonial Commemoration in Tudor Ireland: The case of Sir Henry Sidney', *Sidney Journal*, 29, 1–2 (2011), pp. 131–2.

11 Ibid., p. 131.

12 See Thurley, *Whitehall Palace: An Architectural History*, p. 18. However, it should be noted that the ruinous condition of the Castle meant that lord deputies were often accommodated elsewhere.

13 D. Shaw, 'Thomas Wentworth and Monarchical Ritual in Early Modern Ireland', *The Historical Journal*, 49, 2 (2006), p. 350.

14 E. Hawkins (ed.), *Travels in Holland, the United Provinces, England, Scotland and Ireland MDCXXXIV–MDCXXXV, by Sir William Brereton, Bart.* (Chetham Society, 1844), pp. 140–1.

15 R.G. Asch, 'Wentworth, Thomas, first Earl of Strafford (1593–1641)', in H.C.G. Matthew and B. Harrison (eds), *Oxford Dictionary of National Biography* (Oxford: Oxford University Press, 2004), viewable online: http://www.oxforddnb.com/view/article/29056 (accessed 13 March 2017).

16 W. Knowler, *The Earl of Strafforde's Letters and Dispatches* (London: printed by William Bowyer, 1739), vol. 1, p. 200.

17 Ibid., p. 201.

18 See Knowler, *The Earl of Strafforde's Letters*, p. 112.

19 'From William Lexlingham to the earle of Denbigh Master of the great Wardrobe for providing hangins for the Lo: Deputy of Ireland', March 1632, Records of the Exchequer, National Archives of the United Kingdom, E402/2751.

20 See Shaw, 'Thomas Wentworth and Monarchical Ritual', p. 347, also n. 49. Van Dyck did not paint the state portraits of Charles I and Henrietta Maria until 1636. The portraits that were presented to Wentworth by the King prior to his departure for Ireland, would have been painted before this date.

21 Ibid., p. 347.

22 See Shaw, 'Thomas Wentworth and Monarchical Ritual', p. 349.

23 S. Thurley, 'Revolutionary State? Royal Palaces in Cromwell's England', transcript of lecture, 11 March 2015, Museum of London, viewable online: https://www.gresham.ac.uk/lectures-and-events/revolutionary-state-royal-

palaces-in-cromwells-england (accessed 10 April 2017).

24 'The Irish Sword of State', in C. Blair (ed.), *The Crown Jewels: The History of the Coronation Regalia in the Jewel House of the Tower of London* (London: The Stationery Office, 1998), vol. 2, p. 353.

25 Ibid.

26 See 'The Irish Sword of State', p. 353.

27 See Keay, *The Magnificent Monarch*, pp. 94–5.

28 J. Fenlon, *Goods and Chattels* (Kilkenny: The Heritage Council, 2003), p. 109

29 R. Loeber, 'The Rebuilding of Dublin Castle: Thirty critical years, 1661–1690', *Studies*, 69, 273 (Spring 1980), p. 45.

30 See Fenlon, *Goods and Chattels*, pp. 100–1.

31 Ibid., p. 92

32 See Fenlon, *Goods and Chattels*, p. 100.

33 T. Barnard, 'The Viceregal Court in Later Seventeenth-Century Ireland', in E. Cruickshanks (ed.), *The Stuart Courts* (Stroud: Sutton Publishing, 2000), p. 258.

34 'An Estimate of the Charge of two several estates [i.e. canopies], chairs, stools, and cushions [for the throne-room in Dublin Castle]', MS Carte, Bodleian Library, 53, f. 134.

35 See Fenlon, *Goods and Chattels*, pp. 92–3. For a description and illustration of 'Turkeywork', see P. Thornton, *Seventeenth-Century Interior Decoration in England France & Holland* (New Haven and London: Yale University Press, 1983), pp. 109–11.

36 See Fenlon, *Goods and Chattels*, p. 101.

37 Ibid., pp. 100–1.

38 See Fenlon, *Goods and Chattels*, p. 100.

39 Ibid., p. 101.

40 Memorandum concerning the rebuilding of the Presence Chamber at Dublin Castle, August 1679, MS Carte, Bodleian Library, 38, f. 393v.

41 For Robinson see R. Loeber, *A Biographical Dictionary of Architects in Ireland 1600–1720* (London: John Murray Ltd, 1981), pp. 88–97.

42 R. Loeber, 'Sir William Robinson', *Quarterly Bulletin of the Irish Georgian Society*, 17, 1–2 (January–June 1974), p. 4.

43 E. McParland, *Public Architecture in Ireland 1680–1760* (New Haven and London: Yale University Press, 2001), p. 94.

44 J.B. Maguire, 'Dublin Castle: Three centuries of development', *Journal of the Royal Society of Antiquaries of Ireland*, 115 (1985), p. 16.

45 'An Inventory of the Kings Goods in the Castle of Dublin', May 1693, National Archives of Ireland, Wyche 2/142. I am grateful to Dr Edward McParland for sending me this information.

46 Ibid.

47 E. MacLysaght (ed.), *Teague land, or, A Merry Ramble to the Wild Irish: Letters from Ireland, 1698* (Dublin: Irish Academic Press, 1982), p. 74.

48 See Thurley, *Hampton Court*, p. 153.

49 Ibid., p. 206.

50 Inventory of Dublin Castle, 1705, National Library of Ireland, MS 2524.

51 Inventory of Dublin Castle, 1707, National Library of Ireland, MS 2521, ff. 199–209.

52 Ibid.

53 Inventory of Pictures being returned from Dublin to Kilkenny, 1707, National Library of Ireland, Ms 2521, ff. 213v.

54 Inventory of Dublin Castle, 1705, National Library of Ireland, MS 2524.

55 See Barnard, 'The Viceregal Court', p. 258.

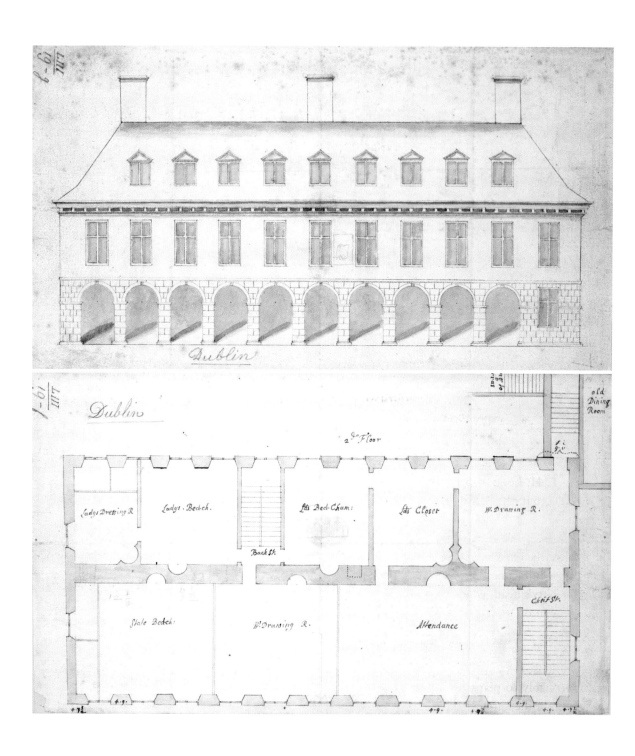

Dublin

Dublin

2d Floor

old Dining Room

Ladys Dressing R   Ladys Bedch.   Lds Bed-Cham: Lds Closet   W. Drawing R.

Back St.

State Bedch: W. Drawing R.   Attendance   Cheif St.

Two

'Trophys and Festoons'
The Lost Presence Chamber
1684–1788

Patricia McCarthy

The Presence Chamber, located in the State Apartments at Dublin Castle, was a room in which the lord lieutenant, or viceroy, in his role as representative of the sovereign, received guests. Furnished with royal regalia, it was the highest-ranking space in the Castle. The room that is the subject of this essay came into being as a result of a fire at Dublin Castle in 1684 and was destroyed by another in 1941. Long before that, however, its function had been relocated to the room next to it, the Battle Axe Hall, which is known today as the Throne Room.[1]

The fire of 1684 destroyed the south-eastern range of buildings in the Upper Castle Yard, in which an earlier presence chamber was located. That room was described in 1635 by Sir William Brereton as 'a room indeed of state', and it was noted that the dining room 'where is placed the cloth of estate over my Lord Deputy's head, when he is at meat' was located next to it.[2] This arrangement is shown on a plan of 1673 (see Fig. 01.08). There was some delay in rebuilding after the fire of 1684 but, eventually, work got underway. The surveyor general, William Molyneux (1656–1696), who held the post jointly with Sir William Robinson (fl. c. 1643–1712), executed the building between 1687 and 1688, probably to plans by Robinson.[3] Drawings from the British Library, prepared within the surveyor general's office in the 1680s show an eleven-bay, arcaded,

Facing page, from top: Fig. 02.01. Elevation of the old State Apartments, Dublin Castle, c. 1680. © The British Library Board, Maps K.Top.53.19.g.

Fig. 02.02. Plan of the first floor of the old State Apartments, Dublin Castle, c. 1680. © The British Library Board, Maps K.Top.53.19.f.

two-storey range with dormer windows and, on the first floor, a four-bay room at the front annotated 'Attendance' – another name for the Presence Chamber (Figs 02.01 & 02.02).[4] Next to it was the Withdrawing Room and, beyond that, the State Bedchamber with two closets. The main staircase in this block adjoined the Presence or Attendance Chamber. No description of the room after this rebuilding has come to light but John Dunton, a visitor to the Castle in 1696, remarked upon 'the several stately rooms one of which is called the Presence chamber and has a chair of state with a canopy over it'.[5] The only information regarding its contents at this time comes from an inventory taken in 1693 by Sir Cyril Wyche, chief secretary to the departing viceroy, Henry Sidney, Viscount Sidney (1641–1704) who served from 1692 to 1693. The inventory included 'Two pieces of fine Tapestry hangings', 'One Canopy of State', 'One State Chayre, footstool, Cushions of red sarge [serge], with Cases' and 'one Turkey workt Carpet'.[6] These items were prefixed by 'brought over' (from England, presumably).[7] Sometimes viceroys left items in the Castle, which might be purchased by their successors. When James Butler, 1st Duke of Ormond (1610–1688) was relieved of his duties as viceroy in 1669, his wife, supervising the removal of the Ormond goods at the Castle, was optimistic that her husband's replacement would buy for his use 'the bedsteads for servants, tables and such lumber … all the locks and keys I likewise paid for, and particularly those belonging to my Lord's closet and my own chamber'.[8] This was not unusual. In London, when Sarah Churchill, Duchess of Marlborough (1660–1744) had to give up her lodgings in St James's Palace after falling out with Queen Anne, she was careful to remove the brass locks 'of my own buying and which I never heard that anybody left for those that were to come after them'.[9]

On the departure of Arthur Capel, 1st Earl of Essex (1631–1683) in 1677, a record was compiled of the goods he sold to his successor. It was labelled as 'An Inventory of Goods bought at ye Castle of Dublin from ye Earle of Essex his Steward for ye use of his Grace James Duke of Ormond on ye 18th day of August 1677'.[10] Among the goods in the Presence Chamber, there was 'Old Red Baise about the Windowes', valued at nine shillings, and a 'Chymney Peece', valued at three pounds.[11] In an inventory taken the following year, 1678, of items in the Castle belonging to the 1st Duke of Ormond, 'six guilt Sconces' were noted in the same room.[12]

By now, entertaining in style at the viceregal court was well established under the Earl and Countess of Essex during their viceroyalty from 1672 to

1677, followed by Ormond, who served for several periods as viceroy up to 1685. Ormond's court was quite dazzling; he brought furniture, carpets, tapestries, silver and pictures from his various houses to furnish the Castle, together with a huge personal entourage.[13] It was said that in the fire of 1684 he lost furniture and effects to the value of £10,000.[14] This gives an indication that there must have been little or no furniture or goods of any real value in the State Apartments at this time, except for what the viceroys themselves supplied.

Ormond's son, Richard Butler, 1st Earl of Arran (1639–1686), who witnessed the 1684 inferno, described the Castle in a letter to his father as 'the worst Castle in the worst situation in Christendom'.[15] A verse composed by Thomas Parnell in 1715 confirms that not a great deal had changed since the 1680s:

> This House [the Castle] and Inhabitants both well agree
> And resemble each other as near as can be;
> One half is decay'd, and in want of a prop
> The other new built, but not finish'd a-top.[16]

In 1746, under the Viceroy Philip Dormer Stanhope, 4th Earl of Chesterfield (1694–1773), work was begun on a plan by the surveyor general, Arthur Jones Nevill (d. 1771), to build a new entrance front to the State Apartments in the Robinson-Molyneux range. It was to include a new 'great staircase' and a Battle Axe Hall, as the existing structures were 'not only in a most ruinous Condition' but were 'in immediate Danger of falling …'[17] Other parts of the Castle were in a similar condition including, in 1749, the rest of the State Apartments. On 14 February 1749, Nevill wrote to Chesterfield's successor and relative, William Stanhope, 1st Earl of Harrington (c. 1683–1756), who served as viceroy from 1746 to 1750, to inform him of the condition of the State Apartments (Fig. 02.03). In his correspondence he stated:

> The Presence Chamber and the Drawing Rooms next to the State Appartments in H.M.'s Castle of Dublin have not been fitted up or furnished since King Williams Reign the Ceiling Floors and Furniture are now so bad that they are not fit for the Reception of Your Excy and the Nobility and Gentry of this Kingdom'.[18]

Fig. 02.03.
James Worsdale, *William Stanhope, 1st Earl of Harrington*, 1746–1750.
© National Portrait Gallery, London.

He attached an estimate for 'fitting them up & New Furnishing them'.[19] Harrington wrote to the Lords of the Treasury on 24 February appealing for funds:

> And as the Presence Chamber and State Appartments adjoining to it are in a Condition extreamly unsuitable to the purposes for which they are used The Floors and Ceilings being worn Out and the Furniture ... which was put up before or soon after the Revolution being Entirely Decayed I inclose likewise the same Officers Estimate of new fitting up and Furnishing those appartments ... the whole amounting to the sum of [£] 2385.15.8. [20]

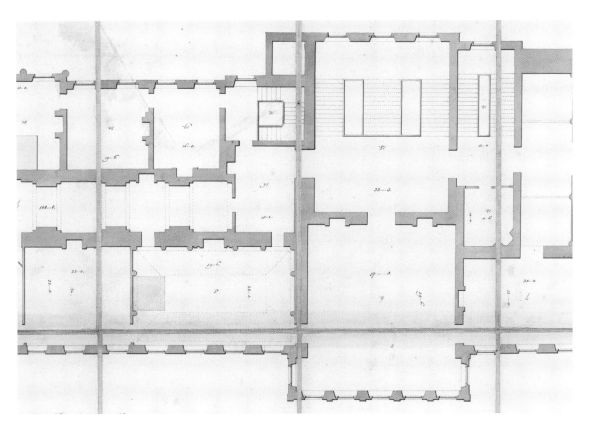

Fig. 02.04.
Euclid Alfray, 'Plan of the Upper State Story of the Castle, Dublin', 1767.
Courtesy of the National Archives of Ireland.

The substantial funds were duly sent and work got underway. The Presence Chamber was fit for use by September 1751.[21]

In the much later 'Plan of the Upper State Story of the Castle, Dublin' by Euclid Alfray dated 1767 (Fig. 02.04), the Presence Chamber (labelled as number five) is clearly to be seen with its canopy of state and coved ceiling, to the left of the new Battle Axe Hall (labelled as number six), behind which is the new and very grand imperial staircase (labelled as number fifteen).[22] Nevill ensured that the standard sequence, as adopted in English royal palaces at the time, of staircase, guard room, audience chamber and private rooms, including the viceroy's drawing room, was maintained.[23]

Newly discovered estimates in Derbyshire Record Office give some idea of the refurbishment proposed for the State Apartments in February 1749. In the letter written by Nevill and dated 14 February, he attached section drawings of the Presence Chamber and the two drawing rooms next to it. Unfortunately, the sections have not come to light, and the attached estimate for fitting up and furnishing the three rooms is not always specific about what relates to any one particular room, so raising a number of questions. The 'new Wainscott' listed probably lined the walls as a dado from the floor to the tops of the pedestals; '12 three Quarter Dorick Cols' and '114 Feet of Dorick Entablature', relate to the Presence Chamber.[24] An estimate of £34.2.6 was for the 'Enrichments in the Ceiling [of the Presence Chamber]', and £12 was for the 'Carved Trophy over the Chimney'.[25] The floor was to be of 'Perquiting [parquet]' at a cost of £87.8.0.[26] Were the 'five Drops between the windows' for the Presence Chamber? [27] Did the '6 Trophys and Festoons' at £60 relate to the stucco in the cove of the ceiling?[28] Though not mentioned in this document, it is likely that the original windows, which were probably mullioned and transomed (see Fig. 02.01), were replaced with sliding timber sashes at this time.[29]

The newly refurbished rectangular Presence Chamber had a coved ceiling, decorated in a somewhat bizarre manner (Fig. 02.05).[30] On the flat bed of the ceiling was a geometric pattern of interlocked circles and half-circles that contained bands of foliage and crossed palms: within the five circles along the centre were five rosettes or roses, from the central one of which hung a chandelier. The rather busy cove was a mix of terms, swags of foliage, royal insignia and large-winged bird-like creatures. The emblems of royalty – crown, sceptres and palm leaves – were located over the chimneypiece and repeated directly opposite on the window wall. The shield with a harp (representing Ireland) was located in the cove on the short side of the room where it would have been directly over the canopy and throne. A Doric order of ten engaged columns resting on pedestals lined three of the walls; the fourth wall was the window wall of four bays.[31] This created some dissonance as the opposite wall was of five bays, with the chimneypiece at its centre. To counteract this, Doric capitals were placed on corbels (or consoles) rather than on engaged columns on the window wall (Fig. 02.06).[32] The five drops between the windows that were specified by Nevill may have been these corbels, or decorative pieces that were placed beneath them. In the metopes of the Doric frieze there were six-pointed stars, laurel wreaths, crossed palms and what appear to have been quivers of arrows crossed with

Above: Fig. 02.05. Ceiling of the old Presence Chamber, Dublin Castle, 1886–1923. Courtesy of the Irish Architectural Archive.

Below: Fig. 02.06. The old Presence Chamber, Dublin Castle, detail of corbel, 1941. Courtesy of the Office of Public Works Library.

looped and knotted rope.[33] Some of these motifs bear a loose resemblance to those in the chancel frieze at the nearby St Werburgh's Church, which have a curiously Masonic appearance (Fig. 02.07). Joseph Jarratt (*d.* 1774) oversaw the reinstatement of St Werburgh's following a fire in 1754 and it is perhaps significant that he was also working on the State Apartments at Dublin Castle, as deputy to the surveyor general, Thomas Eyre (*d.* 1772), in the same decade. In a photograph taken prior to the 1941 fire, it appears that parts of the frieze and entablature were gilded, as were the Doric capitals, while the roses on the flat ceiling and much of the decorative elements within the cove were either gilded or polychromatic (see Fig. 02.05).[34]

Regarding furniture, another estimate dated 9 February 1749 lists what was required for the room:

A Crimson Velvet Canopy with the Kings Arms Disposed in Gold
Embroidery gold Lace &c.   £240.0.0
A Large State Chair Carved and Guilt cover'd with Velvet and Laced with
Gold   £17.10.0
2 State Stools and a foot Stool Covered with Velvet and Laced with Gold
                                                           £13.0.0
A Large Turkey Carpet to fix under the Canopy   £23.0.0
4 pr Crimson & Vangran Window Curtains Lined with Stuff and laced with
Silk Lace &c.   £47.10.0
A Large Carved and Gilt Chandelier   £30.0.0[35]

Fig. 02.08.
Frederick Nash,
*The Council
Chamber or
Drawing Room, St
James's Palace,*
c. 1800–20.
Royal Collection
Trust/© Her
Majesty Queen
Elizabeth II 2017.

The first four items above were essential for a Presence Chamber. The canopy of state in England comprised the canopy itself, above the throne, and a long cloth (the 'Cloth of State') that hung behind it, against the wall. It was made of a rich fabric, such as damask, brocade or velvet, as was proposed for Dublin Castle, and embroidered with the coat of arms of the monarch. The carpet mentioned above would have covered the platform or area on which the throne and footstool rested on the parquet floor, and crimson was a suitably 'royal' colour for the curtains in this important room.[36] A comparable arrangement can be seen in a watercolour of a presence chamber at Kensington Palace (Fig. 02.08). It is probably not surprising that inventories of Irish houses from the early part of the eighteenth century have shown that, between wall hangings, curtains and upholstery, damask was the principal fabric used in drawing rooms, and red the predominant colour.[37] The throne likely replaced that which can be seen in a portrait of the 4th Earl of Chesterfield by Stephen Slaughter (1697–1765), which is dated 1746 and still hangs at the Castle today (Fig. 02.09).

Fig. 02.09.
Stephen Slaughter, *Philip Dormer Stanhope, 4th Earl of Chesterfield*, 1746.
Courtesy of the Office of Public Works, Dublin Castle.

The estimate of 9 February was signed by Richard Harford, and approved by Nevill, as engineer and surveyor general. Harford's name appears from 1743 to 1744 in the *Journals of the House of Commons of the Kingdom of Ireland* when he fitted up the servants' hall at the Castle for a ball, and the Council Chamber 'for an entertainment for his Majesty's birthday being 30 October 1743'. [38] That year he was also paid for 'works & repairs' at the Castle for the then viceroy, William Cavendish, 3rd Duke of Devonshire (1698–1755).[39] In 1750 he was described as an 'upholder', a term used for the craft of upholstery, a furniture supplier, and one who would be the equivalent of today's interior designer.[40] Payments were made to him and, sometimes jointly, to Mark Forward, both of whom were regularly employed at the Castle, and who may have been in business together.[41] Forward is listed in *A Dictionary of Eighteenth-Century Irish Furniture-Makers* as an upholder with an address at Abbey Street, Dublin, where he is described as a 'Freeman of the City of Dublin as an Upholder by Service, Michaelmas 1731', and he was paid £233 for furniture and/or furnishings for the State Apartments at Dublin Castle in 1753.[42]

Apart from the items listed above, it can be assumed that the Presence Chamber would have contained few items of furniture, not just to facilitate the substantial numbers of people who regularly assembled there, but also to focus attention on the throne and its canopy. The only person who might have been seated would have been the viceroy. As the earliest known view of the room is an engraving dating from 1888 (Fig. 02.10), by which time it was being used variously as an ante-drawing room and a dining room, the full extent of the original furnishing scheme can only be guessed at. By 1888 the throne

and canopy had long since been discarded, double doors had been opened in their place and viceregal portraits hung around the room, with side tables placed beneath some of them. There was also a handsome Ionic chimneypiece and, of particular note, a pedimented overmantel relief. Attributed to the prominent woodcarver John Houghton (*fl.* 1730–1750s), whose name appears in accounts for work at the Castle in the 1740s, the panel is made of oak and pine and dates from 1750/1 (Fig. 02.11).[43] This is very likely the carved trophy over the chimney referred to in Nevill's estimates. Its design is taken from a drawing of an overmantel for the Stone Hall in Isaac Ware's *The Plans, Elevations and Sections, Chimneypieces and Ceilings of Houghton in Norfolk*, published in 1735 (Fig. 02.12). The frame is similar to another overmantel relief by Houghton, which he made for Bishop Clayton's house (now Iveagh House) in Dublin, where it remains, but without the broken pediment. While the Iveagh House relief shows a Bacchanalian scene, that at Dublin Castle is more appropriately sober, depicting a scene from the life of the Roman emperor, Marcus Aurelius. While the subject

Fig. 02.10. 'The Dining Room' (old Presence Chamber), Dublin Castle. *The Graphic*, 14 April 1888.

Fig. 02.11.
John Houghton (attr. to), carved overmantel, *c.* 1749–51.
Courtesy of the Office of Public Works, Dublin Castle.

Fig. 02.12. Isaac Ware, 'Hall Chimney-Piece', Houghton Hall, Norfolk, 1735. Metropolitan Museum of Art, New York, Harris Brisbane Dick Fund, 1925.

Fig. 02.13.
Waterford Glass chandelier, 1787.
Photograph by Terry Murphy,
courtesy of Waterford Treasures Museums.

matter referring to this enlightened leader might seem apposite, the inscription is, as Róisín Kennedy observes, 'militaristic in style', showing him more as a conquering hero.[44] The overmantel survived the fire of 1941 as it had been removed to the landing at the top of the main staircase between 1888 and 1915. It has recently been fully conserved.

An interesting item that may have hung in the Presence Chamber only in its last days as such (in the late 1780s, before it became an ante-drawing room) was a thirty-two-light glass chandelier. It was commissioned in 1787 by Charles Manners, 4th Duke of Rutland (1754–1787) who was viceroy from 1784 until his death in 1787, and given as a gift to the Castle.[45] The glass manufactory in Waterford, which later became known as Waterford Glass, was founded in 1783 by George and William Penrose. A kinsman of theirs, the architect Thomas Penrose (1740–1792), was appointed inspector of civil buildings in 1784, in which capacity he would later, in the 1780s, oversee the conversion of the Battle Axe Hall in the Castle to the new Presence Chamber. O'Dwyer has made the point that it was probably no coincidence that Rutland visited the glassworks in Waterford, where he placed an order for the chandelier, which cost £277.[46] It was a quite a *coup* for the burgeoning business. In 1825 the chandelier was hanging in the new Presence Chamber where it was described by a visitor as 'a magnificent glass lustre'.[47] The chandelier appears in an earlier illustration in *Walker's Hibernian Magazine* entitled 'Catholic Congratulation' and dated 14 January 1795 (see Fig. 03.03). Following renovations at the Castle in the second quarter of the nineteenth century, the chandelier returned to Waterford and now hangs, in 'truncated form', in the Council Chamber of the City Hall (Fig. 02.13).[48]

Before discussing how the Presence Chamber functioned, it might be useful to look at a letter dated 27 November 1758 from the surveyor general Thomas Eyre to Richard Rigby, secretary to the viceroy John Russell, 4th Duke of Bedford (1710–1771). Eyre suggests how the new layout of, and additions to, the State Apartments would affect the ducal couple and some of their staff. He recommends that:

> ... the Lord Lieutenant will keep his Levee and the Dutchess her Drawing Room in those Appartments that are Contiguous to the ballroom [in the south-western range]. That the Aid [*sic*] de camps and Gentlemen who have business with my Lord Lieutenant shall wait in the presence Chamber on the right hand side of the Battle Axe hall. That his Grace will dress himself and See Company in the room adjoyning to it, that the next to that may be his Bed Chamber and the Room beyond that may be her Grace's Dressing Room ... I confess that Some Inconveniency will attend this disposition from the Necessity that both their Graces will be under of Crossing the Battle Axe Hall, either to Levee or the drawing room ...[49]

This would suggest that the viceroy would have his levee in the drawing room next to the Ball Room (now St Patrick's Hall), and not in the Presence Chamber. Both the levee and the 'drawing-room' were occasions attended by substantial numbers of people.

'Levee' was a French term, adopted at the court of King Charles II, which referred to the waking and dressing of a monarch in preparation for visits from male members of the nobility and gentry, and from officials and members of the military, who were presented to the sovereign. This was adapted at the Dublin court, where the levee was held twice or three times per week and on various occasions during the year, though George Townshend, 1st Marquess Townshend (1724–1807), as viceroy from 1767 to 1772, found them tedious, and held them on Sundays only.[50] A satirical verse from 1757 describes how, three times a week:

> All the *Beau Monde*, in Crouds, resort,
> 'Twixt Twelve and One, to pay their Court:
> And, though it's more than Middle-Day,
> Fashion will have this call'd Levée ...

The verse continues with a description of those who attend:

Now fills the Hive, the Buz increases;
These come for Pensions, those for Places
Yet ask them all, they all declare
Respect and Custom bring 'em there.
Some walk, some stand, some sit in Windows
To whisper Tales or Innuendo's:
I mean the lower Class: the Great,
When they desire a *tete a tete,*
Steal from us to the next Apartment ...[51]

'Drawing rooms', usually held weekly, were at this time hosted by the wife of the viceroy, mainly for the wives and daughters of the nobility and gentry who had already been presented at court, or who were being introduced for the first time.[52] This had been established by Catherine of Braganza, the wife of King Charles II, in the late seventeenth century when she moved her social gatherings from her own presence chamber to her more intimate withdrawing room.[53] Mrs Delany, wife of the Dean of Down, was most displeased when Charlotte Townshend, Duchess of Bedford (*d.* 1770) turned up late for her 'morning' drawing-room at the Castle in May 1760: 'Waited with very fine ladies in *beaten silver* and glittering with jewels, till half an hour after three: then the door was opened, and the word "approach" was given'.[54]

One very important function held in the Presence Chamber was the swearing in of the Lord Mayor of Dublin. Among the papers in the archive at Alnwick Castle is one that describes in detail the ceremony that took place there on 30 September 1763 during the viceroyalty of Hugh Percy, 2nd Earl of Northumberland (1714–1786):

The Lord Mayor, Lord Mayor Elect, Recorder, Sheriffs Elect, Aldermen &c. came to the Castle at [unspecified] o Clock, being the Hour appointed by the Lord Lieut. and were shown into the State Dining Room by [the] Gentleman Usher, who afterwards acquainted the Ld Lieutenant of their being come. His Excellency immediately came from his Chamber into the Presence Chamber, attended by his Aid du Camp, Gentleman Usher, Gentleman of the Bedchamber, and Lieut of the Battle Axes. The Steward, and the Comptroller,

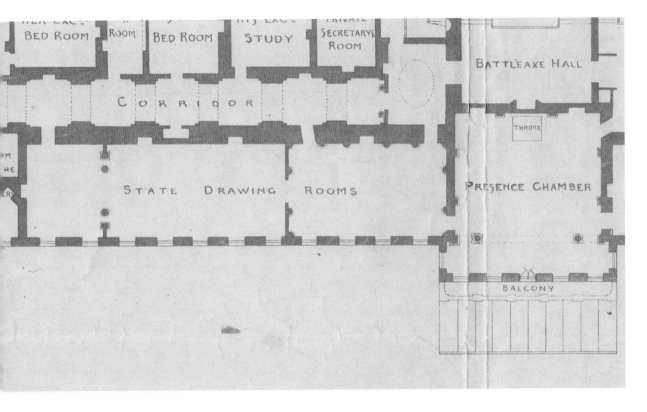

Fig. 02.14.
Plan of the first floor of Dublin Castle, 1911, detail.
Courtesy of the Office of Public Works Library.

with their White Staves, the two Gentlemen-at-Large and [3] Pages, attended in the Presence Chamber. [The Usher] acquainted the Lord Mayor that the Lord Lieutenant was ready to receive them, and they came into the Presence Chamber, without having been introduc'd, preceded by their own Officers, viz. Sword bearer, Macebearer and the City Marshall with the Keys of the City Gates. When the Lord Mayor entered the Presence Chamber the Lord Lieut put on his Hat and they came forward, making three Reverences, the last at the Foot Cloth, at which time the Lord Lieut. took his Hat off and putting it on again the City regalia were deposited at his Feet.[55]

Fig. 02.15.
The old Presence Chamber, Dublin Castle, as a hospital ward, *c*. 1915. *Souvenir Album presented to the Marquis and Marchioness of Aberdeen and Temair*, 1915.
Courtesy of the National Library of Ireland.

The recorder then made a speech presenting the mayor to be sworn in, the oath of office was read and later taken by the new Lord Mayor. According to Joseph Robins, the viceroy always received the Lord Mayor and entourage while seated on the throne as a particular mark of respect and, after the ceremony, a sideboard with wine and cakes was provided for the occasion.[56]

This Presence Chamber remained as such for another twenty-five years. In the late 1780s, Thomas Penrose oversaw the conversion of the Battle Axe Hall into what is now the Throne Room for the then viceroy, George Nugent-Temple-Grenville, 1st Marquess of Buckingham (1753–1813). As a result of this refurbishment, a double doorway was created where the canopy of state had been, which led into the State Drawing Room, and the 'lost' Presence Chamber began a new chapter as an ante-drawing room (Fig. 02.14). It was a chapter that would close by degrees. From 1915 to 1919 the room was appropriated for use, along with the rest of the State Apartments, as a Red Cross Hospital ward (Fig.

Fig. 02.16.
The old Presence
Chamber, Dublin
Castle, as a
courtroom of the
Irish Free State,
1923–31. Courtesy
of the Office of
Public Works
Library.

02.15). Following Irish independence in 1922, it served as a courtroom from 1923 to 1931. A photograph taken during that time shows the emblem of the Irish Free State below the eighteenth-century plasterwork harp in the cove (Fig. 02.16). Finally, in the early hours of 24 January 1941 an accidental fire in the State Apartments consigned it to history:

> Part of the old State chambers in Dublin Castle blazed furiously in the early hours of this morning ... a huge column of smoke, sparks and flames shot up over the building, casting a red glow over the ancient Chapel Royal and the historic buildings adjoining.[57]

A photograph taken shortly after records the extent of the destruction (Fig. 02.17).

Fig. 02.17.
The old Presence Chamber, Dublin Castle, following its destruction by fire, 1941.
Courtesy of the Office of Public Works Library.

I would like to thank the following for their help with this chapter: Myles Campbell, William Derham, David Griffin, J.B. Maguire, Kevin Mulligan and Freddie O'Dwyer.

Endnotes

1 The Battle Axe Hall derived its name from the weapons carried by the ceremonial bodyguard of the viceroys.

2 F. O'Dwyer, 'The Ballroom at Dublin Castle: The origins of St Patrick's Hall', in A. Bernelle (ed.), *Decantations: A Tribute to Maurice Craig* (Dublin: The Lilliput Press, 1992), pp. 152–3.

3 E. McParland, *Public Architecture in Ireland 1680–1760* (New Haven and London: Yale University Press, 2001), p. 94; C. Casey, *Dublin: The City within the Grand and Royal Canals and the Circular Road with the Phoenix Park* (New Haven and London: Yale University Press, 2005), p. 350.

4 See E. McParland's analysis of this in *Public Architecture*, pp. 93–4.

5 J.B. Maguire, 'Dublin Castle: Three centuries of development', *Journal of the Royal Society of Antiquaries of Ireland*, 115 (1985), p. 16.

6 'An Inventory of the Kings Goods in the Castle of Dublin', May 1693, National Archives of Ireland, Wyche 2/142. My thanks to Dr John Montague for this reference.

7 Ibid.

8 *Calendar of the Manuscripts of the Marquess of Ormonde, K.P. preserved at Kilkenny Castle* (London: Historical Manuscripts Commission, 1904), New Series, vol. 3, p. 441.

9 P. McCarthy, *Life in the Country House in Georgian Ireland* (New Haven and London: Yale University Press, 2016), p. 70.

10 J. Fenlon, *Goods & Chattels: A Survey of Early Household Inventories in Ireland* (Kilkenny: The Heritage Council, 2003), p. 87.

11 Ibid., p. 92.

12 See Fenlon, *Goods & Chattels*, p. 100.

13 J. Robins, *Champagne & Silver Buckles: The Viceregal Court at Dublin Castle 1700–1922* (Dublin: The Lilliput Press, 2001), p. 6.

14 J. Fenlon, 'Episodes of Magnificence: The material worlds of the Dukes of Ormonde', in T. Barnard and J. Fenlon (eds), *The Dukes of Ormonde, 1610–1745* (Woodbridge: Boydell & Brewer, 2000), p. 146.

15 See Maguire, 'Three centuries of development', p. 15.

16 T.C. Barnard, '"Grand Metropolis" or "The Anus of the World"? The Cultural Life of Eighteenth-Century Dublin', in P. Clark and R. Gillespie (eds), *Two Capitals: London and Dublin 1500–1840* (Oxford: Oxford University Press, 2001) p. 190.

17 See McParland, *Public Architecture*, p. 104.

18 Letter to William, Earl of Harrington from Arthur Jones Nevill, 14 February 1749, Derbyshire Record Office, D3155/C1100. My thanks to Dr Myles Campbell for this reference.

19 Ibid.

20 Letter to the Lords of the Treasury from William, Earl of Harrington, 24 February 1749, Derbyshire Record Office, D3155/C1097. My thanks to Dr Myles Campbell for this reference.

21 See McParland, *Public Architecture*, p. 104.

22 Alfray's plan of 1767 shows how this south-east range was doubled in size in the late 1750s by the addition of a ceremonial corridor behind the Presence Chamber and the rest of the Robinson-Molyneux range, and suites of rooms on the other side of the corridor, overlooking the gardens.

23 See Casey, *Dublin*, pp. 351–2; see also A. Keay, *The Magnificent Monarch: Charles II and the Ceremonies of Power* (London: Continuum, 2008).

24 'An Estimate for New fitting up and furnishing the Presence Chamber and Two Drawing Rooms in the State Appartments of His Majesty's Castle of Dublin', 14 February 1749, Derbyshire Record Office, D3155/C1100.

25 Ibid.

26 'An Estimate for New fitting up and furnishing the Presence Chamber and Two Drawing Rooms in the State Appartments of His Majesty's Castle of Dublin', 14 February 1749, Derbyshire Record Office, D3155/C1100.

27 Ibid.

28 'An Estimate for New fitting up and furnishing the Presence Chamber and Two Drawing Rooms in the State Appartments of His Majesty's Castle of Dublin', 14 February 1749, Derbyshire Record Office, D3155/C1100.

29 G. Hickey, 'Reconstruction at Dublin Castle, 1941–1969', unpublished P.G. Dip. thesis, Trinity College Dublin, 2008, p. 17; available at the Irish Architectural Archive, ABRC/2008.6.

30 See McParland, *Public Architecture*, p. 104; O'Dwyer called the room 'something of an architectural hybrid', see O'Dwyer, 'The Ballroom at Dublin Castle', p. 163.

31 This included one column in each of only two corners of the room.

32 See McParland, *Public Architecture*, p. 104.

33 O'Dwyer refers to 'garter' stars in the frieze as a possible concession to the incoming viceroy, Lionel Sackville, 7th Earl of Dorset, viceroy from 1750 to 1755, who was a member of the Order of the Garter. However, garter stars have eight points, while those in the Presence Chamber frieze had six. See O'Dwyer, 'The Ballroom at Dublin Castle', p. 163.

34 My thanks to Joseph McDonnell for this observation.

35 'An Estimate for Furnishing the Presence Chamber and two Drawing Rooms in H.M's Castle of Dublin by Order of Arthur Jones Nevill Esqs. Engr & Surveyor General', 9 February 1749, Derbyshire Record Office, D3155/C1101. My thanks to Dr Myles Campbell for this reference.

36 The 'State Chair' or throne mentioned in the estimate pre-dates the present throne that is said to date from 1821, when it was probably installed for the visit of King George IV; R. Kennedy, *Dublin Castle Art* (Dublin: Office of Public Works, 1999), p. 29.

37 See McCarthy, *Life in the Country House*, p. 142.

38 *The Journals of the House of Commons of the Kingdom of Ireland* (Dublin: Printed by Abraham Bradley, 1763) vol. 8, p. 754.

39 Ibid., pp. 751–2.

40 A receipt signed by a Richard Harford and dated 21 April 1762, made out to George Lucy of Charlecote Park, Warwickshire, for fabrics supplied, was found recently in Warwickshire County Record Office (ref. L6/1311). It is not clear if this is the same person. My thanks to Dr Myles Campbell for this reference.

41 In 1783 a John Harford was listed as being in business at 41 Abbey Street, Dublin; see S. Watson, *The Gentleman's and Citizen's Almanack* (Dublin: Printed for Samuel Watson

and Thomas Stewart, 1783), p. 43.

42 J. Rogers, 'A Dictionary of Eighteenth-Century Irish Furniture-Makers', in The Knight of Glin and J. Peill, *Irish Furniture* (New Haven and London: Yale University Press, 2007), p. 275; 'General Accompt of Thos Eyre late Engineer and Surveyor General of what money he received and paid from his covenant in office 1752–62', Irish Architectural Archive, Acc. 86/149, p. 5.

43 See *The Journals of the House of Commons*, pp. 759–765. For a detailed description of the overmantel see Kennedy, *Dublin Castle Art*, pp. 86–7.

44 See Kennedy, *Dublin Castle Art*, p. 86.

45 F. O'Dwyer, 'Making Connections in Georgian Ireland', *Bulletin of the Irish Georgian Society*, 38 (1996/97), p. 18. The chandelier is described in detail in D. Ó Ceallacháin, 'The Waterford Chandelier: An elegant glass lustre of the Waterford manufactory', in J.M. Hearne (ed.), *Glassmaking in Ireland: From the Medieval to the Contemporary* (Dublin and Oregon: Irish Academic Press, 2010), pp. 165–8.

46 See O'Dwyer, 'Making Connections', p. 18.

47 G.N. Wright, *An Historical Guide to the City of Dublin, Illustrated by Engravings and a Plan of the City* (London: Baldwin, Craddock & Joy, 1825), p. 7.

48 See O'Dwyer, 'Making Connections', p. 18.

49 Letter to Richd Rigby from Thomas Eyre, 27 November 1758, 'Private Letter Book 1756–65', Irish Architectural Archive, Acc. 86/149, pp. 74–5.

50 See Robins, *Champagne*, p. 59.

51 The 'next Apartment', according to a footnote in the poem, is described as 'A Room at the East End of the Presence-chamber'; *The Prelude to a Levee; Calculated for the Meridian of the Castle of Dublin* (Dublin: 1757), p. 12.

52 See Robins, *Champagne*, p. 49.

53 See Keay, *The Magnificent Monarch*, p. 126.

54 A. Day (ed.), *Letters from Georgian Ireland: The Correspondence of Mary Delany, 1731–68* (Belfast: Friar's Bush Press, 1991), p. 62.

55 Account describing the swearing-in of the Lord Mayor of Dublin, 30 September 1763, Archives of the Duke of Northumberland, Alnwick Castle, Northumberland, DNP: MS 35, f. 328. See also 'Form of Swearing in the Lord Mayor of the City of Dublin in the presence of the Lord Lieutenant, c. 1750', National Library of Ireland, Genealogical Office Ms 4, pp. 155–6.

56 See Robins, *Champagne*, p. 50.

57 *Irish Press*, 24 January 1941.

Three

'Sketches of their Boundless Mind'

The Marquess of Buckingham and the Presence Chamber at Dublin Castle, 1788–1838

Myles Campbell

Such, Egypt, were thy sons! divinely great
In arts, in arms, in wisdom, and in state.
Her early monarchs gave such glories birth,
Their ruins are the wonders of the earth.
Structures so vast by those great kings design'd,
Are but faint sketches of their boundless mind …[1]

Thursday, 18 September 1788, was a day no more remarkable in Dublin than any other. Readers of the city's newspapers would learn of the usual cycle of life's beginnings and endings, which are no less familiar to their twenty-first century successors. In Earl Street, a fire had put an end to a soap and candle business.[2] In Back Lane, a woman's career as a pedlar of forged coins had been cut short by a vigilant shopkeeper and a column of policemen.[3] Yet one or two beginnings and endings were perhaps more particular to this Georgian city than others. One was the death of a doctor's servant from the excessive consumption of pears.[4] The other was the beginning of an architectural transformation at the city's designated focus of fashion, Dublin Castle. According to the optimistic correspondent of *The Dublin Evening Post*, this architectural apotheosis would soon render the Castle equal to the richest royal residences of ancient Egypt. The 'seat of Vice-Majesty', he gushed, 'will no longer be branded with imputation – as the assylum of sober dullness – and shrival economy – nor his Excellency [the

Facing page: Fig. 03.01. Entrance to the State Apartments, Dublin Castle. Photograph by Davison & Associates, courtesy of the Office of Public Works, Dublin Castle.

lord lieutenant, or viceroy] considered to imitate the Persian Monarch, who hides his royalty to encrease the veneration of the world'.[5]

The viceroy in question was the English peer and politician George Nugent-Temple- Grenville, 1st Marquess of Buckingham (1753–1813). He would play a central role in this kingly production. Its main act would be the making of a new Presence Chamber at the Castle. Buckingham had previously served as Irish viceroy from August 1782 to May 1783 (as Earl Temple) and following his elevation to a marquessate, he was re-appointed in November 1787. 'All', wrote the correspondent, 'will be splendour and magnificence ... and in the language of the poet – the representation of Majesty will "throw all his glories open to their view"'.[6]

The somewhat oblique allusions to a poet and to the ancient King of Persia in this account are obscure but significant. They have their source in the work of the English poet and playwright Edward Young (1683–1765). Like the epigraph that introduces this essay, they are drawn from Young's long-forgotten play, *Busiris, King of Egypt,* which was first performed in 1719. *Busiris* is the story of the mythological Egyptian king who aimed to eclipse the splendour of the neighbouring Persian court. In order to do so, he created a kingdom rich in palatial architecture and 'Blazing to heaven in diamonds and gold'.[7] Secretly reviled as cruel and proud by his courtiers, he was ultimately blinded by the lustre and artifice of his own court, failing to recognize his loyal courtiers as the conspirators who would bring about his downfall. In his dying moments, he proclaimed his immortality, asserting that his name would live forever in the 'Triumphant columns' he had built.[8]

It has been observed that 'by castigating Busiris's love of riches and passion for power' in the early 1700s, Edward Young was creating a piece of 'political propaganda' that challenged the legitimacy of King George I, as the Hanoverian successor to the British throne.[9] By the same token, Young's play was now being invoked in the Dublin of the 1780s to mount a veiled but vituperative attack on the legitimacy of the Marquess of Buckingham as Viceroy of Ireland. Viewed in this context, the colourful announcement of Buckingham's new Presence Chamber at Dublin Castle takes on a different hue. By casting him in the role of the tyrannical Busiris, it would appear that *The Dublin Evening Post* heralded his great new room not as the Castle's apotheosis but as its nadir. Beneath the surface, it seemed to greet it as little more than a veneer, concealing an unpopular viceroy's apparently narcissistic motivations in creating it. In this context, the

Presence Chamber can only be fully understood in relation to the turbulent social, political and cultural climate of Ireland in the 1780s that contributed to Buckingham's unpopularity. The aim of this essay is to explore the room's creation and legacy, as well as the motivations behind its inception, as a means of better understanding that climate and the minds that shaped it.

Hair-dressers and Grizettes: The Old Guard Chamber

To understand the factors that influenced the creation of the Marquess of Buckingham's new Presence Chamber at Dublin Castle is to first understand what it was designed to replace. Despite its unique significance as the nucleus of royal ceremony in Ireland before 1922, surprisingly little is known about the origins of the Presence Chamber, which is today more commonly referred to as the Throne Room. Tentative references have linked its inception to campaigns of improvement at Dublin Castle in the late 1780s, but little substantive evidence has emerged to indicate a precise date. New evidence makes it clear that the room was conceived by the Marquess of Buckingham as a replacement for the existing old Presence Chamber at the Castle, in September 1788. A few days after Buckingham's ambitious plans to transform the State Apartments were vaguely announced in *The Dublin Evening Post*, *The Freeman's Journal* could confirm that the creation of the new Presence Chamber was to be part of his scheme.[10] Buckingham had given orders for the room to be laid out 'in a stile of superior elegance'.[11] It would be created in the space then occupied by the Castle's Battle Axe Hall, or Guard Chamber.

Relatively little is known about this old Guard Chamber. Located behind the pedimented entrance to the State Apartments, it occupied the five central bays of the first floor, on the south side of the Upper Castle Yard (Fig. 03.01). Its central position, at the summit of the grand imperial staircase leading to the state rooms, made it a suitable space for the screening and filtering of courtiers by the viceroy's Battle Axe guards. Having successfully passed through the Guard Chamber, visitors could then enter the dining room to the west, if attending a dinner, or the Presence Chamber to the east, if arriving for a viceregal levee or drawing room. A plan of these spaces drawn by Euclid Alfray in 1767 illustrates the convenience of the arrangement (see Fig. 02.04). This sequence of regal apartments, accessed from a guard room, was entirely analogous to the disposition of spaces in English royal palaces, such as Hampton Court Palace and Windsor Castle.

The physical and visual character of the old Guard Chamber is more difficult to evoke. In March 1746 it was said to be 'not only in a most ruinous Condition' but, in common with the rooms adjacent to it, 'in immediate Danger of falling'.[12] Following its deliverance from this fate through a subsequent campaign of rebuilding, from 1746 to 1747, it was later described, in the 1780s, simply as 'spacious'.[13] A late-eighteenth-century commentator recalled it, perhaps with a tinge of nostalgia and bias, as 'a magnificent hall' that had been obliterated to make way for the 'totally unnecessary' Presence Chamber that took its place.[14] As the space representing the nominally defensive but largely ceremonial Battle Axe Guards, and as the first state room encountered by courtiers at Dublin Castle, the Guard Chamber was almost certainly lined with weaponry to create an appropriate, if somewhat fictive, impression of fortification. An early-nineteenth-century watercolour of the Guard Chamber at Windsor Castle offers some idea of how this arrangement, which was typical in English royal palaces, might have been applied at Dublin Castle (Fig. 03.02).

Fig. 03.02. Charles Wild (after), *King's Guard Chamber, Windsor Castle,* published 1818. Royal Collection Trust/© Her Majesty Queen Elizabeth II 2017.

Something of Buckingham's motivation in replacing the Guard Chamber with a new Presence Chamber might be gleaned from two descriptions of the less than dignified use to which it was being put by the late 1780s. Its conversion, according to one priggish critic would, in future, 'preclude the male and female mob of hair-dressers and grizettes [flirtatious, working-class women], who generally crowded the hall on days and nights of public solemnity'.[15] This supposedly courtly space was likewise satirized by another commentator, as a room that 'on festivals only served for a receptacle for servants, the crowds of whom exceedingly embarrassed the company in their access to the state apartments'.[16] Few viceroys were as sensitive to the regulation of court etiquette as Buckingham. Acutely aware of the power of the press in Dublin, his letters show that he followed newspaper reports of his courtly entertainments with keen interest, sometimes cutting and keeping a report if it flattered him, or writing in dismay to his brother, the future British Prime Minister, William Grenville (1759–1834), if it did not.[17] Buckingham is very likely to have greeted these judgements on his Guard Chamber as an affront to his high standards and a threat to his court's reputation. Towards the end of his first viceroyalty, in March 1783, he had written with bluster to his brother of the splendour of the court he had kept at Dublin Castle:

> We shall have quitted this space at the very pinnacle of our glory; and shall leave a great many friends jealous of our honour and regardful of our memory; and who will not patiently suffer any slur to be thrown on the splendour of these six months of your brother's government, which I am confident are not to be paralleled.[18]

Notoriously conceited and self-indulgent, Buckingham revelled in the pomp and pageantry of his viceregal position. It has been observed that during his first term in office, from 1782 to 1783, 'the splendour of the Irish court reached new heights of ostentation …'[19] His second term, from 1787 to 1789, was to be no different and it remained important to him that the viceregal apartments at the Castle 'should reflect the opulence of the court's regime'.[20]

Buckingham had good reason for encouraging high standards of social etiquette at Dublin Castle, principally on account of his need to salvage an ailing reputation, and reverse his growing unpopularity as viceroy. From the beginning of his first viceroyalty in 1782, he had worked hard to ensure his popularity, but with only limited success. As part of these efforts, he had persuaded King

George III to establish the Order of St Patrick, an Irish order of chivalry designed to cultivate the support of Irish peers. Surviving letters of thanks from the first knights to be admitted to the Order, in 1783, have come to light in the National Library of Ireland. They demonstrate the immediate success of Buckingham's strategy, and the personal gains it brought him. In thanking him for the honour, Henry de Burgh, 12th Earl of Clanricarde (1743–1797), swiftly pledged his loyalty to Buckingham in return:

> Fully satisfied of your Excellency's friendly Disposition towards the Interests of Ireland, I shall consider it as much a Duty, as it is my inclination, to give my utmost support to your administration, in every measure which may correspond with that Idea.[21]

Henry Loftus, 3rd Earl of Ely (1709–1783), in his letter of thanks, gave Buckingham a similarly large share of credit: 'I shall at all times be mindfull that it is to your Excellency I am indebted for this Distinguished mark of his Majesty's Favor'.[22] Despite its brilliance, this popularity would soon fade. Notwithstanding his selection as one of the first knights of the Order, James Caulfeild, 1st Earl of Charlemont (1728–1799), in his criticism of Buckingham, captured the growing drift. 'He knows a great deal', Charlemont noted, 'but is too fond of communicating that knowledge ... He is proud and too apt to undervalue his equals ...'[23]

Compounding Buckingham's flaws was the fact that he also 'lacked charm', and was 'vain and impetuous'.[24] His personal circumstances did not help matters. In 1775, he had married the Irish heiress Lady Mary Elizabeth Nugent (*d.* 1812), daughter of Robert Nugent, 1st Earl Nugent (1709–1788). Although the marriage was economically advantageous, it has been said that his wife was 'seen as a closet Catholic, and this contributed to Buckingham's unpopularity in Ireland'.[25] There seems to be some evidence to support this claim. A newly identified inventory of the Viceregal Lodge at the Phoenix Park during Buckingham's first viceroyalty, records an unusually high number of religious pictures. The inventory was taken on 31 October 1782, and differentiated between items that were the property of the state and those that belonged to Buckingham and his wife. Among the family's numerous religious pictures in the Saloon were 'St Francis'; a 'Madona'; the 'Holy Family, Virgin Mary, Elizabeth and Child Jesus'; and 'Our Saviour in the Garden'.[26] In the Dining Room were representations of the 'Magdalene full length'; 'Abraham looking for Rebecha'; and 'Our Saviour tortured by the Soldiers'.[27] This high concentration of religious imagery may indicate the kind of devotional practices that are more closely associated with the Roman Catholic than the Anglican Church.

Extremely hungry for social advancement and having 'already failed to make a success at Westminster', Buckingham knew that the Irish viceroyalty was a step towards elevation in the peerage.[28] He could little afford any slur on the manners of his court at Dublin Castle if he was to achieve his life's goal of attaining a dukedom. At the end of his first viceroyalty in 1783, he wrote to his brother, William, listing the roll call of former viceroys who had been awarded for their services in this office, and pressing him to solicit honours from King George III on his behalf. 'Lord Shelburne has the Garter', he complained, 'Lord Thurlow a pension, Lord Grantham the same, Townshend a peerage, as marks of the King's satisfaction; would it be improper or impossible to state that I am returning (such as I am) without any feather?'.[29] Hopeful of the dukedom, he settled for a marquessate. Yet all was not lost. A return to power as viceroy in 1787 presented him with a lifeline that, if carefully exploited, could yet lead to his ennoblement as the Duke of Buckingham.

In this context it was now more imperative than ever that Dublin Castle should present an image of the viceroy's exceptional good manners and discernment, in the hope that the King might interpret it as an image incommensurate with the position of a mere marquess. Politically astute and a very hard worker, Buckingham was a man of 'considerable ability' but it was 'his tragedy' that these abilities 'were not matched by personal equilibrium, self-control and discretion of language'.[30] As part of a campaign of sweeping reforms in 1788, Buckingham attempted to bring about a radical reorganization of the Church of Ireland based on Church of England models. This swiftly brought him into serious conflict with senior clergy, including the influential Archbishop of Cashel, Charles Agar (1735–1809). Agar objected to many of Buckingham's ideas, condemning them as 'very ill-suited' to the established Church in Ireland.[31]

Further clashes were to come when Buckingham launched a full enquiry into the finances of the Irish Ordnance Office at Dublin Castle. 'All is bustle and confusion at the Castle', wrote one contemporary observer, '[and] words cannot express the consternation that prevails in every department in the Ordnance … the various officers remain in a state of the most humiliating suspense'.[32] According to a contemporary report, this enquiry came about after Buckingham had been on his way to dine with John Scott, Baron Earlsfort, later 1st Earl of Clonmell (1739–1798) and his wife, one evening in 1788. While passing through Harcourt Street, Buckingham's carriage had suffered a delay due to the volume of coaches drawing up outside a grand house where a ball was taking place. On later enquiring about the owner of the house, he was informed that it belonged to a clerk of the Ordnance Office. Buckingham was suspicious of this lavishness and may well have feared being overshadowed by someone of such junior rank. 'That's very extraordinary', he is said to have remarked, 'if, without any other resources, he can keep such an expensive house and see such splendid company, he must be a surprising manager!'[33] His controversial ordnance enquiry soon followed. As relationships between the viceroy and the Irish ecclesiastical and administrative institutions began to break down, a damaging rift also emerged between Buckingham and King George III. 'I cannot say what I suffer', wrote Buckingham in October 1788, 'while my situation and the public service are trifled with ... by the King's jealousy'.[34] The stakes could scarcely have been higher for Buckingham, as he now set about repairing and rebuilding his profile. It has been said that by this time he had made himself 'almost universally obnoxious' in Ireland.[35] It is perhaps no coincidence that at this critical juncture he resolved to magnify his majesty through the creation of a new Presence Chamber and a remodelled St Patrick's Hall at Dublin Castle. In such a necessarily noble setting, there could be no place for the old Guard Chamber with its imputations of vulgar or uncivilized assembly.

In addition to improving the social tone of Buckingham's court, the removal of the semi-public Guard Chamber allowed for the design of a larger, more tasteful Presence Chamber than the existing one of 1749. It has been noted that, 'Unexpectedly, for an upstairs room or a presence chamber', the architectural order of the 1749 Presence Chamber was Doric.[36] The second most plain and primitive of the five orders of classical architecture, its squat proportions and military associations lent the room little of the majestic character associated with its function. The slender forms and elegant volutes of the Ionic or Corinthian orders would have struck a much more regal note. Compounding the old Presence Chamber's architectural unsuitability was its old-fashioned rococo ornament (see Fig. 02.15). The anachronistic and naive style of this room and the possible suggestions of aesthetic ignorance to which it might easily give rise, could scarcely have escaped the attention of so discerning an aesthete as Buckingham. Always mindful of the power of architecture to shape the image of its patron, he 'believed that a great family demanded great houses'.[37] New evidence shows that in addition to directing the creation of the new Presence Chamber, Buckingham defrayed the entire cost of it 'at his own expence'.[38] This would suggest that he applied the same dictum when shaping a great palace for a great vice-king. At a fraction of Buckingham's vast fortune, the new Presence Chamber, and the positive publicity it might generate, would be cheap at any price, particularly for a viceroy 'whose excesses were renowned'.[39] Such a room, with him enthroned at its centre, would serve as a more fashionable, formal and fitting backdrop to the majestic profile he had been at pains to cultivate since first arriving in Ireland, in 1782. His intention is clear from a letter written to his wife at this time. 'Dublin', he noted, 'is thinning very fast but my fête will keep many in town. The magnificence of it will be beyond every thing ever seen in Ireland'.[40] At a stroke, two old spaces would now be confined to memory and a new one conceived, as *The Freeman's Journal* put it, in a manner more 'suitable to the necessary state of the Viceregal residence'.[41]

Gay though not Gaudy: The New Presence Chamber

Work on Buckingham's new Presence Chamber began at the end of September 1788 and was completed in January 1789. An obscure engraving of it published exactly six years later, in January 1795, provides the only known visual record of how it would have appeared in Buckingham's time (Fig. 03.03). As part of Buckingham's interventions, the doors that formerly opened into the old Guard Chamber from the great staircase had been blocked up. In their place, a new carved timber canopy of state, featuring a lion and a unicorn each clutching an Irish harp, had been installed in the middle of the south wall. Either side of this canopy, above the twin chimneypieces, were large mirrors surmounted by crowned harps and classical swags, presumably executed in timber or plaster. At the centre of the room was a chandelier described by James Malton as 'an elegant glass lustre, of the Waterford Manufactory'.[42] It had been purchased for the old Presence Chamber by Buckingham's predecessor, Charles Manners, 4th Duke of Rutland (1754–1787), in 1787. At a cost of £277, its monetary value alone deemed it worthy of recycling. The entire space was articulated by a giant order of fluted Corinthian pilasters supporting a frieze of oak-leaf swags and lion masks, all crowned by a beefy modillion cornice. That none of these architectural elements were carried over from the old Guard Chamber is clear from a newly identified account of the room, published in the autumn of 1788:

Fig. 03.03.
'Catholic Congratulation, 14th January, 1795'. *Walker's Hibernian Magazine: or, Compendium of Entertaining Knowledge*, January 1795.
Courtesy of the National Library of Ireland.

> The new Presence Chamber is adorned with a number of Corinthian pilasters, four on each side, in white and gold; the cornice is composed Corinthian, and the cieling [*sic*]... is not to be painted, but finished in gilt stucco.[43]

Another observer noted that the pilasters were 'fluted' and reported that the two fireplaces opposite the windows, which on account of the room's size were 'not more than was necessary', were about to receive 'statuary marble chimney-pieces'.[44] As the transformation of the room neared its climax and progress became apparent, the expectations that had been entertained of an architectural metamorphosis began to be met. 'The Castle', it was optimistically stated, 'will, when finished in the superb taste originally designed, be inferior to few houses of Royal residence in point of elegance'.[45]

To his undoubted satisfaction, Buckingham was soon being hailed in the press as something of an architectural tastemaker, who had fashioned 'a very fine reception-chamber'.[46] The room's modern, elegant and rational Neoclassical forms were the full expression of the tentative ideas represented in the astylar Wedgwood Room, which had been built in the State Apartments a decade earlier. As such, they represented an architectural advancement for Dublin Castle and bore all the necessary hallmarks of Buckingham's discernment. An indirect product of the recent studies of Giovanni Battista Piranesi (1720–1778) and of the excavations at Pompeii, which 'had so attracted ... Buckingham on his Grand Tour of 1774', they symbolized his progressive cultural outlook.[47] In their scale and form, they made the spaces adjacent to them, which only forty years earlier had been *de rigueur*, seem archaic and provincial. Enlightenment architecture had come to Dublin Castle and Buckingham was credited as its chief luminary. The gilded stucco ceiling, only a tantalizing sliver of which is visible in the 1795 engraving of the room, was lauded as 'an elegant composition, light though magnificent, and gay though not gaudy'.[48] The marble chimneypieces were heralded similarly as 'superb'.[49] Buckingham could now enjoy full credit for what was reported as 'the magnificence suitable to the audience chamber of the Representative of Majesty in Ireland'.[50]

Amid this initial fanfare of praise for the architectural fabric of Buckingham's new Presence Chamber, none was reserved for the room's architect, whose name went entirely unrecorded and who does not appear to have left behind any drawings for it. Although it was repaired and remodelled by degrees in 1825, 1839, 1959 and in the 1960s, much of the room's original architectural fabric

Fig. 03.04.
Canopy of State,
Throne Room,
Dublin Castle,
c. 1788.
Photograph
by Davison
& Associates,
courtesy of the
Office of Public
Works, Dublin
Castle.

Fig. 03.04.
Canopy of State,
Throne Room,
Dublin Castle,
c. 1788.
Photograph
by Davison
& Associates,
courtesy of the
Office of Public
Works, Dublin
Castle.

Fig. 03.05.
Pilaster and entablature, Throne Room, Dublin Castle, 1788, detail.
Photograph by Davison & Associates, courtesy of the Office of Public Works, Dublin
Castle.

still survives as a clue to its authorship. Buckingham's canopy of state remains largely as it appeared in the engraving of 1795. It features a crowned half-dome, which projects on a robust entablature carried by generous consoles (Fig. 03.04). It also has running guilloche ornament that once framed the embroidered royal arms behind the throne. The pilasters, frieze and cornice have also endured (Fig. 03.05). In several respects, their forms recall the work of the highly influential British architect James Wyatt (1746–1813). In particular, the swagged frieze with its lion-mask paterae has parallels with that found inside Wyatt's Darnley Mausoleum in Kent. It also appears to anticipate the comparable forms of the frieze in the Saloon at Castle Coole, Co. Fermanagh (Fig. 03.06). The inventive capitals of the pilasters, too, might be said to have a loose relationship to the stylized and rather 'novel' Corinthian capitals of Wyatt's Cupola Room at Heaton Hall, Lancashire (Fig. 03.07), themselves rough quotations from the Italian Renaissance architect Donato Bramante (1444–1514).[51] Yet for all its approximate similarities to Wyatt's work there is a naivety in the handling of the

Left: Fig. 03.06. The Saloon, Castle Coole, Co. Fermanagh.
© National Trust Images/Andreas von Einsiedel.

Right: Fig. 03.07. The Cupola Room, Heaton Hall, Lancashire.
Courtesy of Country Life Picture Library.

Presence Chamber that betrays a less assured hand. The positioning of the lion masks in the frieze directly over each of the capitals is a confident response to the verticality and weight of the pilasters below them. However, their placement in the angles of the frieze, as a means of acknowledging and attempting to define the corners of the room, which are without pilasters, is rather more gauche (see Fig. 09.24). It leaves the whole relationship between pilasters and frieze feeling unresolved. That one of the standard hallmarks of Wyatt's practice, the repetition of the patterns of the frieze in the entablatures of the doors, appears to have been eschewed, doubles the dissonance and almost certainly rules out his involvement.

In several recent studies, the room has been confidently attributed to the Irish architect Thomas Penrose (1740–1792).[52] Though circumstantial, the evidence is compelling. From 1784 until his death in 1792, Penrose served as Inspector of Civil Buildings, which would have automatically placed him at the viceroy's disposal in the event of any modifications being ordered at Dublin Castle. Perhaps more significantly, Penrose worked as James Wyatt's Irish agent for fifteen years, from 1772 to 1787.[53] This may readily explain the Wyattesque character of the room. In that capacity he executed a drawing for the bedroom lobby at Lucan House, Co. Dublin, which shows a pair of grisaille overdoors of a type similar to those illustrated in the 1795 print of the Presence Chamber (Fig. 03.08). The drawing for Lucan is signed and dated April 1776.[54] Crucially, Penrose produced a signed plan of the first floor of the State Apartments at Dublin Castle in November 1789. The plan clearly identifies what had been the old Guard Chamber as the 'Audience Chamber', thereby confirming Penrose's familiarity and probable association with the recent work (Fig. 03.09). A newly identified record demonstrates that Buckingham and Penrose enjoyed some form of professional or personal relationship. It was a relationship that was sufficiently healthy for Buckingham to appoint Penrose to the responsible position of Commissioner of the State Lottery.[55] The appointment was made on 19 August 1788, just a month before the commencement of works on the new Presence Chamber. Convincing though this body of evidence is, there is still room for speculation.

Having undertaken to pay for the work himself, Buckingham would have been eager to ensure that his investment represented good value for money. This very personal influence over the project may well have extended to the selection of the architect. It also cannot be ignored that at the time of the room's development, Buckingham's protégé, the Italian artist and architect Vincenzo Waldré (1740–1814), was working on his colossal ceiling paintings just two rooms away,

Fig. 03.08.
Thomas Penrose,
design for the
Bedroom Lobby,
Lucan House, Co.
Dublin, 1776,
detail.
Courtesy of the
National Library of
Ireland.

Fig. 03.09.
Thomas Penrose,
plan of the first
floor of Dublin
Castle, 1789,
detail of the
Presence Chamber.
© The National
Archives, UK,
WORK 31/20.

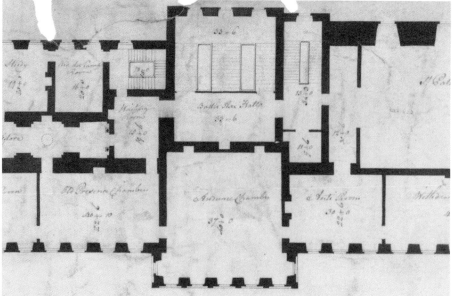

in St Patrick's Hall. Waldré was very familiar with Buckingham's preferred Neoclassical idiom, having designed a spectacular music room for him at Stowe, Buckingham's palatial country seat in Buckinghamshire (Fig. 03.10). After Penrose, he is the most likely contender for the distinction of having designed the Presence Chamber. In any case, regardless of its uncertain authorship and certain minor imperfections, the new Presence Chamber was in keeping with Buckingham's ambitious aims for his 'fête' at Dublin Castle. It was the general impression rather than the individual effects that carried the day. Buckingham had made what was viewed as a bad room a good one and, at the expense of

Fig. 03.10. The Music Room, Stowe House, Buckinghamshire. Courtesy of the Stowe House Preservation Trust.

his anonymous architect, had taken the credit for it. The extent to which he did so is evident from a contemporary newspaper article. In a glowing account that would undoubtedly have prompted Buckingham to reach for his scissors and scrapbook, *The Dublin Journal* trusted that the Presence Chamber, together with the ongoing improvements to St Patrick's Hall, would be interpreted as a triumph that was fully 'creditable to the Viceroy'.[56]

Happy for the Kingdom: Buckingham as Patron of the Arts

It has been observed that for the German philosopher Georg William Friedrich Hegel, 'architecture was a medium only half articulate, unable to give full expression to the Idea, and hence relegated to the level of pure symbolism, from which it must be redeemed by statuary and ornament'.[57] Similarly, for the Marquess of Buckingham, architecture was not the only channel through which an idea of his taste, erudition and largesse could be conveyed. An enthusiastic patron of the fine and decorative arts, he was fully alive to the power of art as a tool in the fashioning of his public image. The grandiose architectural settings he devised were only as expressive as the paintings, textiles, sculpture and decorative schemes he routinely commissioned to complement them. Only through the *Gesamtkunstwerk*, or 'total work of art', could the true breadth of his patronage achieve its full manifestation. The new Presence Chamber was to be no different and Buckingham would set out to furnish it with items that reflected his support for the arts in Ireland. The benefits of this were self-evident, and strongly influenced his approach to design, decoration and furnishing at Dublin Castle. In August 1788, *The Freeman's Journal* issued a robust defence of his support for Irish artisans:

> His Excellency ... has constantly almost appeared in the manufactures of this country, in private as well as public, giving the most extensive orders for various rich suits, and strictly enjoining, that all the cloaths of his household, as well as every article of refitting up, and furnishing the Castle, should be of Irish manufacture. Happy for the kingdom, had her own nobility and gentry shown a tenth part of this zeal![58]

A month later, there was more praise when he arranged for an order of linen to be commissioned from John Carleton and Co. of Lisburn, Co. Antrim, for the household of King George III at Windsor Castle. The action was greeted as a 'very valuable and distinguished compliment' and a gesture of 'friendship' towards the country.[59] A measure of the story's import was that it was also reported outside of Dublin, in the Kilkenny-based *Finn's Leinster Journal*, where the products commissioned were referred to as 'the finest sets of house linen'.[60] Buckingham's insistence on sourcing Irish furnishings and fabrics for Dublin Castle not only helped to augment his own popularity, but also helped to set a trend that would be followed by other conscientious viceroys in the nineteenth century. Newly identified letters show that at least two later viceroys followed his example. In February 1831, the new viceroy Henry William Paget, 1st Marquess of Anglesey (1768–1854) wrote to the Board of Works (later the Office of Public Works or OPW), which managed Dublin Castle. In his letter, he stipulated that 'every article' commissioned for a state building in Ireland, including Dublin Castle, 'should be of Irish Manufacture'. [61] Similarly, in September 1838, a directive was issued by the then viceroy Constantine Henry Phipps, 2nd Earl of Mulgrave, later 1st Marquess of Normanby (1797–1863), that new furniture for the State Drawing Room at Dublin Castle 'should be purchased in Dublin, when such can be obtained sufficiently well executed'.[62]

Buckingham's support for Irish textile manufacturers can be traced to his first viceroyalty, as Earl Temple, from 1782 to 1783. Among the lucrative commissions awarded in that period was one for 'four new suits of Irish manufacture ... for each of his numerous retinue', whom, it was said, he would 'not permit to wear any cloaths ... other than the produce of Irish looms'.[63] A year later, he was ordering 'several hundred yards of figured linings' for his house at Stowe.[64] The order was given to the Master of the Corporation of Weavers in Dublin. The original records of the Corporation of Weavers in the Royal Society of Antiquaries of Ireland allow the Master in question to be identified as Henry Williams. The records show that Williams was first elected Master on 26 March 1781 and was re-elected for a second year on 25 March 1782.[65] Even small orders were invariably placed with local manufacturers. An original record of one such order has recently come to light. On 8 April 1783, Hannah Lagraviere of 13 Skinner Row (now Christchurch Place), Dublin, received a payment of £60.0.4 from Buckingham, for trimmings for the household livery at Dublin Castle.[66] According to her signed bill, which has survived among Buckingham's papers, she provided twelve dozen pieces of broad livery lace, fourteen dozen pieces of narrow livery lace, fourteen 'baggs' for the grooms of the chamber, twenty-six 'baggs' and thirteen yards of ribbon for the footmen, and three orange sword

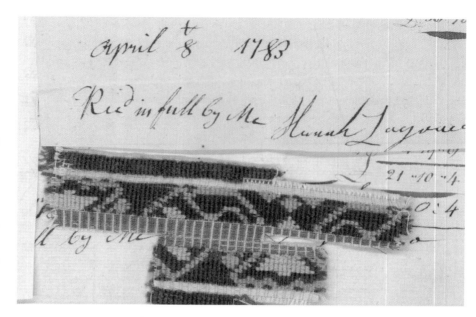

knots for the pages.[67] Remarkably, a rare sample of her trimming has survived with the bill. It suggests a rather vivid palette of orange, green and yellow for Buckingham's livery at the Castle (Fig. 03.11).

Buckingham's efforts to source local products such as these are easily understood in the context of the challenges facing the arts and the manufacturing industry in Ireland in the eighteenth century. By the 1780s, the castigation of Irish patrons for their eschewal of Irish products and services, in favour of European imports, had reached fever pitch. 'Is there a prince in *Germany* or *Italy*', enquired one writer as early as 1729, 'who may not, without Disparagement to his Rank or Grandeur, Ride in such a *Coach* or *Chariot* as I can have made or finish'd in *Dublin*? Is there a Subject of *Britain*, that need blush to appear dress'd in a choice of *Irish Holland* or *Broad-Cloth*?'[68] In 1738, Samuel Madden offered a chilling summary of the problems as he saw them:

> Betwixt the monstrous Mismanagement of the Splendour and Expence of the Rich in foreign Countries or Commodities and the Idleness and Laziness of the Poor, the Tradesmen, Labourer and Husbandmen (chiefly for want of Encouragement) we have been ground to Pieces as between the upper and the nether Millstone.[69]

By 1759, the argument was still evolving. 'In the case of building', wrote Henry Brooke, 'and in truth, in many others; we are (from our inherent hospitality) apt to set too high a value on foreigners: of whom some have appeared to be nothing more than forward prating, superficial pretenders'.[70] To his benefit and credit, Buckingham made sure that he was on the right side of this argument.

Continuing his publicity-winning formula as he prepared to decorate his new Presence Chamber, Buckingham visited what was referred to as 'the Glass House on the North Strand', in November 1788.[71] This visit was said to be 'preparatory to his bespeaking a set of magnificent lustres, for St. Patrick's-hall, and the new rooms at the Castle'.[72] The premises in question can be identified as those of Messrs Chebsey and Co.[73] Whether any of these lustres were ultimately commissioned and installed in the new Presence Chamber is not known but the report, which mentioned that Buckingham was attended on his visit 'by a number of the nobility', sent out the correct message of patriotic example regardless.[74] Later in the same month, it was communicated that in another patriotic gesture, Buckingham had engaged 'the uncommon talents of Mr. De Grey' to paint four pictures 'to be placed over the doors in the new presence chamber at the Castle'.[75] The artist in question was the chief exponent of grisaille painting in Ireland, Peter de Gree (1751–1789).[76] Praised by Sir Joshua Reynolds (1723–1792) as 'a very excellent painter in chiaro-oscuro in imitation of basso-relievos ...', de Gree was a Flemish artist who was invited to Ireland in 1785.[77] He had come to Dublin at the invitation of Buckingham's popular predecessor, the 4th Duke of Rutland. Under Rutland's auspices, he had been designated keeper of an intended new national gallery, which failed to materialize due to Rutland's sudden death in 1787.[78] By the beginning of December 1788, de Gree's commission for the Presence Chamber was being reported in detail:

> The basso relievo figures which Mr De Gree is painting by order of his Excellency the Marquis of Buckingham, to be put up over the door[s] of the new Presence Chamber, are the Four Seasons, strikingly designed, and rendered so seemingly independent of the canvas, that to the nicest eye, they are the deception of relief, highly finished by the sculptor's chisel, and starting forward with unexampled beauty and boldness.[79]

Notwithstanding de Gree's nationality, his employment by Buckingham was cited in the newspapers as another example of 'how warmly' the viceroy was 'inclined to countenance the arts' in Ireland.[80] By the time of de Gree's death in January 1789, only one of the four pictures, *Autumn*, had been completed.[81] Its whereabouts are unknown.

In commissioning the grisailles from de Gree, it is possible that Buckingham was inspired by the Saloon at Buckingham House (later Buckingham Palace), London, which had been ornamented with similar grisaille overdoor paintings only a year earlier (Fig. 03.12).[82] Buckingham would almost certainly have been familiar with the space on account of its function as a presence chamber for Queen Charlotte, and may have been seeking to pay the King and Queen a compliment by emulating it at Dublin Castle. De Gree's untimely death was an initial blow to any such intentions. However, as the 1795 engraving of Buckingham's Presence Chamber shows, a similar scheme for the spaces over the doors does appear to have been carried out. The full-length male portrait illustrated in the same engraving is almost certainly the painting of

Fig. 03.12.
James Stephanoff,
Buckingham House: The Saloon,
1818.
Royal Collection Trust/© Her Majesty Queen Elizabeth II 2017.

King George III referred to in a later description of the room from 1821.[83] It was placed opposite a matching full-length portrait of Queen Charlotte. This practice had parallels with the display of portraits of King Charles I and Queen Henrietta Maria in the Presence Chamber at the Castle during the viceroyalty of Thomas Wentworth, 1st Earl of Strafford, in the 1630s. There can be little doubt that these twin portraits are those from the studio of Allan Ramsay (1713–1784) that remain in the Dublin Castle collection today. They may have been installed in the new Presence Chamber by Buckingham as a further paean to the royal couple, but given his often turbulent relationship with the King, they may have been more useful to him as illustrations of the weight of his own office. The 1821 description of the room records two additional features that almost certainly dated from Buckingham's scheme of 1788; walls of a 'light blue colour' and 'elegant' window cornices 'emblematic of the order of St. Patrick'.[84]

Fig. 03.13. John Keyse Sherwin, *The Installation Banquet of the Knights of St Patrick*, 1785, sketch. © National Gallery of Ireland.

During the festivities surrounding the foundation of the Order of St Patrick in 1783, Buckingham had proudly used Dublin Castle for the grand installation dinner on St Patrick's Day, 17 March. A painting of this assembly in St Patrick's Hall was produced at Buckingham's request by the English artist John Keyse Sherwin (1751–1790), in 1785 (Fig. 03.13).[85] In common with a portrait of him by Robert Hunter (*c.* 1715/20–1801), now in the Deanery of St Patrick's Cathedral, Dublin, it depicts Buckingham in his distinctive light blue robes as the Grand Master of his new order of knights (Fig. 03.14). Buckingham felt a deep sense of pride in having convinced King George III to establish what he flippantly and frequently referred to as 'my Order'.[86] Strictly speaking, it was, of course, the sovereign's order. Throughout the nineteenth century, Buckingham's Presence Chamber would be used periodically for the investiture of new Knights of St Patrick (see Fig. 04.22). This practice is a reminder of the Presence Chamber's little-known but important connection to an order that is more commonly associated with St Patrick's Hall and St Patrick's Cathedral. Much like the emblems of the Order that once enriched the room's window cornices, and the inimitable shade of St Patrick's blue that appears to have coloured its walls, it is a legacy that reflects Buckingham's pride in the Order, as much as in himself for creating it. It has been said of St Patrick's Hall, that 'the provision of opulent premises, appropriately decorated, was key to lending this new chivalric body a veneer of "history and legitimacy"'.[87] The same may be true of Buckingham's new Presence Chamber of 1788.

It would be misleading to claim that self-promotion was the only motivation that shaped Buckingham's approach to ornamenting the Presence Chamber and benevolently patronizing the arts in Ireland. There can be no doubt that he was naturally generous and paternalistic and there is much evidence to demonstrate this. During his time in charge of Stowe, this extraordinary house is said to have 'reached the heights of its numerous house parties and extravagant entertainment, with dinners and dances for hundreds at the slightest excuse'.[88] Buckingham also nursed a genuine passion for art, architecture and music, and sought to create interiors and entertainments that would inspire and delight. Despite these altruistic motivations, there is also evidence that he was aware of the political gains to be made from using the arts to build his reputation, and that he acted accordingly. This was most apparent in a celebration held during his first viceroyalty at Dublin Castle. In honour of the Queen's birthday, St Patrick's Hall was 'new fitted up ... and ornamented with painted festoons of flowers'.[89] There

Fig. 03.14.
Robert Hunter,
*George, Marquess
of Buckingham,
first Grand Master
of the Order of St
Patrick*, 1783.
Photograph
by Davison &
Associates,
courtesy of St
Patrick's Cathedral,
Dublin.

Fig. 03.15.
Vincenzo Waldré,
*King George
III flanked by
Hibernia and
Britannia*, 1788–
1802.
Photograph by
Mark Reddy,
Trinity Digital
Studios, courtesy of
the Office of Public
Works, Dublin
Castle.

was a lavish banquet in the Gothic Supper Room, where a 'new scene of splendor was exhibited'.[90] In addition to the delights of the tables, one of the most striking features singled out for comment by *The Dublin Evening Post* was a transparent painting:

> The room was well decorated round with numerous beautiful and well-engraved devices; in the middle window was a transparent painting, representing Britannia and Hibernia plighting faith to each other ... with Peace descending from above with an olive branch.[91]

Fig. 03.16.
Sir Joshua Reynolds, *The Temple Family*, c. 1780–2.
© National Gallery of Ireland.

The day after the ball, Buckingham wrote to his brother, William, expressing satisfaction at the effect of this transparent painting. Its subject had apparently been selected for political effect. 'Our ball', he bragged, 'was the fullest and most splendid ever seen ... hardly a lady of quality absent; and on my part every thing was done as you will imagine. The enclosed which I have just cut from the *Dublin Evening* [*Post*] will shew you that my transparency has its effect'.[92] The theme of Britannia and Hibernia in a state of concord was evidently one he considered especially effective. It would later form the centrepiece of Vincenzo Waldré's ceiling paintings in St Patrick's Hall, which, it is now clear, were commissioned by Buckingham not in 1787, as has been thought hitherto, but in September 1788.[93] Executed on a scale that dwarfed the efforts of 1783 and bordering on political propaganda, this astonishingly precocious work would be the ultimate realization of Buckingham's aspirations as a patron (Fig. 03.15). By the time he came to commission the Presence Chamber and the ceiling of St Patrick's Hall, Buckingham had fully grasped the power of the arts to forge his public persona.

In the years between 1782 and 1788 there had been numerous grandiose artistic projects. There were portraits. One, by Sir Joshua Reynolds, showed him, together with his artistic wife, who was reputed to have been a pupil of Reynolds, very much as 'the eighteenth-century Grand Seigneur' (Fig. 03.16).[94] The inclusion of the Borghese Vase in the background speaks of their cultivation and affinity with antique classicism. Several portraits of Buckingham found their way into private, civic and national collections.[95] Others took the form of more modest prints

Fig. 03.17. 'Earl Temple'. *The Hibernian Magazine: or, Compendium of Entertaining Knowledge,* October 1782. Courtesy of the National Library of Ireland.

that appeared in Irish periodicals, and helped keep his genteel image alive in the public consciousness (Fig. 03.17).[96] There was also music. In 1783, having discovered that the trumpeters and drummer responsible for the Irish State Music were now living in England, Buckingham suggested that the band should be reorganized and expanded. The result was an enlarged band of six trumpets, seven violins, two French horns, two hautboys, fours bass viols, a dulcimer and a kettle drum.[97] However, with the remodelled St Patrick's Hall still incomplete by the end of January 1789, nothing had yet compared to the ambition of the new Presence Chamber. In early January 1789, *The Dublin Evening Post* thought it 'very doubtful' that the Presence Chamber would be completed in time for the opening of the new session of the Irish Parliament, when it would be required for viceregal levees.[98] Its fears proved unfounded, and the room was fit to host its inaugural levee by the end of the month, on Sunday, 25 January.[99] Dour Doric in the old Presence Chamber had been eclipsed by courtly Corinthian in the new one. Buckingham, from mediocrity, had made majesty. The architecture and decoration of the new Presence Chamber proclaimed his social, political and cultural position at the apex of Irish society. But who would heed that proclamation?

Something Preying upon his Mind: Buckingham's Collapse

For a brief interval during the winter of 1788/9, Buckingham's new Presence Chamber appeared to be ameliorating the reputation he had recently damaged through public quarrels with the Church of Ireland and the Ordnance Office. As has been demonstrated, it cast him in the role of a master of court etiquette, a connoisseur of modern architectural fashions and a philanthropic patron of the arts in Ireland. Despite this, not all the newspapers expressed unreserved enthusiasm for the new room. One commentator opined that the doors were 'poor and paultry, and utterly inadequate to a room of state', recommending that their panels should instead be 'formed of looking glass'.[100] Another was critical of the lack of Irish artists working on the Presence Chamber project, noting that '*foreign manufacture* at the fountain of fashion – the Court' could be 'productive of no good influence'.[101] Others deplored the effect the new room had on circulation in the State Apartments. 'Instead of the former grand entrance', wrote one columnist, 'you must now pass through a lobby which was before merely the landing ... of the great stair-case, which at present resembles the confined lobby of a decent prison'.[102] This new space on the landing at the top of the main imperial staircase had been created as a surrogate lobby for the Battle Axe Guards (see Fig. 03.09). The guards had been displaced by the works to turn their old Guard Chamber into the Presence Chamber. There is little record of the new lobby other than a contemporary account describing it as a space 'inclosed in glass cases to form a contemptible waiting-room', the creation of which was 'exceedingly to be lamented'.[103] Notwithstanding its evident unpopularity as an aesthetic blight on the Castle's principal staircase, the OPW Papers show that this makeshift area remained in place until as late as 1864. On 27 June of that year, a plan was agreed to remove it and restore the staircase to its original appearance.[104] The work was estimated at £65 and involved the provision of a new timber handrail and cast-iron balusters, all of which remain in place today.[105]

Some critics also used Buckingham's relocation from the Castle to temporary lodgings at the Royal Hospital, Kilmainham during the creation of the new Presence Chamber, as a further source of criticism in this period. When Lady Buckingham had the misfortune to go into labour in the less than salubrious surroundings of this old soldiers' hospital, in January 1789, before she and her husband had returned to the Castle, satirists wasted little time in sketching a bawdy cartoon. It illustrated the level to which the King's representative in Ireland had sunk (Fig. 03.18). Yet in spite of these minor tribulations, Buckingham carried on, confidently anticipating the new Castle season that would allow him to display his improvements. In jubilant spirits, he had little expectation of the crisis that was about to befall him.

Fig. 03.18.
William Holland (published by), *The Vice Q –'s delivery at the Old Soldier's Hospital in Dublin*, 1789. © The Trustees of the British Museum.

Towards the end of 1788, King George III had begun a slow descent into a bout of serious mental illness. By November 1788, his condition had worsened and the daily business of the British and Irish parliaments had become severely impeded as a result. On Thursday, 19 February 1789, the Irish Parliament resolved to transmit an address to London, inviting the Prince of Wales to assume the government of Ireland in place of his ill father. That evening, at four o'clock, members of both houses of Parliament processed to Dublin Castle to deliver their address to the viceroy, for transmission to London. It is ironic that this, the event that sealed Buckingham's fate in Ireland, is almost certain to have been one of the first that took place in his new Presence Chamber. Responding to the parliamentary delegation, Buckingham stated that he was 'obliged to decline transmitting this Address to Great Britain', claiming that he did not consider himself 'warranted' to do so.[106] He would later write in confidence to his brother that he had taken this fateful step in the context of pressure brought to bear on him by, among others, the Prime Minister, William Pitt (1759–1806). Having been pressed to take action, he had reached a judgement that he felt was 'essential to the King's service' and 'in every point of view … indispensable'.[107] Later that evening, *The Dublin Evening Post* informed its readers that such was the boldness of Buckingham's move, that impeachment was already being talked of.[108] The situation deteriorated rapidly. Two days later, it was being said that a more daring measure had seldom been attempted by any viceroy in Irish history, than Buckingham's move to 'wantonly' and 'weakly' block the Parliament of Ireland in this way.[109] By 26 February, it was the view of the press that Buckingham's position as viceroy was no longer tenable and that he must be removed from office. It was said that this would 'mark the spirit of the people, and be a caution to his successors not to dare to provoke the indignation of Irishmen'.[110] Buckingham's administration was in crisis. Brazenly he hung on until a reprieve came in the form of the King's recovery, in early March, but the damage had been done.

Several newly identified records show that Buckingham served his final few months as Viceroy of Ireland in much the same state as he had always done. There were balls and banquets, and fireworks in celebration of the King's return to health, but they were too little too late. The artifice of pomp and ceremony that had sustained him before was now found wanting at every turn. His fireworks display at St Stephen's Green on St Patrick's Day 1789, recognized by the newspaper as 'an effort to remove an expiring popularity', was thoroughly ridiculed as 'destitute of taste in the design', and dismissed as 'mean and disgusting'.[111] His ball at the Castle that night saw the new Presence Chamber appropriated for 'cortillons' and 'French dances' in an attempt to maintain the usual gaiety.[112] There was some praise for a transparency of the King's arms, which appeared in the exterior pediment of the Presence Chamber:

> The front of the Castle, over the great entrance, was distinguished by a very handsome transparency, the king's arms, well painted, supported on one side by a figure of Britannia, and on the other by that of Hibernia, and underneath the words, LONG LIVE THE KING.[113]

However, the prevailing interpretation of the event was negative.

In one final attempt to curry favour, Buckingham wrote to his brother in May to announce a spectacular ball he was planning. 'I have ordered', he chirped, 'a most magnificent *fête* for the Queen's real birthday on 18th May; pray take care that the compliment is not lost. We serve upwards of 560 covers, all in St. Patrick's Hall, to a supper partly hot, the rest cold'.[114] Although still clearly working to maximize the publicity value of his artistic endeavours in the highest places, he was now beset by a telling sense of unease and insecurity. 'I am anxious', he conceded, 'for many reasons, to establish the reputation of the ... most splendid entertainments, which I shall have given this winter'.[115] Buoyed by the prospect of this event, Buckingham became delusional:

> I can quit this wretched kingdom with a high head; I can deliver to my successor the King's sword in full vigour and powers; and I feel that I have taught to the Government a lesson on the subject of this Aristocracy which is invaluable, if properly used.[116]

In the event, the ball was spectacular but it was Buckingham who had been taught the lesson. Vincenzo Waldré excelled himself in the design of a massive arcade crowned by 'the best fancied scroll-work' supporting a 'Regal Coronet'.[117] He decorated this arcade with 'illuminated suns ... which, with stars that accompanied them, seemed to float in the air'.[118] There were copious quantities of fresh flowers, strawberries, nectarines, peaches and pears. There were orange trees that extended to twelve feet in height. A band played in the Presence Chamber, and at either end of St Patrick's Hall, there were also Buckingham's trusty transparencies, which featured images of the King and Queen. These, along with the rest of the decorations, were also the work of Waldré.[119] Though undoubtedly impressive, they were still not enough. A final, poorly attended and lacklustre celebration of the King's birthday prompted *The Dublin Evening Post* to conclude: 'Such a celebration … is worthy [of] the Lord of –Bucks'.[120]

Faced with an unforgiving public and parliament, Buckingham descended into what can now be understood as a bout of acute depression. On 5 June 1789, he wrote to his brother of the onset of this debilitating state of mind:

> I cannot describe to you how much my health has already suffered, and how much I lose ground hourly by reflexions of the most unpleasant nature which hourly press upon me. In this unfortunate state of mind I have looked impatiently to Hobart's arrival [Robert Hobart (1760–1816), 4th Earl of Buckinghamshire, Chief Secretary for Ireland], that I might go … to any new scene sufficiently removed from Dublin … I feel how much you will be distressed by this letter, but it is really made necessary by my situation, which is only relieved by the affectionate and constant attentions of my wife. I struggle against it, but I fear that nothing but … a cessation of business and of anxiety can relieve me.[121]

On 9 June, the Irish attorney general, John FitzGibbon, later 1st Earl of Clare (1748–1802) wrote that Buckingham was 'very much out of order' and 'so much depressed' that even minor exertion was affecting him to 'a very alarming degree'.[122] That same day, Lady Buckingham outlined the deterioration in his condition and what she saw as the probable reason for it, in a letter to his brother: 'The dejection of his spirits is greater than you can have any idea of … there seems to be something preying upon his mind which retards his recovery … From what he sometimes drops, I think he is much hurt at the King's not having *marked* any satisfaction at his conduct'.[123] In the context of this advanced level of personal and social insecurity, and desperation for acclaim, it is perhaps understandable why Buckingham had lavished so much time, money and energy on creating a more impressive Presence Chamber and courtly environment at Dublin Castle. But it had all come to nothing. Dejected and desolate, Buckingham resigned as Viceroy of Ireland and departed Dublin Castle in October 1789.

In the final analysis, he was not judged kindly and several satirical rhymes were penned at his expense. One unpublished verse offered a bleak assessment of his tenure. It threw into sharp contrast his inadequacies, in comparison to the virtues of his predecessor:

> Ye Papists & Ye Presbyters, your tythes are in the lurch still
> For tho' his wife's a Roman, he'll make Ye pay the Church still...
> At length he'll leave our Country as same as Wales or Scotland
> O what a mighty difference between Buckingham [and Rutland].[124]

To make matters worse, King George III was 'adamant in his refusal of a dukedom'.[125] Buckingham was crestfallen and described himself as 'the most disgraced *public man* ...'[126] Following George III's final descent into a total mental collapse later in life, the old King is reputed to have said in one of his soliloquies, 'I hate nobody, why should anybody hate me?', before pausing and adding, 'I beg pardon, I do hate the marquess of Buckingham'.[127] Like Busiris, King of Egypt, Buckingham had been defeated by the equals he had undervalued and those whose loyalty he had taken for granted. He would never hold high political office again. Having withdrawn to the shadows, he died of diabetes on 11 February 1813.

Surmounted by the Crown: The Presence Chamber after Buckingham
After Buckingham's lifetime, his Presence Chamber at Dublin Castle continued to be the principal stage for royal and viceregal ceremonial in Ireland, until the twentieth century. Under the custom established by Buckingham, courtiers entered the Presence Chamber from the east through the ante-room, or old Presence Chamber, before proceeding through the space and into the Dining Room, or Portrait Gallery, to the west. Many of its functions changed little over the years, with viceregal inauguration ceremonies and levees generally following the same pattern until the twentieth century. However, there were occasional deviations from the established programme of events, such as the christening of the son of the viceroy, Charles Chetwynd-Talbot, 2nd Earl Talbot (1777–1849) in the room, in March 1818.[128] The selection of the Presence Chamber for a religious ceremony of this nature has parallels with similar practices in Buckingham Palace, where Queen Victoria's eldest daughter, Victoria, Princess Royal, was christened in the Throne Room. Other novel events included the State Trumpet Dinner of 1826. It was given in what was referred to as 'the Grand Presence Chamber, in the first style of elegance'.[129] One of the most controversial

moments in the room's history came in April 1833, when a new government coercion bill, roundly criticized as a 'curfew law', was introduced by the then viceroy, the 1st Marquess of Anglesey.[130] It was designed to curb recent outrages in Co. Kilkenny and had received royal assent in London a few days earlier. The use of the Presence Chamber for the announcement of a political measure of this sort was highly unusual. However, it is worth remembering that since Ireland's assimilation into the United Kingdom in 1801, a vacuum had been left behind by the abolition of the Irish Parliament, which had served as the forum for political discourse. Notwithstanding the profound nature of such events, lighter moments did occasionally punctuate the solemnity. At the inauguration of the new Lord Mayor of Dublin, Mr Alderman Hodges, on 30 September 1836, an excitable crowd undermined the regal dignity of the space. 'At the conclusion of his Lordship's address', it was reported with some amusement, 'the crowd in the Presence Chamber, forgetting the place, broke into a simultaneous cheer'.[131]

The unrivalled highlight in the room's history in the early nineteenth century came on 20 August 1821, when it accommodated the state levee of the new monarch, King George IV. It was in preparation for this momentous occasion that a new throne was installed. Little is known about the earlier throne it replaced, other than that it had been 'covered with crimson velvet, richly ornamented with gold lace ...'[132] For all the physical and symbolic prominence of the new throne, which remains in the room today, there is a similar paucity of original information relating to it. Its maker was not recorded and no evidence of its design has yet been identified, despite careful analysis of contemporary Board of Works records. Its grandiose Regency form was clearly developed with reference to its function as a receptacle, not only for the viceroy and British monarch, but also for the Irish Sword of State, which rested on two specially designed projecting tendrils (Fig. 03.19). An account of the Presence Chamber issued in advance of George IV's levee also failed to mention the exact circumstances in which the throne had been commissioned. However, it provides much detail on the room's appearance by this date:

> The throne is most richly gilt, burnished in oil gold, and picked out with white – The top, of a most gorgeous and glittering canopy, is mounted with the Royal lion and the unicorn, and these are surmounted by the Crown – the back of the Throne is covered with the richest crimson velvet, with the Arms of the Sovereign most splendidly embroidered in pure gold. The drapery

Fig. 03.19. Throne, Throne Room, Dublin Castle, *c.* 1821.
Photograph by Davison & Associates,
courtesy of the Office of Public Works, Dublin Castle.

round the canopy is profusely embroidered, and edged by a deep gold fringe; the chair, or seat, is elevated, and there are two easy ascending steps, forming a circle round the Throne. The cushion, which is edged with gold, is of a crimson colour. The platform is covered with a Turkey carpet.[133]

As has been mentioned, light blue walls formed a backdrop to twin portraits of the late King George III and Queen Charlotte at this time. Apart from the introduction of the new throne, the Presence Chamber appears to have remained virtually unchanged since its completion by Buckingham thirty-two years earlier.

Extravagance even in Small Things: The Marquess Wellesley, Buckingham's Heir
In October 1839, the room would undergo a radical overhaul designed to reflect Ireland's status as part of the United Kingdom. New evidence in the OPW Papers shows that before these major interventions, there was one final, significant alteration to Buckingham's original scheme. On 26 May 1825, the Secretary to the Board of Works informed its architect, Francis Johnston (1760–1829), that he had received proposals from several builders for taking down and reconstructing the front of the Presence Chamber, including the portico, which, by then, was at risk of collapse.[134] The correspondence shows that by 10 June the proposals of Messrs E. Carolin had been accepted. The cost of the building work was estimated at £2,833.10.2 and an additional £204.15.0 was set aside to cover the cost of new chimneypieces for the room.[135] These twin chimneypieces, slightly altered, remain in situ today (see Fig. 04.11). Their simple Roman fasces have connotations of power that are consistent with the room's original function. Significantly, the building works also necessitated the replacement of Buckingham's original ceiling of gilded stucco. The task of executing a replacement ceiling fell to George Stapleton (1777–1844). He was awarded the commission, on the basis of his estimate of £221.0.10.[136] Stapleton's new ceiling was said to be 'remarkable for its delicate tracery and exquisitely carved devices, illustrative of the Order of St. Patrick'.[137] Some impression of its appearance can be ascertained from an early Ordnance Survey map, the survey work for which was carried out in 1838. It shows a florid decorative composition that was somewhat at odds with Buckingham's restrained Neoclassical space (Fig. 03.20).

Work progressed swiftly and on 1 December 1825, the viceroy, Richard Colley Wesley, 1st Marquess Wellesley (1760–1842), was petitioning the Board of Works to have the newly restored room 'new canvassed and papered'.[138] His request was

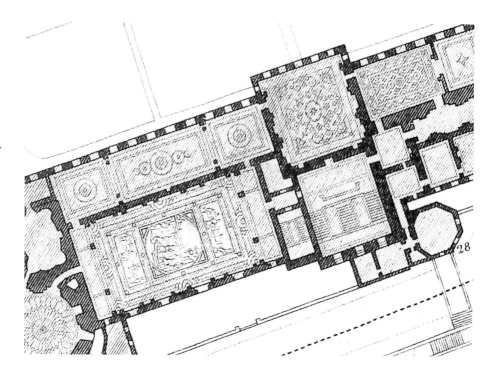

duly granted at the beginning of 1826. A surviving set of estimates produced by Francis Johnston for finishing the work shows that the new wallpaper was patterned and had been selected as an alternative to the 'coloured' [painted] walls that, according to Johnston's notes in the margin, had 'required to be renewed every two or three years'.[139]   No record of the pattern or colour of this new wallpaper has survived. Seven new roller blinds for the windows, crimson cloth for covering the dais supporting the throne, and paint for the woodwork in the room, were also estimated for. The total cost was £149.16.0.[140] By 30 March 1826, the finishing touches were being applied. These included 'ten looking glasses, to be placed behind the lustres', as requested by Wellesley, for the modest cost of £35.00.[141] The only other piece of furniture known to have been commissioned for the room before the remodelling of 1839 was a double ottoman of a somewhat domestic character. It can be seen in later nineteenth-century photographs of the space (see Fig. 04.02). Its production was sanctioned by the Secretary to the Board of Works on 12 March 1829, following a specific request from the then viceroy Hugh Percy, 3rd Duke of Northumberland (1785–1847).[142] Its introduction into the Presence Chamber hints at slightly more comfortable and perhaps less formal arrangements for levees and presentation ceremonies during Northumberland's viceroyalty.

It was fitting that, as the viceroy who presided over the alterations to the Presence Chamber in 1825, the Marquess Wellesley had been a close personal friend of Buckingham. The elder brother of the Duke of Wellington, he had been one of the fifteen men selected by Buckingham to become the founding Knights of the Order of St Patrick. During his two terms as viceroy, from 1821 to 1828 and again from 1833 to 1834, Wellesley maintained the grand traditions of his earlier stint as Viceroy of India, by spending prodigiously. Unlike Buckingham, he did so not from his private purse, which was always depleted, but from the rather healthier public one. It has been said that his jewellery, heavy facial rouge, painted lips and artificially blackened eyebrows 'betrayed extravagance even in small things'.[143] His official portrait at Dublin Castle would appear to corroborate this interpretation (see Fig. 06.04). Wellesley 'no doubt believed that the trappings of power were essential to the exercise of power'.[144] Abundant evidence of this survives in the OPW Papers. It shows that in addition to directing the costly refurbishment of the Presence Chamber, he was frequently engrossed in developing lavish furnishing schemes and entertainments for the rest of the State Apartments.

In March 1824, Wellesley requested new furniture for the State Apartments to the value of £444.17.9.[145] In February 1825, he petitioned the Board of Works for a suite of new carpets, at an estimated cost of £290.6.8.[146] However, these requests paled into insignificance when, in December of that year, his extravagance reached new heights with a request for furniture and works in the State Apartments, to the value of £1,377.4.1.[147] In 1826, he submitted numerous requests, seeking, among other things, the restoration of Buckingham's vast ceiling paintings in St Patrick's Hall.[148] Wellesley's extraordinary spending continued unabated until the beginning of 1828, when the Under-Secretary for Ireland, William Gregory (1762–1840), brought the situation to a head. On 27 January, the Secretary to the Board of Works was obliged to write to Gregory to justify the spending on the viceroy's apartments, which, he conceded, was 'certainly very great'.[149]

In many ways Wellesley's tenure at Dublin Castle had echoes of Buckingham's grand regime of the 1780s, but by the late 1820s, no doubt as a result of Gregory's intervention to curb Wellesley's profligacy, the executive powers of the viceroy in matters relating to interior decoration, were curtailed. The dilution of this privilege was made almost absolute on 15 October 1831, when the Board of Works was abolished and replaced by the Office of Public Works. Radical changes in personnel soon followed. Overseeing the day-to-day activities of this new institution was its parsimonious secretary, Henry Paine. As the early records of the OPW show, Paine would operate a scrupulous system of financial controls within which there was little room for discretionary viceregal splendour.[150]

Defer Repairing: The Dwindling of Funds

A mark of this new, more conscientious approach to the management of finances at Dublin Castle can be perceived in the discussions surrounding proposed improvements to the interior of the Presence Chamber in the late 1830s. By 1838, Henry Paine had, under a certain amount of duress, allowed some funds to be re-allocated towards the construction of a new balcony on the room's exterior.[151] As well as providing a viewing platform for the viceroy, the balcony would offer shelter to those alighting from carriages at the main entrance to the State Apartments below it. Paine's decision was taken in response to a direct

Fig. 03.21. Jacob Owen (attr. to), design for Throne Room balcony, Dublin Castle, 1837–8. Courtesy of the Office of Public Works Library.

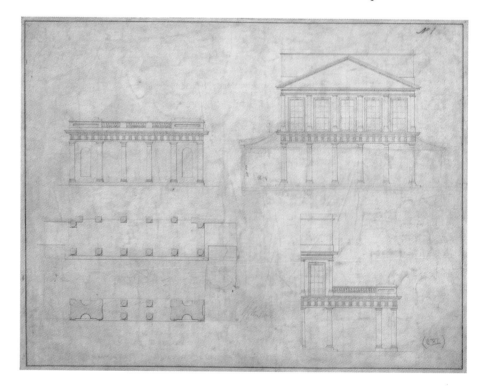

request from the then viceroy, the 2nd Earl of Mulgrave and his wife, Maria, Countess of Mulgrave (1798–1882).[152] An unexecuted design from this period, for a projecting five-bay Doric balcony, survives in the OPW Library (Fig. 03.21). This grandiose early proposal featured a central three-bay loggia flanked by piers containing niches, and supporting a balustrade. Although unsigned, the design was almost certainly the work of the OPW architect, Jacob Owen (1778–1870). On 24 January 1838, Henry Paine expressed concerns about the suitability of the design, on the basis that it would render the Entrance Hall in the State Apartments 'very dark'.[153] It was promptly rejected.

A compromise was eventually reached whereby a shallow balcony with a cast iron and glass canopy was constructed later that year. Although architecturally incongruous and undistinguished, the new balcony extended the reach of the Presence Chamber into the public sphere and cost less than the original design (see Figs 04.01 & 09.05). The additional expense incurred in the balcony's construction, coupled with inaccuracies in the architectural estimates for 1838, provided Paine with the leverage he needed to cancel the planned remodelling of the interior of the Presence Chamber. On 4 May 1838, Paine wrote to Jacob Owen, stating:

> As the funds in the Estimates were not intended to cover the cost of the Workmen applied for you must postpone improvements in the Presence Chamber … Perhaps His Excellency [the viceroy] would think it right to defer repairing the Presence Chamber until next year …[154]

Thus was Buckingham's room given a stay of execution for one additional year. To any of the naturally profligate or design-conscious viceroys of the 1820s and 1830s, like Wellesley and Mulgrave respectively, the extravagant era of Buckingham and his palatial Presence Chamber at the Castle, must have seemed like a golden age and a distant memory.

Conclusion

In attempting to characterize architecture as an art form, Roger Scruton has observed that it 'imposes itself whatever our desires and whatever our self-image' and that, moreover, 'it takes up space: either it crushes out of existence what has gone before, or else it attempts to harmonize'.[155] As he took one last look at his newly minted Presence Chamber in Dublin Castle, in October 1789, the Marquess of Buckingham was very likely conscious of a similar truth. He had sought to crush and expunge the memory of an undignified guard chamber through the making of a great new room. In doing so, he had attempted to conjure a novel self-image that would be as beguiling and fresh as the new Presence Chamber itself. Yet, ultimately, he had gained little from his efforts. His dividend could scarcely have been more than the memory of a costly personal investment that had never been given the time to bear fruit. In the final analysis, it was perhaps evident that all but the architecture of the room would endure and impose itself. With the inevitable erosion of cultural memory surrounding the room's history that followed over the centuries, which was compounded by the extinction of its original function in 1922, it could hardly have been otherwise. With the passage of time, the circumstances of the room's development and the reasons behind its creation have become obscure, whatever Buckingham's possible aspirations to the contrary.

In seeking to retrieve them, this essay has demonstrated that despite the focus on his well-publicized faults and foibles, the ultimate judgement of Buckingham should arguably take into account his rich and enduring legacy as an architectural patron. His great painted ceiling by Waldré in St Patrick's Hall remains the most important eighteenth-century scheme of its type in Ireland. Now, the Presence Chamber, too, can take its rightful place among the catalogue of personal contributions he envisaged, resourced and made tangible at Dublin Castle. As this essay has shown, Buckingham's legacy as a patron of the arts, in the case of the Presence Chamber, was built on the confluence of various complex factors in late eighteenth-century Ireland. These were at once, social, cultural, political and, perhaps above all, personal. The richness of his endowment is a reminder that such viceregal legacies cannot, and should not, be simplified or conflated. The case of Buckingham underscores the very active and influential role of the viceroy as a patron of the arts in Ireland and the example this could set, as a means of stimulating Irish artistic production. The benefits of this for artisans such as Hannah Lagraviere, Chebsey and Co., Peter de Gree and Henry Williams were not merely abstract but took the form of real commissions for real money. New evidence has shown that Buckingham's insistence on sourcing Irish furniture and fabrics for Dublin Castle would later be echoed by Irish viceroys in the nineteenth century. Their influential support for Irish cultural production, which has often gone unnoticed, challenges the notion of the viceregal court as a mostly Anglo-centric entity that routinely deferred to Britain in matters of elite consumption.

Yet whatever the benefits for Irish artisans, the Presence Chamber of 1788–9 was, first and foremost, about Buckingham. It was an idea conceived in his mind, as an expression of his self-image and a product of his private purse. By the 1830s, the appropriation of this viceregal prerogative by a reformed public administration, meant that the Presence Chamber would never again express so emphatically the character of one individual. It had become an expression not of narrow self-interest but of the wider interests of the expanded United Kingdom of Great Britain and Ireland, an entity bigger than any single personality or nation within it. As such, the room's evolution offers an insight into the freedoms once enjoyed by the most powerful men in Georgian Ireland, to use the architecture of the state as a tool in the making of majesty. Like Busiris, King of Egypt, to whom he was so memorably and amusingly compared, Buckingham's name has indeed been written as much in 'triumphal columns' as in the annals of Irish history.[156] Yet the paucity of cultural memory surrounding aspects of his story over two centuries is a useful reminder that, in the words of Edward Young, 'Structures so vast by those great kings design'd, Are but faint sketches of their boundless mind'.[157]

I would like to express my deep gratitude to the Hall Bequest Trust and the Georgian Group for their generosity in awarding me the inaugural George B. Clarke Prize, which has helped to support the research for this essay. I am also very grateful for the help and advice of Anna McEvoy, Roger Potter, Annabel Westman, David McKinstry, Ludovica Neglie, Rafael Cathoud, Dr Anna Moran and the late Giles Waterfield.

Endnotes

1   E. Young, *The Works of the Author of the Night-Thoughts* (London: J. Buckland & W. Bowyer, 1774), vol. 2, p. 3.
2   *Freeman's Journal*, 18 September 1788.
3   Ibid.
4   *Freeman's Journal*, 18 September 1788.
5   *Dublin Evening Post*, 18 September 1788.
6   Ibid.
7   See Young, *The Works of the Author*, p. 8.
8   Ibid., p. 94.
9   C. Gallien, 'Recycling the Orient in Eighteenth-Century British Literature: The case of Busiris by Edward Young', *Études Anglaises*, 63, 4 (October–December 2010), pp. 394–5.
10 *Freeman's Journal*, 20 September 1788.
11 *Dublin Journal*, 18–20 September 1788.

12 E. McParland, *Public Architecture in Ireland 1680–1760* (New Haven and London: Yale University Press, 2001), p. 104.

13 *Dublin Evening Post*, 30 October 1788; *Dublin Journal*, 30 October–1 November 1788.

14 Anon., 'Description of the Houses of Lords and Commons of Ireland, and of Dublin Castle', *The Weekly Entertainer*, 31 (2 July 1798), p. 15.

15 *Freeman's Journal*, 28 October 1788.

16 *Dublin Journal*, 30 October–1 November 1788.

17 See, for example, *The Manuscripts of J.B. Fortescue, Esq., preserved at Dropmore* (London: Historical Manuscripts Commission, 1892), vol. 1, pp. 197, 432.

18 Ibid., p. 204.

19 J. Robins, *Champagne & Silver Buckles: The Viceregal Court at Dublin Castle 1700–1922* (Dublin: The Lilliput Press, 2001), p. 68.

20 Ibid., p. 77.

21 Letter to Earl Temple from the Earl of Clanricarde, 18 January 1783, National Library of Ireland, Mss Joly 39–40.

22 Letter to Earl Temple from the Earl of Ely, 17 January 1783, National Library of Ireland, Mss Joly 39–40.

23 R.W. Davis, 'Grenville, George Nugent-Temple-, first marquess of Buckingham (1753–1813)', in H.C.G. Matthew and B. Harrison (eds), *Oxford Dictionary of National Biography* (Oxford: Oxford University Press, 2004), vol. 23, p. 728.

24 P. Geoghegan, 'Grenville, George Nugent Temple (1753–1813)', in J. McGuire and J. Quinn (eds), *Dictionary of Irish Biography* (Cambridge: Cambridge University Press, 2009), vol. 4, p. 261.

25 Ibid.

26 'Inventory of the Furniture in the Lord Lieutenant's House in the Phoenix Park taken October 31 1782', Stowe Papers, Huntington Library, California, STG CL&I, box 13, folder no. 12.

27 Ibid.

28 See Geoghegan, 'Grenville', p. 261.

29 See *The Manuscripts of J.B. Fortescue*, p. 205.

30 A.P.W. Malcomson, *Archbishop Charles Agar: Churchmanship and Politics in Ireland, 1760–1810* (Dublin: Four Courts Press, 2002), p. 230.

31 Ibid., p. 235.

32 Anon., 'Extract of a letter from Dublin, Aug. 30', *The Edinburgh Magazine, or Literary Miscellany*, 8, 45 (September 1788), p. 129.

33 Ibid.

34 See *The Manuscripts of J.B. Fortescue*, p. 358.

35 See Malcomson, *Archbishop Charles Agar*, p. 230.

36 See McParland, *Public Architecture*, p. 104.

37 See Davis, 'Grenville', p. 730.

38 *Dublin Journal*, 18–20 September 1788.

39 G. O'Brien, 'Revolution, Rebellion and the Viceroyalty 1789–99', in P. Gray and O. Purdue (eds), *The Irish Lord Lieutenancy, c. 1541–1922* (Dublin: University College Dublin Press, 2012), p. 116.

40 C. Casey, *Dublin: The City within the Grand and Royal Canals and the Circular Road with the Phoenix Park* (New Haven and London: Yale University Press, 2005), p. 356.

41 *Freeman's Journal*, 28 October 1788.

42 F. O'Dwyer, 'Making Connections in Georgian Ireland', *Bulletin of the Irish Georgian Society*, 38 (1996/97), p. 18.

43 *Dublin Journal*, 30 October–1 November 1788.

44 *Dublin Evening Post*, 30 October 1788.

45 *Dublin Journal*, 24–27 December 1788.

46 *Dublin Evening Post*, 18 November 1788.

47 M. Bevington, *Stowe House* (London: Paul Holberton Publishing, 2002), p. 51.

48 *Dublin Journal*, 30 October–1 November

1788.

49 Ibid.

50 *Freeman's Journal*, 29 November 1788.

51 J.M. Robinson, *James Wyatt: Architect to George III* (New Haven and London: Yale University Press, 2012), p. 84.

52 See O'Dwyer, 'Making Connections', p. 18; also Casey, *Dublin*, p. 355.

53 See Robinson, *James Wyatt*, p. 103.

54 P. McCarthy, *Life in the Country House in Georgian Ireland* (New Haven and London: Yale University Press, 2016), p. 64.

55 *Freeman's Journal*, 19 August 1788.

56 *Dublin Journal*, 30 October–1 November 1788.

57 R. Scruton, *The Aesthetics of Architecture* (London: Methuen & Co., 1979), p. 5.

58 *Freeman's Journal*, 14 August 1788.

59 *Freeman's Journal*, 9 September 1788.

60 *Finn's Leinster Journal*, 13 September 1788.

61 Letter to William Murray from R. Robinson, 3 February 1831, Board of Works letter book, National Archives of Ireland, OPW1/1/2/4.

62 Letter to Jacob Owen from Henry R. Paine, 3 September 1838, OPW letter book, National Archives of Ireland, OPW1/1/2/6.

63 *Freeman's Journal*, 19 September 1782.

64 *Freeman's Journal*, 18 February 1783.

65 Ballot book for elections of Masters and Wardens of the Corporation of Dublin Weavers, 1761–1806, Royal Society of Antiquaries of Ireland, RSAI/BV/WVRS/013.

66 Bill for livery lace, 20 January 1783, Stowe Papers, Huntington Library, California, STG CL&I, box 13, folder no. 12.

67 Ibid.

68 Patriophilus, *Considerations on the Act for Encouraging in-land Navigation in Ireland* (Dublin: William Smith, 1729), p. 25.

69 S. Madden, *Reflections and Resolutions Proper for the Gentlemen of Ireland* (Dublin: R. Reilly, 1738), pp. 15–16.

70 C. Casey, '"Such a Piece of Curiosity": John Aheron's *A General Treatise of Architecture*', *The Georgian Group Journal* (1995), p. 78.

71 *Dublin Journal*, 11–13 November 1788.

72 Ibid.

73 I am grateful to Dr Anna Moran for this observation.

74 *Dublin Journal*, 11–13 November 1788.

75 *Freeman's Journal*, 29 November 1788.

76 P. McCarthy, 'Decorative Painting 1600–1900', in N. Figgis (ed.), *Art and Architecture of Ireland: Volume II, Painting 1600–1900* (New Haven and London: Yale University Press, 2014), p. 69.

77 Ibid.

78 C. Barrett and J. Sheehy, 'Visual Arts and Society, 1850–1900', in W.E. Vaughan (ed.), *A New History of Ireland VI: Ireland under the Union II, 1870–1921* (Oxford: Oxford University Press, 2012), p. 436.

79 *Dublin Journal*, 2–4 December 1788.

80 *Freeman's Journal*, 29 November 1788.

81 W.G. Strickland, *A Dictionary of Irish Artists* (Dublin: Irish Academic Press, 1989), vol. 1, p. 271.

82 See J.M. Robinson, *Buckingham Palace: The Official Illustrated History* (London: Royal Collection Publications, 2000), pp. 19–20.

83 *Morning Post*, 8 August 1821.

84 Ibid.

85 N. Figgis, 'The Contribution of Foreign Artists to Cultural Life in Eighteenth-Century Dublin', in J. Fenlon, R. Kenny, C. Pegum and B. Rooney (eds), *Irish Fine Art in the Early Modern Period* (Dublin: Irish Academic Press, 2016), pp. 207–8.

86 P. Galloway, *The Most Illustrious Order: The Order of Saint Patrick and its Knights* (London: Unicorn Press, 1999), p. 16.

87 B. Rooney, 'Vincent Waldré: Sketch for the Ceiling of St Patrick's Hall in Dublin Castle', in B. Rooney (ed.), *Creating History: Stories*

of Ireland in Art (Dublin: Irish Academic Press, 2016), p. 179.

88 See Bevington, *Stowe House*, p. 17.

89 *Dublin Evening Post*, 20 February 1783.

90 Ibid.

91 *Dublin Evening Post*, 20 February 1783. Transparencies were described in the eighteenth century as 'paintings on silk &c., with such thin transparent colours, as admit the light to pass through the picture; these are much used for decorations, illuminations, &c., and by means of artificial and brilliant light placed behind them, they have a very gay and sprightly effect'. See C. Taylor, *The Artist's Repository and Drawing Magazine, Exhibiting the Principles of the Polite Arts in their Various Branches* (London: T. Williams, 1784), p. 137.

92 See *The Manuscripts of J.B. Fortescue*, p. 197.

93 Vincenzo Waldré's arrival in Dublin to begin work on the ceiling paintings in St Patrick's Hall was first recorded in *The Dublin Evening Post*, 18 September 1788: 'A number of artists have arrived from England–by the special nomination of his Excellency the Marquis of Buckingham, for the purpose of decorating the rooms at the Castle … The ball-room alone, it is said, will cost more than a thousand guineas. Mr Waldrea, the principal painter, imported on this occasion, is esteemed by AMATEURS to be the first in his profession–he has just completed some necessary embellishments at the Marquis of Buckingham's beautiful seat at Stowe'.

94 J. Gilmartin, 'Vincent Waldré's Ceiling Paintings in Dublin Castle', *Apollo*, 95 (January 1972), p. 43.

95 See, for example, R. Walker, *Regency Portraits* (London: National Portrait Gallery, 1985), vol. 1, pp. 72–3; M. Clark, *The Dublin Civic Portrait Collection: Patronage, Politics and Patriotism, 1603–2013* (Dublin: Four Courts

Press, 2016), pp. 77–8.

96 See Anon., 'An Account of the Earls Temple, embellished with a Striking Likeness of the Present Earl', *The Hibernian Magazine* (October 1782), pp. 505–6; Anon., 'Memoirs of the The Right Hon. Earl Temple', *London Magazine, or Gentleman's Monthly Intelligencer* (October 1782), pp. 451–2.

97 R.B. McDowell, 'The Court of Dublin Castle', in R.B. McDowell, *Historical Essays 1938–2001* (Dublin: The Lilliput Press, 2003), p. 6.

98 *Dublin Evening Post*, 3 January 1789.

99 *Dublin Journal*, 24–27 January 1789.

100 *Dublin Evening Post*, 30 October 1788.

101 *Dublin Evening Post*, 18 September 1788.

102 See Anon., 'Description of the Houses', p. 15.

103 *Dublin Evening Post*, 30 October 1788.

104 Letter to Major Bagot from E. Hornsby, 27 June 1864, OPW letter book, National Archives of Ireland, OPW1/1/2/29.

105 Ibid.

106 *Dublin Evening Post*, 19 February 1789.

107 See *The Manuscripts of J.B. Fortescue*, p. 467.

108 *Dublin Evening Post*, 19 February 1789.

109 *Dublin Evening Post*, 21 February 1789.

110 *Dublin Evening Post*, 26 February 1789.

111 *Dublin Evening Post*, 17 March 1789.

112 *Dublin Evening Post*, 19 March 1789.

113 *Finn's Leinster Journal*, 21 March 1789.

114 See *The Manuscripts of J.B. Fortescue*, p. 471.

115 Ibid.

116 See *The Manuscripts of J.B. Fortescue*, p. 470.

117 *Freeman's Journal*, 19 May 1789.

118 Ibid.

119 *Freeman's Journal*, 19 May 1789.

120 *Dublin Evening Post*, 6 June 1789.

121 See *The Manuscripts of J.B. Fortescue*, pp. 476–7.

122 Ibid., p. 478.

123 See *The Manuscripts of J.B. Fortescue*, p. 478.

124 Verse referring to the Marquess of Buckingham, Macartney-Filgate Papers, Public Record

Office of Northern Ireland, D2225/7/38N.

125 See Davis, 'Grenville', p. 729.

126 Ibid.

127 See Malcomson, *Archbishop Charles Agar*, p. 231.

128 *Caledonian Mercury*, 19 March 1818.

129 *Belfast Newsletter*, 2 May 1826.

130 *Freeman's Journal*, 8 April 1833.

131 *The Examiner*, 9 October 1836.

132 J. Warburton, J. Whitelaw and R. Walsh, *History of the City of Dublin* (London: printed for T. Cadell & W. Davies by W. Bulmer & Co., 1818), vol. 1, p. 471.

133 *Morning Post*, 8 August 1821.

134 Letter to Francis Johnston from R. Robinson, 26 May 1825, Board of Works letter book, National Archives of Ireland, OPW1/1/2/3.

135 Letter to Francis Johnston from R. Robinson, 10 June 1825, Board of Works letter book, National Archives of Ireland, OPW1/1/2/3.

136 Ibid.

137 *Freeman's Journal*, 26 December 1839.

138 Letter to Francis Johnston from R. Robinson, 1 December 1825, Board of Works letter book, National Archives of Ireland, OPW1/1/2/3.

139 'Estimate of the probable expense of furniture required in the State Drawing Rooms & c., Dublin Castle', 1826, Registered Papers of the Office of Chief Secretary of Ireland, National Archives of Ireland, CSO/RP/1826/551.

140 Ibid.

141 Letter to Francis Johnston from R. Robinson, 30 March 1826, Board of Works letter book, National Archives of Ireland, OPW1/1/2/3.

142 Letter to William Murray from R. Robinson, 12 March 1829, Board of Works letter book, National Archives of Ireland, OPW1/1/2/4.

143 P. Brynn, 'The Marquess Wellesley', unpublished PhD thesis, Trinity College Dublin, 1977, vol. 1, pp. 98–9.

144 Ibid., p. 99.

145 Letter to Francis Johnston from R. Robinson, 18 March 1824, Board of Works letter book, National Archives of Ireland, OPW1/1/2/3.

146 Letter to Francis Johnston from R. Robinson, 3 February 1825, Board of Works letter book, National Archives of Ireland, OPW1/1/2/3.

147 Letter to Francis Johnston from R. Robinson, 22 December 1825, Board of Works letter book, National Archives of Ireland, OPW1/1/2/3.

148 Letter to Francis Johnston from R. Robinson, 8 June 1826, Board of Works letter book, National Archives of Ireland, OPW1/1/2/4.

149 Letter to William Gregory from R. Robinson, 27 January 1828, Board of Works letter book, National Archives of Ireland, OPW1/1/2/4.

150 See, for example, letter to Matthew Winter from Henry Paine, 26 February 1834, OPW letter book, National Archives of Ireland, OPW1/1/2/5.

151 Letter to Jacob Owen from Henry Paine, 4 May 1838, OPW letter book, National Archives of Ireland, OPW 1/1/2/6.

152 Letter to Thomas Drummond from Henry Paine, 24 January 1838, OPW letter book, National Archives of Ireland, OPW 1/1/2/6.

153 Ibid.

154 Letter to Jacob Owen from Henry R. Paine, 4 May 1838, OPW letter book, National Archives of Ireland, OPW 1/1/2/6.

155 See Scruton, *The Aesthetics*, p. 15.

156 See Young, *The Works*, p. 94.

157 Ibid., p. 3.

Four

'Quite Like a Palace'

The Presence Chamber at Dublin Castle
1838–1911

Graham Hickey

The modern-day appearance of the Throne Room, which was known for most of the nineteenth century as the Presence Chamber, is the achievement of a major campaign of alterations carried out during the late 1830s under two successive lords lieutenant or viceroys. The incumbents in question were Constantine Henry Phipps, 2nd Earl of Mulgrave, later 1st Marquess of Normanby (1797–1863), and Hugh Fortescue, Viscount Ebrington, later 2nd Earl Fortescue (1783–1861). These works took place as part of a wider series of improvements undertaken in the State Apartments at Dublin Castle during the 1820s and 1830s, but they may also be viewed against a changing administrative backdrop, where conflicting viceregal regimes expressed political sympathies through the panoply and decoration of court.

The primary impetus for these changes, as much practical as it was ceremonial, was likely to have been the preparation of the State Apartments for the reception of the new monarch, Queen Victoria, who came to the throne in June 1837 and was crowned in June 1838. Expectation of a royal visit to Ireland may have provided the opportunity to refashion the Marquess of Buckingham's existing Neoclassical Presence Chamber into a bombastic showpiece of imperial strength. By default, or strategic intent, the newly configured room managed to accomplish

Facing page:
Fig. 04.01.
Entrance to the State Apartments, Dublin Castle, after 1867.
Courtesy of the National Library of Ireland.

an indigenous aesthetic – one that, in spite of the imperialist overtones, exhibited a distinctively Irish character. It is a rare example of ceremonial interior architecture in Ireland that has survived relatively unaltered to the present day (see Fig. 09.24).

Since the mid-eighteenth century, the Presence Chamber in Dublin Castle had been used as a formal space for the reception of public deputations by the viceroy and for his ceremonial investiture at the beginning of his appointed term. The room hosted levees during the court season and was pressed into use during balls, the voluminous crowds of which commandeered most of the public rooms in the State Apartments. Both the adjacent old Presence Chamber, reconstructed from 1749 to 1751, and the new Presence Chamber, formed in the 1780s, were personal manifestations of the status and power of their commissioners: William Stanhope, 1st Earl of Harrington (*c.* 1683–1756) and George Nugent-Temple-Grenville, 1st Marquess of Buckingham (1753–1813) respectively. Arguably, their contemporary decorations *à la mode* represented the taste and cultivation of the individual men more than the public office they held – their respective presence chambers reading as elegant drawing rooms with canopies of state in a nod to the power of their positions.

The change in role of the viceroy to largely one of figurehead in the decades after the Act of Union in 1800 provided a cue change for the future approach to ceremonial decoration in the Presence Chamber. Personal aristocratic patronage and bombast were supplanted by the burgeoning bureaucracy of the Board of Works (known from 1831 as the Office of Public Works or the OPW), which was responsible for the upkeep of Dublin Castle, and by the machinery of permanent government in Ireland. While the viceroy was still consulted on any proposed works at Dublin Castle and politely asked to provide schedules of expected expenditure when establishing annual financial estimates, the OPW and its architect directed works ultimately. Between 1832 and 1856, Jacob Owen (1778–1870) occupied the latter position and was responsible for major physical changes at Dublin Castle during this time.

That is not to say that personal aggrandizement by successive viceroys did not continue to play a role in the enhancement of the ceremonial infrastructure at Dublin Castle. It is, perhaps, no coincidence that the major improvements of the 1830s undertaken in the State Apartments, in particular to the Presence Chamber, took place during and immediately following the elevation of the Earl of Mulgrave to the title of 1st Marquess of Normanby, in June 1838. Many of the alterations pointedly aggrandized the setting in which the incumbent's formalities could be more theatrically played out.

A sizeable component of these works was the construction of the new State Drawing Room to the east of the old Presence Chamber (see Fig. 02.14). This work was well underway in 1838, albeit at a sluggish pace. In September of that year, the OPW wrote to Jacob Owen in London: 'it is probable the works in the Drawing Room at the Castle will be delayed longer than you expect, if a judgement may be formed from the present appearance of things'.[1]

At the beginning of 1838, the OPW had been presented with a related headache with a request from Mulgrave to have plans devised for a porte-cochère in front of the main entrance to the State Apartments, which was to incorporate a balcony accessible from the Presence Chamber (see Fig. 03.21). Not only would this require structural intervention into the Presence Chamber, but the projected cost – ranging from several hundred to £1,000, depending on the nature of construction – was not accounted for in the financial estimates for 1838.[2] Additionally, the Comptroller of the viceroy's household had requested further alterations and furnishing for the State Apartments, probably necessitated by the improvements ongoing in various state rooms, placing more pressure on budgets for the year.[3]

It was decided to opt for an economical balcony design to meet Mulgrave's request, which was under construction by October 1838 at a cost of £246.4.1.[4] Constructed of cast iron and cantilevered off the Portland Stone entrance front with a series of ribbed brackets, and topped out with a cast-iron balustrade, this deft solution demonstrated Owen's training as an engineer and as an architect (Fig. 04.01). The addition of the balcony also had deeper symbolic meaning, forming part of the wider ceremonial re-ordering of the Presence Chamber inside. It established the room not only at the centre of the Dublin Castle complex but also at the heart of public life; a place where Mulgrave and his household could review public parades and address gathered crowds within the controlled environs of the Upper Castle Yard – all, perhaps, with an eye to Mulgrave's elevation in the peerage later that year. Significantly, the balcony pre-dated by a decade the original public balcony designed by architect Edward Blore (1787–1879) for the principal front of Buckingham Palace, London, incorporated at the suggestion of Prince Albert.[5]

Even this modest balcony was a costly overrun for the OPW, and a direction was issued to Owen in May 1838 to 'postpone the improvements in the Presence Chamber contemplated when the annual estimates were framed ...'[6] The letter concluded: 'Perhaps His Excellency would think it right to defer repairing the Presence Chamber until next year when the general renewal will take place'.[7] This is one of the first indications of a plan being masterminded for the re-ordering of the Presence Chamber, which, as correspondence records, did indeed proceed in 1839.

By 1 October 1839, the work was certainly under way, with *The Freeman's Journal* reporting that the Presence Chamber was 'in course of repair'.[8] On St Stephen's Day, 26 December 1839, the same newspaper excitedly elaborated on these changes:

> The improvements making at Dublin Castle, previous to the court season, which is expected to be very gay, are progressing rapidly. The presence-chamber will undergo a complete renovation. The ceiling of this splendid apartment, remarkable for its delicate tracery and exquisitely carved devices, illustrative of the Order of St Patrick, will be remodelled and richly gilt – also the pannels, which are divided into compartments for mirrors and historical paintings. The internal decorations promise to be of the most magnificent character; the hangings are of a superb description – a rich crimson damask tabouret – design, the Rose, Thistle, and Shamrock – emblematical of the united kingdom. The throne and canopy of state are also to be of the same material, tastefully mantled with crimson velvet. Our readers will be much pleased to learn that, in accordance with the Lord Lieutenant's express wish, they are to be of *Irish manufacture*, the Board of Public Works having, with their usual good-feeling, promptly attended to his Excellency's suggestion. The order has devolved on Messrs. Atkinson and Co, the extensive Poplin Manufacturers, and we have no doubt will be executed with their usual good taste and judgment.[9]

The re-ordering of the Presence Chamber may have had its roots in an earlier remodelling undertaken in 1825/6 when the front portion of the room extending into the Upper Castle Yard was effectively rebuilt by the architect to the Board of Works, Francis Johnston (1760–1829), and his assistant, William Murray (1789–1849). This work had included securing 'in a proper manner the ceiling and roof thereof'.[10] The surviving queen-post roof hidden above the Throne Room today appears to date from this remodelling. Following the structural stabilization, new stucco work was commissioned from George Stapleton (1777–1844) to make good the new ceiling, which may have been an economical endeavour given that the quote for the job specified 'part of Presence Chamber and Grand entrance Portico and Hall', all for the price of £221.0.10.[11] It is Stapleton's decorative ceiling that appears to be depicted on the Ordnance Survey map of Dublin for 1838 (see Fig. 03.20).

Owen's late 1830s reordering of the Throne Room was, almost certainly, directly influenced by the newly completed suite of State Apartments in Buckingham Palace. This spectacular enfilade of state interiors was commissioned by King George IV from architect John Nash (1752–1835) as part of the wider transformation of the former Buckingham House into the present Buckingham Palace. In spite of the intervening short reign of King William IV, Queen Victoria was the first monarch to actually reside in Buckingham Palace. As the Palace interiors remained unfinished upon her succession to the throne in 1837, works were swiftly undertaken to complete them for her use. The courtly procession of state rooms conceived by Nash and completed by Edward Blore represented a remarkable new phase in the aggrandizement of royal ceremonial. This sequence consisted of a lavish array of highly integrated, purpose-designed interiors that co-ordinated architecture, decoration and furnishing in an emphatically theatrical manifestation of majesty.

The letter books of the OPW record Owen being in London in September 1838 at the same time as the improvements to the Dublin Presence Chamber were being planned, prompting the possibility that he was inspecting the new Palace interiors with an eye to enhancing Dublin Castle.[12] By then, the State Dining Room in Buckingham Palace was the final room being completed to the designs of Blore, under Queen Victoria's direction. Notably, the supplier of papier mâché ceiling enrichments for that room, Charles F. Bielefeld of London, was the same supplier of similar decorations for the new State Drawing Room then under construction in Dublin Castle.[13] He was also the provider of comparable enrichments for the Viceregal Lodge (now Áras an Uachtaráin), Dublin.[14] Owen was overseeing both of these projects at the time.

Owen's alterations to the Presence Chamber in Dublin Castle directly reflect the design, layout and symbolism of Nash's new Throne Room in Buckingham Palace. In spirit, as much as in physical arrangement, the Dublin room closely follows the precedent of its London counterpart: regimentally disposed and laden with representative devices (Fig. 04.02). The central theme of Owen's decorative

Fig. 04.02.
The Throne Room, Dublin Castle, 1867–1902.
Courtesy of the National Library of Ireland.

scheme is the United Kingdom of Great Britain and Ireland, represented by national emblems – the English rose, the Scottish thistle and the Irish shamrock – incorporated in various aspects of the room's decoration.[15] This reflects Nash's similar 'bold display of heraldry' representing the three kingdoms in the coved ceiling in Buckingham Palace, framing the monarchy as a unifying force between nations (Fig. 04.03).[16] In effect, the Dublin room was 'rebranded' to align more

Fig. 04.03.
The Throne Room, Buckingham Palace.
Royal Collection Trust/© Her Majesty Queen Elizabeth II 2017.

closely with the London example, transmuting an interior once intended to eulogize the Order of St Patrick to a more conscious stage for the pageantry of the modern monarchy under Queen Victoria.

In time-honoured tradition at Dublin Castle, Owen adopted a prudent approach to re-ordering the Presence Chamber, recycling elements where possible from the previous decorative scheme. This included retaining the giant order of Corinthian pilasters lining the walls of the room, the medallion and swag frieze, and the heavy modillion cornice, all dating from the 1780s. The essential layout of the room was also retained, comprising the throne and canopy to the centre, flanked to each side by the chimneypieces of 1825, and the symmetrical arrangement of double-leaf doors arranged on the east and west walls.

The most dramatic intervention, and a feature that appears to have been directly inspired by the Throne Room at Buckingham Palace, was Owen's insertion of a coved ceiling in place of the former flat stuccoed ceiling (Fig. 04.04). Such lofty ceilings were a hallmark of Nash's theatrical interior style and were an effective device for injecting opulence and architectural distinction into a state apartment. The precise date for the creation of the coved ceiling in the Presence Chamber at Dublin Castle has remained a persistent enigma, sustained by the depiction of the previous stucco ceiling on the Ordnance Survey map as late as 1847. This is further confused by a drawing signed by Owen of a ceiling similar to the present one, entitled 'Sketch of the Proposed New Ceiling, Presence Chamber, Dublin Castle', dated August 1847. It depicts the present cove with the flat plane of

Fig. 04.04. Coved ceiling, Throne Room, Dublin Castle. Photograph by Davison & Associates, courtesy of the Office of Public Works, Dublin Castle.

the ceiling occupied by a decorative scheme that may have been intended to be executed in paint or stucco (Fig. 04.05). Another complication is an article in the 1849 edition of *Transactions of the Institution of Civil Engineers*, which recounts in considerable detail the mode adopted by Owen for raising the roof and inserting the cove of the Presence Chamber.[17] The article was published a full decade after the major alterations in the Presence Chamber in 1839, yet no date is given for when the ceiling was *actually* modified. While all of the above may point to alteration works around 1848 – after the publication of the 1847 Ordnance Survey map, and before the publication of the *Transactions* article – in fact, most evidence points to the erection of the coved ceiling as part of the 1839 transformation.

There is no specific record of the coved ceiling in the OPW records for the 1830s or the 1840s. However, it is barely conceivable that such a dramatic intervention would be made to the Presence Chamber so soon after the room was comprehensively remodelled in 1839. There would also have been insufficient space under the previous flat ceiling to accommodate the suite of substantial

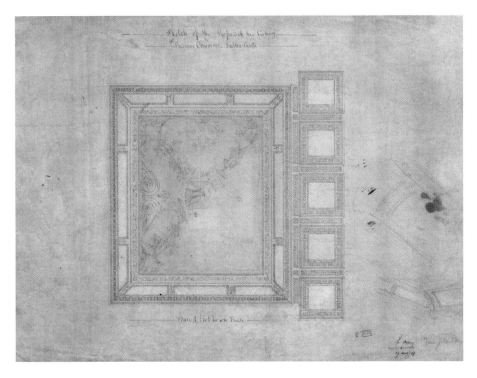

Fig. 04.05. Jacob Owen, 'Sketch of the Proposed new Ceiling, Presence Chamber, Dublin Castle', 1847. Courtesy of the Office of Public Works Library.

chandeliers commissioned for the room in November 1839. The likely explanation is that the 1847 Ordnance Survey map was not updated to reflect the new coved ceiling erected in 1839, only one year after the previously surveyed 1838 map. Accepting this scenario, the 1847 Ordnance Survey map can be taken to depict Stapleton's stucco ceiling of 1825, and not Owen's coved ceiling that was likely present in the room from 1839. Owen's 1847 sketch of a proposed ceiling appears to recycle an earlier drawing, probably dating to the late 1830s. The hard, bold lines of the cove in this sketch contrast with the softer, unfinished forms of the ornaments proposed for the central flat plane of the ceiling. This would suggest that the cove was already in place, and that the drawing of it was reused to depict an intended stucco or painted scheme that was not executed.

The account of raising the Presence Chamber roof in *Transactions* details Owen's economical method for creating the new cove. This was achieved by cutting down the existing flat ceiling, while ensuring that the trussing was disconnected from the ceiling joists, allowing the cornice to remain in situ. The existing queen-post framed roof was then ingeniously raised on screw jacks and quickly secured in its higher position by building up new brickwork underneath. Following this, the cove was inserted, connecting the ceiling with the existing cornice. Owen's structural acrobatics demonstrate not just his skills as an engineer, but also highlight the effort he was willing to exert to limit the cost of the endeavour. Dynamically recycling a roof, renewed only fourteen years previously, reinforces the proposition that the new coved ceiling *was* erected in 1839 – a project that demanded a creative design response to financially justify the intervention.

Owen's remodelled Presence Chamber, which was in use by 13 January 1840, was a *tour de force* of ceremonial state architecture, and remains one of the most unique decorative interiors in Ireland.[18] Ostensibly contrived as a statement of royal patronage and control, it also represented a remarkable collage of Irish craft skills and materials, and denoted a high point of the idiosyncratic Irish William IV style as it transitioned into Victoriana. Its eccentrically baroque wall mirrors and flamboyant set of chandeliers with emphatically bold silhouettes, perfectly capture the eclecticism of the age and the clash of concepts in Irish interior furnishings of the period. This distinctive aesthetic was driven partly by a culture within the OPW to procure furnishings and decorative finishes of Irish, and particularly of Dublin, manufacture wherever possible. Writing to Owen in September 1838, the Secretary to the Board of the OPW stated:

On the subject of Paper Hangings for The Lord Lieutenant's apartments [State Apartments] at the Castle ... I am directed to acquaint you that the Board are very anxious to carry into effect the wishes of The Lord Lieutenant and his Predecessors, that the Furniture and other articles required by the Board should be purchased in Dublin, when such can be obtained sufficiently well executed; and they would therefore wish every exertion to be used by you to have Paper of the particular Pattern (or the nearest to it) approved by Her Excellency, manufactured in Dublin, as it is a Branch of Work which the Tradesmen of Dublin understand well.[19]

Remodelling the eighteenth-century Presence Chamber had been anticipated in 1838 under the viceroyalty of the Earl of Mulgrave; however, substantial works were not executed until after the appointment of his successor, Hugh Fortescue, Viscount Ebrington, in March 1839. Ebrington was broadly disliked amongst the Irish, with his Unionist outlook starkly contrasting with the nationalist politics of his fêted predecessor.[20] Something of his uncompromising character can perhaps be discerned from the stern official portrait of him at Dublin Castle (Fig. 04.06). This was certainly evident during the inauguration of the Lord Mayor of Dublin in the Presence Chamber in October 1840, where Ebrington deviated from the typically polite format of the ceremony. On the subject of repealing the Union of Great Britain and Ireland, he stated that he would rather see war in Ireland: 'if driven to the dreadful alternative of civil war, or the dismemberment of the empire, I should prefer the former as the less evil'.[21] It is a tantalizing prospect that the overtly Unionist tone of the decoration deployed in the Presence Chamber towards the end of 1839 was a manifestation of Ebrington's politics, and of his antipathy towards the leader of the repeal movement in Ireland, Daniel O'Connell (1775–1847). It suggests that the new viceroy may have had a direct hand in the incorporation of the Union-inspired motifs throughout the room. It is a curious coincidence that Ebrington happened to be the nephew of the 1st Marquess of Buckingham, whose Presence Chamber of the 1780s he was now radically overhauling, perhaps, similarly, to reflect his own particular interests.

What is clear is that inspiration for the wider redesign and new layout was absorbed from Nash's Throne Room at Buckingham Palace. All of the core elements of the London room were borrowed by Owen: a lofty coved ceiling, a symmetrical arrangement of mirrors and furnishings, and a giant central chandelier

Fig. 04.06.
T. W. Jones,
*Hugh, 2nd Earl
Fortescue*, 1839.
Courtesy of the
Office of Public
Works, Dublin
Castle.

complemented by an attendant suite of four smaller chandeliers. It is likely that the Palace's influence also extended to some of the construction materials, given that large quantities of Charles Bielefeld's papier mâché ornamentation were imported from London in 1838 to decorate the ceiling of the Castle's new State Drawing Room.[22] This wonder material of its age was favoured by Blore for creating his ebullient palace interiors, and the enrichments applied to Owen's Presence Chamber ceiling closely conform to many of Bielefeld's catalogue designs. These include the garlands of flowers and ribbons placed between the panels on the cove and the virile band of vines framing the central coffer (Fig. 04.07).

A more radical intervention that may also have been influenced by the Buckingham Palace Throne Room is the pair of freestanding columns framing the window bay of Owen's Presence Chamber. It has previously been suggested that these columns were inserted by Johnston during the renovations of 1825/6 to support a sagging beam spanning the room, related to the wider reconstruction of the entrance front at that time.[23] However, the columns and the beam do not feature on any Ordnance Survey map of the period and there was no structural

Fig. 04.07. Coved ceiling, Throne Room, Dublin Castle, detail. Photograph by Davison & Associates, courtesy of the Office of Public Works, Dublin Castle.

Fig. 04.08.
The Throne Room, Dublin Castle, looking west. Photograph by Davison & Associates, courtesy of the Office of Public Works, Dublin Castle.

rationale for their insertion, given that the room featured an unbroken flat ceiling and a singular roof structure above. This suggests that the columns and beam were, in fact, installed by Owen in 1839 as a means of compartmentalizing the window area from the main volume of the room. This would have diverted attention away from the east and west walls, whose symmetry was compromised by the projecting window bay (Fig. 04.08). In this single gesture, Owen would have managed to formalize the space, incorporate additional structural support for his new cove, and inject a courtly air of classical antiquity with free-standing columns. This was the reverse of the arrangement in the Buckingham Palace Throne Room, where the throne there was placed in a ceremonial bay isolated from the central coved volume, but it achieved a similar effect.

It may also be assumed that the curiously dumpy capitals of the columns in the Dublin room, which do not match the capitals of the surviving pilasters

Left: Fig. 04.09. Corinthian capitals, Throne Room, Dublin Castle. Photograph by Davison & Associates, courtesy of the Office of Public Works, Dublin Castle. Right: Fig. 04.10. Ceiling over the window bay, Throne Room, Dublin Castle. Photograph by Davison & Associates, courtesy of the Office of Public Works, Dublin Castle.

from the 1780s, are off-the-peg, papier mâché products ordered by Owen from Bielefeld's extensive lines (Fig. 04.09). The positioning of the columns towards the extremities of the room, rather than as part of an evenly spaced columnar screen, also bears the hallmarks of Owen's occasionally gawky hand. Behind these, the flat ceiling of the window bay was executed in a series of coffers dressed with a Greek key to the soffits and these enrichments may also have been moulded from papier mâché (Fig. 04.10). Entombed in the attic space above this ceiling are areas of lath and plaster that almost certainly comprise tantalizing remnants of Stapleton's 1820s ceiling – a happy survivor of the requirement to retain existing joist structures during the cove-inserting operation of 1839.

The complexity of creating a rigidly ceremonial interior that synthesized art, architecture and furnishing within an existing immovable framework was clearly on the minds of Owen and other officials in the OPW during the re-ordering.

In correspondence to the Under-Secretary for Ireland, Thomas Drummond, in October 1839, it was noted:

> Among other items is one for putting in order the Presence Chamber in the Castle; and in the proposed arrangements there is a difficulty in providing for 4 compartments above the doors. It was suggested to the Comrs [Commissioners of the OPW] by Capt Williams Master of the House to His Excy [the viceroy] that some eleven Italian Paintings were to be had, admirably calculated for the object, having been manifestly proposed for similar situations.[24]

The correspondence goes on to say that among this collection of eleven paintings was a set consisting of eight. Although only four were required for the spaces above the doors of the Presence Chamber, it was observed that the four remaining pictures from this set would be 'perfectly applicable to other vice regal apartments'.[25] The paintings by the Bolognese artist, Gaetano Gandolfi (1734–1802), were subsequently secured from the well-known Gernon family firm of picture dealers, restorers and cleaners for the sum of £89.5.0, which was paid in November 1839.[26] Ultimately, six of these eight paintings found their way into the Presence Chamber, where they remain today (see Figs 05.01, 05.03, 05.04, 05.06, 05.08, 05.09). The inclusion of these paintings as a central component of the new decorative scheme for the Presence Chamber suggests a gradual evolution towards its final composition, rather than execution to a strictly prescribed plan. Their vividly Baroque style was at odds with the existing Neoclassical character of the room, and it is a credible proposition that the design approach to re-ordering the room may have been changed to match their aesthetic. Notably, orders for the suite of flamboyant chandeliers and for a pair of florid mirrors for the east and west walls were placed just over one month after the availability of the paintings was first brought to the attention of the OPW.[27]

Similarly, the order for the giltwood 'wreaths of Flowers Branches & c.' surrounding the four Gandolfi roundels above the doors was placed with Cornelius Callaghan of 24 Clare Street on 12 November 1839.[28] However, a different cabinetmaker, Cornelius de Groot, was paid £8 for two 'richly carved double wreaths' in January 1840.[29] Presumably, these are the two wreaths that frame the Gandolfi ovals positioned on the south wall over the fireplaces, suggesting a subsequent decision to include these in the room. Originally, these may have been placed centrally, in a lower position over the chimneypieces, before being moved

Fig. 04.11.
The Throne Room,
Dublin Castle,
looking south,
detail.
Photograph
by Davison
& Associates,
courtesy of the
Office of Public
Works, Dublin
Castle.

Fig. 04.12.
Cornelius
Callaghan, carved
mirror frame,
Throne Room,
Dublin Castle,
1839.
Photograph
by Davison
& Associates,
courtesy of the
Office of Public
Works, Dublin
Castle.

upwards when the crown-shaped mirrors were installed, probably for Queen Victoria's first royal visit in 1849 (Fig. 04.11). As no record of their installation has emerged in the OPW Papers, the latter do not appear to have formed part of the original 1839 design for the room, and they somewhat confuse the otherwise formal aesthetic.

Cornelius Callaghan appears to have been an established glazier and furniture maker or supplier, specializing in mirrors and giltwood furnishings. His name appears frequently in the OPW Papers as a glazier at Dublin Castle throughout the 1820s.[30] His death was recorded on 13 August 1845 'in the 75th year of his age ... sincerely and deservedly regretted.'[31] He may have been the son of another Cornelius Callaghan, 'house painter, glazier, map and printseller', who was trading in Dublin during the late eighteenth century.[32] For the 1839 re-ordering of the Presence Chamber, Callaghan was charged with supplying the 'two large Glass Frames with the Queen's arms & c' positioned on the east and west walls of the room, which, combined with the four wreaths, cost £122. They were to be 'put up in the Presence Chamber at Dublin Castle by the latter end of December next [1839]'.[33] The vast silvered plates in the mirrors appear to have comprised a separate order, recorded on 1 November 1839, for '2 Ravenhead Pier glasses of the best quality. 120 inches by 60 inches for the sum of £132.3.7'.[34] These were to be 'delivered at the Castle of Dublin within 6 weeks from this date' – precisely pre-empting the delivery of the Callaghan frames which presumably were fitted with the plates on location to avoid risk of breakage.[35] On 27 April 1840, the OPW settled the account of 'Thomas Mooney & Son' for the period

Fig. 04.13. Cornelius Callaghan, carved mirror frame, Throne Room, Dublin Castle, 1839, detail. Photograph by Davison & Associates, courtesy of the Office of Public Works, Dublin Castle.

Fig. 04.14.
Cornelius
Callaghan, carved
foliate frame,
Throne Room,
Dublin Castle,
1839.
Photograph
by Davison
& Associates,
courtesy of the
Office of Public
Works, Dublin
Castle.

up to January 1840, which included '2 silvered plates' of the same dimensions, and a 'discount off for Cash', plus 'silvering' and 'expenses', amounting to a final cost of £136.4.7.[36] Mooney & Son may, therefore, have acted as an agent for Ravenhead Glass (of Lancashire, England) in Dublin.

Callaghan's mirrors strike a curiously strident Louis XV note that is at odds with the rigid classicism of the adjacent pilasters (Fig. 04.12). Their curvaceous rococo flourishes are typical of the idiosyncratic expression of Irish furniture

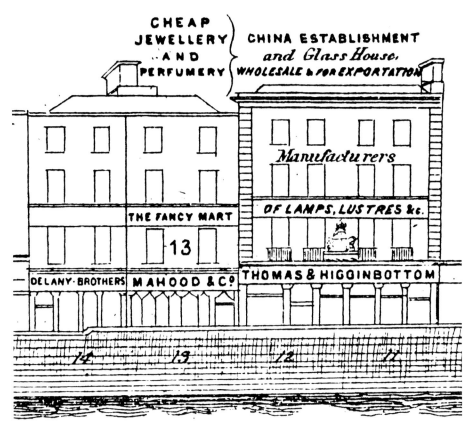

Fig. 04.15.
Premises of
Higginbotham,
Thomas & Co.,
Wellington Quay,
Dublin. Henry
Shaw, *New City
Pictorial Directory*,
1850.

design of the 1830s and 1840s. This suggests that the main body of the mirrors may have been one of Callaghan's catalogue designs, modified with the royal arms and a cluster of shamrocks, a rose and a thistle (Fig. 04.13). The same design approach to fashioning the shamrocks can be observed on Callaghan's picture wreaths alongside (Fig. 04.14).

The most dominant furnishing intervention made during the 1839 re-ordering was a spectacular set of five chandeliers supplied for the room by the Dublin firm of Higginbotham, Thomas and Company, which traded near Dublin Castle from 12 Wellington Quay (Fig. 04.15). The company had operated in various incarnations since its establishment in 1787, primarily trading in china, delft and glassware, including ironstone, earthenware and bone china.[37] The firm was a regular supplier to the OPW and features in accounts related to lustre

Fig. 04.16.
The Throne Room, Dublin Castle, 1867–1902.
Courtesy of the National Library of Ireland.

and lamp installation and maintenance. For much of the twentieth century, the central chandelier hung alone in the Presence Chamber, sustaining a perception that the smaller chandeliers, which had been scattered to other locations, had been intended for other state buildings. Remarkably, the entire suite, which is a dominant feature in nineteenth-century photographs of the Presence Chamber (Fig. 04.16), was made specifically for the room in 1839.

The lighting in Buckingham Palace must have been a major influence on the decision to commission such a theatrical lighting arrangement for the Presence Chamber. While the Palace scheme consists of five mannerly, cut-glass Regency chandeliers with attenuated profiles, the Dublin set was composed of five ormolu chandeliers in a spectacularly heavy, monumental style. Densely clustered in their original hang – with four single-tier, eighteen-light chandeliers suspended at a low level from the four corners of the upper part of the coved ceiling, and a giant two-tier, twenty-four-light chandelier hung from the centre – they presented a *mise en scène* of remarkable vigour and ostentation. The silhouette of each chandelier eschews predictable Empire rigidity in favour of a characterful eccentricity that borders on the grotesque. This is generated by a series of scrolling, foliated arms radiating from emphatic bulbous cores, terminating in flower-head flourishes that enclose the candle holders. Reflecting the patriotic theme of the room's re-ordering, each chandelier features a wreath of intertwining national plants, roses, thistles and shamrocks encircling the base, while the uppermost parts culminate in a swirling mass of acanthus leaves over which tumble further leaves, topped by a proud coronet-like arrangement evoking a regal cluster of feathers (Fig. 04.17). For added spectacle, the central chandelier originally featured a bowl-like lustre of glass beads at its base. This was later replaced with cast-metal acanthus leaves to match the smaller chandeliers. Undoubtedly, the commission from Higginbotham, Thomas and Company was one of the most prestigious of its day and the resulting lighting suite represents an important surviving example of nineteenth-century Irish craftsmanship. The tender from Higginbotham's to manufacture the chandeliers, which included a specification to hold candles, was accepted in November 1839 with a requirement that they be hung in place 'on or before the 1st of January 1840'.[38] Following installation, the account was duly settled by 27 April 1840, for the amount of £116 for the central chandelier and £50 each for the smaller chandeliers.[39]

Also paid on that date was an apparently separate commission from Higginbotham's for '4 candelabras with loose branches made to order' amounting

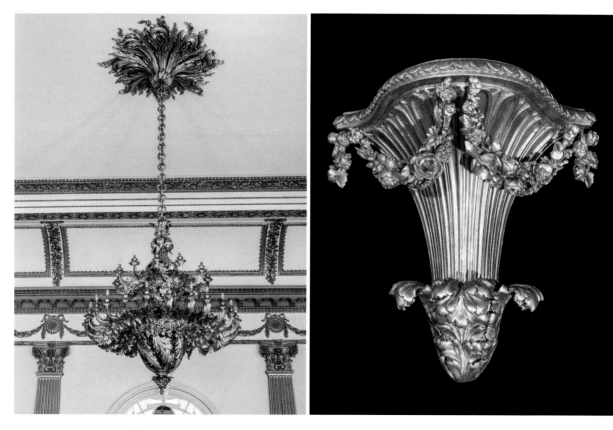

Left: Fig. 04.17. Higginbotham, Thomas & Co., central chandelier, Throne Room, Dublin Castle, 1839. Photograph by Davison & Associates, courtesy of the Office of Public Works, Dublin Castle.

Right: Fig. 04.18. Carved wall bracket, Throne Room, Dublin Castle, before 1840. Photograph by Davison & Associates, courtesy of the Office of Public Works, Dublin Castle.

to £42.[40] These candelabra were probably intended for the gilt wall brackets (Fig. 04.18) positioned to each side of the Callaghan mirrors and visible in nineteenth-century photographs of the room. A set of four candelabra from the Presence Chamber that remain at the Castle today was hosted on these brackets in the later Victorian period, and are likely to be the original specimens commissioned from Higginbotham's (Fig. 04.19).

Fig. 04.19. Higginbotham, Thomas & Co. (attr. to), candelabrum, Throne Room, Dublin Castle, 1839–40. Photograph by Davison & Associates, courtesy of the Office of Public Works, Dublin Castle.

A curious episode occurred within months of the chandeliers being installed, one that demonstrated the power that could be wielded by a viceroy impervious to resulting headaches for officials. OPW correspondence from August 1840 details a request by Ebrington to have the newly installed chandeliers 'altered so as to be lighted with oil lamps'.[41] By the 1840s, both oil and gas were well-established forms of interior lighting, but the Presence Chamber chandeliers had been specifically made to accommodate candles, presumably to amplify the glittering regal atmosphere in the most ceremonial of the Castle's state rooms. By contrast, a new suite of oil-fuelled chandeliers had been commissioned for St Patrick's Hall in December 1835.[42] The OPW at that time expressed disapproval of 'gas for such purposes'.[43] Modifying the Presence Chamber chandeliers would have been a considerable undertaking, as they had not been designed to host an oil reservoir or oil supply pipes. A pragmatic retrofit would likely have entailed the addition of glass shades mounted on individual reservoirs at the end of each arm. The modifications were duly ordered from Higginbotham's, with their bill of 14 December 1841 amounting to a staggering £194.15.0 – almost two-thirds of the cost of the initial order for making the chandeliers.[44] A number of mid-nineteenth-century prints and later photographs depict the chandeliers with glass shades. A further payment of £10 to Higginbotham's is recorded in April 1842 for 'altering lamps in the Presence Chamber', suggesting that the modifications were a drawn-out affair.[45]

Payments for new contents for the State Apartments continued during 1840 and into 1841. These included orders for '2 silvered plates' from Thomas Mooney and Son at a discounted cost of £136.4.7; '2 carved gilt baskets' from Cornelius de Groot costing £3.10.0; gilding by Gervas Murray amounting to £302.7.4; 'tabinet for furniture' at a cost of £140.5.0; and an intriguing order for 'moon lamp glasses' from E.S. Irwin totalling £10.2.0.[46] A new carpet was also commissioned for the Presence Chamber, with the OPW expressing a preference for Irish carpeting in government buildings where it was 'as good and cheap as others'.[47] The celebrated cabinetmaking firm Williams and Gibton (as it was named by the 1830s) also features in the accounts. While few commissions are itemized, it is likely that the firm made some furnishings for the Presence Chamber. In November 1839, they won the commission to replace the royal coat of arms behind the throne, with a warning 'that the Board [of the OPW] approve of the arms being forthwith embroidered, but they expect that the execution will be better than the last'.[48] The firm may also have furnished the

Fig. 04.20.
Williams & Gibton
(attr. to), carved
console table,
State Reception
Room, Áras
an Uachtaráin,
Dublin, *c.* 1839.
Photograph by
Graham Hickey.

areas underneath Callaghan's mirrors on the east and west walls. Nineteenth-century photographs depict the mirrors floating slightly above the dado level, as if hung to accommodate the top of a console table. Such an architectural treatment, which Williams and Gibton were well placed to facilitate through their mannerist style of furniture, would have lent a formality appropriate to the ceremonial function of the room. These tables may be the pair of gilt consoles that survive in the State Reception Room at Áras an Uachtaráin (formerly the Viceregal Lodge) today (Fig. 04.20). Wildly expressive and robust in stature, the tables typify the eccentric streak in Irish furniture of the period, and match the florid style of the Callaghan mirrors. Their general construction also suggests a hasty workshop assembly to accommodate a specific location, while their dimensions perfectly match the width of the Callaghan mirrors and the height of the dado rail in the Throne Room.

No documentary evidence has been uncovered to date about the decorative scheme adopted for the Presence Chamber in 1839. A requisition from December

1825 notes that the room was to be 'new canvassed and papered', indicating that the walls were to be lined with a stretched canvas onto which wallpaper could be applied, a standard decorating solution for prestigious interiors.[49] Later, in July 1848, the OPW requested that Owen furnish 'without delay ... a sketch of the mode proposed for decorating the cornice and walls of the Presence Chamber at the Castle' and expressed the opinion that 'white and gold' would be 'more appropriate than furniture of many colours'.[50] The letter confusingly conflates the decoration of the room with furniture upholstery, but it is perhaps indicative of a white and gold scheme applied to the room or more specifically to its architectural features. The exact nature and colour of the wall covering in 1839 remains elusive. It is only in 1857 that the first *direct* reference to white-painted walls emerges: 'The Presence Chamber is now being canvased ... if the walls are to be finished dead white, I would recommend that a good ground of oil paint should first be made, and that they should be finished in distemper white instead of white paper, which is not likely to make so good a piece of work'.[51] Could the remodelled Presence Chamber of 1839 originally have followed the example set by Nash at Buckingham Palace, with a vibrant crimson? If the colour remains elusive, documentary records – as well as the pragmatic hand of the OPW – at least suggest that paper was the wallcovering most likely to have been used.

Queen Victoria visited Ireland in the summer of 1849 in the midst of the Great Famine, propelling the Presence Chamber into the ceremonial limelight. Anxious to keep costs down, the administration of the Viceroy George Villiers, 4th Earl of Clarendon (1800–1870) undertook a minimum of upgrading at the Viceregal Lodge where the Queen stayed.[52] It is likely that less still was spent at the Castle given the recent enhancement of a number of the principal State Apartments. These were pressed into use for a 'drawing room' at which, according to Queen Victoria, 'one thousand six hundred ladies were presented'.[53] A grand levee was also held in the Presence Chamber, at which a remarkable 2,000 gentlemen were presented over the course of several hours, preceded by loyal addresses from various bodies.[54] Queen Victoria recounted afterwards: 'Everything here as at St. James's Levée. The staircase and throne-room quite like a palace ... Two thousand people were presented!'[55]

For the second half of the nineteenth century, the Presence Chamber settled into a comfortable and relatively undisturbed existence as a stoical observer of a predictable changing of the guard. In all, eighteen viceroys, four of whom served two terms, were sworn into office and departed from the room between the recall of Ebrington in 1841 and Queen Victoria's death in 1901. The arrival of a new viceroy followed a fairly standard routine as he journeyed from Kingstown (now Dún Laoghaire) by train to Westland Row station, Dublin. Depending on the popularity of the individual and the wider political climate, the final stage to Dublin Castle could be a low-key affair or could be accompanied by full military honours and assembled crowds, as occurred for William à Court, 1st Baron Heytesbury (1779–1860) on his arrival in July 1844. The street outside the station was lined with the First Royal Dragoons where the Lord Mayor tendered the keys of the city to Heytesbury, before the viceroy was escorted to the Castle in a procession of carriages via Nassau Street and College Green. *The Freeman's Journal* reported: 'The procession then entered the Castle, where the Lord Lieutenant was received by the Gentleman Usher, and conducted to the Presence Chamber, where their Excellencies the Lords Justices received his lordship, sitting covered under the canopy as Chief Governors'.[56] The newspaper went on to report the details of the ceremonial procedure, one that remained relatively consistent for the rest of the nineteenth century:

> After a short conference, their Excellencies the Lords Justices intimated to Lord Heytesbury that the members of her Majesty's Most Hon. Privy Council were assembled in the Council Chamber, and in readiness to administer the oaths to his lordship in the usual manner; and a procession was then made from the Presence Chamber to the Council Chamber ... The Throne-room, where Lord Heytesbury was sworn in was crowded by the nobility and gentry, who gained admission to it shortly before His Excellency's arrival.[57]

Following the reading of oaths, Heytesbury was invested with the collar and insignia of the Order of St Patrick on behalf of the Queen, before returning to the Presence Chamber where he was seated on the throne, and the Sword of State and maces were placed underneath the canopy. This final act was accompanied with three rounds of a twenty-one-gun salute by the ordnance, answered by infantry assembled in Dame Street and College Green. A levee was then held in the Presence Chamber before Heytesbury retiring, without escort, to the Viceregal Lodge.[58] Something of the formality of these occasions can be gleaned from a print recording the welcome speech presented to the new viceroy, John Poyntz Spencer, 5th Earl Spencer (1835–1910) by the Lord Mayor and Corporation of the City of Dublin on 21 January 1869 (Fig. 04.21).

Fig. 04.21.
'The Lord
Lieutenant holding
a State Reception
at Dublin Castle'.
*The Illustrated
London News*, 30
January 1869.

The Presence Chamber was a regular feature in the Castle's social calendar during the mid-nineteenth century. It played host to a constant round of levees, typically held around two o'clock in the afternoon and attended by men only, as distinct from 'drawing rooms', to which women were also admitted. Attendance at a levee was segregated into two groupings: the privileged 'Private Entree', consisting of the viceregal household, high-ranking members of the aristocracy and administration in Ireland, and the broader 'Public Entree', comprising a diverse array of public officials, religious and educational heads, military figures and members of the legal fraternity.[59] Drawing rooms were also held in the Presence Chamber, such as that held by George Howard, 7th Earl of Carlisle (1802–1864) in January 1857, which began at nine o'clock in the evening. The dress of the ladies present was reported in great detail. Of particular note were

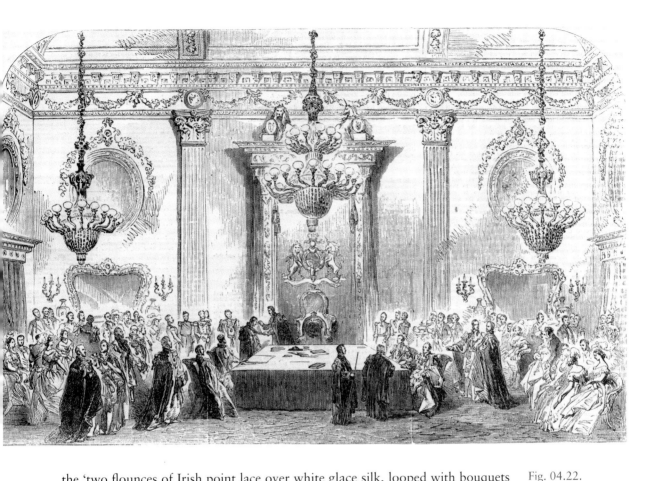

the 'two flounces of Irish point lace over white glace silk, looped with bouquets of silver flowers' worn by Lady Burke of Mount Street, Dublin, and the 'feathers and lace lappets; ornaments, diamonds and rubies' displayed by Dowager Lady Harty of Prospect House.[60] The Presence Chamber was also pressed into use for larger events, such as the St Patrick's Ball held in the State Apartments in March 1845, at which 900 people were present.[61] On that occasion, dancing was held in 'St. Patrick's Hall and the presence chamber', while other state rooms hosted the more sedate provision of refreshments, tea and coffee, and a vast supper spread across the 'long drawing room [Portrait Gallery], billiard-room [Wedgwood Room] and round-room [Gothic Supper Room]'.[62]

In between the arrival and departure of each viceroy, the Presence Chamber accommodated another major ceremonial event in the life of Dublin Castle: the

Fig. 04.22. 'Investiture of the Order of St. Patrick, at Dublin Castle'. *The Illustrated London News*, 10 March 1855.

investiture of new members of the Order of St Patrick. These included Archibald Acheson, 3rd Earl of Gosford (1806–1864) and Richard Dawson, 3rd Baron Cremorne, later 1st Earl of Dartrey (1817–1897), who were invested in March 1855 (Fig. 04.22). The room was commonly re-titled the 'Chapter Room' for these ceremonies and furnished with a chapter table and stalls to the centre, which were overseen by the Ulster King of Arms and witnessed by other members of the Order.[63]

In the quiet hours between these august ceremonies of state, the Presence Chamber also played host to less stately, but no less memorable occasions, as recounted by Lord Fredric Hamilton, son of the viceroy, James Hamilton, 1st Duke of Abercorn (1811–1885):

> My brother and I were not allowed in the throne-room on ordinary days, but it offered such wonderful opportunities for processions and investitures, with the sword of state and the mace lying ready to one's hand in their red velvet cradles, that we soon discovered a back way into it. Should any of the staff of Lord French, the present Viceroy, care to examine the sword of state and the mace, they will find them both heavily dented. This is due to two small boys having frequently dropped them when they proved too heavy for their strength, during strictly private processions fifty-five years ago. I often wonder what a deputation from the Corporation of Belfast must have thought when they were ushered into the throne-room, and found it already in the occupation of two small brats, one of whom, with a star cut out of silver paper pinned to his jacket to counterfeit an order, was lolling back on the throne in a lordly manner, while the other was feigning to read a long statement from a piece of paper. The small boys, after the manner of their kind, quickly vanished through a bolt-hole.[64]

Another entertaining, if even less dignified episode in the room's history, was recorded by Percy Fitzgerald, who worked at Dublin Castle in the mid-nineteenth century. Fitzgerald recalled how, during the tenure of the 7th Earl of Carlisle, who served as viceroy from 1855 to 1858, and again from 1859 to 1864, the balcony of the Presence Chamber was put to a somewhat inglorious use. While viewing the crowd in the Upper Castle Yard on St Patrick's Day, Carlisle is said to have 'rushed into the room beyond and reappeared laden with cakes, bread, &c., which he actually threw down to the mob – amid the yells and shouts of the rest, who struggled and fought for the morsels'.[65]

Routine maintenance and minor renewal of decorative features and furnishings in the Presence Chamber remained constant throughout the nineteenth century and into the twentieth century. The introduction of oil lighting in 1840, and the later adoption of gas lighting, generated a perennial battle against a film of soot and scorch marks on the walls and ceiling. In 1857 it was reported:

> The Presence Chamber walls, it is proposed to be finished in plain dead white colour – and as the walls require to be constantly cleaned, it is suggested they be done in distemper, which can be easily renewed. It is submitted also for the Lord Lieutenant's directions, whether it would not be advisable to remove the gas lights from over the door of the Presence Chamber, as from their proximity to the walls, and the frames, the gas is injurious.[66]

Seven years later, approval was given to convert the oil chandeliers in the State Apartments to be fuelled by gas, with an amendment subsequently issued to also alter 'the lighting in the Presence Chamber'.[67] Presumably this involved converting the existing chandeliers to gas, but may conceivably have referred to adding new lighting to the room.

Another extensive renewal of decoration in the State Apartments was begun at the end of 1866 by John Battersby, contractor, of St Stephen's Green, with upholstery by Messrs Fry and Son of Westmoreland Street, Dublin. Several adjustments in the Presence Chamber were reported:

> ... the canopy over the throne has been re-embellished in white and gold; the carvings, on the carved ceiling have all been re-gilt, and the fluted pillars set in the same colours. Crimson brocatelle of the richest kind is the fabric used in the furniture ... and the window hangings of the same rich material. The frames of the medallions have been gilt, and the pictures finely renovated.[68]

Following the completion of these works in February 1867, little appears to have changed in the room until January 1888, when a similar renewal took place. The furniture of the Presence Chamber was re-upholstered in silk poplin 'specially manufactured' by Messrs Fry and Company 'in an Oriental design' and was displayed in their shop window in Upper Sackville Street (now O'Connell Street).[69] In keeping with tradition, the colour of the new upholstery was a 'rich crimson'.[70] One final effort at keeping up appearances seems to have been made

Fig. 04.23.
'The Throne
Room', Dublin
Castle. *The
Graphic*, 21 April
1888.

on the eve of the visit of King George V and Queen Mary in 1911. *The London Journal* reported: 'for the first time in its existence Dublin Castle is really looking like a royal residence … The Throne Room is newly decorated with crimson tabourette, specially woven in Dublin'.[71]

Photographs and illustrations from the final years of the nineteenth century depict the Presence Chamber architecturally unaltered from its completed state in 1839, with the exception of the crown-shaped mirrors that likely date from the 1840s. One major difference, however, is a pitiful decline in court presentation, where strictly disposed formal furniture yielded to the creeping influence of suburban domesticity. Shapeless Victorian sofas, buttoned and tasselled upholstery, undersized candelabra, and the icon of mass production – the bentwood chair – all populated the room in a stark manifestation of a dying administration (Fig. 04.23). In spite of this, the essential ensemble conceived by Jacob Owen in the late 1830s survived remarkably unscathed into the new century. His eccentric interpretation of the disciplined, high Regency, Nash interiors at Buckingham Palace may be viewed as a distinctly Irish manifestation of court decoration, synergizing the protocols of royalty with the indigenous skill and aesthetic of Dublin artisans and manufacturers. The result is a scene of animated magnificence.

Endnotes

1   Letter to Jacob Owen from Henry R. Paine, 3 September 1838, OPW letter book, National Archives of Ireland, OPW1/1/2/6.

2   Letter to Thomas Drummond from Henry R. Paine, 24 January 1838, OPW letter book, National Archives of Ireland, OPW1/1/2/6.

3   Letter to Jacob Owen from Henry R. Paine, 4 May 1838, OPW letter book, National Archives of Ireland, OPW1/1/2/6.

4   Account entry, 4 October 1838, OPW account book, National Archives of Ireland, OPW2/1/12/3.

5   The balcony was removed during remodelling of the State Apartments from 1964 to 1968.

6   Letter to Jacob Owen from Henry R. Paine, 4 May 1838, OPW letter book, National Archives of Ireland, OPW1/1/2/6.

7   Ibid.

8   *Freeman's Journal*, 1 October 1839.

9   *Freeman's Journal*, 26 December 1839.

10   Letter [to Francis Johnston] from R. Robinson, 8 April 1826, OPW letter book, National Archives of Ireland, OPW1/1/2/3.

11   Letter to Francis Johnston from R. Robinson,

26 May 1825, OPW letter book, National Archives of Ireland, OPW1/1/2/3.

12 Letter to Jacob Owen from Henry R. Paine, 3 September 1838, OPW letter book, National Archives of Ireland, OPW1/1/2/6.

13 C. Casey, *Dublin: The City within the Grand and Royal Canals and the Circular Road with the Phoenix Park* (New Haven and London: Yale University Press, 2005), p. 355.

14 Ibid., p. 295.

15 Wales was generally considered a principality of the United Kingdom.

16 J.M. Robinson, *Buckingham Palace: The Official Illustrated History* (London: Royal Collection Publications, 2011), p. 70.

17 J. Owen, 'An Account of the Mode adopted for Raising the Roof of the Presence Chamber, Dublin Castle', *Transactions of the Institute of Civil Engineers of Ireland*, 3 (1848/49), pp. 32–4.

18 The Presence Chamber was used for a levee; see *Freeman's Journal*, 13 January 1840.

19 Letter to Jacob Owen from Henry R. Paine, 3 September 1838, OPW letter book, National Archives of Ireland, OPW1/1/2/6.

20 J. Robins, *Champagne & Silver Buckles: The Viceregal Court at Dublin Castle 1700–1922* (Dublin: The Lilliput Press, 2001), p. 119. See also P. Gray, 'A "People's Viceroyalty"?: Popularity, theatre and executive politics 1835–47', in P. Gray and O. Purdue (eds), *The Irish Lord Lieutenancy c. 1541–1922* (Dublin: University College Dublin Press, 2012), p. 170.

21 *Freeman's Journal*, 22 October 1840.

22 Letter to Charles Bielefeld from Henry R. Paine, 22 December 1838, OPW letter book, National Archives of Ireland, OPW1/1/2/6.

23 F. O'Dwyer, 'A Guide to the State Apartments & Architectural History of Dublin Castle' (OPW, unpublished Ms, 1990).

24 Letter to Thomas Drummond from J.T. Burgoyne, 8 October 1839, OPW letter book, National Archives of Ireland, OPW1/1/2/6.

25 Ibid.

26 Account entry, 9 November 1839, OPW account book, National Archives of Ireland, OPW2/1/12/5.

27 Letters to Jacob Owen from Henry R. Paine, 12 November 1839, OPW letter book, National Archives of Ireland, OPW1/1/2/6.

28 Letter to Jacob Owen from Henry R. Paine, 12 November 1839, OPW letter book, National Archives of Ireland, OPW1/1/2/6.

29 Account entry, January 1840, OPW account book, National Archives of Ireland, OPW2/1/12/6.

30 Account and ledger entries, 1820s, OPW account books, National Archives of Ireland, OPW2/1/1/7 and OPW2/2/3/9.

31 *Irish Examiner*, 13 August 1845.

32 J. Rogers, 'A Dictionary of Eighteenth-Century Irish Furniture-Makers', in The Knight of Glin and J. Peill, *Irish Furniture* (New Haven and London: Yale University Press, 2007), p. 292.

33 Letter to Jacob Owen from Henry R. Paine, 12 November 1839, OPW letter book, National Archives of Ireland, OPW1/1/2/6.

34 Letter to Jacob Owen from H.R. Paine, 1 November 1839, OPW letter book, National Archives of Ireland, OPW1/1/2/6.

35 Ibid.

36 Account entry, 27 April 1840, OPW account book, National Archives of Ireland, OPW2/1/12/6.

37 K. Curry, 'Empire of China', *Irish Arts Review*, 21, 1 (Spring 2014), pp. 116–23.

38 Letter to Jacob Owen from Henry R. Paine, 12 November 1839, OPW letter book, National Archives of Ireland, OPW1/1/2/6.

39 Account entry, 27 April 1840, OPW account book, National Archives of Ireland, OPW2/1/12/6.

40 Ibid.

41 Letter to Jacob Owen from Henry R. Paine, 20 August 1840, OPW letter book, National Archives of Ireland, OPW1/1/2/6.

42 Letter to Messrs Perry and Company from Henry R. Paine, 30 December 1835, OPW letter book, National Archives of Ireland, OPW1/1/2/5.

43 Letter to Thomas Edge from Henry R. Paine, 30 November 1835, OPW letter book, National Archives of Ireland, OPW1/1/2/5.

44 Account entry, 13 March 1841, OPW account book, National Archives of Ireland, OPW2/1/12/6.

45 Account entry, April 1842, OPW cash ledger, National Archives of Ireland, OPW2/2/5/2.

46 Account entries, 1840/41, OPW account book, National Archives of Ireland, OPW2/1/12/6.

47 Letter to Jacob Owen from Henry R. Paine, 9 January 1841, OPW letter book, National Archives of Ireland, OPW1/1/2/6.

48 Letter to Messrs Williams and Gibton from Henry R. Paine, 26 November 1839, OPW letter book, National Archives of Ireland, OPW1/1/2/6.

49 Letter to Francis Johnston from R. Robinson, 1 December 1825, OPW letter book, National Archives of Ireland, OPW1/1/2/6.

50 Letter to Jacob Owen from J. Walker, 5 July 1848, OPW letter book, National Archives of Ireland, OPW1/1/2/9.

51 Letter to the OPW from James H. Owen, 8 December 1857, OPW Papers, National Archives of Ireland, OPW[5]18599/57.

52 See Robins, *Champagne*, p. 124.

53 Queen Victoria with Arthur Helps (ed.), *Leaves from the Journal of our Life in the Highlands, from 1848 to 1861* (New York: Harper & Brothers, 1868), p. 239.

54 Ibid.

55 See Queen Victoria with Arthur Helps, *Leaves*, p. 238. See also J.H. Murphy, *Abject Loyalty: Nationalism and Monarchy in Ireland during the Reign of Queen Victoria* (Washington: The Catholic University of America Press, 2001), p. 94.

56 *Freeman's Journal*, 27 July 1844.

57 Ibid.

58 *Freeman's Journal*, 27 July 1844.

59 *Freeman's Journal*, 7 April 1840.

60 *Belfast Newsletter*, 31 January 1857.

61 *Freeman's Journal*, 28 March 1845.

62 Ibid.

63 *Irish Times and Daily Advertiser*, 14 June 1860.

64 F. Hamilton, *The Days before Yesterday* (London: Hodder & Stoughton, 1920), p. 80.

65 P. Fitzgerald, *Recollections of Dublin Castle & of Dublin Society by a Native* (London: Chatto & Windus, 1902), p. 62.

66 Letter to Captain Williams from E. Hornsby, 12 December 1857, OPW Papers, National Archives of Ireland, OPW[5]19067/57.

67 Letters to James H. Owen from E. Hornsby, 30 November and 3 December 1864; OPW letter book, National Archives of Ireland, OPW1/1/2/30.

68 *Irish Times and Daily Advertiser*, 12 January 1867.

69 *Irish Times*, 25 January 1888.

70 Ibid.

71 *London Journal*, 22 July 1911.

Five

'Admirably Calculated for the Object'

Gaetano Gandolfi's Paintings in the
Throne Room at Dublin Castle

Ludovica Neglie

This essay aims to shed light on the history of the Italian Baroque paintings that adorn the Throne Room in Dublin Castle. These canvases, which have hung in the room since 1839, were described for much of the nineteenth and twentieth centuries as being by various 'great masters', including Angelica Kauffmann (1741–1807) and Vincenzo Waldré (1742–1814).[1] It was only in 1995 that the paintings were re-identified as being the work of the Bolognese artist Gaetano Gandolfi (1734–1802), when his signature was revealed during cleaning.[2] Building on the efforts of the 1990s, this essay seeks to give a clear account of their fascinating and complex story. Drawing on newly identified sketches for the paintings, and exploring new avenues of enquiry, this study will elucidate the circumstances of the original commission as well as contextualizing the remarkable journey of these paintings to Dublin Castle.

Gaetano Gandolfi was born on 31 August 1734 in San Matteo della Decima, in the Emilia-Romagna countryside, where his father worked as an agent on the estate of the Villa Fontana.[3] Gaetano moved to Bologna with his brothers, Ubaldo (1728–1781) and Rinaldo (b. 1718), where the latter worked as a clockmaker, while Gaetano and Ubaldo studied art. Gaetano was thirteen when he arrived in Bologna, and in 1747 he started his studies at the Accademia

Facing page: Fig. 05.01. Gaetano Gandolfi, *Odysseus and the Winds*, 1766. Photograph by Davison & Associates, courtesy of the Office of Public Works, Dublin Castle.

Clementina, the most important art academy of the city at that time.[4] Named after Pope Clemente XI (1649–1721), it was founded as a public academy in 1710 thanks to the efforts of its creator, Giampiero Zanotti (1674–1765). The academy functioned as an association of artists and as a place where they could gather to work independently, as well as to exchange personal creative ideas. This intention to institutionalize art training, followed as a model the methods of the Accademia degli Incamminati, founded in 1590 by the two Carracci brothers, Annibale (1560–1609) and Agostino (1557–1602). This was a private establishment, mainly devoted to the artistic representation of nature, the so-called *vero naturale*.[5] In particular, this was achieved through an idealistic synthesis of everyday reality, with the classicism of Raphael and the Renaissance tradition, as a reaction to Mannerism.[6] The Roman Accademia di San Luca, founded in 1577, also served as an important model for the Clementina, sharing with it the objective of elevating the figure of the artist above the mere activity of the craftsman. Informed by the legacy of the great Bolognese art of the past, and of the sixteenth century in particular, the Accademia Clementina transmitted old ideas to a new generation of artists, and in doing so created a contemporary school of Italian art.

It is in this context that the Gandolfi brothers began their artistic training. The sources of the time – in particular Calvi, Grilli and Martinelli – report that the painter Ercole Lelli (1702–1766) was one of Gandolfi's masters.[7] Gaetano's apprenticeship with Lelli, and his studies in human anatomy, were fundamental to his development as a draughtsman. His debut, however, was with sculpture, earning him the academy's annual Marsili Prize at the age of seventeen in 1751.[8] Gaetano's artistic research and academic training evolved towards the study of sixteenth-century classicism, where he constantly tried to retrieve the essence of local traditions. For Gaetano, this method did not undermine the originality of his work, and he was awarded the Fiori Prize in 1752, 1753, 1755 and 1756.[9] His skill clearly did not go unnoticed.

In 1760, Antonio Buratti, a rich Venetian merchant, patron and collector, took Gandolfi as his protégé and paid for his studies for one whole year in Venice. Buratti also commissioned him to produce drawings of the most celebrated altarpieces of Bologna, with the idea of creating an album, but in the end, this was never realized.[10] Gandolfi was twenty-five when he was sent to Venice to study the work of the great masters of the Venetian school, in 1760. Unfortunately, there are few records relating to his time there. Those that survive, in the Venice

State Archives, record his stay at Buratti's palace in that period.[11] During his year in Venice, Gandolfi gained great experience of the characteristics of Venetian painting, in particular, the use of diffused light and vibrant colouring. Much of his practice was in the drawing and copying of canvases, frescoes and statues, specifically the work of Giovanni Battista Tiepolo (1696–1770). This stay exerted a marked influence on his later works and represented an important addition to his already extensive training.

The development of Gandolfi's technique can be traced in paintings such as *The Liberation of St Peter* (1760–5, Yale University Art Gallery, New Haven), 'with its emphasis on virtuoso brushwork rather than the precise contours typical of the Bolognese tradition'.[12] The Venetian influence can be seen in the work produced by Gandolfi throughout the 1760s. He gradually moved away from it in the following decade, returning to the influences of his initial training, but he never abandoned it completely. Its survival can be seen in *The Marriage at Cana* (1775, Pinacoteca Nazionale di Bologna), which was evidently derived from a painting of 1563, on the same theme, by Paolo Veronese (1528–1588). Veronese's famous canvas now hangs in the Louvre, Paris, but would almost certainly have been seen by Gandolfi in its original setting at the church of San Giorgio Maggiore in Venice.[13] The 1760s were crucial years for the development of Gandolfi as a leading artist in Bologna. In 1765 he finally became one of the academicians in the Accademia Clementina, after having been refused three times.[14] During those years the work of the two Gandolfi brothers was very similar in style. While their drawing techniques were comparable, their works were still distinguishable, mainly on account of the different palette of colours they used. Gaetano had a preference for primary colours whereas Ubaldo favoured secondary ones.[15] The late 1760s and early 1770s was a pivotal period in Gandolfi's career, marked by several awards and acknowledgements in Italy and beyond. Following his appointment at the Clementina, his talents were further recognized through an important international commission. *The Triumph of Venus* was painted for a Russian patron, reputedly Prince Nikolai Borisovich Yusupov (1750–1831), and it clearly represented a growing appreciation of his work beyond his native Italy.[16] It is in this context that the paintings now in Dublin were realized.

The mythological paintings now in the Throne Room at Dublin Castle were painted by Gandolfi in 1766 and 1767. They occupy the spaces above the doors and chimneypieces on the room's east, west and south walls (see Fig. 09.24). Their subject matter is in line with the artistic production of eighteenth-century

Fig. 05.02.
Gaetano Gandolfi,
*Odysseus receiving
a bag of winds
from Aeolus,
c.* 1766.
© Victoria and
Albert Museum,
London.

Italian artists, who were mainly concerned with religious scenes or mythological tales. The set consists of two ovals, *Odysseus and the Winds* and *Iris at the Death of Dido*, and four roundels, *Jupiter abducting Ganymede*; *Juno and the Peacocks*; *Minerva with her Sacred Bird, the Owl*, and *Mars with his Sacred Animals, the Wolf and the Woodpecker*.

Of these six paintings, the two ovals portray scenes inspired by episodes from two of the most important epic poems of classical literature: Homer's *Odyssey* and Virgil's *Aeneid*. In *Odysseus and the Winds* Gandolfi represents the hero receiving the bag of winds from the god Aeolus, in order to facilitate his return to Ithaca, on the condition that he does not open the bag (Fig. 05.01). During the night, while the exhausted Odysseus was sleeping, his companions opened the bag thinking that he could have been hiding some treasures given by Aeolus, which he did not want to share. Upon the opening of the bag, the winds escaped and pushed the ship back, just as it was in sight of Ithaca. The painting is signed by Gandolfi and is dated 1766.[17] A surviving preparatory drawing reveals that the oval composition was intentional from the outset (Fig. 05.02). It differs little from the finished canvas, and was drawn on the back of a draft of an apparently unrelated letter dated 12 November 1766.[18]

The second oval shows *Iris at the Death of Dido* and depicts the final moments of the famous Queen of Carthage. Aeneas, the mythical founder of Rome, had been called back by the god Jupiter to fulfil his destiny, forcing him to leave his lover, Dido (Fig. 05.03). At first she begged him to stay but after his departure she cursed him, predicting the never-ending hatred and war between their two countries. It is thought that Virgil's contemporaries traced the origins of the Punic Wars, and the hatred between Rome and Carthage, to this mythological tale. Gandolfi chooses to depict one of the Queen's final moments, full of pathos, as she embraces her sister Anna for the last time before killing herself with Aeneas's sword and then throwing herself on the pyre. Iris, the goddess Juno's messenger, is portrayed cutting a lock from the Queen's hair. In Virgil's poem, Aeneas sees the smoke while sailing away from Carthage and suspects what has just happened. The painting is signed simply 'Gandolfi'.[19] No preparatory drawing has yet come to light for this painting.

The roundel showing *Jupiter abducting Ganymede* depicts the myth of Jupiter kidnapping Ganymede, the most beautiful of the mortals, from Troy, to make him a servant of the gods on Mount Olympus (Fig. 05.04). In contrast to more typical depictions of this subject, Jupiter, king of the gods, is shown not in the

Fig. 05.03.
Gaetano Gandolfi,
*Iris at the death
of Dido*, *c.* 1766.
Photograph
by Davison
& Associates,
courtesy of the
Office of Public
Works, Dublin
Castle.

Above:
Fig. 05.04.
Gaetano Gandolfi, *Jupiter abducting Ganymede*, 1767. Photograph by Davison & Associates, courtesy of the Office of Public Works, Dublin Castle.

Left:
Fig. 05.05.
Gaetano Gandolfi, *Jupiter abducting Ganymede*, *c.* 1767. Private collection.

form of an eagle but instead appears in a chariot drawn by two eagles. In many Greek myths, Jupiter would take the form of an animal to seduce mortals. The roundel is signed by Gandolfi and is dated 1767.[20] A preparatory drawing for this composition was sold by Christie's in Paris on 21 March 2002, and is now in a private Bolognese collection (Fig. 05.05). Before its sale the drawing was attributed to Ubaldo Gandolfi; however, it has become apparent that it is a work by Gaetano, since it has now been linked conclusively to the Dublin Castle series.[21]

A second roundel, *Juno and the Peacocks,* shows Juno, wife of Jupiter, in a chariot drawn by a pair of peacocks. In her right hand she holds aloft two crowns and a string of pearls, while in her left hand she proffers various fruits and what appears to be an olive branch (Fig. 05.06). This canvas bears Gandolfi's signature and the date 1767.[22] Only one difference stands out in the surviving preparatory drawing, in which Juno holds in her hand a single apple instead of the large bundle of fruit (Fig. 05.07). In the mythological tale of the Judgement of Paris, it was Venus who was awarded the golden apple of discord. Perhaps at risk of confusing Juno with Venus, the single apple of the drawing became a larger assortment of fruit in the finished canvas.

The third roundel depicts *Mars with his Sacred Animals, the Wolf and the Woodpecker*. Close observation reveals that Mars is seated on a chariot, which is being drawn by two wolves that are tethered to it, while the woodpecker rests atop the god's helmet (Fig. 05.08). This canvas is not signed or dated, but obviously forms part of the series of roundels.

The final roundel in the Throne Room is a representation of *Minerva with her Sacred Bird, the Owl*. She, too, is depicted in a chariot that is drawn by two animals, in this case a pair of owls. On her helmet is a sphinx and behind her are four putti, three of which are holding respectively a book, dividers, and what close inspection reveals to be fasces (Fig. 05.09). This canvas is neither signed nor dated, but like *Mars*, obviously forms part of the Dublin Castle series of roundels. The rediscovery of the preparatory drawing for this canvas during the course of research for this essay allows for a deeper understanding of its development. Unlike the other paintings for which sketches survive, *Minerva* was evidently painted with virtually no deviation from the preparatory study. The drawing is in the collection of the Minneapolis Institute of Art and, unlike the others, is prominently signed by Gandolfi (Fig. 05.10). In addition, it carries an inscription, 'Monsù Giò. Bolangier', on the reverse, which could suggest an

Above: Fig. 05.06.
Gaetano Gandolfi, *Juno and the Peacocks*, 1767. Photograph by Davison & Associates, courtesy of the Office of Public Works, Dublin Castle.

Left: Fig. 05.07.
Gaetano Gandolfi, *Juno riding in a car drawn by a pair of peacocks*, c. 1767. © Victoria and Albert Museum, London.

Fig. 05.08.
Gaetano Gandolfi,
*Mars with his
Sacred Animals,
the* Wolf *and the
Woodpecker*,
c. 1767.
Photograph
by Davison
& Associates,
courtesy of the
Office of Public
Works, Dublin
Castle.

incorrect attribution to the French artist Jean Boulanger of Troyes (1606–1660), who was also known as Giovanni, and who was active in Modena and Bologna in the seventeenth century. However, given how prominently Gandolfi's name appears on the sketch, the other inscription may refer to a previous owner.

In addition to the six canvases in the Throne Room, two others formed part of the original set purchased by the Office of Public Works (OPW) for Dublin Castle in 1839: *Vulcan at his Forge* and *Venus and the Three Graces*, which due to a lack of space in the Throne Room, were placed in the adjacent old Presence

Fig. 05.09.
Gaetano Gandolfi,
*Minerva with her
Sacred Bird, the
Owl, c.* 1767.
Photograph
by Davison
& Associates,
courtesy of the
Office of Public
Works, Dublin
Castle.

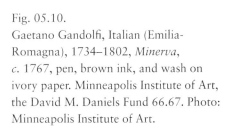

Fig. 05.10.
Gaetano Gandolfi, Italian (Emilia-
Romagna), 1734–1802, *Minerva,
c.* 1767, pen, brown ink, and wash on
ivory paper. Minneapolis Institute of Art,
the David M. Daniels Fund 66.67. Photo:
Minneapolis Institute of Art.

Chamber or Ante-Drawing Room after their purchase. There they remained until at least 1867, when they were recorded by *The Irish Builder*.[23] Although the report was quite precise in its description of some of the artworks at the Castle, it mistakenly described these two paintings as 'frescoes of Vulcan at his forge and Psyche', thereby confusing the medium of both and the subject matter of the latter.[24]

These two paintings were moved out of the Ante-Drawing Room at some stage after 1867 and before 1897. A newly identified inventory demonstrates that they were certainly not on display in any of the State Apartments at Dublin Castle in May 1897.[25] It is perhaps conceivable that they were two of the five pictures

Fig. 05.11. Gaetano Gandolfi, *Vulcan at his Forge*, 1767. Photograph by Davison & Associates, courtesy of the Office of Public Works, Dublin Castle.

Fig. 05.12.
Gaetano Gandolfi, *Vulcan at his forge*,
c. 1767. © Victoria and Albert Museum,
London.

with 'scriptural subjects' described as being in storage at that time.[26] A second inventory, of the viceroy's other residence, the Viceregal Lodge (now Áras an Uachtaráin), taken the previous month, makes no mention of them.[27] By 1904 they were apparently at the Viceregal Lodge, where they stayed until the viceroy left the country on the establishment of the Irish Free State in 1922.[28] Following this, they were placed in storage.

Vulcan at his Forge made its way to the Papal Nunciature in the Phoenix Park (formerly the Under-Secretary's Lodge).[29] It stayed there until the 1970s, before being returned to the OPW when the Nunciature was moved to another location. The canvas was finally recognized as part of the Throne Room series in 1999, when Róisín Kennedy and Michael Wynne examined the preparatory drawing for it at the Victoria and Albert Museum, London.[30] Only after this complex journey did the painting return to hang in the State Drawing Room at Dublin Castle, which neatly adjoins the Throne Room where its sister canvases are displayed. This roundel depicts the god Vulcan working at his forge but, somewhat unexpectedly, he is balanced on a chariot drawn by a three-headed dog (Fig. 05.11). The painting differs from the preparatory drawing by the addition of three intertwined figures leading the dog (Fig. 05.12).

Venus and the Three Graces was eventually given on loan to the American Legation at the Phoenix Park (previously the Chief Secretary's Lodge) and was last recorded there in 1928.[31] Despite extensive searches, no trace of it has since been found. An inventory from 1934 for the American Legation does survive, but unfortunately, it only lists the personal property of the minister.[32] Some sense of the style and composition of the lost *Venus and the Three Graces* might be gleaned from a similar painting in Osterley Park, London. Labelled as *Venus descending from Her Swan-Drawn Chariot* (*c.* 1770, Osterley Park, London), it is ascribed to both Gandolfi brothers, but it is almost certainly to be attributed only to Gaetano (Fig. 05.13).[33] At first glance it is unlikely to be the lost Dublin picture, not least due to its relatively small size. The Dublin roundels are 101 cm in diameter, while the Osterley Park painting measures 60 cm x 76 cm. The Osterley Park picture can also be connected with the famous Festive Carriage

Fig. 05.13. Gaetano Gandolfi (attr. to), *Venus descending from Her Swan-Drawn Chariot, c.* 1770. © The National Trust.

Fig. 05.14. Gaetano Gandolfi (1734–1802), *The Triumph of Venus*, *c.* 1768–9. Princeton (NJ), Princeton University Art Museum. Pen and brown ink and brush and brown wash over traces of graphite, on light tan paper, mounted down; 23.5 × 34.5cm. (9 1/4 × 13 9/16 in.). Gift of Frank Jewett Mather Jr, x1976-64. © 2017. Princeton University Art Museum/Art Resource NY/ Scala, Florence.

that Gaetano Gandolfi had realized for the wealthy Bolognese Senator Vincenzo Marescalchi, in 1769.[34] This canvas may be a study for, or a replica of, the painting realized for the carriage mentioned above, preparatory sketches for which are at Princeton Art Museum and in a private collection (Fig. 05.14).[35] Nonetheless, the similarities between this picture and the Dublin Castle roundels are compelling. All depict a single god on a chariot; all of these chariots are drawn by pairs of animals, or in the case of *Vulcan*, a three-headed animal; and all have an obviously circular composition. It is possible that it could be a preparatory study for the missing Dublin Castle *Venus*, and was later recycled, and possibly extended, in the development of the carriage scheme.

The quality of these paintings is superb and they are among the most extraordinary examples of Gandolfi's artistic maturity. The mellowness of the tones, the softness of the draperies, the range and competent use of the colours, all demonstrate the high level his art had reached by the late 1760s and explain why he was the artist of choice at the time in Bologna. Old stretcher marks on the canvases reveal that they were adapted before being hung in the Throne Room: the ovals were originally rectangular in shape and the roundels were

Fig. 05.15.
Gaetano Gandolfi
(1734–1802), *Self-Portrait*. Bologna,
Pinacoteca
Nazionale. ©
2017. Photo
Scala, Florence,
courtesy of the
Ministero Beni e
Att. Culturali e del
Turismo.

square.[36] Despite this size reduction, the composition has not been affected. The similar composition and theme of the five roundels suggest that they were part of one series. Those that are dated are from 1767. The two oval canvases do not conform to these patterns and as one of them is dated 1766, it is likely that they were part of a separate, slightly earlier series.

The question of the origin of the paintings is necessarily connected with the relationship between Gandolfi and the English world. Despite suggestions that they may have been commissioned for an Italian palazzo, it is now clear that they were realized 'per un Inglese' ('for an Englishman'), as Gandolfi himself wrote.[37] Marcello Oretti, one of the artist's first biographers recorded that he produced eight paintings of 'istorie profane' ('profane tales') for an English patron.[38] Oretti obtained this information from the artist himself in a handwritten note that Gandolfi had left him in around 1770, but unfortunately, he did not leave any further information on the identity of the individual. The patron may have been British or Irish, as 'Inglese' was often casually used to refer to Irish as well as to British travellers in Italy at the time.[39]

Gandolfi's contacts with English society pre-date and post-date the commission of the Dublin paintings. He certainly went to London in 1787, at the invitation of Richard Dalton (*c.* 1715–1791), the artist, art dealer and later librarian to King George III.[40] He visited many places that must have been sources of inspiration for him, such as the British Museum, the library at Buckingham House, the Foundling Hospital and Somerset House, where the Society of Antiquaries and the Royal Academy were housed.[41]

The following year he was back in Italy, as Augusto Zanotti wrote that 'in 1788 he wanted to see his friends in London again', asserting also that he did not work on this trip.[42] A self-portrait, believed to date from 1788, captures him at work in this period (Fig. 05.15). By January 1789 he was certainly back in London, as a newly discovered letter written by Richard Dalton to George Augustus Clavering-Cowper, 4th Earl Cowper makes clear. The letter, which has been identified by Myles Campbell of Dublin Castle, offers a deeper insight into Gandolfi's working methods and his English experience:

> A very singular character, Signr Gaetano Gandolfi from Bologna, the most Capital Draughtsman I ever met with and who has enriched His Majesty's collection with Drawings after the most Capital Pictures at Bologna, although unknown at Rome, Florence & other parts of Italy having shut himself up in his own house, would raither [*sic*] have painted in fresco or oil in proportion for five pound than made Drawings for twenty. He suddenly took it in his head to come and see England, after he had painted a Picture per il Duomo di Pisa, dividing his profit between himself & family, and came with a portmanteau … with a fine Drawing after Ludi Carracci and most capital heads of his own

Invention with a Pen which he Draws with the facility as a man of business writes a letter. Just after I had carried him [to] Windsor, this melancholy accident [the mental illness of King George III] hapned [*sic*], so now all works of art are at a stand, from the present situation of affairs as the Papers inform you at large. Therefore I'm a getting him to make repetitions of several of those valuable Drawings, which he otherwise would never have done and any artist who should chance to come to England in His wretched situation could not meet with the least encouragement.[43]

Despite the King's illness, Gandolfi's English stay was nevertheless productive. It is likely that, during this stay, Dalton managed to introduce Gandolfi to the uppermost circles of English elite society.

Richard Dalton originally met Gaetano Gandolfi in Bologna and he was both a client and a friend to the artist.[44] Dalton first stayed in Venice in 1759, where he took an interest in the collection of Consul Joseph Smith (*c.* 1682–1770), before returning in 1764 to Bologna, where he had previously studied.[45] While there, he commissioned from Gandolfi copies in ink of the most famous altarpieces of Bologna for the Royal Library in Buckingham House.[46] Dalton always held Gandolfi in high esteem and admired him; it is therefore understandable that he should invite him to London, in order to gain him commissions. A letter addressed to Philip Yorke, 2nd Earl of Hardwicke (1720–1790), shows that Dalton had acquired a drawing by Gandolfi on his behalf in the 1780s, to enrich the Earl's collection.[47] It represents further evidence of Dalton's secondary role as art dealer, not only for the King but also for other members of the English aristocracy. Dalton was thus the key figure in the relationship between Gandolfi and the English upper class, and could easily have been the mysterious commissioner of the Dublin Castle paintings. Although those of the paintings that Gandolfi inscribed with a date are from 1766 and 1767, the handwritten note left by Gandolfi, and reported by Oretti, bears the date 1764. This date, scribbled at the side, might have been added later or it could refer to the year in which the commission began, the same year that Dalton was in Bologna.[48] If Dalton was involved with the commission, it is more likely that he acted as a channel, commissioning them on behalf of someone else.

Richard Dalton died on 7 February 1791 in his residence at St James's Palace. His own collection was sold at Christie's, with the sale beginning on 9 April 1791.[49] The lots sold on the first day included historical artefacts, such as the sword of the Prince of Wales from 1616, Indian daggers, Algerian pistols, and the armour of King Henry V that had been removed from the Tower of London by King Charles II himself in the previous century.[50] Among the other lots there were various antique objects such as lamps, vases and marbles, and two royal portraits of Anne Boleyn and King Henry VIII.[51] The items sold on the second day comprised of 111 works of art owned by Dalton at the time of his death. A great many of them were the work of the most important artists of the preceding centuries, including Canaletto (1697–1768), Titian (c. 1488–1576), Rubens (1577–1640), Rembrandt (1606–1669), Guercino (1591–1666), van Dyck (1599–1641), and Rosalba Carriera (1673–1757). Such a collection clearly showed the impeccable taste of Dalton and his passion for the arts, which he had proven throughout his life as a patron and friend of many artists. Unfortunately, the Gandolfi paintings do not appear to have been part of this list. Despite the absence of any works by Gandolfi, there can be no doubt that Richard Dalton admired his art greatly.

It is possible that further connections were formed between Gandolfi and the British circle in Venice during his stay there in 1760. Joseph Smith was the British Consul in Venice between 1744 and 1760 and, beyond his political duties, he devoted much energy to art dealing. He also promoted artists and represented them, often influencing their commercial success, as in the case of Canaletto.[52] He was not the only British representative or dealer in Venice. There were several other important enablers and collectors, such as Sir James Gray, John Murray, John Strange, John Udny and the Irishman Owen McSwiney. It was through the efforts of these art dealers that the majority of Italian artworks flowed to Britain. The drawing collection of Consul Smith was acquired by King George III in 1765 for £10,000, and was considered the 'most important royal purchase of art in the eighteenth century'.[53] This resulted in a large amount of Italian works ending up in the Royal Collection, where they remain. Another important collection of prints and drawings purchased by King George III was the Roman collection of Cardinal Albani.[54] They were kept at Buckingham House, where he started forming a new library that became 'the core of the future British Library'.[55] Since the commissioner appears to have been 'an Englishman', it is equally possible that he was a privileged gentleman who could have commissioned them in person while on the Grand Tour in Italy. The British and Irish ruling classes were deeply influenced by Italian art and ideas and the formation of their new collections often began with artefacts brought back from Italy.[56]

A further hypothesis that can be advanced about the identity of the mysterious commissioner centres on the figure of James Caulfeild, 1st Earl of Charlemont (1728–1799). He was an exceptionally important patron of art and architecture and was well acquainted with Richard Dalton.[57] It is possible that Charlemont commissioned the paintings through Dalton to decorate the interior spaces of his new residence, Charlemont House, Dublin, begun in 1763. Although this may be unlikely because the house remained unfinished due to lack of funds, the timing is right, with the Dublin Castle paintings dating from the 1760s.[58] Charlemont had two other houses, Roxborough House (later Castle), Co. Tyrone, and Marino House, Dublin, both of which have since been demolished. He was a man of culture, a patron of the arts, and was highly conversant with classical culture. He spent nine years in Italy and the Mediterranean world on his Grand Tour, but was back in Ireland by 1755, which suggests that if he did commission the paintings in the 1760s, Dalton was indeed his channel to Gandolfi.

A veil of mystery still surrounds the journey of the paintings from when they were commissioned in the 1760s until they appeared in Dublin in the 1830s. The purchase of the set for the newly remodelled Throne Room at Dublin Castle was prompted at the beginning of October 1839. Having been made aware of their availability, the OPW subsequently consulted the Under-Secretary for Ireland, Thomas Drummond, on the matter:

> Among other items [in the annual estimates for 1839] is one for putting in order the Presence Chamber in the Castle; & in the proposed arrangements there is a difficulty in providing for 4 compartments over the Doors. It was suggested to the Commrs [of the OPW] by Capt Williams Master of the Horse to his Excy. that some eleven Italian Paintings were to be had, admirably calculated for the object, having been manifestly prepared for similar situations. On inspecting them the Commrs at once laid the idea of purchasing them aside on the presumption that the cost wd be too heavy but upon enquiry finding that the eight of which the set consists might probably be purchased & lined & cleaned for a sum not exceeding £100 an amt. that the Estimates will admit of, they are decidedly of opinion that such a sum wd be extremely well laid out for the purpose.[59]

Drummond sanctioned the purchase on 15 October.[60] The eight paintings were then duly acquired from a Mr Gernon for the sum of £89.5.0.[61] This could either have been James Gernon, who was then trading as a picture dealer and restorer at 34 Molesworth Street, Dublin, or his brother John, then advertising as an auctioneer, valuator and picture restorer from 9 D'Olier Street, Dublin.[62] The choice may have fallen on that specific atelier as the Gernon family was well acquainted with the OPW through Michael Gernon, father of James and John, who had cleaned pictures for the organization in the 1820s. For instance, on 23 September 1825 he was paid a total of £38.13.6 for cleaning and repairing pictures at the State Apartments in Dublin Castle and the Viceregal Lodge.[63]

There is no evidence that the identity of Gandolfi as the author of the pictures was known to either the dealer or the OPW at the time of the purchase. It seems unlikely as the paintings were sold for only £89. On the other hand, Baroque paintings of this sort were out of fashion by that time. As previously noted, the whereabouts of the paintings before they ended up in the dealer's hands are still unknown and no information appears to survive on how or where Mr Gernon acquired them. Dr Michael Wynne suggested that 'they may have become available as the result of the remodelling of a country house'.[64] There can be little doubt that they had a home in either Britain or Ireland before falling into the hands of Mr Gernon.

Thomas Drummond is perhaps the most interesting figure connected with the purchase of Gandolfi's paintings for Dublin Castle. He was a Scot, a native of Edinburgh, and was educated as a military engineer at the Royal Military Academy in Woolwich. He was a man of steady work and great intelligence, throwing himself fully into whatever he was doing.[65] In May 1839, *The Freeman's Journal* recorded that the Throne Room in Buckingham Palace contained portraits of the late King George III and his consort Queen Charlotte.[66] However, it relied more on the spectacle of its architecture than on the beauty of its paintings to create an impression, as it still does today (see Fig. 04.03). Drummond's choice of paintings for the Dublin Castle Throne Room just a few months later was rather different and, if we allow the term, *neutral*. He probably opted for subject matter that could be interpreted as a suitably showy, but generic rather than specific, celebration of the monarchy. The Gandolfi paintings, with their rather vague associations of regal power and majesty, would have easily suited this purpose. They were fine examples of Italian painting and, in the hierarchy of academic art, were considered to be in the highest genre on account of their subject matter. Mythological subjects could have easily offered an allusive and allegorical representation and celebration of the monarchy through what Fintan

Cullen refers to as 'the safe distance of the past'.[67] The past, and moreover an abstract one in this case, provided 'a sense of security' for the very reason that it did not 'spill over into the present'.[68]

Choosing a contemporary subject could have been a delicate task because of the political climate in Ireland at the time. For the same reason, references to the issue of Britain's rule of Ireland were not usually to be found in history painting. But it is of Dublin Castle and the British administration that we speak, and the choice fell to a British servant of the Crown in Ireland. Royal portraits, like those in the Throne Room at Buckingham Palace, would in theory have been the most suitable for the Dublin Castle Throne Room, given its function. Indeed, since the 1780s large paintings of King George III and Queen Charlotte, like those at Buckingham Palace, had hung in the Dublin room. They were still there in November 1838 when, as the OPW account books show, the landscape painter William Howis (1804–1882) was paid £5 for cleaning and varnishing them.[69]

Why then did Drummond not select royal portraits for the remodelled room? Why did he choose to represent the monarchy through mythological images? More importantly, why were the two royal portraits of King George III and Queen Charlotte removed from the Throne Room during the renovations and not put back in place afterwards, especially since they had just recently been restored? Instead, the figures in Gandolfi's paintings took their place as the only protagonists on the Throne Room's walls. Drummond's choice, and its suggested neutrality, is also interesting in light of his political sympathies. There were other places in the United Kingdom where he could have pursued his political career but, as his mother had said, 'he had a partiality for Ireland'.[70] Daniel O'Connell (1775–1847) was a friend of Drummond and they worked together for the Catholic cause. From the beginning, Drummond 'had established a government which was at once strong, just and rational … ruling for the people by the people … introducing constitutional authority into Ireland and always consulting and considering the Representatives of the people'.[71] Therefore, political and social context considered, it is comprehensible why such a man, whose 'kindly nature and strong sense of justice' had always made him work for the well-being of his beloved Ireland, should not make the same kind of political and cultural choices that other British officials had made before him.[72]

For instance, George Nugent-Temple-Grenville, 1st Marquess of Buckingham (1753–1813), during his second term as viceroy in 1787–89, commissioned the painted ceiling in St Patrick's Hall at Dublin Castle from the Italian artist Vincenzo

Waldré. Its outright celebratory subject matter echoed what has been described as 'the fundamental principle of Britain's Irish policy: the preservation of control'.[73] The central panel depicts *George III supported by Liberty and Justice* (see Fig. 03.15), while the two rectangular side panels represent scenes from ancient Irish history, *Saint Patrick converting the Irish to Christianity* (Fig. 05.16) and *King Henry II receiving the submission of the Irish Chieftains* (Fig. 05.17). Ranging from the historical to the allegorical, 'their unity of purpose is readily discernible: an ancient culture both Christian and loyal, Ireland can reap untold benefits while remaining firmly within the imperial orbit'.[74] The side Buckingham had taken represented an incontrovertible celebration of the monarchy. In particular, the panel depicting the oath of fidelity to King Henry II taken by the Irish chieftains, aimed to remind Irishmen in influential positions that 'privilege came with responsibilities, in this case a debt to the Crown' and that 'refusal to honour that debt or a threat to shake that connection would only lead to disaster'.[75] The fact that the side panels portrayed 'concluded history', allowed them to act as a metaphor, and to stand in for the present, making their message more palatable.[76]

Fig. 05.16. Vincenzo Waldré, *Saint Patrick converting the Irish to Christianity*, 1788–1802. Photograph by Mark Reddy, Trinity Digital Studios, courtesy of the Office of Public Works, Dublin Castle.

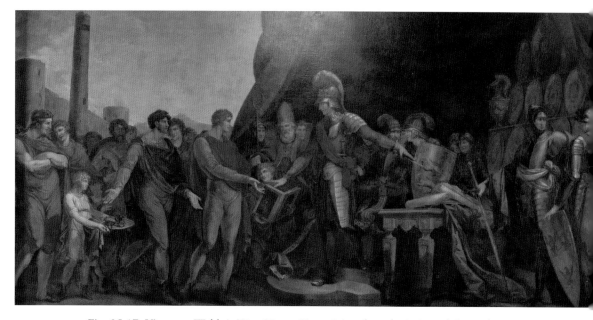

Fig. 05.17. Vincenzo Waldré, *King Henry II receiving the submission of the Irish Chieftains*, 1788–1802. Photograph by Mark Reddy, Trinity Digital Studios, courtesy of the Office of Public Works, Dublin Castle.

As visual tools, the ceiling panels in St Patrick's Hall encourage reconciliation and unity through the pledge of loyalty to the Crown in a time of political instability, celebrating at the same time the Knights of St Patrick who were to gather in the room. Whereas the clear choice made by Buckingham in this example represents a manifest political statement, the hypothesis advanced here is that Drummond might have disguised his opposing political sympathies by means of an apolitical and inoffensive artistic choice for the Throne Room.

It might be argued that to search for a meaning, and to try to interpret Drummond's choice of paintings as a purposeful one, is perhaps futile. There might be no specific reason at all why the Gandolfi paintings were chosen; it might have been because they were reasonably priced and were very fine examples of Italian art. It might have been that they easily fitted the physical space for which they were purchased, as well as meeting the thematic requirements of this majestic room. On the other hand, Drummond's choice of vaguely regal mythological scenes might be viewed as a conscious side-stepping of the problems posed by the politically charged nature of official portraiture. However, it is undeniable that by placing them in the Throne Room, Drummond imbued Gandolfi's paintings with a royal significance that they probably would not have enjoyed had they been placed somewhere else. The context in this case endowed them with a meaning that, otherwise, could have been totally different.

In conclusion, after the several new findings and arguments raised in this essay are taken into account, a number of questions still remain. Who commissioned the paintings in the 1760s? Where is the missing canvas of *Venus and the Three Graces*, which disappeared from record in 1928? Where are the preparatory drawings that, based on the fact that they exist for five of the eight paintings, must also exist for the missing *Venus*, for *Mars with his Sacred Animals* and for *Iris at the Death of Dido*? What, precisely, is the relationship between the Osterley Park *Venus* and the missing Dublin picture of the same subject? These are questions that only further study can hope to answer. Despite them, there can be no question that Gaetano Gandolfi's paintings were, indeed, 'admirably calculated for the object' of adorning the most *majestic* space in Ireland. All things considered, they are, and will remain, the crown jewels of the Throne Room at Dublin Castle.

Endnotes

1   Anon., 'Improvements at the Castle', *The Irish Builder*, 9, 171 (1 February 1867), p. 29.

2   R. Kennedy, *Dublin Castle Art* (Dublin: Office of Public Works, 1999), p. 27; M. Wynne, 'Six Gaetano Gandolfis in Dublin Castle', *The Burlington Magazine*, 141, 1155 (June 1999), pp. 352-4.

3   M. Cazort, 'The Gandolfi: An introduction', in M. Cazort (ed.), *Bella Pittura: The Art of the Gandolfi* (Ottawa: National Gallery of Canada, 1993), p. 12.

4   D. Biagi Maino, *Gaetano Gandolfi* (Bologna: Allemandi, 1995), p. 13.

5   P. De Vecchi and E. Cerchiari, *Arte nel Tempo: Dalla Crisi della Maniera al Rococò* (Milan: Bompiani, 2004), p. 584.

6   Ibid.

7   See Biagi Maino, *Gaetano Gandolfi*, p. 13.

8   P. Bagni, *I Gandolfi: Affreschi, Dipinti, Bozzetti, Disegni* (Bologna: Nuova Alfa Editoriale, 1992), p. 213.

9   Ibid.

10 See Bagni, *I Gandolfi*, p. 13.

11 Ibid., p. 215.

12 See Cazort, 'The Gandolfi: An introduction', p. 15.

13 See Biagi Maino, *Gaetano Gandolfi*, p. 30.

14 Ibid.

15 See Cazort, 'The Gandolfi: An introduction', p. 15.

16 D. Biagi Maino, *Gaetano e Ubaldo Gandolfi: Opere Scelte* (Bologna: Umberto Allemandi & C., 2002), p. 37.

17 See Wynne, 'Six Gaetano Gandolfis', p. 352.

18 P. Ward-Jackson, *Italian Drawings, Volume Two: 17th–18th century* (London: Her Majesty's Stationery Office, 1980), p. 143.

19 See Kennedy, *Dublin Castle Art*, p. 27.

20 Ibid., p. 25.

21 See Biagi Maino, *Gaetano e Ubaldo Gandolfi*, p. 24.

22 See Wynne, 'Six Gaetano Gandolfis', p. 352.

23 See Anon., 'Improvements at the Castle', p. 29.

24 Ibid.

25 Inventory of the State Apartments at Dublin Castle, 10 May 1897, National Archives of Ireland, OPW[5]6540/98.

26 Ibid.

27 Inventory of pictures at the Viceregal Lodge, 27 April 1897, National Archives of Ireland, OPW[5]6540/98.

28 See Biagi Maino, *Gaetano e Ubaldo Gandolfi*, p. 85.

29 M. Wynne, 'Gandolfi's "Vulcan" in Dublin Restored', *The Burlington Magazine*, 142, 1169 (August 2000), p. 501.

30 See Biagi Maino, *Gaetano e Ubaldo Gandolfi*, p. 86.

31 See Wynne, 'Gandolfi's "Vulcan"', p. 501.

32 Inventory of personal property of F.A. Sterling in American Legation, Dublin, 7 March 1934, National Archives of Ireland, OPW[5]8588/34.

33 Donatella Biagi Maino, in conversation with the author, maintains that the work is by Gaetano Gandolfi only.

34 See Biagi Maino, *Gaetano Gandolfi*, p. 39.

35 M. Cazort, 'The Art of Embellishment: Drawings and paintings by Gaetano and Mauro Gandolfi for a festive carriage', *Record of the Art Museum, Princeton University*, 52, 2 (1993), pp. 28–35.

36 See Wynne, 'Six Gaetano Gandolfis', p. 354.

37 See Biagi Maino, *Gaetano e Ubaldo Gandolfi*, p. 22.

38 Ibid.

39 E. McParland, *Public Architecture in Ireland 1680–1760* (New Haven and London: Yale University Press, 2001), p. 6.

40 See Cazort, 'The Gandolfi: An introduction', p. 18.

41 See Biagi Maino, *Gaetano Gandolfi*, p. 109.

42 A. Zanotti, 'L'Angelo della Famiglia - l'ultimo dei Pittori Carracceschi', *Bollettino Mensile della Parrocchia di S.Egidio in Bologna*, 8–10 (August–October 1929), unpaginated.

43 Letter to 4th Earl Cowper from Richard Dalton, 13 January 1789, Records of the Earls Cowper, Hertfordshire Archives and Local Studies, DE/P/F310/29.

44 See Biagi Maino, *Gaetano Gandolfi*, p. 41.

45 Ibid.

46 See Biagi Maino, *Gaetano Gandolfi*, p. 41.

47 Letter to Philip Yorke, 2nd Earl of Hardwicke from Richard Dalton, 9 November [17]86, Hardwicke Papers, The British Library, Add MS 35624, f. 297.

48 See Biagi Maino, *Gaetano e Ubaldo Gandolfi*, p. 22.

49 Catalogue of the picture collection of Richard Dalton auctioned by Christie's, London, 9–11 April 1791 (London: Christie's, 1791).

50 Ibid.

51 See catalogue of the picture collection of Richard Dalton.

52 S.L. Morrison, 'Smith, Joseph', in H.C.G. Matthew and B. Harrison (eds), *Oxford Dictionary of National Biography* (Oxford: Oxford University Press, 2004), vol. 51, p.

234.

53 J. Brewer, *The Pleasures of the Imagination: English Culture in the Eighteenth Century* (London: Harper Collins, 1997), p. 219.

54 A. Wilton and I. Bignamini, *Grand Tour: The Lure of Italy in the Eighteenth Century* (London: Tate Gallery Publishing, 1996), p. 33.

55 Ibid., p. 20.

56 See Wilton and Bignamini, *Grand Tour*, p. 12.

57 R. Musielak, *Charlemont's Marino: Portrait of a Landscape* (Dublin: Office of Public Works, 2014), p. 11.

58 C. Casey, *Dublin: The City within the Grand and Royal Canals and the Circular Road with the Phoenix Park* (New Haven and London: Yale University Press, 2005), p. 150.

59 Letter to Thomas Drummond from J.T. Burgoyne, 8 October 1839, OPW letter book, National Archives of Ireland, OPW1/1/2/6.

60 Ibid.; see note in margin of letter.

61 Letter to Captain Williams from H.R. Paine, 22 October 1839, OPW letter book, National Archives of Ireland, OPW1/1/2/6.

62 See entry on Michael Gernon in 'British Picture Restorers, 1600–1950', National Portrait Gallery, London, http://www.npg.org.uk/research/programmes/directory-of-british-picture-restorers/british-picture-restorers-1600-1950-g.php (accessed 2 March 2017).

63 Record of payment to Michael Gernon, 23 September 1825, OPW day book, National Archives of Ireland, OPW2/2/3/9.

64 See Wynne, 'Six Gaetano Gandolfis', p. 352.

65 L. O'Dea, 'Thomas Drummond', *Dublin Historical Record*, 24, 4 (September 1971), p. 113.

66 *Freeman's Journal*, 13 May 1839.

67 F. Cullen, 'Visual Politics in 1780s Ireland: The role of history painting', *Oxford Art Journal*, 18, 1 (1995), p. 58.

68 L. Gibbons, 'A Shadowy Narrator: History, art and romantic nationalism in Ireland 1750–1850', in C. Brady (ed.), *Ideology and the Historians* (Dublin: The Lilliput Press, 1991), p. 120.

69 Record of payment to William Howis, 26 November 1838, OPW account book, National Archives of Ireland, OPW 2/1/12/4.

70 R. Barry O'Brien, *Thomas Drummond, Under-Secretary in Ireland 1835–40: Life and Letters* (London: Kegan Paul, Trench & Co., 1889), p. 75.

71 See O'Dea, 'Thomas Drummond', p. 119.

72 See O'Brien, *Thomas Drummond*, p. 196.

73 See Cullen, 'Visual Politics', pp. 59–60.

74 Ibid., p. 67.

75 See Cullen, 'Visual Politics', p. 71.

76 Ibid., p. 58.

Six

Where Crown Met Town

The Presence of Lay Catholics and
the Uncrowned Monarch of Ireland
in the Chamber, c. 1795–1845

Sylvie Kleinman

Facing page:
Fig. 06.01.
'Catholic
Congratulation,
14th January, 1795'.
*Walker's Hibernian
Magazine: or,
Compendium
of Entertaining
Knowledge*,
January 1795.
Courtesy of the
National Library of
Ireland.

The January 1795 issue of *Walker's Hibernian Magazine* opened with a fine 'descriptive engraving' entitled *Catholic Congratulation, 14th January, 1795*. It depicts the immensely popular, recently arrived but soon-to-be-recalled lord lieutenant, or viceroy of Ireland, William Wentworth-Fitzwilliam, 4th Earl Fitzwilliam (1748–1833), receiving the lay Catholic Committee of Dublin in a room unmistakable to those familiar with it: the Presence Chamber, or Throne Room, of Dublin Castle (Fig. 06.01).[1] The appointment of this reform-minded Whig, 'heavily influenced by Edmund Burke', had fuelled widespread expectations of full Catholic emancipation, but Fitzwilliam had moved too speedily on the question after his investiture.[2] His dismissal after only six weeks plunged Ireland into a state of confusion and crisis against the backdrop of the war with France, and traditional narratives have seamlessly linked the ensuing bitterness and mounting disorder to the emergence of the United Irish revolutionary conspiracy, and the 1798 Rebellion itself. Though the Fitzwilliam débâcle has been debated at length by scholars of the period, this rare visualization of a fleeting but optimistic moment in Anglo-Irish relations has been overlooked to date. Its primary function was to illustrate the facing text, but the *Congratulation* is also the earliest known visual record of decorative features of the Presence Chamber (discussed elsewhere in this volume). It equally provides a wealth of insights on this forgotten practice, in the history of contacts at Dublin Castle between the representative of the Crown and the Irish people, while presenting several challenges to widely held assumptions about the closed nature and futility of the so-called mock court. Overall it is a unique view of something happening in the Presence Chamber in the eighteenth century, and incites us to question many constructs in Irish history. One is how it blurs the boundaries in the rigid caste system.[3] As far as can be ascertained, none of the Catholics present that day were aristocrats; their chairman, Edward Byrne (c. 1739/40–1804), was one of the wealthiest merchants in Ireland, and at his death in 1804 he had paid more tax than anyone else in the land.[4] They appear to have been received privately, and not in the semi-public bustle of a levee, the sphere for encounters which has received far more attention, like the glamorous balls. The image will be discussed below in terms of its quality as historical reportage, and also frames a tantalizing question. Given the demonstrable overlap between the Catholic Committee and prominent United Irishmen, by now banned and meeting covertly, were there any committed republicans, or indeed future rebels, in the Presence Chamber that day?

In popular memory the landmark royal visit by King George IV in 1821 marked the symbolic entrée into high society of Daniel O'Connell (1775–1847), by then the 'celebrity lawyer of the day' and unrivalled champion of the people, but already infamous in the eyes of the establishment for his ferocious attacks on the governance of Ireland (Fig. 06.02).[5] Not only did he never espouse republicanism, his 'messianic leadership' came to embody an uncrowned monarchy of Ireland.[6] He is the subject of another image, the

Fig. 06.02.
John Gubbins, *Daniel O'Connell, c.* 1815.
Courtesy of Dublin City Council.

barely veiled meaning of which sits as a polar opposite to the congenial but deferential *Congratulation*. Its title, *The 'Uncrowned Monarch's' next Levee*, evokes a form of strictly regulated audience held in Ireland, semi-publically, by the viceroy.[7] Harmlessly amusing as it may seem at first glance, almost indirectly flattering to both the protagonists who are handsomely portrayed, the print, published by *Punch*, is actually a biting political satire of the realpolitik of Anglo-Irish relations in June 1845. It depicts Sir Robert Peel (1788–1850), the Tory Prime Minister of Britain, about to kiss the loosely offered hand of his long-term sparring partner Daniel O'Connell, the eponymous counter-monarch of Ireland. He and his political associates in the movement to repeal the Union of Great Britain and Ireland, had just staged an elaborate event at the Rotunda, Dublin, on 30 May 1845, the very name of which was an unprecedented provocative affront to the establishment and the Crown. Billed as a national levee, it is regarded by one authoritative scholar of the period, James H. Murphy, as nothing less than a 'parody of the rituals of the viceregal court'.[8] In Ireland, before 1922, there could be but one venue for such a 'levee', the Presence Chamber of Dublin Castle, a space to which, as will be seen, O'Connell was no stranger.

Catholic Congratulation as Historical Reportage

Earl Fitzwilliam was greeted in Ireland by 'unbounded' public exaltation on 4 January 1795, and the centre of Dublin had been illuminated for his arrival.[9] In the Castle, it may have been possible, at dusk, to catch glimpses of some windows lit up with themed transparencies on Parliament Street and Cork Hill from the north-facing windows of the Presence Chamber. The room is mostly considered 'inwardly', in terms of the select rituals which unfolded *inside* the building, but anyone in it was by no means disconnected from the sights and sounds of the city. High hopes of reform had 'rendered the manifestations of the public satisfaction rather more lively than usual on such occasions'.[10] At Fitzwilliam's first levee there was 'a most numerous attendance of the first fashion and consequence', and in keeping with the spirit of concessions to Ireland and fostering Catholic loyalism to Britain, as war raged with France, Fitzwilliam knighted a prominent member of the Catholic nobility.[11] He immediately aroused animosity due to his dismissals of senior Ascendancy office-holders not aligned, as he was, with the Portland faction of the Whigs, and alienated Irish country squires by insisting on 'a rigorous and foppish ceremonial' at the Castle.[12] Some elites probably welcomed his revival of the 'etiquette of Full Dress at levees', which would have 'salutary consequences' for traders, but would especially restore 'grandeur and dignity to the state of the Irish court', which had been lapsing 'into the plain and negligent fashion of the times'.[13] *The Freeman's Journal*, then owned by the infamous 'Sham squire' Francis Higgins (1750–1802), the most productive informant to the Castle during the troubled second half of the 1790s, was vocal about this prevailing negligence in dress and 'confusion of ranks in society'.[14] The 'growing disrespect of the *Cannaille* [rabble] for their superiors', was the result when men of high birth lost the dignity of demeanour by adopting 'the coarse manners of Plebeians [and] the garb of grooms or farmers'.[15] Fitzwilliam had even apparently sent away the Lord Chancellor John Fitzgibbon, later 1st Earl of Clare (1749–1802) for 'appearing in boots and breeches'.[16] Anti-Catholic and one of the Castle 'junto' reviled by the progressive as an enemy of liberty, Fitzgibbon embodied the unaccountable Protestant Ascendancy, and was dismissed from office by Fitzwilliam. This never took full effect, but the reprimand of his sartorial nonchalance must have exacerbated political tensions.

In the days before Fitzwilliam received the Catholics, the court chamberlain John Hasler published press notices that levees at the Castle would be suspended until further notice. The radical polemicist and United Irishman William Drennan (1745–1820), a physician and accoucheur (male midwife) living nearby at 11 Dame Street, knew that the viceroy had been 'indisposed'.[17] Yet Fitzwilliam received a deputation of Presbyterian Dissenters on 12 January, which Drennan was to have joined as one of their Strand Street congregation, as part of their own efforts to achieve full civic rights. Though less vocal after a brief stint in prison in 1794 (he was acquitted of seditious libel), he had published an open letter to Fitzwilliam delivered to the Castle that same day, and so had thought it prudent not to go.[18] The pamphlet rationally pleaded for a more universal system of education, but his critique of the ignorance of the people expanded into a bitter indictment of the previous administration. It had nurtured religious animosities to divide a people who were in the process of uniting, and Drennan explicitly condemned the squirearchy of Ireland, 'the *cast* of *political* country gentlemen ... who ... make interest ... in the levee or the anti-chamber', often 'cringing at court for revenue places'.[19] His metaphors conveniently echo themes of this discussion, symbolically referencing the inner spheres of courts where power is brokered. Drennan privately revealed details about the Dissenters' address to Fitzwilliam congratulating him on his viceroyalty, but noted that:

Only a few were admitted into the closet where his excellency was, indisposed, as he has been, really or affectedly, ever since he came, and the rest were obliged to cool their heels in the ante-chamber. I hear his answer was much longer than the address.[20]

Committed since the 1780s to the total reform and independence of Irish politics, Drennan had watched the Catholics processing towards the Castle, but to him they 'looked stiff, awkward and out of place even in their own carriages which are always tawdry and dirtily gilt'.[21] The press had reported that a numerous and 'highly respectable body of Roman Catholics' had first assembled at the Rotunda, and their train of carriages to the Castle had been 'uncommonly long'.[22] This observation would recur throughout the nineteenth century in reference to the traffic jams on Dame Street on levee or ball days. The liberal *Dublin Evening Post* stated that the body 'to the amount of two hundred thousand' had been 'affably received at the Castle'; this awe-inspiring figure is only possible if droves of supporters had travelled up from the provinces, but seems highly improbable.[23] Such a turnout would certainly have elicited comments elsewhere. The (very) radical *Morning Post* provided a crucial detail, stating that they had been 'graciously received by Earl Fitzwilliam in the presence chamber, the closet *not being sufficiently capacious*' [author's emphasis] to accommodate them.[24] Receiving loyal addresses in either room was not in fact simply a logistical matter, as will be seen below, during King George IV's visit of 1821. After leaving the Castle, the 'populace stopt the carriage of Mr. Byrne', their chairman, freed the horses and 'drew the vehicle' themselves back to the Rotunda where the Catholics re-assembled; in one version of events, Byrne had been drawn 'in triumph'.[25] Over the next few days, various papers reprinted both the loyal address of the Catholics of Dublin to the viceroy, as well as Fitzwilliam's answer, but no further details on the audience itself have emerged.[26]

Despite recent interdisciplinary shifts and a growing interest in print culture, the press is still underutilized by historians, especially as a rich source of visual material. Incisive research on Irish periodicals for this period provides us with a better understanding of the market in which the *Congratulation* image was produced, though the identity of the artist remains a mystery.[27] By 1795, *Walker's Hibernian Magazine: or, Compendium of Entertaining Knowledge* was one of the most successful monthly titles of its time, also operating a highly lucrative lottery ticket agency from its premises nearby at Cicero's Head, 79 Dame Street.[28]

The *Hibernian* aimed to provide readers with a 'fund of entertainment', and a 'faithful register of public events both foreign and domestic'.[29] Its features were mostly cultural though, and it also targeted a female readership, given the regular inclusion of embroidery patterns. There was no 'direct' reporting, it generally steered clear of controversy, and no commentary was added to the *Congratulation* print and the accompanying texts, the Catholic address and Fitzwilliam's response (both general and aspirational). Yet in itself commissioning the print reveals a wish to echo the prevailing optimism of progressive public opinion. The *Hibernian* stood out from other Irish periodicals due to the frequency and, occasionally, the high quality of its prints, advertising them as 'beautifully engraved by Irish artists', though regrettably neither their names nor those of the engravers are ever provided; apart from portraiture, Irish scenes were in fact infrequent.[30] Also published were portraits of notable individuals like viceroys and generals, but in addition prominent Irish and English radicals, alongside proceedings of treason trials, like that of Archibald Hamilton Rowan (1751–1834) in 1794, or Theobald Wolfe Tone (1763–1798), after his death in 1798. William Drennan himself had been pursued for his portrait around the time of his trial in June 1794 by a 'John' Walker, presumably of the *Hibernian* enterprise; he was so determined to get Drennan's 'countenance' that he made it known that he would even publish a counterfeit.[31] Clearly there was a profit to be made by selecting material that reflected Ireland's political turmoil but also conveyed, in the case of these 'chic rebels', a certain frisson. A compelling facet of the rise of portraiture during the Enlightenment was the public character and the increased visibility of commoners. Images of political heroes like Henry Grattan (1746–1820) were ubiquitous, but new forms of popular notoriety were also driven by upward social mobility. In fact Edward Byrne had already been singled out for portrayal in the *Hibernian* back in November 1792, as nationwide elections for delegates to the landmark Catholic Convention in Dublin were underway.[32]

Who would have accessed the publication? It would have been read at home by private subscribers, perhaps at the Eagle tavern on Eustace Street frequented by both United Irishmen and Castle informers, or in any of Dublin's innumerable coffee shops and booksellers' premises. Possibly, Daniel O'Connell (still studying law in London in 1795), had perused it after joining the Dublin Library Society, located at 6 Eustace Street, in 1796.[33] But booksellers famously also displayed prints, and the increasingly popular genre of satires or cartoons, in their shop windows, so the visibility of the *Congratulation* may not have been limited to the elites. Given the attention to detail, copies could have been offered for sale to some of the individuals depicted. It appears that the unknown artist intended them to be recognizable, just as Francis Wheatley (1747–1801) had when composing his now iconic action scenes of the Volunteers at College Green and the inside of the House of Commons.[34] These have been discussed by Fintan Cullen as historical *reportage* and compelling forms of visual politics at a time of major shifts in Irish identity, depicting a genuine event of recent memory, in a 'recognisable location', and in which were featured easily identifiable leaders of society.[35] The print conforms to this increasingly popular genre of representing history in the making; but 'action' scenes such as these remained extremely rare in any of the Irish illustrated periodicals until the next century.

As the war with France intensified, the government was eager to prevent further alienation which could push Protestant and Catholic reformers and radicals even closer together. Historians could define the theme of the *Congratulation* as concession from above, though it projects several messages. In terms of the Castle's history, it appears to be the first of only two visualizations identified of *any* deputation presenting a loyal address to any viceroy, even after the advent of photography (see Fig. 04.21). Fitzwilliam had found the Catholic question 'already in agitation' when he arrived, and generally addresses of 'affection and respect' poured into the Castle from 'every corner of the kingdom', all 'religious and political opinions blended', and all through the month of February.[36] Catholics organized on a county basis, and those of Co. Kildare were championed by no less than the progressive William Fitzgerald, 2nd Duke of Leinster (1749–1804); evidently an *habitué* of the levees, he had personally 'waited' on Fitzwilliam at the Castle to present his county's address.[37] Given the wealth of some of the core members of the Dublin Catholic Committee, considered below, the *Hibernian* no doubt had another motivation, quite simply to sell: this January 1795 issue was advertised in other papers, and described the *Congratulation* as 'a beautiful and exact representation of the principal Roman Catholics of the City of Dublin' presenting their address to Fitzwilliam.[38] This selling point of exactitude makes the anonymity of the artist all the more frustrating.

The viceroy, Earl Fitzwilliam, aged forty-seven in January 1795, stands out from all the others in the *Congratulation* due to his welcoming stance and outstretched hand, though nothing in his dress or demeanour indicates his preponderant status (nor considerable personal wealth). Apart from Fitzwilliam and the leading Catholics, identifying anyone else, namely among his household, is only safe speculation. The official published list of his staff appears to have been printed before his various sackings, and may not reflect the realities on the day; apart from gentlemen of the bedchamber and the gentleman usher, it is difficult to ascertain who would normally have attended him at this type of audience, the protocol of which differed from levees.[39] Though survey histories overlooked these addresses, Joseph Robins did not, and discussed their protocol, which differed as 'faiths diverged from the principles of the Established Church', and also depended on the personal attitude of individual viceroys.[40] While Presbyterians and Quakers were received in the viceroy's chamber, i.e. as 'select visitors', it was nonetheless 'without ceremony'.[41] Frederick Howard, 5th Earl of Carlisle (1748–1825) had received Huguenots in the Presence Chamber and stood under the state canopy, but as no steward or comptroller attended them carrying wands, this was a sign that they were 'given less than full honours'.[42] John Russell, 4th Duke of Bedford (1710–1771) had received Catholics in 1759, after which they were usually received in the viceroy's personal office, or 'closet', again 'without ceremony by the gentleman usher'.[43] Protocol closely followed that of the Court of St James's in London, where the closet had a backstairs entrance, allowing the monarch to meet selected visitors 'in private', which could also imply they were 'not entitled to any particular degree of public recognition'.[44] Cautiously accepting both the *Morning Post*'s insight on the closet as the original intended venue for the 1795 event and the *Hibernian*'s puff that the print was exact, we do note that this reception of an address was unusual in that it took place *in* the Presence Chamber but more or less 'privately', i.e. not during a levee. This *may* explain why Fitzwilliam is not standing in front of (or even near) the state canopy; indeed the Catholics processing in from the viewer's right are (albeit not deliberately) masking the dais and the throne in the background, though the location of these is still discernible. In his correspondence with Whitehall, an anxious Fitzwilliam spoke of the political tensions and only made a vague and indirect reference to this event. Of his staff, he may have especially asked supportive members of his household to attend, as he was eager 'to keep clear of any engagement'.[45] Seemingly, some well-known (and possibly highly placed) 'intolerant characters' had 'roved about the purlieus of the mansion' that day with chagrined countenances.[46] Apart from the two men behind him who appear to be in civilian dress, we certainly notice at least two if not three dashing officers standing around 'decorously' in their military regalia, two to the far left of the scene and one to Fitzwilliam's own left.[47] Of the two men standing behind the viceroy one may be his private secretary, the Reverend Thomas Lewis O'Beirne (1747–1824). He was an Irish Catholic who converted to Anglicanism, took Holy Orders, then became active in Whig circles; he had gained precious experience as first chaplain and private secretary to William Cavendish-Bentinck, 3rd Duke of Portland (1738–1809), Fitzwilliam's mentor, during his Irish viceroyalty in 1782. O'Beirne was soon to be elevated to the bishopric of Ossory, and was a well-placed advisor on Catholic grievances in Ireland who had briefed Fitzwilliam before his posting; the latter did set the founding of the Catholic seminary at Maynooth, Co. Kildare, in motion before his recall. If having one's gentleman usher and master of ceremonies present was part of the protocol of receiving what we could regard as 'political' delegations, Fitzwilliam would have been privileged to have the seasoned Sir Boyle Roche (1736–1807), who had held that position since 1778 and for which he was 'pre-eminently qualified by his handsome figure, graceful address, and ready wit'.[48] Roche had also vehemently opposed the Catholic Convention in 1792. Legendary for his famous bulls and ludicrously contradictory statements, he may have advised his anxious viceroy before meeting the Catholics with one such pronouncement, namely that 'the best way to avoid danger is to meet it plump'.[49]

It is unclear how many Catholics were in the deputation and escorted inside and upstairs into the State Apartments; though there are nine in the print at the head of the procession, we get the sense that more will advance into the chamber. Only their chairman, Edward Byrne, who presented the address to Fitzwilliam, and Hugh Hamill, who 'pronounced it', are mentioned in contemporary press reports. Unlike many of the leading activists of the Catholic Committee, Edward Byrne was certainly never a United Irishman, even in their early, moderate phase, and he later rejected armed rebellion. Emblematic of the extraordinary success of Catholic merchants of his generation, he had interests abroad in textile manufacturing, but his fortune had been made from distilling and sugar baking. At his death it was said that his property was 'almost incalculable', and that he had paid 'into the Revenue larger sums than any individual in this country'; yet he had been blackballed from joining the merchants' guild in 1793, even though Catholics were now eligible.[50] Shrewd and indefatigable, he had been involved in Catholic agitation for rights since 1773 and rose to prominence in 1791, when a select committee split from the aristocrats who had until then fronted Catholic agitation, such as lords Kenmare and Fingall. Byrne and another major figure, John Keogh (1740–1817), represented a far less deferential and more assertive generation of self-made men who had found Kenmare's petition to the viceroy, John Fane, 10th Earl of Westmorland (1759–1841), in December 1791 insidious and servile. Little is known of Hugh Hamill, a Dublin merchant who had represented Drogheda at the landmark 1792 Catholic Convention, or why it was he who had read out the address.

One of the great ironies of the history of these times is that two of the most valuable and insightful sources emanate from polar opposites of the political spectrum. These are Francis Higgins's confidential letters to the Under-Secretary for Ireland Edward Cooke (1755–1820), which unfortunately only begin on 29 March 1795, and Theobald Wolfe Tone's detailed diaries.[51] Hamill was appearing regularly in Higgins's information as a key organizer and a host of radical lay Catholics pressing for rights; though never assumed to be a United Irishman, Hamill had welcomed Lord Edward Fitzgerald (1763–1798) and others conspiring with Wolfe Tone (in exile) for a French invasion.[52] Frustratingly, Tone's journals for early 1795 have never been found; both he and Higgins, each for their own reasons, would most certainly have commented on the Catholic deputation. Tone, who had been the highly influential agent and secretary to the Catholic Committee, from 1792 to 1793, was re-contacted by them on Fitzwilliam's appointment, and undoubtedly discussed this deputation with some of them. He may even have written the address itself, as he had in March when accompanying them to London to petition King George III for Fitzwilliam's reinstatement. Compromised in a treason trial in 1794, Tone was already planning his exile; it would have been inappropriate for him to go to the Castle that day, and in hindsight if he had, he surely would have commented on it.

The name of the secretary of the Catholic Committee, Richard McCormick, appears after Byrne's at the bottom of the manuscript version of the address, which Fitzwilliam forwarded to the Home Secretary, the Duke of Portland, in London.[53] A successful poplin manufacturer, he had been a major player in Catholic agitation since 1789, and the secretary of the committee which organized the Convention in 1792, the so-called Papist congress which had so alarmed the Ascendancy.[54] But McCormick was also a trusted associate of Tone, and an active United Irishman, who seems to have espoused separatism and a seditious alliance with France as early as the outbreak of war in 1793. McCormick had also served as a major in the Volunteers of Dublin in the 1780s, a rare honour at the time for prominent Catholics but not as unusual as has been assumed. Within weeks of Fitzwilliam's recall, Higgins was reporting that McCormick was involved in, and hosting, meetings (which included leading United Irishmen) to incite 'working people to riot' and hiss the new viceroy, John Jeffreys Pratt, 2nd Earl Camden, later 1st Marquess Camden (1759–1840), who arrived on 31 March 1795.[55] McCormick typified the radical agitator who had proceeded through 'constitutional' channels, but who had rapidly turned militant after Fitzwilliam's recall; he fled to France in February 1798 shortly before a major series of arrests.

Of the core members of the Dublin committee who in all probability attended, the following appear in Higgins's information but should also be mentioned in their own right. John Keogh was a very successful silk merchant of immense wealth who resided at the finely decorated Mount Jerome House, Dublin; a leading member of the Catholic Committee since 1779, he would travel with a Catholic deputation to the King in London in March 1795, as he had done in 1793. It seems virtually certain that he would have been among the delegation. But he too was especially close to Tone and supportive of his efforts, and probably at one stage an active United Irishman, though escaping arrest in 1798. John Sweetman was a prosperous brewer of porter with premises at St Stephen's Green, a collector of fine art, and one of the more radical Catholic activists. By 1796 he was one of a core group of militarized United Irishmen and was arrested in 1798 and banished in perpetuity; his exceptional art collection was seized. Though more names could be suggested, we conclude with William James Macneven, a physician, intellectual polymath, prominent United Irishman and unrepentant republican. He was banished in perpetuity after 1798, and after serving briefly in Napoleon's Irish Legion, emigrated to the United States. Macneven was one of the nine-man Dublin committee which had swiftly mobilized Catholics around the island, in December 1794, to meet and gather petitions, after Henry Grattan had returned from London, buoyant with the news that they would be 'relieved of all their remaining disabilities'.[56] Keogh had been the one to suggest fielding a Catholic candidate for Parliament, as the only actual impediment was the offensive oath of office. As emancipation had still not been won in 1828, an alliance of Catholics and liberal Protestants seized history by running Daniel O'Connell. His victory, leadership and embodiment of Irish nationhood totally transformed Irish history, but it is the forgotten episodes of his presence in Dublin Castle, and various affronts to symbols of sovereignty, which will now be considered.

O'Connell's Lessons in the Power of Monarchy

That Castle society – like Dublin – was transformed by the Union of Great Britain and Ireland, with the exodus of Anglo-Irish aristocrats and the rise of new elites from the emerging commercial and professional middle classes is certain, even if Catholics were still rare among these 'new Paddies' appearing at functions.[57] The spirit of conciliation imbued many aspects of the heavily planned ceremonials in Dublin for the visit of King George IV (Fig. 06.03). James Murphy views the occasions for experiencing spectacle, during this visit, as O'Connell's first interface with his many lessons 'in the power of monarchy' and its capacity to 'destabilize' political opponents.[58] At the Castle, preparations for George IV's 'grand' levee were complex, but not only due to the logistics of having nearly 3,000 persons presented.[59] Encounters within certain spheres in the State Apartments would allow the sovereign to reach out to his subjects, while projecting subtle political messages. Prior to receiving loyal addresses, the King had sent for Arthur James Plunkett, 8th Earl of Fingall (1759–1836). In the intimacy of the closet (but relayed well beyond), the King informed him that he would be investing him with the Order of St Patrick, fully satisfied as he was with the 'loyalty and demeanour' of the Catholics of Ireland.[60] Fingall, the premier Catholic peer of Ireland, had also been agitating for the rights of his coreligionists since the 1780s, albeit employing methods far too patrician and deferential for Byrne and Keogh back in the early 1790s, and for O'Connell from 1805 onwards. Fingall's name had topped the list Fitzwilliam had drawn up for the unprecedented dinner he had hosted at the Castle in 1795, at which Catholics had outnumbered Protestants.[61] The investiture was symbolically important, the King's intention being to 'give full effect to the conciliation of parties' in Ireland, and a knighthood of St Patrick for a Catholic was paired with (for some perhaps tagged on to) a baronetcy for Abraham Bradley King (1773–1838), the Lord Mayor of Dublin.[62] King had only just resigned from the Orange Order the previous month, having complied with the groundswell of opinion and banned the dressing of the statue of King William III at College Green on 12 July, which went ahead regardless, as he was explaining himself to the Werburgh Street Orange Lodge.[63] But Fingall's investiture provoked reaction from both extremes, and Lord Byron (1788–1824) commemorated the visit with contempt. He penned a 'swingeing satire', *The Irish Avatar*, which his friend Thomas Moore could not:

Fig. 06.03.
Sir Thomas
Lawrence and
studio, *King
George IV (1762–
1830) in Field
Marshal's Uniform*,
c. 1813–15.
© National Trust
Images.

> Wear Fingal thy trapping …
> Will thy yard of blue riband – poor Fingall – recall
> The fetters from millions of Catholic limbs?[64]

After the investitures, but before the levee in the Presence Chamber, the elders of the Dissenters first, and then the Quakers, were introduced in sequence into the closet to present their loyal addresses to George IV, the Quakers 'suffering their hats to be taken off before entering the presence'.[65] Their plain attire and formal peculiarity of manner had seemingly excited 'much observation' among the brilliant cortege of a crowded court, reminding us of the importance of the Castle's stairwells and corridors as connected spheres of shared, yet ritualized presence. With disregard for the actual demographics of Ireland, the closet reception of the Catholic bishops came last; but press reports elaborately conveyed that they had not been dressed 'in their full canonicals, as was supposed, but wore small black silk cloaks, and their gold chains and crosses'.[66] They had been treated with marked respect in the Palace and by the immense concourse of persons who filled the yards and neighbouring streets. Catholics of all ranks could feel pride (and increased loyalism) at what accounts referred to as the first 'public' recognition of that body; the term may seem contradictory given the very regulated access to these closet encounters, yet the projection of regal goodwill was one of the successes of the visit. Our greater awareness of the mechanics of these addresses helps us to deconstruct, too, the (failed) efforts deployed behind the scenes to get both bodies of Catholics, bishops and laity, to present a joint address. But the 'Catholics at large' had made a 'persevering application' to have *their* address also presented 'at a closet audience', and having declined the amalgamation, were obliged to present theirs at the far more public, and densely packed, levee.[67] After these closet addresses, the King entered the Presence Chamber, and the levee commenced, with Thomas North Graves, 2nd Baron Graves (1775–1830), Lord-in-Waiting, presenting a suitably long list of nobility, gentry, and military men. These were followed by city and county addresses from around the island, and the name of Daniel O'Connell's brother, John, appears among them as the presenter of the address from Co. Kerry. Among the 'gentlemen who went up with the Catholic address', the aristocrats among them took precedence, after which Daniel O'Connell himself was finally named in press reports; in keeping with the formulaic tradition, all 'met with a gracious reception from his Majesty and all had the honour of kissing hands'.[68]

Fig. 06.04.
Sir Thomas
Lawrence (after),
*Richard, Marquis
Wellesley, K.G.,*
after 1811.
Photograph
by Davison
& Associates,
courtesy of the
Office of Public
Works, Dublin
Castle.

Regrettably, there are no personal insights of any kind on the royal visit and his presence at the levee to be gleaned from O'Connell's otherwise revealing correspondence.[69] George IV's Dublin landing at Howth and departure from Dún Laoghaire (duly renamed Kingstown) were seemingly occasions for O'Connell's first scrutinized displays of fulsome loyalty, seized upon by lampoonists for years to come. At Howth he would have kneeled dangerously low; at Kingstown, to present the King with a crown of laurel, he had (in one cutting version of the story) even 'followed him (literally) into the sea … kneeling in the water to do so'.[70] When this last ridiculous story resurfaced in 1833, O'Connell had been honour-bound to pointedly deconstruct the calumny in the press. Acquitting himself of 'unbecoming servility', O'Connell stated that he had presented the wreath in a tent, and at the end 'farthest from the water'.[71] Possibly awestruck, O'Connell had perhaps only reflected afterwards on this, his first levee. He might have remembered it in a manner similar to Elizabeth Burke-Plunkett, Countess of Fingall (1866–1944) who would later recall the Throne Room as 'picturesque on such an occasion. I saw it clearly later. Not then, when it swam before my frightened eyes'.[72] But his letters do reveal vivid details of future encounters with royals or viceroys, starting with Richard Colley Wellesley, 1st Marquess Wellesley (1760–1842) who served as viceroy from 1821 to 1828, and again from 1833 to 1834 (Fig. 06.04).

O'Connell and the Old Dotard

Overshadowed by his illustrious younger brother Arthur Wellesley, 1st Duke of Wellington (1769–1852), Wellesley, like Fitzwilliam, had brought with him (in December 1821) sweeping changes and high expectations of Catholic emancipation. He swiftly installed liberal Protestants in the offices of attorney general and solicitor general, and appointed Anthony Richard Blake (1786–1849), a highly successful Irish Catholic barrister, to his Castle 'cabinet'.[73] Blake broke new ground for Catholics when made chief remembrancer of the exchequer for life, in 1823, and later when he became a commissioner for education, but precisely how and why he came to acquire the tantalizing title of 'backstairs viceroy' merits further investigation. O'Connell described Blake as a 'very particular friend of his' who was to introduce him to Wellesley at his first levee on 8 January 1822.[74] He intended on attending all of Wellesley's levees, O'Connell informed his uncle, as it would cost him nothing but would perhaps bring *'fair play'* in his profession as a lawyer. His uncle replied the following week (to a lost letter) that he was pleased with the 'kind reception' he had met with at the Castle, which augured favourably for Catholics.[75] In fact a Catholic congratulatory address – only one among many – had been presented to Wellesley at this levee after having been adopted at a meeting the day before, on O'Connell's motion. In one press report, members of this deputation are not listed, but O'Connell's name does appear towards the end of a very long list of guests at the levee 'set down in order of arrival'; thus we note that O'Connell had arrived before the Honourable Mr Hely Hutchinson (presumably Christopher, 1767–1826, MP for Cork and an O'Connellite), and Richard Ponsonby, Dean of St Patrick's Cathedral (1772–1853).[76]

Attendance at Wellesley's levee on 24 December 1822 was vital to mark support for the viceroy, who had just been victim of the notorious 'bottle riot', when Orangemen pelted him with a quart bottle and part of a watchman's rattle during his first state visit to the Theatre Royal on 14 December. They were venting their outrage at the government's earlier banning of their pet ritual, the dressing of the statue of King William III at College Green, but afterwards the city went 'wild' about writing addresses in support of Wellesley, O'Connell wrote to his wife Mary.[77] O'Connell had, on 11 July, written to Wellesley alleging that the ritual was illegal, and urging him to ban it.[78] Following the riot, he decided to merge the Catholic demonstration of support with that of the 'general body of citizens', resulting in a joint loyal address to Wellesley from liberal Protestants and Catholics, an especially significant reconfiguration of the manner in which the latter could profess themselves loyal subjects.[79] The context gave rise to O'Connell's most vivid description of a function, which has remained hidden from the Castle's history until now, and though the occasion called for sombre patriotism, his depiction is both informative and entertaining.

The deputation had assembled at the Mansion House, Dublin, and 'went up at about two o'clock in great procession to the Castle'.[80] O'Connell would have his 'second turn out in Court dress' (his first was presumably in honour of George IV), but would not wear a powdered wig, and though twenty to thirty were in court dresses, the rest were in plain clothes.[81] The Catholic hierarchy, including eighty-three-year-old Archbishop Troy (1739–1823), the Archbishop of Dublin, and his co-adjutor Daniel Murray (1768–1852), soon to replace him, wore the 'dresses in which the King received them'.[82] O'Connell kept free of the opening 'scene' at the Castle, the great scramble for refreshments which he found 'quite a bear garden'.[83] A 'quantity' of wine and cakes was demolished in high style and a tall college lad from Connaught, having had his share, made a nuisance of himself thereafter.[84] When Wellesley arrived around three o'clock they were 'ushered into a large room called St Patrick's Hall', with three rows of rising seats at the sides, 'one above the other', and a canopy and throne at the end of the room.[85] As the deputation filled the centre of the room, Wellesley, surrounded by a suite in superb uniforms, ordered a chair for Archbishop Troy. The viceroy's admirable response to the Lord Mayor's address prompted 'bursts of applause', which O'Connell believed to be 'very much out of rule'.[86] Then the levee began, at which all those in court dress were admitted, the 'collegian' from Connaught getting in by means of his cap and gown, 'notwithstanding his thick shoes and worsted stockings'.[87] As Wellesley 'went round the circle bowing to each of us', the collegian followed 'with his nose occasionally almost in the Marquis' face'.[88] It was provoking and ludicrous, O'Connell told his wife Mary, but when the lad 'fastened on Dr Troy', who could not get rid of him, O'Connell 'interfered' and took him off.[89] An aide-de-camp came, and 'got a beefeater or battle-axe guard man to take my worthy collegian into custody and turn him out', he wrote.[90] O'Connell, perhaps while searching for his own name in the newspaper accounts of the levee, noted that the incident had not been 'noticed' in the press, but that it was still laughable.[91] The proudest moment of this event was personal and parental, and projected O'Connell's vision of an Ireland where the rigid caste system of the past may have been displaced, and he was proud to be at its core: their eldest child Maurice (then aged nineteen) had made 'his first appearance at the Castle' and he too drank a couple of glasses of '*royal* wine'.[92] His reference to the viceroy going around the 'circle' is noteworthy. It corroborates an earlier account of this practice in Ireland recorded by Marc Marie, Marquis de Bombelles (1744–1822), a French diplomat and habitué of the French court, back in 1784. He had attended the levee of Charles Manners, 4th Duke of Rutland (1754–1787) on 4 November 1784, and entered a brief but well-observed note in his journal, after explaining that notice was given in the papers two or three days in advance:

> The Vice Roy enters followed and preceded by about twenty aide de camps, dressed in ceremonials, with the insignia of his orders ... the room in which he receives is decorated with a dais, but ordinarily he does not sit and circles among the persons present [il ... fait le Cercle parmi les personnes présentes].[93]

By early January 1823, O'Connell had been invited to dinner at the Viceregal Lodge: Wellesley had written apologizing for not having spoken to him 'at his last levée', aware of this oversight.[94] From our perspective, the Presence Chamber was being redefined as a sphere for potentially productive networking, in which Catholics could feel less and less alienated.

O'Connell also conveyed how sectarian politics in Dublin were palpable during these Castle functions. In March 1823, 'of course in Court dress', he had been received with marked kindness by Wellesley at a most crowded levee.[95] The 'Orangemen', despite rumours, had not had the courage to stay away, afraid of losing their places, and so 'cringed with as much sycophancy as if the Lord Lieutenant was of their own "kidney"'.[96] O'Connell found the sight amusing enough, but reminded Mary that he had felt:

> ... very cold in my white silk stockings although I had warm ones underneath
> ... Darling heart, I felt I was lucky in being able to get from court [the Four
> Courts] there. The crowd was nearly as great as at the King's Levée, and Dr.
> Troy and Dr. Murray were there in full canonicals. [97]

The grand levee of January 1824 revealed some complacency: by now it seemed acceptable for O'Connell not to go near 'the old dotard' (Wellesley was then sixty-four).[98] O'Connell was totally disenchanted with Wellesley for various reasons and refused to drink his health while presiding at a charity dinner (in effect, a direct insult), as it was safer to be his enemy than his friend.[99]

The suppression of the Catholic Association and continuous efforts to vote through emancipation brought O'Connell twice to London in the spring of 1825. Between giving evidence at Westminster commissions and winning over animated public meetings with the cream of British reformers, his presence in London was heavily publicized. With other leading champions of Catholic rights, and his son, he attended a royal levee and found himself once again before King George IV. To his wife he wrote: 'I am this moment come in from the levée. It was greatly crowded so that my hand is unsteady as I write … Your son Maurice, you will easily believe, looked very well in his court dress. He kissed the King's hand immediately after me'.[100] Thus O'Connell was fast becoming a habitué of the fluid passage through levees at Dublin or London, but the following year had missed the St Patrick's night ball of 1826, to which his wife and daughters had been invited. He had enquired if his daughter Kate had liked the ball and whether

Fig. 06.05.
John Partridge, *Queen Victoria*, 1842. Photograph by Mark Reddy, Trinity Digital Studios, courtesy of the Office of Public Works, Dublin Castle.

Marianne Patterson, Marchioness Wellesley (1788–1853) said anything to them, or, he wondered, 'was it like a levée, a curtsey and away?'[101]

O'Connell's election to Westminster in 1828 (by which time disabilities against Dissenters, but not Catholics, had been repealed) made Catholic emancipation inevitable and prompted the resignations of Wellington and Peel. O'Connell reminisced that the King's constitution was 'utterly broken'; he began referring to himself as merely the 'Dean of Windsor', Wellington as 'King Arthur', but O'Connell as 'the King of Ireland'.[102] This last uncrowned monarch dutifully attended the first royal levee after the passing of Catholic emancipation in 1829, which gave rise to a celebrated anecdote, as George IV was said to have been overheard by a courtier muttering, 'There is O'Connell! – G–d damn the scoundrel!'; some versions softened this last word to 'fellow'.[103] The most foregrounded issue in the monarchy's relations with Ireland for the next decade, according to James Murphy, would be 'policy toward O'Connell', now among a handful of public figures dominating the political sphere.[104] The problem of dealing with him (generally) could become especially awkward during ritualized face-to-face encounters, but a totally new, and gendered, dynamic between the monarchy and his embodiment of Irish demands for justice set in with the accession of Queen Victoria in 1837 (Fig. 06.05).

The Liberator of Ireland in his Capacity as Lord Mayor

O'Connell's avuncular and effusive professions of loyalty to this 'darling little Queen' have been the subject of ample debate, and often barely veiled derision of his unwavering monarchism, though it is worth recalling that she was three years younger than his youngest son Daniel (Fig. 06.06).[105] Murphy's compelling exploration of 'gender and the O'Connell monarchy' opens with a reminder that O'Connell was 'prominent in the throng' before St James's Palace the day her accession was proclaimed, waving his hat 'with conspicuous energy'.[106] Eight months later, he revealed in private correspondence that the Queen was determined to conciliate Ireland, and having 'expressed a wish to see' him, he would attend her next levee.[107] Victoria recorded her experience of this particular levee in a letter to her uncle King Leopold of Belgium because '*O'Connell*', she emphasized, was 'The only person who I was very anxious to see and whom I was much interested to have seen'; when presented, he 'of course … kissed hands'.[108] It had been 'quite a treat' for her, and she was impressed by his good-humoured countenance and appearance, confirming that he looked 'very like

Fig. 06.06.
J. McCormick (published by), *He Stoops to Conquer*, 1837–47.
Courtesy of the National Library of Ireland.

his caricatures', an allusion to his ubiquitous presence in political satires (a phenomenon yet to peak in the early 1840s).[109] Though relations were soon to sour, Victoria left another vivid record of when he came before her as Lord Mayor of Dublin in April 1842, to present an address of congratulations from Dublin Corporation on the birth of the Prince of Wales. She described the white wand in his hand and his crimson robe, but also his 'fine deep voice', impressive manner, and 'strong Irish brogue'.[110]

O'Connell's election, in 1841, as the first Catholic mayor – and chief magistrate – of Dublin since Sir Terence MacDermott (*d.* post-1699) in 1689, raised the paradox of him wearing King William III's chain of office and being 'enrobed … in the spoils won from Orangeism', as is captured in formal portraits (Fig. 06.07).[111] The Municipal Corporations Act (1840), which had made his election possible, led to the 'discontinuance' of the ancient swearing-in ceremonial of the mayor before the viceroy in Dublin Castle, according to the provision of the charter going back to the reign of King Henry II.[112] This had been part of an elaborate day of ceremonials described in many post-Union histories and guidebooks to the capital. The Lord Mayor and aldermen accompanied by the recorder proceeded in state from the Mansion House, and were joined by the city commons and corporation officers 'in full costume' at the City Assembly House on South William Street, from where they marched in procession to the Castle.[113] After being entertained 'with cake and wine', the mayor was sworn in before the viceroy. Until the 1820s Dublin Corporation had triumphantly championed ultra-Protestantism, and so a (liberal) press account for the last of these crown-led inaugurations on 31 October 1840 cynically referred to the undemocratic body's ritual as the 'annual farce'.[114] The yearly outing of the mayoral 'ginger-bread coach' surrounded by a 'battle-axe guard battalion' had excited the laughter of a few idle onlookers, then the *grand cortege* entered the Upper Castle Yard headed by the city marshall carrying a few old rusty keys 'tied with an Orange ribbon'.[115] The viceroy, Hugh Fortescue, Viscount Ebrington, later 2nd Earl Fortescue (1783–1861), arrived a few minutes after two o'clock and shortly afterwards was introduced into the Presence Chamber, where 'standing at the foot of the throne, [he] was surrounded by the officers of the household'.[116] The recorder, the Right Honourable Frederick Shaw, later 3rd Baronet of Bushy Park (1799–1876), then addressed Ebrington. On behalf of the Corporation, he was to present the incoming Lord Mayor, Sir John Kingston James (1784–1869), 'in order that he might, in his Excellency's presence, take the accustomed oaths, and be invested

Fig. 06.07.
Stephen Catterson
Smith the Younger,
Daniel O'Connell,
1910.
Courtesy of Dublin
City Council.

with the insignia of that high and ancient office'.[117] But Shaw then expressed, at length, reservations about the new legislation. After the swearing-in, Ebrington's reply was not as usual on these occasions 'a matter of mere formality'.[118] Instead, he delivered a speech with an unusually political tone for this space, and conveyed the views of the government on the ongoing agitation for the repeal of the Act of Union. When he stated that the Union was necessary to the 'present security and the permanent stability of the British empire', expressions of applause 'were heard from the numerous assemblage in the Presence Chamber, but they were hushed by the officers in attendance upon his Excellency'.[119] The following year, O'Connell's election as Lord Mayor and his declaration of the oath of office took place at the City Assembly House; the theatre of Anglo-Irish politics had been robbed of an unprecedented scene, his swearing-in at the Castle. Some close associates had asked if there would be a mayoral procession; he replied there *would*, shortly, when they went up to the incoming viceroy's first levee.

By then the Repeal rallies at the Corn Exchange on Dublin's Burgh Quay were also competing with the Castle as the only centre of motion with political legitimacy. Barely a month into his term, O'Connell provoked the establishment by his 'wonderfully insulting' speech on his impending (mayoral) presence at the levee of the new Tory viceroy, Thomas Philip de Grey, 2nd Earl de Grey (1781–1859), who served as viceroy from 1841 to 1844 (Fig. 06.08).[120] In it he juggled with simple language, repeating official titles in a symbolic triad binding him directly to the Queen, if through her intermediary:

> In my official capacity of Lord Mayor, I will feel it my duty to pay every token of respect to the representative of her Majesty. It is as such that I honour the Lord Lieutenant, and not through any feeling of personal respect for his Excellency. In fact, I entertain no respect at all for Lord de Grey; but as, unhappily, he is my Sovereign's representative, I must in my capacity as Lord Mayor approach him![121]

This was the *mise en scène* that led one of his earliest biographers to state: 'Never in the annals of courts did a civic functionary present himself before a viceroy under such whimsically curious circumstances'.[122] A logistical problem on the day of the levee, 17 November 1841, led to misunderstandings and misrepresentations in an already tense atmosphere. The episode even made the London newspapers, extending the sphere of the Presence Chamber beyond Ireland's shores. Because

Fig. 06.08. Frederick Richard Say (attr. to), *Thomas Phillip, Earl de Grey, K.G.*, *c.*1845. Photograph by Davison & Associates, courtesy of the Office of Public Works, Dublin Castle.

so little detail was recorded on what actually went on in the Presence Chamber itself, the broader setting allows us to sense the general atmosphere.

As expected, the Lord Mayor had proceeded 'in state' from the Mansion House, followed, according to *The Times* of London, 'by several of the *Radical* aldermen and town council' [author's emphasis].[123] The streets had been 'thronged to excess' from early morning and eager spectators even perched on rooftops to witness 'so truly novel a scene'.[124] The (at that stage of its long history) liberal *Freeman's Journal* was disdainful of the wealthy viceroy, representing 'the aristocracy and bread-taxers' of the impoverished people; coercive invitations dispatched to the four corners of the island, requested the presence of friends of 'good government'.[125] All depended on a full attendance of 'wigs and gowns, coronets and cocked hats, swords, knee buckles and silk stockings, ruffled shirts and powdered lackeys, whiskered military and peculating plundering placehunters'.[126] Shifting to 'another side of the picture' on which every lover of humanity and liberty delighted 'to dwell', the anonymous and effusive *Freeman's* reporter gushed on about the 'eloquent and indomitable assertor' of the rights of the people, O'Connell.[127] The cheers of the multitude following the procession were deafening as it wound its way up Dame Street, where every window was 'crowded to suffocation by persons eager to get a glimpse of his lordship [O'Connell] and the state equipage', which, taking precedence, had been ushered through by mounted police.[128] Crowds gathered at Cork Hill, the rendezvous for those eager to witness the 'gaudy show' of the carriages arriving; proprietors recognized as political enemies were received 'with a shout of disapprobation', convincing proof that 'all was not gold that glittered'.[129] But when 'his lordship's carriage and cortège entered the Castle gates', the cheering of 'the people' became 'absolutely astounding', and their 'ebullition' uncontrollable, reported the enthusiastic but more restrained *Dublin Evening Post*.[130] Crowds anxious to 'witness the champion of his country' pressed upon the carriage, causing confusion, but thanks to the police, 'the liberator of Ireland – the untiring advocate of national independence and national prosperity', as trumpeted by the *Freeman's*, finally entered the Castle gates.[131] The ensuing noise, as described, clearly delineated competing camps: cheering from without the gates was soon echoed *within* the Castle yard, and was so 'deafening' as to drown out the music of the Hussar band stationed there.[132] Presumably, the persons 'of respectable appearance' allowed by the police to enter the Lower Castle Yard swelled the numbers of the O'Connellites who drowned out the viceroy's musicians. If the *Freeman's* was not mistaken, this cheering even startled 'his Excellency himself who was at that very moment entering the presence chamber'.[133]

O'Connell arrived at the grand entrance to the State Apartments 'amid peals of applause' then ascended the great stairs at one o'clock and entered St Patrick's Hall.[134] But in one report he had delayed a few minutes 'on the lobby', known today as the Battle Axe Landing, to allow other members of his entourage to join him; several 'noblemen and gentlemen' who were 'passing up' bowed to him, and 'not a few' shook his hand.[135] He then 'proceeded to the presence chamber', paid his respects to the 'representative of royalty' and departed.[136] The Tory press later claimed that, with his 'innate modesty', the Lord Mayor had 'demanded the privilege of the private entrée', but the Chamberlain had courteously explained 'he should enter the presence chamber by the route prescribed for the general class of visitors'.[137] The *Freeman's* reporter, having certainly not 'courted' the honour (of an invitation, or entrée) to witness the scene in the Presence Chamber for himself 'when the Lord Mayor's name was announced', relied on the accuracy of a dependable eyewitness.[138] O'Connell gave his card to the gentleman placed on the corridor for that purpose, proceeded through St Patrick's Hall, with the mace, keys and sword borne before him, to the entrance to the Presence Chamber. The tempo then picked up in rhythmic bursts, almost mimicking the fanfare of court trumpets:

> His lordship entered, and was announced – the aides de camp stared – the officers of the household gazed with wonder and amazement – his Excellency bowed – his Lordship bowed and – retired! Thus ended the official duty of the Liberator of Ireland in his capacity as Lord Mayor.[139]

O'Connell exited the 'Vice-Regal Court' and entered his carriage again to rapturous applause, except that 'the band in the yard struck up *Nix my Dolly*, the performance of which created considerable laughter'.[140] The song was an immensely popular operatic ballad sung in rogue's cant by a fictitious criminal hero born in Newgate Gaol. What message precisely the viceroy's band was conveying, and whether the laughter was universal, we may only guess. In the days that followed, O'Connell was forced into denying publically that he had deliberately delayed at the gate 'in order to allow the *rabble* to shout'.[141] This was translated into giving 'the populace … an opportunity to huzza' by the liberal press, which stressed that 'such a thing was absurd' as the delay had occurred 'at the internal staircase'.[142] But, *The Times* pushed on, claiming that the delay 'looked rather suspicious, nonetheless'.[143] On a graver note, it was said that the Lord Mayor had shown disrespect by being 'somewhat later in his attendance than is usual for the first magistrat on such occasions', and by having extended 'a chilling reception' to the viceroy.[144] In a unique twist in the Castle's history, the views of the sword-bearer and mace-bearer were sought, and they denied any report that the viceroy had treated O'Connell 'with withering contempt', according to *The Freeman's Journal*.[145] This highly publicized *cause célèbre* raged on for weeks. It had indeed been 'a day of rare sport at Dublin Castle', defining (through misrepresentation) a new age in the appropriation of leadership which O'Connell embodied.[146]

A National Levee

The event indirectly referenced in *Punch*'s cartoon, *The 'Uncrowned Monarch's' next Levee*, was a commemoration at the Rotunda, Dublin, on 30 May 1845 to mark the anniversary of the release from prison the previous year of the 'Repeal Martyrs'; they had been charged with conspiracy, O'Connell among them (Fig. 06.09). On his release from the Richmond Bridewell, he had been transported through Dublin on an extravagant triumphal car.[147] The event at the Rotunda was elaborate and heavily stage-managed, as is clear from a fine and rare print, published in *The Pictorial Times*; it evidently inspired *Punch*'s spinoff satire (Fig. 06.10).[148] Though the official printed proceedings labelled the event as a 'Commemoration of the 30th of May 1844' for the 'Repeal State Prisoners', it is explicitly referred to four times in the finer print of the main text, and in press reports, as a 'Levee'.[149] It is also described as such in designs by Mr Phillipps for the room's decoration (Fig. 06.11).[150] After a grandiose procession from the Richmond Bridewell to the Rotunda, 'Mr. O'Connell and his Fellow Prisoners' were conducted inside the heavily festooned Pillar Room; during the 'Levee' he received addresses from various delegations around Ireland. In the *Pictorial* print, O'Connell appears clearly in the costume of the '82 club, which honoured the triumph of Henry Grattan, who was instrumental in bringing about legislative independence for the Irish Parliament in 1782. He stands on an elevated platform with, as a dramatic backdrop, a painted scene of the former Parliament House at College Green. The image bore the Repealers' motto: 'It was and shall be', verbalizing their commitment to restoring an Irish legislature; a threat to the Empire. Not visible in the print are the seven chairs on this

Above:
Fig. 06.09.
'Mr. O'Connell's Levee'. *The Pictorial Times*, 14 June 1845. Courtesy of the National Library of Ireland.

Left:
Fig. 06.10.
'The "Uncrowned Monarch's" next Levee'. *Punch*, 28 June 1845. Courtesy of the National Library of Ireland.

THE "UNCROWNED MONARCH'S" NEXT LEVEE.

platform for the Repeal martyrs; 'the chair placed for the Liberator was covered with rich green damask', its frame beautifully gilded and carved with a harp and '82 encircled in shamrocks.[151] In other words, a throne of sorts. The men advancing in robes are most probably the aldermen of Dublin Corporation, also wearing their gold and green '82 uniforms but under 'their scarlet robes of office'.[152] Many delegations representing corporations and the trades followed, paying 'their respects to the Liberator', though it is easy to see how the *Punch* version was derived: the alderman on bended knee and O'Connell are, most certainly, graciously touching hands.[153] Whether kissing ensued is almost immaterial; physical contact was also established when scrolls were successively placed in O'Connell's hand. William Smith O'Brien (1803–1864) seems to have acted as a master of ceremonies, and read out the pledge which all had signed on these scrolls. It asserted their 'national right to a national legislature', as a great nation.[154] They would never desist from seeking the repeal of the Union, by peaceable, moral and constitutional means, and all pledged this in unison. Terence Bellew MacManus (1811–1861), another (future) veteran of the Young Irelander Rebellion of 1848, was also present.

There were, needless to say, 'livid' reports in the press.[155] There had been weeks of political tensions in Parliament over the question of the new Irish Colleges. But the real context was the graciously vague response by Queen Victoria to Dublin Corporation's address, delivered personally on 23 May, in favour of a long-awaited royal visit to Ireland; after months of speculation, she looked forward to such a visit, 'Whenever' she would be welcomed there.[156] The commemoration was timely and O'Connell's spin

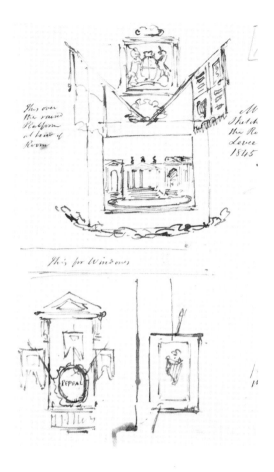

Fig. 06.11.
Mr Phillipps, 'Sketch for decorating the Rotunda for the Levee on 30th May 1845', 1845.
Courtesy of the National Library of Ireland.

doctors seized the opportunity to stage what James Murphy has deemed 'one of the most outlandish burlesques of his career'.[157] There had been 10,000 people in the procession, estimated the Duke of Wellington, and 100,000 lining the streets: 'as impudent a demonstration … as ever witnessed in Ireland'.[158] Worse perhaps was the pledge, the 'declaration of independence', and all this 'under the very nose of executive government'.[159] One paper was especially savage about this 'outrage on royalty', with O'Connell 'sitting in aristocratic state in the throne room of the Rotundo … surrounded by *regalia*'.[160] The fault lay with the viceroy of the day, William à Court, 1st Baron Heytesbury (1779–1860), as that day O'Connell had been the '*de facto* Viceroy over him'.[161] An even more grandiose demonstration followed in Cork on 8 June that year.

In the Anglophone world, usage of the term 'levee' had broadened slightly to encompass any elitist audience or gathering during which it was socially advantageous to be seen, and at which one could court favours or advancement, or simply network. Back in 1789, George Washington (1732–1799), the first President of the United States, had (reluctantly) accepted the lexical appropriation of the vexed term for his official weekly receptions, though it evidently was the antithesis of new American principles. This triggered bitter condemnation by his political opponents among the Democratic Republicans, as they were then known:

> Mr Washington in his public or levee room (which … might soon have been called his *court*) has exactly copied the style of monarchs in the royal nothings of which his brief discourse on these occasions is so full.[162]

The republicans who preceded O'Connell never seem to have wanted to mock regal rituals, or replicate Washingtonian levees. In a lost letter, seemingly about plans for this Rotunda commemoration, O'Connell had replied: 'As to a *levée* it has nothing royal about it'.[163] He seems to have been asked something about a 'sceptre', but he knew nothing of it and 'would of course put an end to such a farce'.[164] The Lord Chancellor and chief judges held levees, and 'foreign princes and *royals*' held them in London, he wrote.[165] But O'Connell was in Dublin, and was the unrivalled 'neo-royal embodiment' of Ireland, and with this national levee he had succeeded in wresting the sacred symbolism of the Presence Chamber from the confines of Dublin Castle.[166]

Conclusion

In his letter to Earl Fitzwilliam on the urgency of political reform, William Drennan had urged the 'minds of statesmen' to 'now move in a wider orbit than the closet, or the anti-chamber'.[167] The *Catholic Congratulation* print, while conveying the deference observed that day by the Catholics in the Presence Chamber at Dublin Castle, opened it up to public scrutiny. There is an extraordinary immediacy to it, akin to photojournalism; a sense of movement from right to left, as we anticipate a train of gentlemen entering. It has been viewed here mainly as a source of political insights, in how it demystified the Presence Chamber. All are upright and standing. The success against the odds of King George IV's royal visit to Ireland has been discussed perceptively by James Loughlin in terms of the celebratory context of Dublin, and the remarkable resignifying of the Castle as the location for events in which 'mutual political alienation' dissolved into common expressions of loyal allegiance.[168] Furthermore, he pointedly refers to the blurring of imaginative barriers between personal and public realms, and the demystification of 'awed loyalty' that 'distance-asserting ritual' is meant to produce between monarch and subjects.[169] Though Loughlin mainly references outdoor events, his analysis of George IV's liminality to his people is compelling in how it allows us to comprehend proximity within designated spaces inside the Castle, closet or Presence Chamber, throughout this discussion. After his election as Lord Mayor of Dublin, Daniel O'Connell had been reminded by his son that he now had 'a legally recognised *lordship* from the people, utterly unconnected with court favour and aristocratic usage'.[170] In the *Punch* image, The '*Uncrowned Monarch's' next Levee*, after the affront of the national levee in Dublin, Prime Minister Robert Peel is seen about to perform the ritualistic traditional courtesy, which ministers of the Crown partook in upon assuming office. But here the courtesy is performed not before Queen Victoria, as had been the case when Peel took office on 30 August 1841, but rather before the 'Uncrowned King', Daniel O'Connell.[171] Again, the theme (apart from O'Connell's literally towering presence, though at that time officially only an MP for Co. Cork) is a concession to Ireland. But the 'kissing hands' ritual, which only a few privileged persons could partake in, is in fact the focal point of the picture. Though it is an ancient regal courtesy performed between sovereigns and subjects, here it is appropriated, amusingly, to convey Anglo-Irish accommodations, brokered solely in the sphere of politicians that extended beyond the walls of the Presence Chamber.

Endnotes

1   *Walker's Hibernian Magazine: or, Compendium of Entertaining Knowledge, for January, 1795*; for details on William Wentworth-Fitzwilliam (1748–1833), 4th Earl Fitzwilliam, and his term as viceroy of Ireland, see, *inter alia*, J. Kelly, 'Fitzwilliam, William Wentworth (1748–1833), 2nd Earl Fitzwilliam (GB), 4th Earl Fitzwilliam (Ire.)', in J. McGuire and J. Quinn (eds), *Dictionary of Irish Biography* (Cambridge: Cambridge University Press, 2009), hereafter *DIB*, viewable online: http://dib.cambridge.org/viewReadPage.do?articleId=a3259 (accessed 11 April 2017); D. Wilkinson, 'Fitzwilliam, William Wentworth, second Earl Fitzwilliam in the peerage of Great Britain, and fourth Earl Fitzwilliam in the peerage of Ireland (1748–1833)', in H.C.G. Matthew and B. Harrison (eds), *Oxford Dictionary of National Biography* (Oxford: Oxford University Press, 2004), viewable online: http://www.oxforddnb.com/view/article/9665, (accessed 10 April 2017); D. Lindsay, 'The Fitzwilliam Episode Revisited', in D. Dickson, D. Keogh and K. Whelan (eds), *The United Irishmen: Republicanism, Radicalism and Rebellion* (Dublin: The Lilliput Press, 1993), pp. 197–208; D. Mansergh, *Grattan's Failure: Parliamentary Opposition and the People in Ireland, 1779–1800* (Dublin: Irish Academic Press, 2005), pp. 176–90; no study on Fitzwilliam references the print.

2   T. Bartlett, *Ireland: A History* (Cambridge: Cambridge University Press, 2010), p. 212; T. Bartlett, *The Fall and Rise of the Irish Nation: The Catholic Question, 1690–1830* (Dublin: Gill & Macmillan, 1992), pp. 202–3.

3   J.H. Murphy, '"Mock Court": The Lord Lieutenancy of Ireland, 1767–1922', *The Court Historian*, 9, 2 (2004), pp. 129–45; C. Dickens, 'The Castle of Dublin', *All the Year Round*, 15, 370 (26 May 1866), p. 463; J. Robins, *Champagne & Silver Buckles: The Viceregal Court at Dublin Castle 1700–1922* (Dublin: The Lilliput Press, 2001), pp. 50–1.

4   C.J. Woods, 'Byrne, Edward 1739/40–1804', in J. McGuire and J. Quinn (eds), *DIB*, viewable online: http://dib.cambridge.org/viewReadPage.do?articleId=a1324 (accessed 10 April 2017), citing *The Dublin Evening Post*.

5   P. Geoghegan, *King Dan: The Rise of Daniel O'Connell* (Dublin: Gill & Macmillan, 2008), p. 198.

6   See Bartlett, *Ireland*, p. 268.

7   *Punch*, 9, 207 (28 June 1845); National Library of Ireland, PD 2120 TX (2) 37.

8   See Murphy, '"Mock Court"', p. 134.

9   *Finn's Leinster Journal*, 7 January 1795, and following. Transparencies of coated paper featured symbolic imagery and inscriptions, ranging from expressions of loyalism to radical patriotic slogans; e.g., for King George III's golden jubilee in 1809, one Hughes, a watchmaker in Grafton Street, had 'exhibited one of the King, crowned by Time', and another of Hibernia pointing to a timepiece: *Freeman's Journal*, 30 October 1809; see also P. Higgins, *A Nation of Politicians: Gender, Patriotism, and Political Culture in Late Eighteenth-Century Ireland* (Wisconsin: University of Wisconsin Press, 2010), p. 328.

10 *Finn's Leinster Journal*, 7 January 1795.

11 *Belfast Newsletter*, 9 January 1795; *Finn's*

Leinster Journal, 7 January 1795, reported that 'Hugh O'Reily, Esq., of Bailinlough, Lieutenant Colonel of the Westmeath militia, A Roman Catholic Gentleman of considerable landed property, is created a Baronet of this kingdom by the Earl Fitzwilliam'.

12 M. Elliott, *Wolfe Tone* (Liverpool: Liverpool University Press, 2013), p. 238.

13 *Freeman's Journal,* 20 January 1795.

14 Ibib.; for Higgins, see C.J. Woods, 'Higgins, Francis ('Sham Squire') (1745?–1802), *DIB,* viewable online: http://dib.cambridge.org/ viewReadPage.do?articleId=a3999 (accessed 10 April 2017); and especially T. Bartlett (ed.), *Revolutionary Dublin, 1795–1801: The Letters of Francis Higgins to Dublin Castle* (Dublin: Four Courts Press, 2009).

15 *Freeman's Journal,* 20 January 1795.

16 See Elliott, *Wolfe Tone,* p. 238.

17 *Freeman's Journal,* 10 January 1795; J. Agnew (ed.), *The Drennan-McTier Letters* (Dublin: Irish Manuscripts Commission, 1998/99), vol. 2, p. 119.

18 W. Drennan, *A Letter to His Excellency Earl Fitzwilliam Lord Lieutenant, &c. of Ireland* (Dublin: Printed by J. Chambers, 1795).

19 Ibid., p. 25.

20 See Agnew, *Drennan Letters,* p. 119.

21 Ibid., p. 120.

22 *Dublin Evening Post,* 15 January 1795, with estimation of numbers; *Finn's Leinster Journal,* 17 January 1795.

23 *Dublin Evening Post,* 15 January 1795; Whitelaw's private census of 1804 estimated Dublin's population at 182,370: see D. Dickson, *Dublin: The Making of a Capital City* (London: Profile Books, 2014), p. 278.

24 *Morning Post or Dublin Courant,* 15 January 1795; this elusive anti-government paper deserves more attention. Its proprietor, Peter Cooney, was jailed in 1789 and 1794 for 'his temerity in lampooning the Castle administration and its supporters'; see Bartlett, *Revolutionary Dublin,* p. 100.

25 *Freeman's Journal,* 15 January 1795.

26 *Belfast Newsletter,* 12–16 January 1795; *Dublin Evening Post,* 15 January 1795; *Finn's Leinster Journal,* 17 January 1795; *Northern Star,* 19 January 1795.

27 J. Archbold, 'Irish Periodicals in their Atlantic Context, 1770–1830: The monthly and quarterly magazines of Dublin, with comparison to those of Edinburgh and Philadelphia', unpublished PhD thesis, Trinity College Dublin, 2008, p. 104.

28 Ibid., p. 166. It is assumed that the John, Joseph and Henry Walker linked to his business were brothers or sons: see M. Pollard, *A Dictionary of Members of the Dublin Book Trade 1500–1800* (London: Bibliographical Society, 2000) pp. 582–4; *Walker's Hibernian Magazine,* January 1796.

29 See Archbold, 'Irish Periodicals', p. 104.

30 It was more or less unrivalled in terms of visual material until the stylish *Anthologia Hibernica* was launched in 1793: see Archbold, 'Irish Periodicals', p. 122. The *Hibernian* published a list of plates in June and December. One notable exception from this list was the 'Representation of the Body of his Grace the late Duke of Rutland lying in STATE in the [Irish] House of Lords', *Walker's Hibernian Magazine,* November 1787, reproduced in Robins, *Champagne,* following p. 56.

31 See Agnew, *Drennan Letters,* p. 62, discussed in F. Cullen, *The Irish Face: Redefining the Irish Portrait* (London: National Portrait Gallery, 2004), p. 159.

32 *Walker's Hibernian Magazine,* November 1792; National Library of Ireland, EP BYRN-ED (1) I, viewable online: http://catalogue.nli. ie/Record/vtls000056960 (accessed 30 March 2017).

33 M. Kennedy, '"Politicks, Coffee and News":

The Dublin book trade in the eighteenth century', *Dublin Historical Record*, 58, 1 (Spring 2005), p. 80.

34 See Francis Wheatley, *The Dublin Volunteers in College Green, 4 November 1779*, 1779-80, National Gallery of Ireland, oil on canvas; the key to his *The Irish House of Commons*, 1780, Leeds Museums and Galleries, oil on canvas, was in fact only created in 1801.

35 F. Cullen, 'Visual Politics in 1780s Ireland: The role of history painting', *Oxford Art Journal*, 18, 1 (1995), p. 59.

36 Letter to the Duke of Portland from Earl Fitzwilliam, 8 January 1795, Home Office Papers, National Archives of the United Kingdom, HO/100/56/39ʳ; D. Taaffe, *An Impartial History of Ireland from the Period of the English Invasion to the Year 1810* (Dublin: Christie, 1811), vol. 4, p. 536.

37 *Dublin Evening Post*, 19 February 1795.

38 *Dublin Evening Post*, 7 February 1795. Patrick Byrne, a leading bookseller, had stated that his only principle in trade 'was to make money of it'; see Archbold, 'Irish Periodicals', p. 45.

39 For a full list of Fitzwilliam's 'Officers of State' and 'Household', see *The City and Country Calendar or Irish Court Registry, for the Year of our Lord 1795* (Dublin: 1795), pp. 50–1; see also Robins, *Champagne*, pp. 50–1; R.B. McDowell, 'The Court of Dublin Castle', in R.B. McDowell, *Historical Essays 1938–2001* (Dublin: The Lilliput Press, 2003), pp. 7–9.

40 See Robins, *Champagne*, p. 50.

41 Ibid., p. 51.

42 See Robins, *Champagne*, pp. 50–1; no date is given for the reception of the Huguenots, but Carlisle's term was from November 1780 to April 1782.

43 Ibid., p. 51.

44 See Robins, *Champagne*, p. 51.

45 Letter to the Duke of Portland from Earl Fitzwilliam, 15 January 1795, Home Office Papers, National Archives of the United Kingdom, HO/100/56/39, f.82ʳ.

46 *Dublin Evening Post*, 15 January 1795.

47 See Robins, *Champagne*, p. 41.

48 Ibid., p. 45; see J. Quinn, 'Roche, Sir Boyle (1736–1807)', in J. McGuire and J. Quinn (eds), *DIB*, viewable online: http://dib.cambridge.org/viewReadPage.do?articleId=a7741 (accessed 10 April 2017).

49 See Quinn, 'Roche, Sir Boyle'.

50 See Woods, 'Byrne, Edward'.

51 For Higgins, see Bartlett, *Revolutionary Dublin*; for Tone, see T. Moody, R. McDowell and C. Woods (eds), *The Writings of Theobald Wolfe Tone* (Oxford: Clarendon Press, 1998; 2001; 2007), 3 vols.

52 See Bartlett, *Revolutionary Dublin*, pp. 170, 333.

53 Letter to the Duke of Portland from Earl Fitzwilliam, 15 January 1795, Home Office Papers, National Archives of the United Kingdom, HO/100/56/39, 143ʳ–145ʳ.

54 See Moody, McDowell and Woods, *The Writings of Theobald Wolfe Tone*, vol. 1, p. 388; vol. 3, p. 563.

55 See Bartlett, *Revolutionary Dublin*, p. 82.

56 See Lindsay, 'The Fitzwilliam Episode', p. 199.

57 See Robins, *Champagne*, pp. 94–6.

58 See Murphy, *Abject Loyalty*, p. 9.

59 *Times*, 24 August 1821.

60 Ibid.

61 'List of persons who came to Dinner [Saturday]', 28 February 1795, Wentworth Woodhouse Muniments, Sheffield City Archives, WWM/F/30/33; see Mansergh, *Grattan's Failure*, p. 294. That this dinner was held in Dublin Castle and not at the Viceregal Lodge is mentioned in William Drennan's correspondence: see Agnew, *Drennan Letters*, p. 130.

62 *Times*, 24 August 1821.

63 J. Hill, *From Patriots to Unionists: Dublin Civic Politics and Irish Protestant Patriotism, 1660–1840* (Oxford: Clarendon Press, 1997), p. 321.

64 R. Kelly, *Bard of Erin: The Life of Thomas Moore* (Dublin: Penguin Ireland, 2008), pp. 361–2.

65 *Times*, 24 August 1821; Anon., 'The King's Visit to Ireland', *The New Annual Register* (January 1822), p. 220; sections of this take up, verbatim, reports from *The Times*.

66 *Times*, 24 August 1821.

67 *Times*, 23 August 1821.

68 *Freeman's Journal*, 21 August 1821; *Finn's Leinster Journal*, 25 August 1821.

69 M.R. O'Connell (ed.), *The Correspondence of Daniel O'Connell, 1815–1823* (Dublin: Irish University Press, 1973), vol. 2, pp. 327–31.

70 'More of O'Connell's Inconsistencies', *The Spectator*, 285 (14 December 1833), pp. 1267–9.

71 The tent is to the lower right in: *To his Most Excellent Majesty George the Fourth King of Great Britain &c. &c. &c.*, National Library of Ireland, PD D25, viewable online: http://catalogue.nli.ie/Record/vtls000147554 (accessed 4 April 2017).

72 The Countess of Fingall and T. West, *Seventy Years Young: Memories of Elizabeth, Countess of Fingall* (Dublin: The Lilliput Press, 1991), p. 62. 'Daisy' Burke married the 11th Earl of Fingall in 1883, who was State Steward at Dublin Castle from 1882 to 1885.

73 See R. Hawkins, 'Blake, Anthony Richard', in J. McGuire and J. Quinn (eds), *DIB*, viewable online: http://dib.cambridge.org/viewReadPage.do?articleId=a0720 (accessed 10 April 2017).

74 See O'Connell, *Correspondence of Daniel O'Connell*, vol. 2, p. 347.

75 Ibid., p. 350.

76 *Freeman's Journal*, 9 January 1822, emphasis as per original; I am indebted to Christopher J. Woods and James Quinn for clarifying that Christopher is the only one of John Hely Hutchinson's five sons who could, on this date, have been styled 'the Honourable': D. Murphy, 'Hely-Hutchinson, Christopher', in J. McGuire and J. Quinn (eds), *DIB*, viewable online: http://dib.cambridge.org/viewReadPage.do?articleId=a4176 (accessed 10 April 2017).

77 See O'Connell, *Correspondence of Daniel O'Connell*, vol. 2, p. 411.

78 P. Brynn, 'The Marquess Wellesley', unpublished PhD thesis, Trinity College Dublin, 1977, vol. 3, p. 1350.

79 See Hill, *Patriots to Unionists*, pp. 326–7; see Geoghegan, *King Dan*, p. 195.

80 See O'Connell, *Correspondence of Daniel O'Connell*, vol. 2, pp. 415–16.

81 Ibid., p. 416.

82 See O'Connell, *Correspondence of Daniel O'Connell*, vol. 2, p. 416.

83 Ibid.

84 See O'Connell, *Correspondence of Daniel O'Connell*, vol. 2, p. 416.

85 Ibid.

86 See O'Connell, *Correspondence of Daniel O'Connell*, vol. 2, p. 416.

87 Ibid.

88 See O'Connell, *Correspondence of Daniel O'Connell*, vol. 2, p. 416.

89 Ibid.

90 See O'Connell, *Correspondence of Daniel O'Connell*, vol. 2, p. 416.

91 Ibid.

92 See O'Connell, *Correspondence of Daniel O'Connell*, vol. 2, p. 416.

93 J. Gury (ed.), *Journal de Voyage en Grande Bretagne et en Irlande, 1784* (Oxford: Voltaire Foundation, 1989), p. 246, author's translation; I am indebted to Christopher J. Woods for providing me with this

source. Bombelles had evidently witnessed the Volunteer review at College Green to commemorate the birthday and landing in Ireland of King William III.

94 See O'Connell, *Correspondence of Daniel O'Connell*, vol. 2, p. 422.

95 Ibid., pp. 443–4.

96 See O'Connell, *Correspondence of Daniel O'Connell*, vol. 2, pp. 443–4.

97 Ibid.

98 M.R. O'Connell (ed.), *Correspondence of Daniel O'Connell, 1824–1828* (Dublin: Irish University Press, 1974), vol. 3, p. 10.

99 See Geoghegan, *King Dan*, p. 210.

100 Ibid., p. 155.

101 See O'Connell, *Correspondence of Daniel O'Connell*, vol. 3, p. 239; by 'them' he must have meant their two eldest daughters Ellen, aged twenty-one, and Catherine (Kate), aged eighteen.

102 See Murphy, *Abject Loyalty*, pp. 10–12, and following.

103 W.J. O'Neill Daunt, *Personal Recollections of the Late Daniel O'Connell* (London: Chapman & Hall, 1848) vol. 1, p. 130.

104 See Murphy, *Abject Loyalty*, p. 12.

105 Ibid., p. 26.

106 See Murphy, *Abject Loyalty*, p. 20.

107 M.R. O'Connell (ed.), *The Correspondence of Daniel O'Connell, 1829–1832* (Dublin: Irish University Press, 1977), vol. 4, p. 134.

108 See Murphy, *Abject Loyalty*, p. 22; Viscount Esher (ed.), *The Girlhood of Queen Victoria: A Selection from Her Majesty's Diaries between the years 1832 and 1840* (London: John Murray, 1912), vol. 1, pp. 286–7.

109 See Esher, *The Girlhood of Queen Victoria*, p. 287.

110 See Murphy, *Abject Loyalty*, p. 23.

111 P. Geoghegan, *Liberator: The Life and Death of Daniel O'Connell, 1830–1847* (Dublin: Gill and Macmillan, 2010), p. 122.

112 See Hill, *Patriots to Unionists*, p. 381; *Freeman's Journal*, 1 October 1840; 'First Report of the Commissioners Appointed to Inquire into the Municipal Corporations in Ireland', *House of Lords Sessional Papers*, 9, 1 (1835), p. 10.

113 J. Warburton, J. Whitelaw and R. Walsh, *History of the City of Dublin* (London: printed for T. Cadell & W. Davies by W. Bulmer & Co., 1818), vol. 2, p. 1063, n. †.

114 *Freeman's Journal*, 1 October 1840.

115 Ibid.

116 *Freeman's Journal*, 1 October 1840.

117 Ibid.

118 *Belfast Newsletter*, 6 October 1840.

119 Ibid.

120 See Geoghegan, *Liberator*, p. 123.

121 W.J. O'Neill Daunt, *Personal Recollections of the Late Daniel O'Connell* (London: Chapman & Hall, 1848) vol. 2, p. 45.

122 Ibid.

123 *Times*, 19 November 1841.

124 *Dublin Evening Post*, 18 November 1841.

125 *Freeman's Journal*, 18 November 1841.

126 Ibid.

127 *Freeman's Journal*, 18 November 1841.

128 *Dublin Evening Post*, 18 November 1841.

129 *Freeman's Journal*, 18 November 1841.

130 *Dublin Evening Post*, 20 November 1841.

131 *Freeman's Journal*, 18 November 1841.

132 Ibid.

133 *Freeman's Journal*, 18 November 1841.

134 Ibid.

135 *Dublin Evening Post*, 18 November 1841.

136 Ibid.

137 *Times*, 20 November 1841.

138 *Freeman's Journal*, 18 November 1841.

139 Ibid.

140 *Freeman's Journal*, 18 November 1841.

141 *Times*, 22 November 1841.

142 *Freeman's Journal*, 20 November 1841.

143 *Times*, 22 November 1841.

144 Ibid.

145 *Freeman's Journal*, 20 November 1841.

146 *Freeman's Journal*, 18 November 1841.

147 *Irish Times*, 11 August 2012.

148 *Pictorial Times*, 14 June 1845, National Library of Ireland, PD 2120 TX (2) 34, viewable online: http://catalogue.nli.ie/Record/vtls000171299 (accessed 4 April 2017).

149 See *The Repeal State Prisoners, Commemoration of the 30th May, 1844* (Dublin: printed by Browne of Nassau Street, 1845).

150 It may have been Thomas Matthew Ray, secretary of the Repeal Association, who had hired 'Mr. Philips principal decorator of the Theatre Royal': *Dublin Evening Post*, 31 May 1845.

151 *Dublin Evening Post*, 31 May 1845; see also *Freeman's Journal*, 31 May 1845.

152 *Freeman's Journal*, 31 May 1845.

153 Ibid.

154 *Freeman's Journal*, 31 May 1845.

155 See Murphy, *Abject Loyalty*, pp. 55–6.

156 Ibid., p. 55.

157 See Murphy, *Abject Loyalty*, p. 55

158 Ibid., p. 56.

159 *Times*, 2 June 1845.

160 *Freeman's Journal*, 2 June 1845, cited in Murphy, *Abject Loyalty*, p. 56.

161 See Murphy, *Abject Loyalty*, p. 56.

162 *Remarks Occasioned by the Late Conduct of Mr. Washington, as President of the United States* (Philadelphia: printed for Benjamin Franklin Bache, 1797), p. 62, n.

163 M.R. O'Connell (ed.), *The Correspondence of Daniel O'Connell, 1846–1847* (Dublin: Irish University Press, 1980), vol. 8, p. 317, emphasis as per original.

164 Ibid.

165 See O'Connell, *Correspondence of Daniel O'Connell*, vol.8, p. 317.

166 J. Loughlin, *The British Monarchy and Ireland: 1800 to the Present* (Cambridge: Cambridge University Press, 2007), pp. 39–40; G. Owens, 'Visualising the Liberator: Self-fashioning, dramaturgy, and the construction of Daniel O'Connell', *Éire-Ireland*, 33/34 (1998), pp. 103–29.

167 See Drennan, *A Letter to His Excellency*, p. 16.

168 See Loughlin, *The British Monarchy and Ireland*, pp. 23–5.

169 Ibid.

170 M.R. O'Connell (ed.), *The Correspondence of Daniel O'Connell, 1841–1845* (Dublin: Irish University Press, 1978), vol. 7, p. 125, emphasis as per original.

171 R. Brazier, *Ministers of the Crown* (Oxford: Clarendon, 1997), p. 81; R.A. Gaunt, *Sir Robert Peel: The Life and Legacy* (London and New York: I.B. Tauris, 2010), p. 101.

Seven

Royal Visits to Dublin, 1821–1911

Pier, Procession, Presence Chamber

Kathryn Milligan

Facing page:
Fig. 07.01.
William Sadler II,
*The Landing of
King George IV at
Howth Harbour*,
1821.
Collection of
Bonner & Partners
Family Trust.
Image courtesy of
whytes.com.

The entry of a monarch or other royal personage into the Presence Chamber at Dublin Castle was an important component of a royal visit. A significant ceremonial moment, this ritual united the physical royal body with two outward manifestations of sovereignty: the throne itself and the Irish Sword of State, conjoined with an imposing and somewhat sanctified architectural space. Here, majesty was made apparent and loyalty declared openly. This essay will consider the Presence Chamber (the name more frequently used for the Throne Room during this time) as a terminus for royal processions, and as part of a series of important locations used on the arrival of a royal party to Dublin. The chief focus will be on the visits of King George IV in 1821, the first and last visits of Queen Victoria (1849 and 1900), the 1868 visit of the Prince and Princess of Wales (later King Edward VII and Queen Alexandra), and the Duke and Duchess of York (later King George V and Queen Mary) in 1897. Retracing the ceremonial aspects of these occasions through the papers relating to their organization, visual representations and written descriptions, the analysis will show how the idea of loyal Dublin was evinced through ritual, visualization, and materialism.[1]

The approach to this topic is informed by two methodologies: the first relating to the study of royal ceremonial and the second to the study of the urban environment, which considers the relationship between the city, architecture, and society. First published in 1983, David Cannadine's essay, 'The Context, Performance and Meaning of Ritual: The British Monarchy and the "Invention of Tradition", *c.* 1820–1977' has shaped the study of royal ceremony. Here, Cannadine identified 'ten aspects of ritual, performance and context ...' which need to be considered in relation to the topic of royal ritual and ceremony.[2] While an examination of the relationship of all these points to royal visits to Ireland lies outside the scope of the present essay, six of Cannadine's principles are of particular relevance. These are:

> ... the type, extent and attitude of the media: how vividly did it describe royal events, and what picture of the monarchy did it convey ... the prevailing state of technology and fashion ... the condition of the capital city in which most royal ceremonials took place: was it squalid and unimpressive, or endowed with splendid buildings and triumphal thoroughfares as a fitting backdrop for ritual and pageantry ... the attitude of those responsible for liturgy, music and organization ... the nature of the ceremonial as actually performed ... [and the] question of commercial exploitation: how far did manufacturers of pottery, medals and other artefacts feel that there was money to be made from the sale of commemorative pieces?[3]

In Cannadine's analysis, these concepts are all linked to a further idea, that of the 'invention of tradition'. Eric Hobsbawm defines an 'invented tradition' as a 'set of practices, normally governed by overtly or tacitly accepted rules and of a ritual or behaviour by repetition, which automatically implies continuity with the past'.[4] As will be demonstrated, royal visits to Ireland can be considered an 'invented tradition', heavily reliant on repeated rituals and the invocation of the past, both of which were established with the visit of King George IV in 1821.

Cannadine's six points relate in a number of ways to the topic of this essay: briefly, over the period from 1821 to 1911, royal visits were covered extensively in the Irish and British newspapers and periodicals, though with an increasing political divide in the early twentieth century. Illustrations of these visits were largely published in London by journals with an imperialistic outlook; as Margarita Cappock has observed in relation to *The Illustrated London News*, this 'ideological stance is reflected in the visual output and the result is, to some extent, a distorted and propagandistic account of these events. Aimed at a predominantly middle-class readership, the publication was fully aware of the power of these images in creating an exaggerated impression of Ireland's allegiance to the Crown'.[5]

Royal visits to Ireland did not rely solely on 'anachronistic modes of transport or dress', but the past was frequently invoked through published accounts of the history of certain traditions; for example, the foundation of the Order of St Patrick.[6] Dress was used to illustrate a connection between the royal person and Ireland, whether through the use of Irish fabrics, such as poplin and lace, or through emblems, such as the shamrock, sometimes intertwined with the English rose and Scottish thistle. To an extent, the visits were associated with modernity and industrial advancement; for example, through the use of the bourgeoning railway system, and innovative light displays. Visits were also strongly militaristic, with fine displays by troops and naval vessels. Contemporary sources suggest that the organizers of these ceremonials were acutely aware of being seen as lacking, or even provincial, and certainly great attempts were made to ensure everything ran smoothly, and performed to the best of everyone's ability. Concern for a successful visit is reflected in the extensive planning process, not just in relation to the main ceremonials, but also in ensuring adequate provisions were provided in the city for the occasion, that troops were in the correct position, or that elements of the royal household were in place prior to the royal party's arrival. Reflecting the changing political context, the fervour for commemorative objects (chiefly medals, ribbons and prints) tailed off during the later visits, but was a significant feature of those in the early to mid-nineteenth century.

Regarding the 'condition of the capital city', Dublin at this time was both 'squalid and unimpressive', and 'endowed with splendid buildings and triumphal thoroughfares'.[7] Ahead of the visit of the Prince and Princess of Wales in 1868, *The Times* printed the following description of the city, stating that:

> Dublin, though capable of much improvement, is quite as well adapted for spectacles of all kinds as London. Its bay magnificent; its river very pretty; its park four times as large as Hyde Park, and four times as beautiful; its public buildings, if anything, are a little too ambitious; its cathedral is large enough to seat three thousand ... ; its streets and squares are laid out better than our own; its railways are numerous, good and well managed; its suburban scenery is enchanting and even grand; its atmosphere healthy, pleasant and clear; its markets are excellent, and its Crystal Palace, where the Royal visitors will open a grand ball in a few days, is in the city instead of being eight miles off.[8]

While not incorrect, this account of the nineteenth-century city ignores the fact that alongside these grand parks, buildings, streets and squares were dilapidated and overcrowded tenements and cabins, with little or no sanitation or cleansing. The declining standard of housing in Dublin's city centre in the nineteenth century has been well documented: Jacinta Prunty has dated the trend for converting houses intended for single-family occupancy into tenements to 'at least the eighteenth century'.[9] The inward migration of people from the countryside into the urban environment during the Famine years intensified the already acute problem, leading to more and more overcrowding. Furthermore, the uneven flow of people moving from the city centre to the new suburbs also exacerbated the crisis in the city centre; very few working-class families moved to the new suburbs, and houses made vacant by the departing middle class were converted for either business use or subsumed into the tenement housing stock.[10]

Cannadine's attention to the presentation of the city resonates with the approach taken by Dana Arnold in her writing on the development of cities in general, and London in particular. Arnold has outlined how:

> The city is not just ... a set of buildings in a specific geographical location – the dialectic between architecture and the city and their interrelation is an indicator of metropolitan identity which is an agglomeration of histories, geographies, social relationships, production, consumption and governmental institutions.[11]

Within this reflexive framework, Arnold shows how the different facets of urban life work together to contribute to a broader sense of identity through dialogue with each other; and how urban space comes to be understood and defined by those who live, work, purchase and govern within it. Arnold's argument can also expand to allow for competing identities to exist within a single urban environment, for example, loyalist and nationalist, and for the mechanisms by which these are created to be examined and understood. Arnold invokes the idea of an 'imagined community', a term coined by Benedict Andersen in his influential study on nationalism.[12] Drawing on the writings of Cannadine and Arnold, the present study will demonstrate how, through the use of the city, its architecture, commercial life, and ceremonial events, royal visits were celebrated in Dublin, even as nationalist sentiment grew in opposition.

Arrival at the Pier: The Landing of a Royal Party

The journey to the Presence Chamber began when the royal party arrived at one of Dublin's coastal towns. Visual depictions and written accounts of the landing of a royal visitor emphasize the sense of spectacle that accompanied this moment, whether through descriptions of those who attended it, the decorative schemes employed, or the size of and reaction of the crowd that gathered to witness it. Providing an adequate opportunity to view the proceedings was important, not only for the main bodies involved – for example, those connected with the harbour, railway line, and the Board of Works (known from 1831 as the Office of Public Works or the OPW) – but also for other businesses that operated in the area. For example, in 1900, the Dublin Steam Packet Company applied to the OPW/Kingstown Harbour for permission to issue tickets for employees and friends to 'witness from the deck of the steamer the ceremony connected with the landing of Her Majesty the Queen'.[13]

Shortly before the visit of King George IV, the Royal Irish Institution had announced a competition for artists, which proposed to pay £500 for the 'best picture on the subject of his Majesty's arrival and landing, which shall be painted in IRELAND by an IRISH ARTIST'.[14] A public welcome had been planned for Dún Laoghaire (known from 1821 to 1920 as Kingstown), Co. Dublin, but due to confusion caused by the death of the King's estranged wife in the days prior to the visit and inclement weather, the King and his entourage arrived rather unexpectedly at Howth on 12 August 1821. Encouraged perhaps by the prospect of the competition prize money, the arrival of the monarch was recorded in paint by William Sadler II (*c.* 1782–1839), in a small panel (Fig. 07.01). In contrast to Sadler's large and detailed depiction of the ceremony surrounding the departure of the King (now in a private collection), the scene represented in this panel distances itself from any representation of what little official welcome there was at the pier-side, and instead takes in an expansive panorama of the headland, with the squadron of ships just visible in the right middle-ground. The main focus of the painting is the broad road that runs down to the pier, flanked on either side by small thatched cottages. Alerted to the arrival of the King by a steam signal, the small group of figures hold their arms up in recognition of the fact, and move towards the landing site.

In contrast, the arrival of Queen Victoria and Prince Albert to Dublin in 1849 was a far greater ceremonial success. While there was no official competition to represent their landing, a wide range of paintings and illustrations were created by contemporary artists, driven in part by the emergence of the illustrated press in the intervening period. George Mounsey Wheatley Atkinson (1806–1884) completed several paintings of the arrival of the royal yacht at Cobh (known from 1849 to 1920 as Queenstown), Co. Cork, as did his lesser-known English contemporary, Philip Phillips (*d.* 1864). In October 1849, *The Times* explained how Phillips 'went expressly to Ireland to collect material to illustrate the various scenes connected with her Majesty's late visit', and how he had recently 'had the honour of laying before her Majesty at Osborne those sketches, as well as some others descriptive of the finest scenery in Ireland'.[15] According to this account, Queen Victoria was well pleased with Phillips's drawings, and commanded that he 'prepare a series of subjects from the sketches presented to her'.[16] Five works depicting this visit by Phillips are now in the Royal Collection. However, this was not the only form in which he presented his scenes of Ireland. In 1850, Phillips's drawings and paintings were exhibited as a 'Grand Moving Diorama' at the Chinese Gallery, Hyde Park Corner, London. The diorama was accompanied by a written account of the visit by Phillips, and contained views of the 'Lake of Killarney, the Gap of Dunloe, the Eagle Mountain, and other localities … not honoured by her Majesty's presence during her late visit'.[17]

The landings of Queen Victoria and the royal party at Cobh, Dublin, and Belfast were all depicted by Phillips. In the view of Kingstown, Phillips positions

Fig. 07.02. Philip Phillips, *The Queen and Prince landing at Kingstown Harbour, Dublin, 6 August 1849*, 1849. Royal Collection Trust/© Her Majesty Queen Elizabeth II 2017.

the viewer on the water, looking towards the pier, adorned by tenting, flags, and crowds of fashionably dressed people enthusiastically greeting the royal family (Fig. 07.02). While there are evident technical shortcomings, for example in the use of perspective and scale, Phillips's painting does successfully convey an atmosphere of welcome, excitement, and perhaps most importantly, of loyalty, at the moment the Queen and her family began their visit to Dublin. A significant amount of planning and preparation had been undertaken by the authorities to ensure that this moment of arrival ran smoothly, and that the appearance of the pier was suitably impressive and welcoming. Despite this, *The Freeman's Journal* did note that '... the whole affair was of a rather meagre and flimsy character'.[18] Their report however, is useful in interpreting Phillips's painting, describing how the pier was 'bisected by the pavilions and canopied passage leading from the edge of the jetty to the broad flight of steps leading up to the terminus'.[19] Something of the colour and texture of the temporary structure can also be discerned from the printed description:

> ... the whole passage, including the expanded spaces at the pavilion and the extent of the upper terrace with its seats, the ante-chamber, and also the platform itself – was covered with carpeting of bright crimson cloth. All along the side of the approach from the jetty, and arranged round the pavilions and the upper terrace were vases and flower pots, filled with flowering exotics. ... In the ante room leading to the carriage platform there were arranged some very elegant designs in flowers and exotic blossoms representing the royal crown and other emblems.[20]

These arrangements were overseen by the OPW, with the co-operation of officials in Kingstown. Plants and flowers were selected and provided by 'The Curator of the College Botanical Gardens, Dr Mackay...', along with a '... splendid Lillium speciosum ... from the gardens of Mrs White, Killakee'.[21] Bouquets for the royal carriage were from 'Mr Bridgford, of Spafield Nursery, Ball's-bridge...', and 'Messrs. Toole and Mackey supplied the choice and beautiful exotics which ornamented the terrace'.[22]

In 1849, and during subsequent visits, the royal party was first greeted on board the royal yacht by the lord lieutenant, or viceroy, other members of the viceregal household, and various officials from the clerical, civil, and military bodies. When, finally, Victoria and Albert set foot on the Kingstown pier in

1849, the moment was marked by the cannon fire from the assembled naval fleet, which 'thundered incessant peels, while the crowds assembled on the jetty waved hats and kerchiefs'.[23] On the occasion of the visit of the Prince and Princess of Wales (later King Edward VII and Queen Alexandra) in 1868, *The Daily Express* (Dublin) reported that the crowd of spectators gathered to witness the landing could be estimated at thirty to thirty-five thousand people.[24] The OPW oversaw the construction of a new pavilion, designed by assistant architect, Enoch Trevor Owen (*c.* 1833–1881), and constructed by 'Mr McDowell, Montgomery-street, Dublin …'[25] As in 1849, however, it seems that the efforts of the organizing committee fell somewhat short of the expectations of the assembled press: *The Illustrated London News* described the pavilion as 'commodious enough, but not very elegant. It was a wooden shed, built in the form of a boathouse, having the floor covered with crimson cloth, and having at the point of landing the letters "V.R.," with the figures "1849," to indicate the spot on which her Majesty the Queen stepped when she first visited her Irish subjects'.[26] This reference to an earlier visit demonstrates how past visits could be evoked on future occasions, creating a sense of continuity and tradition.

The landing of the Prince and Princess of Wales into this new pavilion was sketched by Robert Thomas Landells (1833–1877), and reproduced as an engraving in *The Illustrated London News* (Fig. 07.03).[27] Six sketches by Landells of this visit are extant in the Royal Collection, and five of these were engraved for the popular magazine. Potentially produced from the artist's observations on the spot, or later worked up from smaller thumbnail sketches, the depiction of the landing of the Prince and Princess takes in the broad expanse of the pavilion, and offers a view out to the harbour and the bay beyond, including Howth Head. To either side, figures in official or military dress observe and defer to the two couples that walk between them. The procession to the carriage was led by the viceroy, James Hamilton, 2nd Marquess of Abercorn, later 1st Duke of Abercorn (1811–1885) and the Princess of Wales. They were followed by the Prince of Wales and Louisa Hamilton, Marchioness of Abercorn, later Duchess of Abercorn (1812–1905); Prince George, 2nd Duke of Cambridge (1819–1904); and Francis, Prince of Teck (1837–1900) with Lady Georgiana (1841–1913) and Lady Albertha Hamilton (1847–1932). In keeping with traditions established both by King George IV and Queen Victoria, the Prince and Princess outwardly referenced the country they were visiting, through shamrock adornments and through the use of Irish textiles. The jacket and dress worn by the Princess was

Fig. 07.03. Robert Thomas Landells, *Visit of the Prince and Princess of Wales to Ireland, April 1868: Landing at Victoria Wharf, Kingstown, 15 April*, 1868. Royal Collection Trust/© Her Majesty Queen Elizabeth II 2017.

described as being made of 'deep-blue tabbinet, or poplin, trimmed by Irish lace; and a white bonnet of Irish lace, ornamented by a single rose, surrounded by a bunch of shamrocks...'; similarly, the Prince wore a 'cravat of the Irish colour, green'.[28]

In the account of the arrival published in *The Illustrated London News*, reference is made to the arrival of Princess Alexandra in England for her marriage to Edward, Prince of Wales in 1863. They note that her 'countenance was lighted up with that bright and pleasant smile which won the hearts of people in London on her first arrival in England'.[29] This comment may have been made in reference to the fact that Alexandra had recently recovered from a serious illness; her biographer notes that this was among the first public occasions at which she did not need the aid of two walking sticks; she was also pregnant with her fourth child.[30] It is also suggestive of a visual comparison between Landells's depiction of the couple's arrival in Dublin, and Henry O'Neill's lavish painting, *The Landing of Her Royal Highness The Princess Alexandra at Gravesend, 7 March 1863* (1864, National Portrait Gallery, London, oil on canvas, 132.1 cm x 213.4 cm). Both images use the pavilion structure to frame the royal (or in the case of Landells, royal and viceregal) party, using the natural perspective to include a crowd of admirers and onlookers to both sides, and a sea-view in the background. The pose used by Landells for the Princess of Wales echoes that of O'Neill, although the sketch is on a far more modest scale. Whether Landells was directly referencing O'Neill's painting is unclear, but it would not have been unusual for an illustrator to borrow from the conventions or styles of fine art. O'Neill's painting would likely have been familiar, for example through commercially available prints, but also as a result of his status as a painter to the royal family.

As letters between the OPW and the Harbour Works, Kingstown, for Victoria's visit in 1900 show, the ceremony around the landing of the Queen (or any other royal personage) had changed little in the intervening period. Issues regarding the depth of the water in the harbour, the width of the berth, and the cleanliness of the wharf were discussed at length, as well as a requirement (stipulated by the Captain of the Royal Yacht, who was no doubt conscious of the Queen's advanced years) that there be 'a <u>nearly</u> level platform ... from our gangway to the shore'.[31] In addition to these practical concerns, the two bodies decided on decorations, taking the form of two Venetian masts, with 'lines of suitable flags, bunting, etc.', and illuminations.[32] A flagstaff, 'suitable for flying a large Royal Standard ...' was also to be erected at the harbour.[33] Extra trains, to cater for the 'large number of passengers who will desire to leave Kingstown for Dublin immediately after Her Majesty', were organized by the Dublin, Wicklow and Wexford Railway.[34] A newspaper vendor based in Kingstown applied to supply newspapers and magazines to the royal visitors, but this was rejected by the commissioners of the OPW, who stated that 'the arrangements for the landing of her Majesty the Queen ... do not permit the presentation of newspapers or periodicals by any person'.[35]

Processions and Pomp: The Royal Party in the City

Once the royal party had landed in Dublin, the next aspect of the ceremonial was the formal entry to the city. This ceremony was reserved for a visiting monarch, although some aspects of it were repeated during the welcoming of a new viceroy. The formal entry of King George IV took place a number of days after he arrived in Dublin, with the King having spent the intervening period in relative seclusion at the Viceregal Lodge. On 17 August, the King and his entourage processed from the Lodge, along the North Circular Road, and onto Sackville Street (now

O'Connell Street) via Cavendish Row. A large and temporary triumphal arch had been erected at the junction with Sackville Street, and this served as the official city gates for the ceremonial. The moment of the King's entry is depicted in *George IV of England, Entering Dublin* (1821, National Gallery of Ireland, oil on canvas, 171cm x 279cm) by William Turner de Lond (*fl.* 1820–1837), replete with crowds of people lining the street, windows and rooftops (Fig. 07.04).[36] When fully formed, the procession was made up of around 200 carriages ranked in a strict order of precedence, along with members of the trades including the 'Silk, Ribbon, Stuff, and Tabinet Weavers …' with 'each man dressed or ornamented with the fabric of his trade, and carrying a small flag'.[37]

The procession from the Lodge was preceded by Athlone Pursuivant of Arms, while the Lord Mayor of Dublin led the civic bodies to the city gates. The Lord Mayor's coach is prominently displayed in the centre of de Lond's composition, and the painting includes an exact reproduction of the painted scene on the coach door, attributed to Vincenzo Waldré (1742–1814).[38] Heralded by a trumpeter, Athlone was admitted through the city gates, and on approaching the Lord Mayor stated 'that by the command of his Excellency the Lord Lieutenant of Ireland,

Fig. 07.04.
William Turner de Lond, *George IV, King of England, entering Dublin*, 1821.
© National Gallery of Ireland.

he demanded entrance to the City of Dublin, for his Majesty King George the Fourth'.[39] The Lord Mayor then replied that 'he and every one of his fellow Citizens, most heartily rejoiced that their gracious Sovereign had condescended to honour the City of Dublin with his presence – that the gates should be, on the instant, thrown open, and the Corporation of Dublin would wait, with all humility, to receive his Majesty'.[40] As the royal carriage passed through the gates, the assembled bands struck up *God Save the King*; the King stood in his carriage, and 'repeatedly pointed to the shamrock which decorated the front of his hat …'[41] Waiting for the King were the Lord Mayor, aldermen, sheriffs, common council, and two city representatives, and it is their approach to the carriage that de Lond represents in this painting. The Recorder of Dublin addressed the King, and then the Lord Mayor, 'kneeling, and bareheaded, delivered the Keys of the City and the City Sword to His Majesty. The King immediately re-delivered them saying, "My Lord, I return these Keys and this Sword; they cannot be placed in better hands than yours."'[42]

In 1849, temporary city gates were constructed at Baggot Street Bridge, and this format was also used for Queen Victoria's last visit in 1900; the visits of King Edward VII in 1901 and 1903; and that of King George V in 1911, with a temporary arch constructed at Leeson Street Bridge on these occasions.[43] The style of these temporary constructions varied widely, with the Gothic-style replica of Baggotrath Castle made for the 1900 visit something of a stylistic pinnacle. Perhaps because of its striking design, this arch was also widely represented, with aspects of the entry ceremony appearing in paint, illustration, photography, and newsreel. A watercolour by Percy French (1854–1920), shows the procession moving

Fig. 07.05.
William Percy French, *Queen Victoria's Entry through Dublin's City Gate (a temporary replica of Baggotrath Castle), Leeson St Lower Bridge, April 1900*, 1900.
© National Gallery of Ireland.

Fig. 07.06.
Queen Victoria
in Dublin, April
1900.
Royal Collection
Trust/© Her
Majesty Queen
Elizabeth II 2017.

through the gates towards the city, along with the crowds who turned out to see the cavalcade pass by (Fig. 07.05).[44] While French's painting of the scene gives a sense of the colour and atmosphere, photographs and the Pathé newsreel more accurately convey the militaristic aspects of the occasion. A mounted photograph by Chancellor and Son was taken from behind the double line of soldiers positioned to one side of the arch (Fig. 07.06). In full uniform, and with fixed bayonets, the troops look either straight ahead, or towards the carriage in the middle-ground of the photograph, where Victoria is being presented with the keys to the city. The newsreel footage brings to life the parade of mounted regiments that preceded the arrival of the Queen, and also shows the formal ceremony between the city officials and the monarch. Although silent, the frantic waving of hats and handkerchiefs signals the arrival of the Queen, and the close of the formal ceremony.[45]

The journey across the city, either to Dublin Castle or to the Viceregal Lodge, provided an opportunity for the public to catch a glimpse of the royal party, as well as further opportunities for artists and illustrators to depict the welcoming crowds, even if this loyalty was exaggerated for pictorial and propagandistic

Fig. 07.07.
William Turner de
Lond, *King George
IV, at College
Green, Dublin,
1821*, 1821.
Private Collection.

purposes. The area of College Green provided an aspect that was both visually appealing and symbolic: the openness of the area allowed crowds to gather, with the former Parliament House (now the Bank of Ireland) and Trinity College providing a useful framing device, as well as being indicative of the historical past. The presence of public sculpture could further enhance the symbolic potential of the streetscape. In a watercolour study for a now unknown oil painting, de Lond depicted the procession of George IV against the Bank of Ireland, with William Laffan noting that the 'building stands as a mute reminder of the loss of Irish sovereignty' (Fig. 07.07).[46] The building was to have been decorated with an illustrative transparency, but in the days before the event the bank authorities decided to remove this so that the King would 'have a full and perfect view of the noble Portico of that magnificent Building fronting College-green'.[47] In 1868, *The Illustrated London News* showed the procession of the Prince and Princess of Wales as it passed the monumental, and frequently contentious, statue of King William III, while in *The Graphic*'s illustration of Queen Victoria in College Green in 1900, the raised arm of the sculpture of Henry Grattan, by John Henry Foley (1818–1874), is clearly visible (Figs 07.08 & 07.09).[48] Scenes such as these show the different ways in which the cityscape can read symbolically: whether through architecture, such as the former parliament building, or through

Fig. 07.08.
'Visit of the Prince and Princess of Wales to Ireland: The Royal Procession Passing College-Green, Dublin'.
The Illustrated London News,
25 April 1868.
Courtesy of Trinity College Dublin.

Fig. 07.09.
'The Queen's Arrival in Dublin: Her Majesty Passing the Old Parliament House'.
The Graphic,
14 April 1900.
Courtesy of Trinity College Dublin.

public sculpture, with King William III facing in the direction of Dublin Castle, or Grattan the seat of learning.

A photograph from 1897 shows the progress of the Duke and Duchess of York as they passed the Provost's House and Trinity College. A banner declares 'Frequent Acquaintence [*sic*] Promotes True Friendship', while onlookers raise their hats and handkerchiefs to greet the visitors (Fig. 07.10). Other temporary decorations can be seen, for example the devices around the sign for Thomas Cook, as well as copious strings of bunting and flags. From 1821 onwards, the city was extensively adorned for royal visits. During George IV's visit, public buildings and private homes were decorated with transparencies showing a range of different scenes.[49] Examples of these tableaux were reported in the press, for instance, a Mr Foley of Capel Street showed a transparency of 'his Majesty on his favourite white horse, surmounted by a splendid crown, exceedingly brilliant, with the rose and shamrock', while Mr Murphy of 108 Townsend Street showed 'a full length figure of Hibernia lamenting the loss of that great patriot Henry Grattan'.[50] Sheriff Witford on North Great George's

Fig. 07.10.
The Duke and Duchess of York in Dublin, 18 August 1897.
Royal Collection Trust/© Her Majesty Queen Elizabeth II 2017.

Street showed three transparencies in his windows, one of which was a female figure, representing the city of Dublin: 'she leans forward, and looks anxiously towards her Monarch ... accompanied by three little Cherubs, who are leaning on the City Keys; the Sword and the Mace, as it were, at his Majesty's feet'.[51] On Mary Street, Cornelius Callaghan, a gilder, carver and glazier who worked at Dublin Castle, showed five:

> ... in the centre drawing-room window, a large Crown, G. IV. R. Long live the King; to the right window of do. the figure of Britannia, the Shield and Lion, with the Shamrock, Rose and Thistle ... to the left window of the Crown, the figure of Hibernia and Harp, a handsome pedestal with the Crown on a cushion, the wolf dog near the figure, and the words "Erin Rejoices"; in the right attic window the figure of Peace ... In the left attic window the figure of Europe, and Hibernia playing on the Harp ... The remainder of the windows were handsomely lighted with lustres and lamps, and decorated with laurels [and] above the drawing-room windows a Crown of laurels and roses under which an elegant embroidered flag, G. R. God save the King, Cead Mile Failte.[52]

Other businesses used gas light to draw attention to their buildings: 'Home's Royal Arcade, and Spadacini's Royal Hotel and Coffee House, College-green were again most showily lighted with gas, and various devices ...', and the Kildare Street Club House 'was brilliantly lit with lamps, George Rex, Crown &c.'[53]

In 1849, a formal committee was established in Dublin to decide how the visit of Victoria and Albert would be celebrated. To fund the celebrations, the committee invited subscriptions from members of the public, with the promise that a list of such people would be published.[54] The decision of the committee to request 'general illumination of all the houses in the city ...', was in contrast to other cities around the country, notably Cork and Limerick, where a decision was made not to spend money on such decorations given the ongoing Famine.[55] Opposition to Dublin Corporation's plan was voiced in the press, with one commentator declaring that 'Dublin throws herself not upon her knees to Majesty, but on her face. She spreads, not her cloak ... but gives *herself* to be the gangway'.[56] The debate over whether it was appropriate to spend money on illuminations, and other decorations for the visit is just one example of the political tensions raised by the occasion.[57]

Further to the display of illuminations or other decorative devices, the occasion of a royal visit also provided businesses with the opportunity to capitalize on the general festive sentiment, whether through stocking new lines of goods relevant to the visit, or by putting on special events. These activities can be traced through the advertisement pages of contemporary newspapers and journals, and are consistent across the period from 1821 to 1911. In 1821, one 'M SATCHWELL, SILK MANUFACTURER, 84 DAME-STREET' advertised that 'she has on sale sashes suitable for the reception of his Majesty, as approved by the reception committee …', while 'BROWN, Jeweller to the Most Illustrious Order of St Patrick …', invited members of the nobility to view, in his premises on Fownes Street 'the GRAND COLLARS and STAR, to be worn at the approaching installation'.[58] Brown also invited ladies to inspect 'a beautiful ornament of Irish manufacture, patronized by the LADY MAYORESS …' which they expected she would wear during the King's visit. Anyone wishing to order their own piece of special jewellery, was advised to do so 'without delay, the time now being very limited to prepare the various ornaments'.[59] A shamrock-shaped box of bog-oak, gold, enamel, diamonds and pearls, bearing the hallmark of the Dublin jeweller Matthew West, was also made at this time, and is now in the Royal Collection.

Fig. 07.11. Edward Murray, shamrock-shaped box made for King George IV, 1821. Royal Collection Trust/© Her Majesty Queen Elizabeth II 2017.

It features the Irish inscription 'Go mbeannughudh Dia thu' (meaning 'May God bless you') and was ostensibly produced as an official gift for the King, whose initials appear in the centre of the lid (Fig. 07.11).

The 1849 visit of Victoria, Albert and their children prompted a more particular response from art repositories and printmakers in Dublin. Prior to their arrival in the city, *The Dublin Evening Post* reported that in 'every emporium and print shop for the sale of art in Dublin, portraits of the Queen and Prince Albert are exhibited … and we are assured they command a very ready sale'.[60] Furthermore, the visit appears to have prompted two of the city's leading keepers of repositories, Thomas Cranfield and Adolphe Lesage, to bring highly celebrated artworks to Dublin. The same report in the *Post* noted that 'Alderman Moon, of the City of London, in compliance with the request of Mr Thomas Cranfield, the eminent publisher and print seller of this city, has lent [Franz Xavier] Winterhalter's celebrated painting of the Royal family in domestic life, which he will exhibit in his spacious gallery in Grafton-street, during the Queen's visit'.[61] Similarly, Lesage advertised that 'WINDSOR IN THE MODERN TIME, BY E. LANDSEER', would be exhibited during the visit, being an 'admirable painting, containing portraits of her Majesty, Prince Albert, and the young Princess &c., … This painting is considered one of the best works of this eminent artist'.[62]

Winterhalter's *The Royal Family in 1846* (1846, Royal Collection Trust, oil on canvas, 250.5cm x 317.3cm) was commissioned by Queen Victoria to hang in the dining room at Osborne House, on the Isle of Wight. Outside of this private setting, the finished painting was exhibited to great acclaim in St James's Palace, where 100,000 members of the public came to see it. It is unclear whether the painting exhibited in Cranfield's gallery was the original work, or a copy. The prospect of the painting being seen by an Irish audience arose in February 1848, when *The Dublin Evening Packet and Correspondent* reported that the painting would be lent to Cranfield's through Alderman Moon, having been on exhibit in St James's Palace the previous year, where it was 'visited by all the rank and fashion then in London'.[63] The exhibition of the painting was also announced in *The Pilot*, but a later account noted that it was a 'beautiful copy by Cunningham of this world-famed Picture …' that could be seen.[64] In August 1849, Cranfield announced that he had been 'again entrusted by Alderman Moon, for Private Exhibition in his New Gallery 115, Grafton-street, the above magnificent drawing, exhibited some time ago at her Majesty's request, at St James's Palace'.[65] *The Cork Examiner* also reported that the painting would be shown 'for a few days at Mr. Fletcher's, No 71, Patrick-street …', where patrons could also register for engravings after the picture.[66] Regardless of whether it was the original painting or copies that were exhibited in Dublin in 1849, the desire of Dublin repositories to show these depictions of the royal family speaks to the importance of the visual image in promoting the royal family, and by extension, the wish of the general public to see these artworks.

The 1849 visit also prompted Cranfield and Lesage to produce commemorative prints, and these were brought to public attention within one to two months of the Queen's departure. In September, Cranfield advertised that he was 'preparing for immediate Publication a large and important picture by Kendrick, ARHA, representing the Royal Squadron leaving the Harbour in the order of Sailing, with the LA HOGUE in advance'.[67] The original painting by Matthew Kendrick (*c.* 1797–*c.* 1874), was purchased by Queen Victoria in 1850.[68] An engraving after Kendrick's painting, by Charles Mottram (1807–1876), printed by McQueen, London, and published by T. Cranfield, 115 Grafton Street, Dublin, is also in the Royal Collection (Fig. 07.12).[69] Lesage also advertised his souvenir of the visit, a collection of eight lithographs 'dedicated by permission and under the patronage of her Most Gracious Majesty the Queen'.[70] A collection of maritime views, the advertisement stated that the 'series will be enclosed in an elegant and

Fig. 07.12. Charles Mottram (engraved by), *The Departure of the Queen and the Royal Squadron from Kingstown, August 1849,* 1852. Courtesy of the National Library of Ireland.

appropriate ornamental cover, with two vignettes'.[71] While it is unclear as to whether they were part of the advertised set, lithographs by Jonathan Needham (*fl.* 1858–1870), after Edwin Hayes (1820–1904) showing the departure of the royal party from Kingstown, and published by A. Lesage, 40 Lower Sackville Street, Dublin, and Thomas McLean, 26 Haymarket, are extant in both the Royal Collection and the National Library of Ireland (Fig. 07.13).[72]

Peripheral activities to royal visits were not confined to the city centre: the sense of spectacle was furthered by the presence of large, and well-known naval ships, which accompanied the royal yacht on its journey from Holyhead, Wales (or another port) to Dublin. Part of the channel fleet, the war-ships were inspected by Dublin citizens, and on at least one occasion, created lighting displays as a form of public entertainment. In 1900, the squadron placed lighting on the ships' masts and rigging, creating a silhouette against the night sky.[73] A further light display was illustrated by W.L. Wyllie in *The Graphic*, when the fleet lit up the night sky with a searchlight display. In 1849, the directors of the Dublin and

Fig. 07.13. Jonathan Needham (engraved by), *The Departure of Her Most Gracious Majesty, Queen Victoria from Kingstown Harbour, August 10th 1849*, 1850. Courtesy of the National Library of Ireland.

Kingstown Railway sought to extend the general excitement over the visit of Queen Victoria, and to ensure the part played by the railway company did not go unnoticed. On 18 August, they advertised in *The Evening Packet* that the Royal Carriage, which had 'been an object of admiration to all who had an opportunity of observing it, on the days of her Majesty's arrival and departure ...', would be on public display at Kingstown.[74] Described as a 'really splendid product of Irish taste and manufacturing skill ...', the directors hoped that the carriage would be 'destined to convey her Majesty on the occasion of future Royal visits, along the Dublin and Kingstown Railway'.[75] Throughout the period from 1821 to 1911, the Phoenix Park also played an important role in royal visits, not least because the Viceregal Lodge often hosted the royal party for the duration of their stay. In addition to dinner and garden parties at the Lodge, the more public areas of the park were used for military reviews and, in 1900, for a special children's day, where schoolchildren from around the country were invited to meet the Queen.

Dublin Castle and the Presence Chamber: Monarchs, Princes and Knights
After the noise and colour of the assembled crowd and decorated street, the entry of the royal party into the Dublin Castle complex signalled a return to a more organized and ritualistic form of ceremony. The arrival of George IV into the Castle, following his procession through the city, was recorded in a drawing by Sir T. Hammond, and reproduced as a lithograph by N. Chator & Co., London (Fig. 07.14). The print shows the Upper Castle Yard filled with soldiers on horseback, while the King's open carriage halts at the entrance portico to the State Apartments. One account reported that, in total, the progress of the King and royal party from the Viceregal Lodge to the Castle had taken two and a half hours.[76] As the King entered through the Castle gate, the 'event was notified by a rocket to the battery at the Park, where a royal salute was immediately fired'.[77] *The Freeman's Journal* reported that on alighting from his carriage, the King was presented with the Irish Sword of State by the viceroy, Charles Chetwynd-Talbot, 2nd Earl Talbot (1777–1849), who fell 'to his knees before his Majesty. The King took the Viceroy by the hand, raised him and said – "I receive this Sword that I may again present it to you, my Lord Talbot. Accept it, and I feel assured I cannot entrust it to better hands than yours. Let us proceed"'.[78] Dating to the early 1660s, the Irish Sword of State was an essential piece of regalia and an ensign of royal power (see Figs 01.06 & 01.07). The sword was most frequently used in viceregal ceremonies, and was entrusted to the viceroy on his investiture.

Fig. 07.14.
N. Chater & Co.
(engraved by),
*Entrance of the
King into his Castle
of Dublin, Augt
17th 1821*, 1822.
© National Gallery
of Ireland.

As a symbol of the monarch, the sword preceded the viceroy in processions, and was placed above the throne in the Presence Chamber when the room was in use (see Fig. 04.02).[79]

From here, the King proceeded to the Presence Chamber, and then had the opportunity to survey the spectacle of the procession from the windows facing on to the Upper Castle Yard. While probably exaggerating the numbers of those in attendance, the account of the event does give a sense of the great length and colour of this spectacle:

> ... the procession of the Nobility, the Gentry, the Country Gentlemen, Parishes and Trades, four abreast, amounting as near as it was possible to compute them, to about forty thousand, following the order prescribed to them, entering by the upper, and retiring by lower Castle yard, cheering his Majesty enthusiastically as they passed. The Gentry, full twenty thousand, were mounted on horses caparisoned, some with silk bridles, all with large rosettes of sky blue or pink ribbon.[80]

Following this, the King took his place on the throne in the Presence Chamber, before hearing addresses from a variety of civic and religious bodies. In addition to the viceroy, he was attended to by Robert Stewart, 2nd Marquess of Londonderry (1769–1822); Henry Addington, 1st Viscount Sidmouth (1757–1844); James Graham, 3rd Duke of Montrose (1755–1836); Thomas Taylour, 1st Marquess of Headfort (1757–1829); Charles Ingoldsby Burroughs-Paulet, 13th Marquess of Winchester (1764–1843); and other lords of the bedchamber.[81]

Despite the symbolic importance of the Presence Chamber, there are only two visual representations of the room being used on the occasion of a royal visit. Published in *The Illustrated London News* in 1849, *The Throne-Room of the Castle* shows Queen Victoria, flanked by Prince Albert, receiving guests during the levee (Fig. 07.15). The intention of Victoria to hold a levee during her stay in Dublin had been announced in July, and was governed by strict court regulations. A notice from the Lord Chamberlain's Office, Dublin Castle, was reproduced in

Fig. 07.15.
'The Throne-Room of the Castle, Dublin'. *The Illustrated London News*, 11 August 1849.
Private collection.

the city's main newspapers, and contained instructions for those who intended to go to the event, which was to be a full-dress levee and drawing room:

> Names of Ladies and Gentlemen, with those by whom they are to be presented, must be sent to the Lord Chamberlain's Office, on or before Friday, the 3rd August; and no Lady or Gentleman can be presented, except by someone who has himself or herself personally been presented to her Majesty.[82]

The progress of the Queen, Prince Albert and their attendants from the Phoenix Park to Dublin Castle had not been scheduled as an official procession, but *The Freeman's Journal* reported that it had become so, due to a rumour that 'absolutely prevailed in the early part of the morning that her Majesty's entrance would be one of truly royal splendour'.[83] As had occurred on the journey from Kingstown to the Viceregal Lodge, citizens and visitors lined the route from 'the gates of the Park, Parkgate-street, the entire line of quays, Parliament-street, and the portions of Dame-street and Cork-hill which lay in or near the expected route'.[84] A description of Parliament Street demonstrates how the layout of the city could be advantageously used on ceremonial occasions, with the 'narrowness of its footway and great height of its houses, and also forming a straight vista from Essex-bridge to the Royal Exchange ...' it presented 'one of the most striking as well as brilliant phases in the line of the intended procession ...'[85] At the entrance to the Castle, and alongside the police and mounted military cordon, a brass band of 'one of the dragoon regiment was stationed in front of the state entrance and continued through the day to perform a variety of brilliant music ...'[86] As the Queen and her entourage arrived at the Castle, it was reported that the 'multitudes within and without the gates cheered, the band played the National Anthem, and amidst the most unmistakable evidence of popular regard, her Majesty and the Prince entered, for the first time, her old Castle of Dublin'.[87]

In the Presence Chamber, Victoria received addresses from different bodies, including Dublin Corporation, the graduates of Dublin University (Trinity College) and representatives of the Anglican and Roman Catholic Churches. Following this, presentations of ladies and gentlemen took place, as seen in the image reproduced in *The Illustrated London News*. Printed in black and white, the impact of the colour that the scene would have presented is lost; however, the textures of the different uniforms, fine evening dresses, and the sumptuous decorations is conveyed. It was reported that the Queen wore a 'robe of exquisitely shaded Irish poplin, of emerald green, richly wrought with shamrocks in gold embroidery. Her hair was simply parted on her forehead, with no ornament save a light tiara of gold studded with diamonds and gold'.[88] *The Advocate* reported that she also wore the 'ribbon and star of the order of the St Patrick, and a most superb wreath of diamonds on her head, necklace and ear-rings of diamonds, her hair in bands as represented in the most admired of her portraits'.[89]

In 1868 the Prince and Princess of Wales also received deputations in the Presence Chamber, having travelled directly from Kingstown (via train to Westland Row) to Dublin Castle. Rather than approaching the throne, or standing beside it, reports note that they 'stood with their back to the windows looking out on the square'.[90] The main ceremony of this visit was the installation of the Prince of Wales as a Knight of St Patrick at St Patrick's Cathedral, most notably depicted by Michael Angelo Hayes (1820–1877), with a visit to the Punchestown Races also receiving significant press and artistic attention.[91] Similarly, in 1897, the installation of the Duke of York as a Knight of the Order of St Patrick was also a central ceremonial of the visit. However, on this occasion the focus of the rite was firmly on Dublin Castle.

As had happened in 1868, the Duke and Duchess of York travelled directly to the Castle on arrival in Ireland in 1897; however, no official functions were performed, other than lunch with the viceregal household. Instead, on the third day of the visit, the Duke of York travelled from the Phoenix Park with the viceroy to the Castle, where he received deputations. As Victoria had done in 1849, he stood in front of the throne, rather than sitting on it: in his reply to the addresses received, the Duke thanked those assembled for their 'loyal and cordial sentiments …', and promised to 'convey to her Majesty the Queen the expressions of loyalty to her throne and person which you have all conveyed to me'.[92] Following this ceremony, the installation of the Duke as a Knight of St Patrick took place in St Patrick's Hall. While this rite had previously taken place in St Patrick's Cathedral, it had been transferred to the Castle after the disestablishment of the Church of Ireland in 1869.

A photograph of St Patrick's Hall by Chancellor and Son (part of a set of photographs taken by the firm of the 1897 visit) shows how a canopy and two thrones were set up at the far end of the Hall along with the royal coat of arms (Fig. 07.16). This arrangement echoes that of the Presence Chamber, maintaining a focus on the majesty of the occasion. The ceremony itself was recorded by Amadée Forestier (1854–1930), an Anglo-French artist and contributor to *The*

Fig. 07.16.
St Patrick's Hall,
Dublin Castle,
1897. Courtesy
of the National
Library of Ireland.

Fig. 07.17.
Amadée Forestier
(drawn by), 'The
Duke and Duchess
of York in Ireland:
Investiture of the
Duke of York
as a Knight of
St. Patrick in St.
Patrick's Hall,
Dublin Castle'.
*The Illustrated
London News*,
28 August 1897.
Courtesy of Trinity
College Dublin.

Illustrated London News (Fig. 07.17). Forestier's illustration shows the Duke being presented to his fellow knights after his installation into the Order, by Sir Arthur Vicars, Ulster King of Arms and Knight Attendant of the Order of St Patrick. To the left of the canopy, the Chancellor of the Order, Gerald Balfour, can be seen holding the Irish Sword of State. A larger and more richly detailed watercolour of the same scene by Forestier is extant in the Royal Collection.

Fig. 07.18. Amadée Forestier, *Investiture of the Duke of York with the Order of St Patrick at Dublin Castle, 20 August 1897*, 1898. Royal Collection Trust/© Her Majesty Queen Elizabeth II 2017.

It, in addition, shows the balcony of St Patrick's Hall, and the Duchess of York sitting with the vicereine, Beatrix Cadogan, Countess Cadogan (1844–1907) on the left-hand side of the composition (Fig. 07.18). While the cathedral setting may have lent the installation ceremony a sense of history, the relocation to Dublin Castle, and the performance of the ceremony before the throne, visually and symbolically strengthened the link between the Order, the monarch, and the British administration in Ireland.

The pomp and ceremony of the installation in 1897 is in sharp contrast to the final visit of Queen Victoria to Ireland in 1900. As was to be expected by that date, the visit was extensively covered in the illustrated press, including scenes of time spent in Dublin Castle. These images contrast strongly with those from 1849: greeted by the Cadogans at the entrance to the State Apartments, the elderly Queen was supported by her Indian servant, Abdul Karim, and instead of receiving deputations and presentations in the Presence Chamber, she was shown inspecting the Irish regalia from a wheelchair, in the room (Fig. 07.19). In this final illustration, the canopy and throne appear diminished, the architectural and decorative features of the room are barely shown, save for a few suggestive lines.

Fig. 07.19. 'The Queen's visit to the Lord Lieutenant at Dublin Castle'. *The Sphere*, 28 April 1900. Courtesy of the National Library of Ireland.

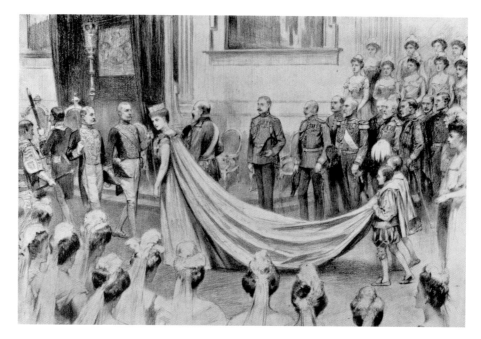

Fig. 07.20. Amadée Forestier (drawn by), 'Their Majesties entering St. Patrick's Hall for the Court Ceremonial on the evening of July 23'. *The Illustrated London News*, 1 August 1903. Courtesy of Trinity College Dublin.

From this date, the Presence Chamber itself was generally overlooked in favour of St Patrick's Hall during royal visits to Ireland. This may have been for practical purposes: both King Edward VII and King George V visited with their consorts, and so two royal chairs were required, and on visits from 1901 to 1911, large numbers of people were presented, requiring a larger space for official functions. The furnishing of the throne, and the form of the ceremonial rites did not change: for example, during the King's morning levee in 1903 the 'throne was placed in the centre of the north-side of the Hall … Over the throne and dais which supported it was a canopy of crimson velvet curtains, with gold embroideries, and surmounted with a crown'.[93] The arrival of the royal party was announced with 'a blare of trumpets …', and after they had taken their places on the dais the viceroy, William Humble Ward, 2nd Earl of Dudley (1867–1932) stood behind the King 'bearing aloft the sword of State …'[94] This ceremony was repeated at an evening court, and was sketched for *The Illustrated London News* (Fig. 07.20). Prior to the visit of King George V and Queen Mary in 1911, *The Sphere* printed a picture article titled 'The Official Thrones of England's Reigning Sovereign in London, Windsor, and Dublin'. The short caption described how 'the Viceroy is but a representative of the Sovereign himself, whether in Ireland or India, and the

Fig. 07.21.
Artists and special
correspondents of
the Royal Visit,
1897.
Courtesy of the
National Library
of Ireland.

throne in either country is in truth the King's throne …', and that 'in addition to the King's throne in the Throne Room of Dublin Castle, there is another royal throne in St Patrick's Hall' (see Fig. 09.12).[95]

This chapter reasserts the importance of the throne and its location in royal ceremonial, along with the power it embodied. By 1911, royal visits to Ireland were met with considerable opposition from nationalist groups, and the visit of that year was the last prior to Ireland's political independence from Britain, in 1922. In the period from 1821 to 1911, the locations used during a royal visit were carefully selected in order to ensure a successful ceremonial: from the party's landing, most usually at a predominantly Unionist suburb, a journey through the city's most salubrious streets and thoroughfares, a stay in the pastoral seclusion of the Phoenix Park, and finally to a levee or ball at the administrative and courtly centre of the British administration in Ireland, Dublin Castle. The presence of the press, written and pictorial, and of visiting artists keen to capture the city *en fête* ensured that the most positive aspects of these visits were recorded for posterity (Fig. 07.21). By considering Dublin Castle in general, and the Presence Chamber in particular, in the wider ceremonial that attended a royal visit, its importance in the public expression of sovereignty and Irish loyalty is revealed.

Endnotes

1   This chapter focuses on the ceremonial aspects of royal visits. For analysis of the political context in which they occurred, see, for example, J. Loughlin, *The British Monarchy and Ireland: 1800 to the Present* (Cambridge: Cambridge University Press, 2007); and J.H. Murphy, *Abject Loyalty: Nationalism and Monarchy in Ireland during the Reign of Queen Victoria* (Cork: Cork University Press, 2001).

2   D. Cannadine, 'The Context, Performance and Meaning of Ritual: The British monarchy and the "invention of tradition", c.1820–1977', in E. Hobsbawm and T. Ranger (eds), *The Invention of Tradition* (Cambridge: Cambridge University Press, 2003), 10th ed., p. 106.

3   Ibid., pp. 106–7.

4   E. Hobsbawm, 'Introduction: Inventing traditions', in E. Hobsbawm and T. Ranger (eds), *The Invention of Tradition* (Cambridge: Cambridge University Press, 2003), 10th ed., p. 1.

5   M. Cappock, 'Pageantry or Propaganda?: The Illustrated London News and royal visitors to Ireland', *Irish Arts Review Yearbook*, 16 (2000), p. 93.

6   See Hobsbawm, 'The Context, Performance and Meaning of Ritual', p. 106.

7   Ibid., p. 107.

8   *Times*, 11 April 1868.

9   J. Prunty, 'The town house as tenement in nineteenth- and early twentieth–century Dublin', in C. Casey (ed.), *The Eighteenth-Century Dublin Town House* (Dublin: Four Courts Press, 2010), p. 153.

10 Ibid., p. 155.

11 D. Arnold, *Re-presenting the Metropolis: Architecture, Urban Experience and Social Life in London, 1800–1840* (Aldershot: Ashgate, 2000), p. xix.

12 See B. Andersen, *Imagined Communities: Reflections on the Origin and Spread of Nationalism* (London and New York: Verson, 2006).

13 Memorandum headed 'Kingstown Harbour', 27 March 1900, OPW file: Visit of Her Majesty the Queen, National Archives of Ireland, OPW/2012/60/4.

14 *Freeman's Journal*, 8 August 1821. This was a vast sum of money to offer, and would have been a major prize for any artist in Ireland given the poor opportunities for sales and patronage in the country at that time. Strickland notes that the Royal Irish Institution had raised £12,000 to create 'a national testimonial in honour of the visit of George IV ...' – the name of the successful artist and artwork is not recorded; see W.G. Strickland, *A Dictionary of Irish Artists* (Dublin and London: Maunsel & Company Limited, 1913), vol. 2, pp. 607–8. In 1828, King's Bridge, a national testimonial to the visit of George IV, was unveiled. The bridge spans the River Liffey, connecting Kilmainham with the Phoenix Park. In 1941 it was renamed 'Sean Heuston Bridge'.

15 *Times*, 5 October 1849.

16 Ibid.

17 *Globe*, 18 March 1850. The following published text accompanied the diorama: 'Philip Phillips, *A Description of the Grand Moving Diorama Representing Ireland on the Visit of Her Most Gracious Majesty, Queen Victoria, H.R.H. Prince Albert and the Royal*

Children: From Sketches Made on the Spot by Mr Philip Phillips, to which is annexed an historical record of the particulars connected with that memorable event; now exhibiting at the Hyde Park Gallery, Hyde Park Corner (London: 1850)'. A copy of this is in the National Library of Ireland.

18   *Freeman's Journal*, 7 August 1849.

19   Ibid.

20   *Freeman's Journal*, 7 August 1849.

21   *The Advocate: or, Irish Industrial Journal*, 22 August 1849. Originally from Scotland, James Townsend Mackay (1775–1862) began his career at Trinity College Dublin in 1802. From 1806, he served as the curator of the Trinity College Botanic Gardens, Ballsbridge, until his death in 1862. See E. Leaney, 'Mackay, James Townsend', in J. McGuire and J. Quinn (eds), *Dictionary of Irish Biography* (Cambridge: Cambridge University Press, 2009), vol. 6, pp. 20–1. It is possible that the 'Mrs White, Killakee' refers to Mrs Anne Salisbury White of Killakee House, Rathfarnham, Co. Dublin (now demolished).

22   *The Advocate: or, Irish Industrial Journal*, 22 August 1849.

23   *Freeman's Journal*, 7 August 1849.

24   *Daily Express* (Dublin), 16 April 1868.

25   *Saunders's Newsletter*, 4 April 1868.

26   *Illustrated London News*, 25 April 1868.

27   Landells was the eldest son of Ebenezer Landells (1808–1860), an engraver, illustrator and magazine owner. Landells frequently contributed to *The Illustrated London News*, most notably providing war sketches from the Crimea in 1856. Additionally, Landells had produced memorial paintings for Queen Victoria between 1857 and 1874.

28   *Illustrated London News*, 25 April 1868.

29   Ibid.

30   G. Battiscombe, *Queen Alexandra* (London: Constable & Company, 1980), p. 94.

31   Letter to the Harbour Master, Kingstown from Admiral Fullerton, Captain, Royal Yacht, 15 March 1900, OPW file: Visit of Her Majesty the Queen, National Archives of Ireland, OPW/2012/60/4.

32   Notes from Kingstown Harbour Board Meeting, 24 March 1900, OPW file: Visit of Her Majesty the Queen, National Archives of Ireland, OPW/2012/60/4.

33   Memorandum to the Superintendent of Works, Kingstown Harbour, 30 March 1900, OPW file: Visit of Her Majesty the Queen, National Archives of Ireland, OPW/2012/60/4.

34   Letter to OPW Secretary from M. Keogh, Dublin, Wicklow and Wexford Railway Company, 29 March 1900, OPW file: Visit of Her Majesty the Queen, National Archives of Ireland, OPW/2012/60/4.

35   Letter to Lord Plunkett, Viceregal Lodge from OPW Secretary, 24 March 1900; letter to D. Stephens, Kingstown from OPW Secretary, 31 March 1900, OPW file: Visit of Her Majesty the Queen, National Archives of Ireland, OPW/2012/60/4.

36   For a recent discussion of this painting, and the depiction of the crowd in nineteenth-century Ireland, see M.J. Boland, 'Creating Order? Painting the crowd in nineteenth-century Ireland', in B. Rooney (ed.), *Creating History: Stories of Ireland in Art* (Dublin: Irish Academic Press & National Gallery of Ireland, 2016), pp. 90–111.

37   *Freeman's Journal*, 18 August 1821.

38   For a full history of the Lord Mayor's coach, see P. McEvansoneya, 'A Colourful Spectacle Restored: The State Coach of the Lord Mayor of Dublin', *Irish Arts Review*, 17 (2001), pp. 80–7.

39   *The Royal Visit, Containing a Full and Circumstantial Account of Everything Connected with the King's Visit to Ireland* (Dublin: Printed by P. Crooks for P. Byrne,

1821), p. 34.

40 Ibid.

41 *The Royal Visit*, p. 36.

42 Ibid., p. 39.

43 In 1853, Victoria was presented with the keys to the city at Westland Row train station.

44 An almost identical watercolour by French is in the Royal Collection, RCIN 920935.

45 'Queen Victoria in Dublin', 4 April 1900, British Pathé, 1674.18, http://www.britishpathe.com/video/queen-victoria-in-dublin (accessed 16 March 2017).

46 W. Laffan, 'George IV at College Green', in W. Laffan (ed.), *Painting Ireland: Topographical Views from Glin Castle* (Tralee: Churchill House Press, 2006), p. 193.

47 *Freeman's Journal*, 17 August 1821.

48 For more on the political and symbolic nature of public sculpture, see P. Murphy, *Nineteenth-Century Irish Sculpture: Native Genius Reaffirmed* (New Haven and London: Yale University Press, 2010), ch. 10.

49 Transparencies were 'scenes painted on paper, Irish linen, fine calico or cambric muslin that were back-lit to create an illuminated effect'. See J. Plunkett, 'Light Work: Feminine leisure and the making of transparencies', in K. Hadjiafxedni and P. Zakreski (eds), *Crafting the Woman Professional in the Long Nineteenth Century: Artistry and Industry in Britain* (London and New York: Routledge, 2016), p. 44.

50 *Freeman's Journal*, 20 August 1821.

51 Ibid.

52 *Freeman's Journal*, 20 August 1821.

53 Ibid.

54 *Freeman's Journal*, 1 August 1849.

55 *Freeman's Journal*, 26 July 1849.

56 *Freeman's Journal*, 2 August 1849.

57 For more on the political context of the 1849 visit see J. Loughlin, 'Allegiance and Illusion: Queen Victoria's Irish visit of 1849', *History*,

87, 288 (2002), pp. 491–513.

58 *Saunders's News-letter*, 8 August 1821; *Dublin Evening Post*, 4 August 1821.

59 *Dublin Evening Post*, 4 August 1821.

60 *Dublin Evening Post*, 31 July 1849.

61 Ibid. 'Alderman Moon' was Sir Francis Graham Moon (1796–1871), a London-based print seller and publisher.

62 *Dublin Evening Packet and Correspondent*, 2 August 1849. The painting referred to is Sir Edwin Landseer's *Windsor Castle in Modern Times; Queen Victoria, Prince Albert and Victoria, Princess Royal*, 1841–3, Royal Collection Trust, oil on canvas, RCIN 406903.

63 *Dublin Evening Packet and Correspondent*, 29 February 1848.

64 *Pilot*, 6 March 1848.

65 *Dublin Evening Post*, 16 August 1849.

66 *Cork Examiner*, 31 August 1849. In October 1849, *The Advocate: or, Irish Industrial Journal* reprinted an article from *The Cork Examiner* which stated that fifty-two people subscribed for an engraving in Cork, '… although the picture was only exhibited here for three weeks …', and that there were seventy subscribers in Dublin, '… although it was exhibited in that city for months, and the Earl and Countess of Clarendon were at the head of the list'; see *The Advocate: or, Irish Industrial Journal*, 3 October 1849. Eileen Black records that in September 1848, a watercolour copy of *Windsor Castle in the Present Day* by Stephen Poyntz Denning was exhibited at Hodgson's, Belfast. Furthermore, in September–October 1849, a copy of *The Royal Family* by 'Cunningham, after the original by Franz Xavier Winterhalter' was also displayed at Hodgson's. These may be the same copies that were exhibited in Dublin and Cork. See E. Black, *Window to an Age: A Chronicle of Art in Belfast 1760–1888* (Belfast: Ulster Historical Society, 2016), pp.

84–6.

67 *Dublin Evening Post*, 13 September 1849.

68 The title given to this painting in the Royal Collection catalogue is incorrect: it shows Kingstown (Dún Laoghaire), rather than Queenstown (Cobh).

69 After Matthew Kendrick, *The Departure of the Queen and the Royal Squadron from Kingstown, August 1849*, Royal Collection Trust, engraving, RCIN 770264.

70 *Freeman's Journal*, 4 September 1849.

71 Ibid.

72 After Edwin Hayes (1797–1864), *Departure of Her Majesty from Kingstown Harbour, 10 August 1849*, published 1 February 1850, Royal Collection Trust, lithograph, RCIN 750944. See also Jonathan Needham (*fl.* 1850–1874) and Edwin Hayes (1819–1904), *The Departure of Her Most Gracious Majesty, Queen Victoria from Kingstown Harbour, August 10ᵗʰ 1849*, published 1 February 1850, National Library of Ireland, lithograph, PD D35.

73 *Weekly Irish Times*, 7 April 1900.

74 *Evening Packet*, 18 August 1849.

75 Ibid.

76 See *The Royal Visit*, p. 43.

77 *Belfast Newsletter*, 21 August 1821.

78 *Freeman's Journal*, 18 August 1821.

79 'The Irish Sword of State', in C. Blair (ed.), *The Crown Jewels: The History of the Coronation Regalia in the Jewel House of the Tower of London* (London: The Stationery Office, 1998), vol. 2, pp. 350–5.

80 *Freeman's Journal*, 18 August 1821.

81 Ibid.

82 *Dublin Evening Post*, 25 July 1849.

83 *Freeman's Journal*, 9 August 1849.

84 Ibid.

85 *Freeman's Journal*, 9 August 1849.

86 Ibid.

87 *Freeman's Journal*, 9 August 1849.

88 Ibid. *The Dublin Evening Post* reported that the Queen's dress was pink; see *Dublin Evening Post*, 11 August 1849.

89 *The Advocate: or, Irish Industrial Journal*, 15 August 1849. Both *The Illustrated London News* and the description given in *The Advocate* seem to either visually or textually reference Winterhalter's portrait of the Queen, completed in 1842. See Franz Xavier Winterhalter, *Queen Victoria (1819-1901)*, 1842, Royal Collection Trust, oil on canvas, RCIN 401413.

90 *Freeman's Journal*, 16 April 1868.

91 See Michael Angelo Hayes, *The Installation of the Prince of Wales as a Knight of St Patrick*, 1872, collection of Lord Iveagh, oil on canvas, currently on display at Farmleigh House, Dublin.

92 *Freeman's Journal*, 21 August 1897.

93 *Evening Star*, 23 July 1903.

94 Ibid.

95 *Sphere*, 24 June 1911.

Eight

(Ad)dressing Home Rule

Irish Home Industries, the Throne Room and Lady Aberdeen's Modern Modes of Display

Éimear O'Connor

By the late nineteenth century, fashion had become 'a great force' with which to invigorate its supporting industries in Ireland – poplin weaving, lace making, and art embroidery – all of which had been in decline since the onset of the Famine.[1] Although the so-called 'Castle season' culminated in a lavish ball held on the evening of St Patrick's Day in the eponymous ballroom at Dublin Castle, 'most of the levées and drawing room parties for ladies were held in the throne room'.[2] Thus, the Throne Room became the centre of the 'great force' of fashion. A liminal space, and yet at the epicentre of style, the Throne Room became a theatre of performance through which passed a parade of *à la mode* fashions. Well aware of the connection between sartorial chic and communication, fashion-conscious Castle season attendees wore garments that proposed a multiplicity of visual signifiers: wealth; social connections; allegiance to the throne; allegiance to Ireland; and allegiance to the philanthropic concerns of the reigning vicereine, wife of the viceroy. Additionally, the records show that from at least 1826 and onwards, it was not at all unusual for the viceroy and vicereine to wear clothes manufactured with Irish materials, and embellished with Irish lace or embroidery, to social gatherings in the Throne Room.[3] Moreover, as monarch presiding over the entire British Empire, and in acknowledgement of her regal relationship with

Facing page: Fig. 08.01. Ishbel, Countess of Aberdeen, 1886. Photograph album given by the Earl and Countess of Aberdeen to Colonel Caulfield. Courtesy of the Office of Public Works, Áras an Uachtaráin.

Ireland, Queen Victoria is known to have patronized Irish home industries, and to have worn, for example, 'a robe of exquisitely shaded Irish poplin of emerald green, richly wrought with shamrocks in gold embroidery', during her levee at Dublin Castle during her state visit in 1849.[4]

By the 1880s the 'authority' on Irish lace was a Mr Ben Lindsey, owner of an establishment known as the Lace Depot on Dublin's Grafton Street.[5] The shop provided a much-needed outlet to lace-making cottage workers around the country. So, too, hand embroidery was popular, such as that made by the Royal Irish School of Art Needlework (RISAN), whose remit since its inception in 1876, and foundation in 1877 as part of the Queen's Institute, was to supply work for women of high class who had fallen on hard times, rather than to support the peasant classes who populated cottage industries such as lace making.[6] The RISAN was reinvigorated by Katrine Cecilia de Grey Cowper, Countess Cowper (1845–1913) during her two-year tenure as vicereine in Dublin Castle. She appears to have been responsible for the introduction of a 'new constitution' intended 'to replicate even more closely the by now firmly established Royal School of Art Needlework (RSAN)' in London.[7] Indeed, the RISAN may even have been an 'affiliate' of the RSAN, which had been established in 1872, with similar aims in terms of design and quality, if not interconnected business arrangements.[8] The RISAN was boosted yet again in the 1890s by Geraldine Bourke, Countess of Mayo (d. 1944) who moved the school into new premises at 20 Lincoln Place, Dublin, and such was its success that by 1902 she was in a position to write that the school now had 'twenty-three workers' and classes were ongoing.[9] By this time there were several well-established dressmakers with a much sought-after royal warrant, or seal of approval, working in Dublin, two of whom, Mrs Sims of Dawson Street, and Miss Manning of Grafton Street, are perhaps the best known. They provided up-to-date garments to fashionistas attending the Castle season, many of which were embellished with Irish lace, and embroidered by the RISAN.

It was not uncommon for the reigning vicereine to display her support for Ireland by wearing Irish-made and embellished clothes, evident as early as 1826, when an observer for *The Freeman's Journal* wrote that the vicereine had worn 'a splendid train of white Irish silver tabbinet, shamrock pattern, richly trimmed with silver, and manufactured by O'Reilly of College Green' while attending the levee in the Throne Room.[10] In 1830, the viceroy and vicereine, Hugh Percy, 3rd Duke of Northumberland (1785–1847) and Charlotte Percy, Duchess of

Northumberland (1787–1866) both attended a 'Drawing Room' at Dublin Castle dressed in 'Irish manufacture, as were the generality of those attending'.[11] But it was not until 1886 that such support was deliberately fused with a paternalistic project to create economic recovery and stability for Ireland's cottage workers. This was concomitant with support for the political zeitgeist of the time: Home Rule for Ireland. Amid the flurry of activity associated with her duties as vicereine, there were many magnificent moments during which Ishbel Hamilton-Gordon (*née* Marjoribanks), Countess of Aberdeen, later Marchioness of Aberdeen and Temair (1857–1939) influenced her public and the press in an entirely modern way that was vastly different in approach to any of her predecessors. While dealing, of necessity, with issues pertaining to context, this narrative focuses on three important instances from amid Lady Aberdeen's extraordinary career in Ireland – 1886, 1893, and 1909 – after which the Throne Room, encompassed as it was into a Red Cross Hospital in 1915, would never be the same again.

During her first tour of duty in Dublin Castle in 1886, which lasted a mere six months, Lady Aberdeen followed precedent and made sure to be seen in garments made from Irish poplin and embellished with Irish lace and embroidery by the RISAN.[12] This tradition also extended to the use of Irish motifs on her garments. These motifs included 'silver and green shamrocks', which featured on a dress worn by her in the Throne Room at Dublin Castle, as she received her guests for the St Patrick's Day Ball of 1886.[13] Having been ousted from the Dublin Throne Room in August 1886, her strength of character emerged when she wore a formal court dress, possibly made by Mrs Sims, and certainly embroidered in gold on a 'cream coloured ground' with 'Celtic sources' by the RISAN, to Queen Victoria's first drawing room of the season in 1888.[14] While 'Celtic sources' might not have displeased the Queen, a patron of Irish home industries, Lady Aberdeen's blatant advertisement in the Throne Room of Buckingham Palace will not have been missed by those who did not support Home Rule. Equally, Queen Victoria had no time for William Gladstone's liberal politics. Just as well then, that Lady Aberdeen's 'Celtic' court dress was only on view in Buckingham Palace for a couple of hours. In her diary for 24 February 1888 she wrote:

> More snow, cold intense … Hurried home to dress for Drawing room. Irish gold embroidered dress and re-arranged emerald tiara quite satisfactory … had to start for Buckingham Palace at 2.30 and got away at 4.40. Changed, went to service [at] Lambeth Palace Chapel [at] 5.[15]

Lady Aberdeen continued to wear Irish-made and embellished garments even after leaving Dublin Castle in 1886, and throughout the second Aberdeen viceroyalty between 1906 and 1915. Poignantly, too, when her youngest brother, Archie, a long-time invalid, died in December 1900, she recorded that his coffin was 'covered with a pall of rich cream Irish poplin, with a cross of gold woven throughout the length'.[16] Her commitment to Ireland, and to Home Rule, and to Irish home industries was heartfelt, genuine, and always ecumenical in approach.

Ishbel's assertiveness regarding her role as vicereine was a continuance of her life thus far. Her father, Dudley Coutts Marjoribanks, was a Liberal MP for Berwick-on-Tweed and on friendly terms with Gladstone, although the issue of Home Rule broke the bond between the two men.[17] But Ishbel remained Gladstone's friend, ally, and political supporter. From an early age she was acutely aware of the importance of service to the community; she ran Sunday school classes for the children of the workers on her family estate, Guisachan, in Inverness.[18] Always concerned for the morality and livelihoods of working girls, in the late 1870s and early 1880s Ishbel often 'went alone into dark alleys off the Strand [London] and persuaded girls to come into the bright mission room for tea, and talk of a new start'.[19] Ishbel and her husband, John Campbell Hamilton-Gordon, 7th Earl of Aberdeen, later 1st Marquess of Aberdeen and Temair (1847–1934), whom she married in 1877, were drawn together through their 'common desire to dedicate' their 'lives to the service of God'.[20] Fundamental to their attitude was a paternal disposition that accepted as a given that 'God had created a hierarchal society and that it was the duty of the wealthy to protect, guide and help the lower ranks, maintaining a firm moral superintendence'.[21] Inherent to their paternalism was the concept of social benevolence. This attitude was 'exemplified' in Scottish 'kailyard' literature, as espoused by 'Free Church minister turned journalist William Robertson Nicoll', who, as it happened, 'encouraged the Aberdeens to write their memoirs' which were published in 1925.[22] Kailyard literature acknowledged 'tacit social norms', including the notion that 'inequality and social hierarchy were acceptable if the upper classes remained in contact with their subordinates and thus open to human feelings prompting them to acknowledge obligations towards the less fortunate'.[23] Thus, the couple involved themselves with several social causes including an organization, based in London, which worked towards the provision of seats for shop assistants, along with the National Home Reading Union, the Parents' National Education Union, the

Canning Town Women's Settlement, and homes for working girls.[24] Significantly, the Aberdeens, or more specifically, Ishbel, co-operated with Gladstone 'in his rescue work with London prostitutes'.[25] Such was the extent of the Aberdeens' paternalism, particularly towards women, that their friend, Gladstone, is reputed to have said that they were 'a very edifying couple'.[26] Moreover, wherever they went, whether Haddo House (the Gordon family home in Aberdeenshire), the Viceregal Lodge in Dublin or to Canada during his sojourn as Governor General, the couple built chapels – permanent in the case of Haddo House, and wooden in the case of Dublin and Toronto. Significantly, the chapels were ecumenical, and always open to tenants and visitors, as well as to the family, a tradition that continues at Haddo House.

The arrival of Lord and Lady Aberdeen at Dublin Castle in 1886, appointed by Gladstone who was now an advocate for Home Rule, heralded changes in the viceregal role concomitant with the political spirit of the time. Lady Aberdeen was astute, clearly politicized in spite of her protestations to be otherwise, and highly experienced in working with those far less privileged. She was well used to addressing the press, and she was in no mind to remain behind the scenes while her husband, to whom she was an equal partner, fulfilled the public role.[27] A naturally confident communicator, she conjoined her inherent 'social benevolence' to her belief in Home Rule, through her engagement with Irish home industries. Her project was to bring about an economic revival, especially among the poorer classes, so that the Irish people could help themselves, but under the caring eye of the 'welfare monarch' presiding over Home Rule. Although she began her tenure as vicereine by wearing Irish-made and embellished garments during the Castle season, it was the inauguration of the Irish Industries Association, of which she was president, in May 1886 that heralded her first, highly intentioned, public relations exercise.

Organized as a garden party at the Viceregal Lodge, rather than in the Throne Room at Dublin Castle, attendees were invited to wear Irish-made and Irish-embellished costume.[28] It would appear to have been the first time that such an event had ever taken place at the Viceregal Lodge, and Lady Aberdeen commissioned a distinctive dress for the occasion. The design of the dress and the accompanying jewellery and adornments had been suggested to Lady Aberdeen by 'Major MacEniry, curator of the Royal Academy', with the intention of rendering her a living, head-to-toe announcement for Irish home industries.[29]

> Mr Johnson of 94 Grafton Street designed the necklace, ear-rings, and torque bracelet, while the fibula and Tara brooches and the girdle were made by Messrs Waterhouse ... Messrs West formed as a head ornament, a gold pin after the headpieces in the Irish Academy; also a chatelaine bag and bunch of keys from similar designs. The Balbriggan stockings were embroidered with shamrocks by Mr Smyth. The untanned Irish leather shoes were fastened with Irish harp buckles, and the white poplin parasol was trimmed with Limerick lace on an Irish yew stick and a Tara brooch handle.[30]

The poplin for the dress was supplied by 'Messrs Atkinson', a Dublin-based company that had been supplying Irish poplin for the Throne Room at the Castle since at least 1839.[31] Made by Mrs Sims, a favourite of Lady Aberdeen's, the dress had a 'petticoat' of the 'richest cream poplin' with 'an overskirt of similar material, superbly wrought with gold work'.[32] The hem of the overskirt was embroidered with a deep band of Celtic-style interlocking circles while the accompanying long and decorative court train featured more naturalistic leaf motifs within Celtic-type swirls along the outer edges. The embroidery was carried out by the RISAN using designs derived from the Book of Kells.[33]

Significantly, while some observers noted that the dress was reminiscent of costumes thought to have been worn by Irish princesses in the thirteenth or fifteenth century, another commentator wrote that the design and embellishment of the dress had been based on a painting by Irish-born artist Daniel Maclise (1806–1870). Entitled *The Marriage of Strongbow and Aoife*, it was completed in 1853.[34] Although not entirely true to the dress Aoife wears in the painting, it is the theme – the strengthening of Ireland by its connection to England, as exemplified through the physical, spiritual, and philosophical joining of Strongbow and Aoife – that was important to Lady Aberdeen's philanthropic concerns, allied with her support of Home Rule. Secondly, and perhaps more provocatively, several photographs were taken of Lady Aberdeen wearing the dress, which, for their formality, might just as well have been taken in the Throne Room (Fig. 08.01). But in another Lady Aberdeen is photographed sitting at a spinning wheel so as to advertise the 'Irish industries of wool, flax, and silk' (Fig. 08.02).[35] These were the industries that, if revived, could help the Irish people to help themselves, and yet, remain subjects under Home Rule. An extraordinary photograph for the time, Lady Aberdeen was the first vicereine to promote visually her combination of concerns using her own image. Dressed to epitomize Ireland, and Irish home

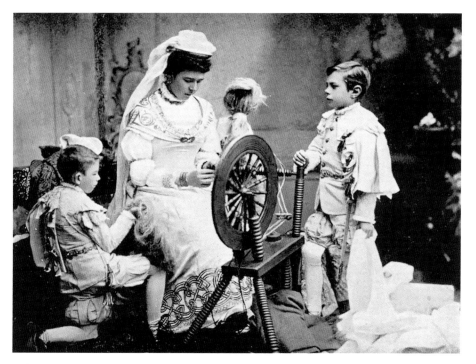

Fig. 08.02.
Ishbel, Countess
of Aberdeen at her
spinning wheel
with the Irish
industries of wool,
flax and silk, 1886.
Marjorie Pentland,
A Bonnie Fechter,
1952.

industries, yet cast as 'a stand-in for a maternally imagined Queen Victoria', it was a thoroughly modern attempt to influence the press, and the public, to stimulate support for her endeavours.[36]

In the meantime, the Gladstones often stayed with the Aberdeens at their weekend home, Dollis Hall in Willesden, in the countryside west of London.[37] Thus, it was to Dollis Hall, and the Aberdeens, that the Gladstones retreated after the failed reading of the Home Rule Bill in July 1886.[38] Parliament was dissolved, and as a result, the Aberdeens had to leave Dublin Castle. But, according to the evidence available in the numerous illuminated addresses that the couple received prior to leaving, Lady Aberdeen had already made an excellent impression. One such address, presented by the Lord Mayor of Dublin, well exemplifies the goodwill towards her:

> By her good example, her wise counsel, and her liberal assistance, she rendered to the public in that time of trial a priceless service. She has initiated an organisation for the promotion of Irish cottage industries from which admirable results are likely to follow. In fact, no week passed during her

Fig. 08.03.
Illuminated address
from the Lord
Mayor and Town
Clerk of Dublin
to the 7th Earl of
Aberdeen, 1886.
© Gordon Family
Archive, Haddo
House. Courtesy
of Alexander,
7th Marquess of
Aberdeen and
Temair.

sojourn amongst us in which some deserving institution or class of people did not receive proofs of her regard, while at the same time, she won for herself the high esteem of all whose privilege it was to be brought into relations with her …

Significantly, the address to the Aberdeens (Fig. 08.03) finished thus:

We hope that in the decree of Divine Providence it may be accorded to Mr Gladstone to complete in that more favourable time the blessed work of justice and of pacification which he so nobly commenced, and if in these happy circumstances we should have the pleasure of seeing your excellency and the Countess of Aberdeen return to resume the high functions which you now lay down, we can confidently assure you that you will receive from the citizens of Dublin and the people of Ireland a hearty welcome.[39]

While intensely saddened, the Aberdeens firmly believed that they would return to Dublin Castle when Gladstone next won an election. As it turned out, to their disappointment, this was not to be, and Lord Aberdeen was instead appointed as Governor General of Canada in 1893. In the interim, Lady Aberdeen, having left Dublin Castle in August 1886 wearing an Irish poplin dress of St Patrick's blue, the make and fit of which was 'as perfect as might be expected from the eminent firm [Manning] to which the task of designing and making had been entrusted', did not abandon her Irish Industries Association.[40] She returned frequently to chair meetings, and to continue the general work of the organization, and was careful to be seen in public in Irish-made clothes. In 1896, for example, she was observed at the Dublin Horse Show wearing a 'magnificent cope' which had been embroidered by the Dalkey Co-Operative Embroidery Society, managed by the Loreto nuns, and based in a building in the grounds of the Loreto convent, Dalkey, Co. Dublin.[41] The enterprise had only begun the year before.

Although no longer in Dublin Castle, Lady Aberdeen was planning a major project to advertise her Irish home industries, and with that in mind, she undertook a tour of Ireland in the early months of 1893. The project came about owing to the success of the Irish home industries section at the International Exhibition, Edinburgh, in 1886, for which Lady Aberdeen was awarded a certificate of merit for the exhibition of Irish Women's Industries (Fig. 08.04). The idea that emerged was that it would be possible to create a greater market in America by involving

Fig. 08.04.
Diploma of honour from the International
Exhibition of Industry, Science and Art,
awarded to Ishbel, Countess of Aberdeen, 1886.
© Gordon Family Archive, Haddo House.
Courtesy of Alexander, 7th Marquess of
Aberdeen and Temair.

Irish home industries in the forthcoming World's Fair in Chicago in 1893. There were several complicating issues regarding the venture, not least that the Irish Industries Association was in competition with Mrs Ernest Hart, who eventually set up a second Irish village in Chicago.[42] Notwithstanding all of that, it was Lady Aberdeen who travelled across the Atlantic in 1892 'to interview the Exhibition authorities at Chicago, and to interest business men connected with Ireland in the U.S.A.'[43] Always well aware of the significance of the press to her project, she made herself constantly available for interview when she got to Chicago. As a former vicereine of Ireland, doors were opened, and her efforts were not in vain:

> Mr. S. Medill, proprietor of the *Chicago Tribune*, and Mr. J. Farwell, to whom Mr. Carnegie had given us introductions, gave us great help, and invited a number of people to meet us at dinner. Mr. Strobel, Mr. Carnegie's partner, brought us into touch with a number of business people who all seemed interested, especially Mr. W. J. Walsh, of the First National Bank, and Mr. Scott, of the *Chicago World*. Mr. H. Gordon Selfridge, who was then a partner of Marshall Field, of Chicago, gave most practical help. He ordered outright [a] wedding dress and vest of Irish lace, and undertook to provide us with wax figures and glass cases. We reminded him of this many years later when he started his great venture in London on St. Patrick's Day.[44]

The Aberdeens raised a lot of money towards creating Ishbel's Irish village throughout that tour of America, which also took in Washington and New York.[45]

They encouraged patriotic sentiment wherever they went. This was evident, for example, in their visit to New York where they were hosted to dinner by a 'newly-constructed Irish body, pledged to moderation and avoidance of physical force', and to undertaking 'to support the Irish Parliamentary Party till Home Rule was given'.[46] The dinner took place at the famous Delmonico's Restaurant, and was attended by 'many ladies of Irish origin' who assured the couple that they would 'support' their 'Irish Industries movement', thereby demonstrably connecting the Irish village at the Chicago World's Fair with Home Rule for Ireland.[47]

When Lady Aberdeen visited Ireland's cottage workers looking for people to bring to Chicago, which she did on many occasions in early 1893, the 'people crowded round her gratefully' because the Irish Industries Association had already 'brought more money into their homes year by year'.[48] On the day the chosen workers were leaving for Chicago a correspondent wrote from Queenstown (now Cobh), Co. Cork, that:

> Lady Aberdeen selected a party of lace makers, dairymaids, and other representatives of the cottage industries of Ireland, and by their aid, hopes to make the Irish village at Chicago one of the brightest spots in the whole of the Columbian Exposition … Deft and dainty workers of every branch of Irish cottage industry have been secured, and the pretty faces, no less than their nimble fingers, are certain to "bring back to Erin" in spirit at least, the hearts of those Irish exiles who will pay the Irish village a visit during the next few months.[49]

As the 'deft and dainty' women left Queenstown harbour to board the *Britannica* clothed in 'cloaks of navy blue, lined with crimson satin, with a deep frill around the shoulders and a turned down collar', they presented a picturesque image: Ireland's clean, tidy, well-dressed, and well-trained cottage-industry women under the parental leadership of Lady Aberdeen, known supporter of Home Rule.[50]

Meanwhile, Gladstone won the general election in 1892, but political machinations behind the scenes meant that he did not nominate Lord Aberdeen to the role of viceroy in Ireland. Although deeply disappointed, the couple took it in their stride, and Lord Aberdeen's appointment as Governor General of Canada was announced during the Chicago World's Fair, which opened on 2 May 1893. Lady Aberdeen's Irish village proved popular with visitors, helped by the fact that the couple often stayed in a small purpose-built cottage on the site where they received their personal guests, special visitors, and a constant stream of interviewers. Although saddened not to be returning to an official role in Ireland, Lady Aberdeen enthusiastically endorsed Irish home industries in Chicago with as much grace and fervour as she had done while in the Throne Room in 1886. Their little cottage in the Irish village had a dedicated visitors' room, which was decorated to present a vision of Ireland, past and present:

> The floor is covered with a hand-loom carpet from Weaver Square, Dublin, and the walls are frescoed in a peculiar shade of green with a frieze of shamrocks … There are prints of Daniel O'Connell, Alexander Pope, Isaac Barre and Jonathan Swift … the furniture is made of Irish oak and is of the kind peculiar to Irish homes … In one corner is a three-cornered cabinet which was at one time the property of William O'Brien … the cabinet is filled with a set of Belleek china … In [another] corner are [Lady Aberdeen's] chair and spinning wheel. The chair is of Irish oak, richly carved, and covered with tapestry made in Ireland long ago …[51]

Controversy arose, however, as a result of Lord Aberdeen's refusal to 'hoist the British flag' over their Irish village.[52] When asked to account for the situation, the manager of the Irish village, Mrs Peter White, stated that Lady Aberdeen's Irish village was:

> The result of individual effort, stimulated by that national sentiment which Lady Aberdeen, the principal promoter, had readily recognized. Funds to establish it were contributed not only by men of all political parties, but also by American gentlemen of Irish sympathies. The (Irish Industries) association [is] non-political in character, and is the work of an incorporated company that is in no way connected with the British Government.[53]

Accordingly, the only flags over Lady Aberdeen's Irish village were 'the star-spangled banner of the United States … and the ancient sunburst flag of Ireland'.[54] Moreover, the Aberdeens' political affiliations were made more evident in Chicago through the public exhibition of a painting from their private collection. Painted in 1890, by Madame Louisa Starr Canziani (1845–1909), the painting featured the couple's two younger sons, Dudley and Archie, dressed as neat and tidy Irish peasants clothed in Irish-made materials. Exhibited as number 113 in the British

Fig. 08.05.
Louisa Starr
Canziani, *Two
little "Home
Rulers", the
Hons Dudley and
Archie Gordon,
sons of the Earl of
Aberdeen*, 1890.
© Gordon Family
Archive, Haddo
House.
Courtesy of
Alexander, 7th
Marquess of
Aberdeen and
Temair, and the
National Trust for
Scotland.

art section, the painting was titled *Two little "Home Rulers", the Hons Dudley and Archie Gordon, sons of the Earl of Aberdeen, lent by the Earl of Aberdeen* (Fig. 08.05).[55] Consequently, most of the Aberdeen family publicized the range of benefits derived from the work of the Irish Industries Association to Irish cottage workers, and to the buying and viewing public, but cleverly rendered concomitant with Home Rule.

Lady Aberdeen's Irish village did well in terms of sales and orders of Irish-made products. Their friend, founder of the Irish Agricultural Organisations Association (IAOS), Horace Plunkett, a firm believer in an ecumenical approach to agricultural co-operation in a manner that aligned well with the Aberdeens' open regard for all religions, and all political viewpoints, examined the accounts for the Irish village. He 'pronounced himself well satisfied with the efficiency and economy with which the whole enterprise had been conducted'.[56] The financial success of the Irish village meant that for the Aberdeens it was 'a great gratification ... to be able to repay in full the £7,500 advanced to us by a few

Irish and American friends which enabled the Irish Village of the World's Fair to be built'.[57] Indeed, the venture purportedly made a £50,000 profit, £30,000 of which went to the authorities in Chicago and towards paying back loans, while 'the sum of £20,000 went to the workers in Ireland'.[58] This was the economic recovery, concomitant with Home Rule in Ireland, which Lady Aberdeen desired. Her success on behalf of Irish home industries was acknowledged during a presentation to award her the 'Freedom of the City of Limerick' in June 1894:

> In the conferring of the Freedom of the City of Limerick on Lady Aberdeen, it is purely because she is a benefactress to our race, and not through any political motives. We give it to her for her goodness, and we give it spontaneously ...[59]

On the other hand, there were people who thought little of Lady Aberdeen's benevolent activities. One critic, R.R. Kane, a well-known Grand Master of the Orange Order in Belfast, wrote that her Irish village was a charitable endeavour 'calculated to favour the impression which political partisans [the Parnellites] wish to make'.[60] Perhaps naively, given the issues over the British flag, and the Aberdeens' clear support for Home Rule, Lady Aberdeen wrote in response to Kane that 'the Irish Industrial Association have ever held it as a fundamental principle that both political and sectarian differences should be wholly and absolutely ignored in our work' and that the organization was not a charity.[61] Rather, it desired to 'develop the home industries of Ireland on business lines' and had therefore 'secured the cooperation of businessmen on its committees'.[62] She invited Kane to join her organization, but he declined by suggesting that Irish workers did not need her charity, and that he supported Irish-made goods by simply buying them when it was appropriate to do so. It was a full-blown controversy that made it into most of the Irish, English, and Scottish newspapers of the time. Although the rumblings against her activities continued, Lady Aberdeen had no qualms about publically rebutting her critics, while at the same time, avowedly maintaining her stance regarding Irish home industries.

Behind the scenes the Aberdeens were putting their own money into developing the market for Irish-made products; the Irish Lace Depot is a case in point. Just before the Aberdeens left for Chicago, Mr Ben Lindsey:

> ... the great authority on Irish lace and whose Irish Lace Depot in Grafton Street, Dublin, had a monopoly of the Irish lace trade, died. His method of

dealing with the lace industries was to tell those in charge to work away and he would come round and see what they wanted. And then he would choose this and that piece and fill his basket, and offer so much for the lot. The convents and the managers of the lace industries dared not refuse for fear of losing his orders.[63]

Although problematic to some extent, because nobody could be sure of their earnings from him, Lindsey's method of work meant that he did not facilitate what was known as the 'putting out system … whereby a merchant or his agent would take materials to a household to be made up and collected within an allotted time, quotas and quantities agreed at the outset'.[64] In operation in many parts of the British Isles, the 'putting out' system was open to abuse by merchants, and could lead to 'sweated labour'.[65] Such was the exploitative nature of 'sweated labour', that the author Henry Mayhew, 'made the link between it and poverty, [and] also between sweated work and prostitution'.[66]

The Aberdeens were informed that an apparent 'syndicate was prepared to purchase the goodwill of the business, and would certainly not consider the welfare of the workers' so an urgent appeal was made to them 'to step in and save the situation'.[67] On the advice of Mr Tom Fitzgerald, 'wise counsellor and as hon. solicitor to the Irish Industries Association', Lady Aberdeen got her life insured for a sum sufficient to buy the business, and they left for Chicago now the 'proud possessors of the Irish Lace Depot'.[68] With the paternalist Aberdeens behind the depot, the aforementioned 'putting out' system, so prevalent in England, and so closely associated with prostitution, could not gain traction in Ireland. The depot was refurbished, and, now complete with an underwear department managed by 'Miss Geoghegan, late of Mrs Manning's', it reopened on 18 December 1893. The shop offered 'the largest selection of Irish laces in the world, as well as a beautiful collection of needlework executed in their homes by girls in the different poorer districts in the country'.[69] Notably, according to Lady Aberdeen, 'the annual profits were £25,000, nearly the whole of which went to the workers, or helped some other industry, such as starting the Kildare Carpet Industry at Naas', thereby continually contributing to her planned economic recovery for Ireland.[70]

Meanwhile, Lord Aberdeen bought a house at the end of Motcomb Street in London, 'so that the ground-floor might be rented from him as an Irish Industries shop. Its green corner windows, where festoons of lace hung among red Connemara cloaks, gave a splash of colour to the Belgravian façade. Inside an equally vivid woman manager from Wexford, with bright blue eyes and a rich brogue, displayed the goods'.[71] Her name was Miss Keatinge. When asked whether the stock was simply for rich people, Miss Keatinge replied on the contrary, noting that on the opening day Lady Aberdeen 'wore a dress of Irish lawn which was greatly admired, though the material only cost 6*d*. a yard … unbleached linen from the Convent of Mercy at Skibbereen and you [could] get it in pale blue or pink at 1*s*. a yard'.[72] The shop was also selling 'hand-knitted ladies stockings at 3*s*. a pair, all wool blankets at 15*s*. a pair: soft warm tweeds at 6*s*. a yard double width'.[73] Lady Aberdeen noted with regard to the London Lace Depot that 'the royal family were always most kind' by giving 'active patronage, and often attending sales' which were held in private London houses.[74]

Never having lost touch with Ireland since 1886, and by now extremely well known for their philanthropic endeavours to aid Irish home industries, the Aberdeens were re-appointed to Dublin Castle by Sir Henry Campbell-Bannerman, beginning their second viceroyalty on 3 February 1906, and remaining in situ until 15 February 1915.[75] The couple truly believed that Ireland would gain Home Rule, and that theirs would be 'the last Viceregal State Entry under the old régime'.[76] But it was now twenty years since their previous sojourn at Dublin Castle, and the political landscape was rapidly changing. Nationalism, and the desire for complete separation from Britain, rather than mere Home Rule, was gaining in popularity.

The following year, 1907, was a busy one for the Aberdeens. The famous lace ball, really a continuation of the 1886 viceregal garden party, in terms of actively encouraging the market at home and abroad for Irish-made poplin, lace, and embroidery, took place in Dublin Castle on 5 March. While it was a stylish occasion, unfortunately, Lady Aberdeen, recently unwell with an attack of rheumatism, could only attend the event 'for a short time' and was 'conveyed to the ballroom in a wheelchair'.[77] Yet, with every intention of catching the eye of the press, attend she did, wearing 'a magnificent robe of deep blue chiffon velvet, lavishly trimmed with Irish point lace made at the Youghal lace industry', while her two young pages, Master Thomas Arnott and Master Ulick de Burgh wore 'pale blue poplin suits, with Irish crochet collars and ruffles'.[78] The lace ball was closely followed by the Irish International Exhibition at Herbert Park, Donnybrook, Dublin, opened on 4 May 1907, at which Lady Aberdeen's Irish Industries Association had a major presence. It was here that Lady Aberdeen formally launched her initiative to try to rid Ireland of tuberculosis. But now labelled 'Lady Microbe' by Nationalists, she became a focus for separatists who did not want Home Rule in any shape or form.[79]

Entirely unfazed by her critics, Lady Aberdeen set about organizing her next major event, and this time, there would be no mistaking her role in the economic revival of Irish home industries through the auspices of the Irish Industries Association. The occasion was advertised as a 'Pageant of Irish Industries', at which all attendees were to attire themselves to represent some aspect of Irish industry, such as, for example, copper; gold and silver; or salt (Fig. 08.06). The dresses worn by the ladies taking part in the pageant were designed by students at the Metropolitan School of Art, Dublin.[80] At the same time, attendees were encouraged to wear clothes, embellishments, and jewellery that had been made in Ireland. Several dress rehearsals took place in St Patrick's Hall at Dublin Castle during the ten days or so before the official pageant at the Castle on the night of 17 March 1909. In fact, the demand for tickets for the event, to which the public had been invited, proved so great that the pageant also took place on the evening of 16 March at 'Royal University Buildings, Earlsfort Terrace' so that

Fig. 08.06. Mineral Quadrille, Pageant of Irish Industries, 1909. © Gordon Family Archive, Haddo House. Courtesy of Alexander, 7th Marquess of Aberdeen and Temair.

a larger audience could see it.[81] Monies raised through the sale of tickets were given in 'aid to the Women's National Health Association of Ireland', which Lady Aberdeen had inaugurated during the previously mentioned Irish International Exhibition in 1907.[82]

But Lady Aberdeen had a more focused purpose in mind for her own dress for the Pageant of Irish Industries. Although Irish businesses had been using trademarks for a long time, it was not until the Trade Mark Act, 1905, that such symbols could be formally registered. There were fake products, purporting to be Irish-made, being offered for sale in Ireland and elsewhere, which was a cause of major concern among Irish businesses. An umbrella group entitled the Irish Industrial Development Association (IIDA), based in Cork, registered an official 'made in Ireland' trademark in 1906. The concept of a national trademark for Ireland was first mooted by Professor Windle, of Queen's College, Cork, in 1904. After competition and discussion, a committee finally chose a symbol designed by a Mr Buckley, which was based on the 'Collar of Morann'. Morann, it was believed, was:

> The Aristides of ancient Ireland; His judgements were so remarkable for their integrity that they were attributed to supernatural inspiration: and as he invariably wore a collar when delivering his opinions, the idea spread abroad that the collar would tighten at any deviation from the truth.[83]

In light of the dishonesty then prevalent, regarding purportedly Irish-made goods, the IIDA felt that the symbolism, and the concept of 'deviation from the truth' that would cause the collar to tighten, was well chosen. Clearly, there had been some collaboration between the Cork-based association and Lady Aberdeen prior to the Pageant. Consequently, when Lady Aberdeen made her entrance at the Royal University and at St Patrick's Hall on the night of the Pageant of Irish Industries, she was wearing 'a most stately and becoming gown of pale saffron Irish poplin ... the bodice draped with most beautiful Clonmacnoise lace, fastened with gold Celtic ornaments and diamonds; the graceful sleeves were the same lace'.[84] Attached to the gown was her official court train, made by Mrs Sims and embroidered by the RISAN in 1886.[85] Most significant, however, was the embroidered detail, presumably by the RISAN, that had been added to the front of the dress (Fig. 08.07). Featuring 'raised gold embroidery on a white poplin ground', the emblem was, in fact, the aforementioned 'Irish national

Fig. 08.07.
Ishbel, Countess
of Aberdeen in
her dress for the
Pageant of Irish
Industries, 1909,
detail.
Courtesy of the
National Library
of Ireland.

trademark', upon which was inscribed, in the Irish language, '*Déanta in Éirinn*' [made in Ireland].[86]

Remembering her 1886 garden-party dress, and how she advertised Irish home industries at that time, perhaps Lady Aberdeen's 'trademark' dress was not unexpected. What is surprising is her public advertisement of the Irish language, throughout two pageants, one through the Throne Room and St Patrick's Hall. Not only did Lady Aberdeen wear the dress in public but, anxious to engage with the media to further advertise her trio of concerns – Irish home industries, Home Rule, and now, the Women's National Health Association, she also permitted the 'Original Irish Animated Picture Company' to create 'a magnificent series of animated pictures of the Pageant'.[87] These were, 'by special arrangement with Lord and Lady Aberdeen, exhibited at their matinee in the Round Room,

Rotunda [Rutland Square (now Parnell Square), Dublin]', on 26 August 1909.[88] The Rotunda management had arranged to 'pay half the gross receipts to the Dublin Samaritan Fund for assisting patients under home treatment for consumption'.[89] The *Déanta in Éirinn* dress was arguably Lady Aberdeen's finest moment in terms of modern modes of display, while at the same time, it offers a glimpse into her connections and interests behind the scenes.

Though the Pageant was considered a success, Lady Aberdeen became embroiled in another controversy, this time regarding the publication of the official souvenir of the event. While the publishers, Messrs Maunsel and Company, were Irish, the pamphlet was 'produced at the initiative of the English branch of the Irish Industries with the approval of the Irish Industrial Development Association', whose secretary had apparently given 'full permission to use the trademark in any way concerned with the pageant'.[90] But the Association had not been informed that the pamphlet would be printed in England; otherwise, it would have 'refused to allow the Irish trademark to be associated with it in any way whatsoever'.[91] Writing from the Viceregal Lodge, Lady Aberdeen stated that the souvenir 'in no sense' pretended to be 'Irish in origin'.[92] Rather, it was the work of 'Mr J. S. Wood, Editor of the *Gentlewoman*' who had been for many years 'the organising secretary of the English branch of the Royal Irish Industries Association'.[93] Moreover, the pamphlet had been published to 'further popularise and make known the too little recognised industries of Ireland, and this, moreover, in Great Britain as much as in Ireland'.[94]

By now involved in setting up a hospital at Peamount, Co. Dublin, for the treatment of adults and children with tuberculosis, Lady Aberdeen continued to wear Irish-made clothes, featuring Irish lace and embroidery, as often as possible. The St Patrick's Day Ball of 1912 at Dublin Castle provided another such opportunity. In the early evening, Lady Aberdeen and her husband 'held a Court' in the Throne Room, where they received their guests.[95] Positioned in front of the throne, Lady Aberdeen wore 'a gown of pale mauve brocade'.[96] Significantly, it was remarked upon in the press that she also wore Irish-made lace lappets from Carrickmacross, Co. Monaghan.[97] Just over one month later, the couple hosted a ball at the Royal Dublin Society (RDS) to raise funds for the RISAN.[98] By this stage the RISAN was in serious financial difficulties (the school did not last much beyond 1915). In 1913 the Aberdeens hosted a drawing room, at which Lady Aberdeen wore a 'gown beautifully embroidered by the Royal Irish School of Art Needlework'.[99] At a formal state ball, held in Dublin Castle to close the season in the same year, she wore a 'green poplin' dress that had been 'handsomely embroidered' by the RISAN.[100] At both of these events Lady Aberdeen and her husband again greeted their guests in the symbolic surroundings of the Throne Room, using the emblems of monarchy to reinforce her support for Irish industries. Just over a year later, following the outbreak of the First World War, her imaginative use of the Throne Room was to take an unexpected turn, and a new plan emerged for the State Apartments at Dublin Castle.

Lady Aberdeen had been involved with the Red Cross Ladies' Committee in Scotland during the Boer War. Having received its Royal Charter in 1908, she became the county president for the Aberdeenshire branch of the Red Cross in 1909.[101] Although living in Ireland, she was well informed of the activities of her branch, and she attended as many as her time would allow.[102] In 1914 Lord and Lady Aberdeen convened a meeting at the RDS, at which it was agreed to call 'on the women of Ireland and on the men not serving with the Army or Volunteers, to qualify for Red Cross work by forming classes'.[103] With Lady Aberdeen as the first president, a 'Red Cross bureau of information was set up at 7 Ely Place [Dublin]', a house that the Aberdeens purchased for their own use, and which also served as a 'receiving centre for garments and hospital comforts', and as classrooms in which to teach first aid.[104] In addition, the senate of the National University gave the organization the use of 29 Lower Fitzwilliam Street 'for the period of the war', which served to accommodate workers, and to make and store garments that were sent to the war front, via the branch headquarters in London.[105] But the best help that the Aberdeens could give to the organization was to provide much-needed hospital accommodation. Thus, a 'telegram was dispatched from the Viceregal Lodge' asking approval of King George V to 'use and equip the State apartments at Dublin Castle as a Red Cross Hospital'.[106] The King gave his immediate approval 'promising a donation of £100'.[107]

In spite of 'an extraordinary and inexplicable campaign' against the plans by individuals who suggested that there were microbes in the walls of the building, the hospital within the State Apartments was formally opened on 27 January 1915.[108] Notwithstanding its ceremonial importance, not even the Throne Room escaped appropriation. With accommodation for 250 patients, 'there was … much competition for the bed under the canopy over the Throne' which the Aberdeens had endowed in 'remembrance of … Captain Hope', who was the first of the Castle staff to 'fall in the war'.[109] The symbolism of this endowment should not go unnoticed; in place of the throne, and the associated pomp and

Fig. 08.08.
The Throne Room,
Dublin Castle,
as a hospital
ward, *c.* 1915.
Courtesy of the
Irish Architectural
Archive.

ceremony, was now a bed in memory of a man killed at war (Fig. 08.08). Rather than being the space in which Lady Aberdeen's Irish sympathies were merely displayed, the Throne Room had now become the space in which they were *enacted*. Extraordinarily, perhaps, it was to this hospital that James Connolly was brought after the Easter Rising in 1916.

Ultimately, it was the Red Cross 'that was to prove to be the cause' of Lady Aberdeen's 'greatest unpopularity with her critics on every side', in spite of her good intentions.[110] Adopting her usual ecumenical approach, she wanted people of all religious persuasions to join the Red Cross. A private note to the editor of *The Freeman's Journal*, sent in October 1914, revealed that she had concerns that the Ulster Unionists wanted to 'capture' the Red Cross in Ireland and run it from London, which would be 'unacceptable to the Irish Volunteer people'.[111] The note found its way into the wrong hands, and was published by Arthur Griffith's newspaper, *Sinn Féin*. It was the postscript to the note, which congratulated the editor of *The Freeman's Journal* for the newspaper's contribution to the 'consummation of hopes' regarding Home Rule. This gave Griffith and, indeed, James Larkin, the fodder they needed to accuse Lady Aberdeen, and *The Freeman's*

Journal of collaboration to create 'the worst curse that could happen to a nation struggling for independence'.[112] When requested by the Red Cross to refute the existence of her private letter, she could not do so. The spat with the organization became public; *The Irish Times* rebuked Lady Aberdeen for her accusations of a Unionist plot to take over the Red Cross. As the wife of the viceroy, it was 'disgraceful' that she could not 'stand aloof' from party politics.[113] Their days in Dublin were numbered. Asquith believed that nine years at Dublin Castle was enough; the couple left in a formal state procession on 15 February 1915. They were gone from office, but characteristically, Lady Aberdeen continued to return to Ireland in the service of her many philanthropic interests until the 1930s.

Looking back, Lady Aberdeen realized that there was:

> ... but little chance of any real revival of the beautiful Irish lace industry, as lace of similar type is made in China and Syria so perfectly that only an accomplished expert can distinguish any difference, and yet the price of this foreign lace is about a fifth of that which has to be charged for Irish lace ... In addition to this formidable competition, the truth is that there is but little Irish lace or crochet now being made, except in some convents and in the Congested Districts Board classes, and lace-workers these days would never accept the wages for which they used to work.[114]

Admittedly the figures are by now difficult to prove, but according to Lady Aberdeen, and to her daughter, Marjorie Pentland, a lot of money reached the cottage workers, lace makers, and embroiderers of Ireland: 'The outcome of these sales and of the London depot between 1888 and 1914 amounted to over £230,000, most of which found its way into the pockets of the Irish workers, the management being very economical'.[115] At the same time, owing to the success of the Irish village in Chicago, the 'profits had flowed back into poor homes all over Ireland; a market for their industries had been established in America'.[116] Through her support of Home Rule, of Irish home industries, and later, of various health initiatives, Lady Aberdeen made much of her role as vicereine of Ireland. Her modern modes of display, which were specifically designed to publicize her amalgamation of concerns – demonstrated in this chapter in three specific events that occurred in 1886, 1893 and 1909 – and most emphatically advertised in the Throne Room at Dublin Castle, were audacious, courageous, and contemporary. Moreover, her 1909 *Déanta in Éirinn* dress, featuring a trademark developed by

ISHBEL ABERDEEN & TEMAIR

an association that was not of her making, but with which she was clearly aligned, indicates something of the extent of her cultural connections and interests. Furthermore, she was at least partially responsible for an economic recovery within the Irish home industries, the narrative of which has been entirely lost to the cause of Irish nationalism, which in turn raises the prospect of further investigation. Accordingly, Lady Aberdeen's use of the Throne Room, symbolic or otherwise, is a narrative that deserves to be present amid the many other (her)stories that have come to light during the Centenary of Commemoration now taking place in Ireland (Fig. 08.09).

The author would like to acknowledge and thank Alexander Gordon, 7th Marquess of Aberdeen and Temair, for permitting access to the Gordon Family Archive, and also to thank Alex Ward (National Museum of Ireland); Barbara Bonini (National Library of Ireland); Myles Campbell and William Derham (Office of Public Works) and Jennifer Melville (National Trust for Scotland).

Fig. 08.09.
Silhouette of Ishbel, Marchioness of Aberdeen and Temair, 1915.
© Gordon Family Archive, Haddo House. Courtesy of Alexander, 7th Marquess of Aberdeen and Temair.

Endnotes

1   J. Helland, *British and Irish Home Arts and Industries 1880–1914: Marketing Craft, Making Fashion* (Dublin: Irish Academic Press, 2007), p. 10.

2   P. Pearson, *The Heart of Dublin: Resurgence of an Historic City* (Dublin: The O'Brien Press Ltd, 2000), p. 101.

3   See, for example, *Freeman's Journal*, 10 March 1826; *Freeman's Journal*, 20 February 1830; *Freeman's Journal*, 9 August 1849; *Freeman's Journal*, 29 January 1874 – articles that describe the reigning vicereine's dresses made with Irish poplin, lace, and sometimes embroidery, worn to drawing rooms and balls

at Dublin Castle.

4   *Freeman's Journal*, 9 August 1849.

5   The Marquis & Marchioness of Aberdeen & Temair, *More Cracks with 'We Twa'* (London: Methuen & Co. Ltd, 1929), p. 233.

6   J. Helland, 'Ishbel Aberdeen's "Irish" Dresses: Embroidery, display and meaning, 1886-1909', *Journal of Design History*, 26, 2 (October 2012), p. 156.

7   Ibid., p. 157. The Cowpers were in Dublin Castle between May 1880 and March 1882.

8   L. Cluckie, *The Rise and Fall of Art Needlework: Its Socio-economic and Cultural Aspects* (Bury St Edmunds: Arena Books, 2008), p. 106. The RSAN archives for the late nineteenth century are no longer extant.

9   The Countess of Mayo, 'Royal Irish School of Art Needlework' in Department of Agriculture and Technical Instruction, *Ireland: Industrial and Agricultural* (Dublin, Cork, Belfast: Browne & Nolan Limited, 1902), p. 440.

10 *Freeman's Journal*, 10 March 1826.

11 *Freeman's Journal*, 20 February 1830.

12 See, for example, Helland, 'Ishbel Aberdeen's "Irish" Dresses', p. 156.

13 *Belfast Newsletter*, 18 March 1886.

14 See Helland, 'Ishbel Aberdeen's "Irish" Dresses', p. 160.

15 M. Pentland, *A Bonnie Fechter: The Life of Ishbel Marjoribanks, Marchioness of Aberdeen & Temair, G.B.E., LL.D., J.P., 1857 to 1939* (London: B.T. Batsford Ltd, 1952), p. 76.

16 Lord and Lady Aberdeen, *'We Twa': Reminiscences of Lord and Lady Aberdeen* (London: W. Collins Sons & Co. Ltd), vol. 2, p. 197.

17 See Pentland, *A Bonnie Fechter*, p. 1.

18 Ibid., p. 14.

19 See Pentland, *A Bonnie Fechter*, p. 39. For remarks about the couple working together in 'the East End of London', see P. Maume, 'Lady Microbe and the Kailyard Viceroy: The

Aberdeen viceroyalty, welfare monarchy, and the politics of philanthropy' in P. Gray and O. Purdue (eds), *The Irish Lord Lieutenancy c. 1541–1922* (Dublin: University College Dublin Press, 2012), p. 201.

20 Lord and Lady Aberdeen, *'We Twa': Reminiscences of Lord and Lady Aberdeen* (London: W. Collins Sons & Co. Ltd), vol. 1, p. 163.

21 See Cluckie, *The Rise and Fall of Art Needlework*, pp. 59–60.

22 See Maume, 'Lady Microbe', p. 202.

23 Ibid.

24 See Lord & Lady Aberdeen, *'We Twa'*, vol. 1, p. 197.

25 See Maume, 'Lady Microbe', p. 201.

26 See Pentland, *A Bonnie Fechter*, p. 81.

27 Informal discussion between Alexander 7th Marquess of Aberdeen and Temair and the author, 9 February 2017.

28 See Aberdeen & Temair, *More Cracks*, pp. 226–7. They wrote that at the same time, and in answer to the general supposition that there were no materials of high enough quality in Ireland, they held an 'exhibition of such materials in the tennis court at the Viceregal Lodge, where manufacturers were invited to display their goods, and which was attended not only by intending guests, but by milliners and tailors and dressmakers, who were surprised at the selection available'.

29 'The Viceregal Garden Party: How to dress in Irish materials', May 1886, Gordon Family Archive, Haddo Estate, 22/4/27.

30 Ibid.

31 *Freeman's Journal*, 26 December 1839.

32 See Helland, 'Ishbel Aberdeen's "Irish" Dresses', p. 159. That the dress was made by Mrs Sims is referred to in 'The Viceregal Garden Party: How to dress in Irish materials', May 1886, Gordon Family Archive, Haddo Estate, 22/4/27.

33 See 'The Viceregal Garden Party: How to dress in Irish materials', May 1886, Gordon Family Archive, Haddo Estate, 22/4/27.

34 See Helland, 'Ishbel Aberdeen's "Irish" Dresses', p. 159. Helland quotes from *Lady's Pictorial*, 20 May 1886, p. 497, in which the author wrote that the dress was 'copied exactly' from the painting in the National Gallery of Ireland.

35 See Pentland, *A Bonnie Fechter*, plate between pp. 50–1.

36 See Maume, 'Lady Microbe', p. 199.

37 See Lord & Lady Aberdeen, '*We Twa*', vol. 1, p. 223.

38 Ibid., pp. 263–4.

39 Illuminated address from the Lord Mayor of Dublin to Lord Aberdeen on the occasion of leaving office in Dublin Castle, undated [1886], Gordon Family Archive, Haddo Estate, C2/16.

40 See Helland, 'Ishbel Aberdeen's "Irish" Dresses', p. 155.

41 Lady B. Balfour, 'Dalkey Co-Operative Society', in Department of Agriculture and Technical Instruction, *Ireland: Industrial and Agricultural* (Dublin, Cork, Belfast: Browne & Nolan Limited, 1902), p. 442.

42 The author acknowledges that there were complications and nuances pertaining to Chicago, especially in view of the role of Mrs Ernest Hart, who first had the idea of an 'Irish village'. These issues are dealt with in detail in É. O'Connor, *Art, Ireland, and Irish America 1893–1939: Culture, Connections, and Controversies* (Dublin: Irish Academic Press, forthcoming 2018).

43 See Lord & Lady Aberdeen, '*We Twa*', vol. 1, p. 300.

44 Ibid., p. 308.

45 See Lord & Lady Aberdeen, '*We Twa*', vol. 1, p. 315.

46 Ibid., pp. 315–16.

47 See Lord & Lady Aberdeen, '*We Twa*', vol. 1, p. 316.

48 See Pentland, *A Bonnie Fechter*, p. 98.

49 *Irish Times*, 14 April 1893.

50 Ibid.

51 *Chicago Record*, 7 June 1893, newspaper cutting, the Gordon Family Archive, Haddo Estate, file number 22/2/10.

52 *Public Ledger*, 30 May 1893, newspaper cutting, the Gordon Family Archive, Haddo Estate, file number 22/2/10.

53 Ibid.

54 *World*, 30 May 1893, newspaper cutting, the Gordon Family Archives, Haddo Estate, file number 22/2/10.

55 *World's Columbian Exposition, 1893, Official Catalogue* (Chicago: W.B. Conkey Company, 1893), part 10, p. 132.

56 See Lord & Lady Aberdeen, '*We Twa*', vol. 1, p. 333.

57 See Aberdeen & Temair, *More Cracks*, p. 233.

58 Ibid., p. 231.

59 *Irish Times*, 9 June 1894, newspaper cutting, the Gordon Family Archive, Haddo Estate, file number 22/2/10.

60 *Belfast Newsletter*, 14 August 1893, newspaper cutting, the Gordon Family Archive, Haddo Estate, file number 22/2/10. See also *Daylight*, 12 August 1893, newspaper cutting, the Gordon Family Archive, Haddo Estate, file number 22/2/10, which describes R.R. Kane as the Grand Master of the Orange Order in Belfast.

61 *Belfast Newsletter*, 14 August 1893, newspaper cutting, the Gordon Family Archive, Haddo Estate, file number 22/2/10.

62 Ibid.

63 See Aberdeen & Temair, *More Cracks*, pp. 233–4.

64 See Cluckie, *The Rise and Fall of Art Needlework*, p. 49.

65 Ibid.

66 See Cluckie, *The Rise and Fall of Art Needlework*, p. 49.

67 See Aberdeen & Temair, *More Cracks*, p. 234.

68 Ibid. Rev. Father T. Finlay, Mr R.A. Atkins of Cork, and Mr Brennan, the Master of the School of Art at Cork and 'an expert in Irish lace and design' undertook the management of the Irish Lace Depot while the Aberdeens were in Canada.

69 *Dublin Daily Express*, 18 December 1893, newspaper cutting, the Gordon Family Archive, Haddo Estate, file number 22/2/10.

70 See Aberdeen & Temair, *More Cracks*, p. 235. Lady Aberdeen writes that the Naas carpet industry had a promising start and did well for a few years, but had to close down during the First World War because of the difficulty in obtaining raw materials.

71 See Pentland, *A Bonnie Fechter*, pp. 94–5.

72 Ibid., p. 95.

73 See Pentland, *A Bonnie Fechter*, p. 95.

74 See Aberdeen & Temair, *More Cracks*, p. 230.

75 See Lord & Lady Aberdeen, '*We Twa*', vol. 2, pp. 175–6.

76 Ibid., p. 177.

77 *Irish Times*, 6 March 1907.

78 Ibid.

79 See, for example, P. Maume, 'Lady Microbe', pp. 199–214.

80 *Irish Examiner*, 12 March 1909.

81 *Evening Herald*, 13 March 1909.

82 *Irish Examiner*, 12 March 1909.

83 *Irish Independent*, 15 March 1909.

84 *Irish Independent*, 16 March 1909.

85 Ibid.

86 *Irish Independent*, 15 March 1909.

87 *Irish Independent*, 27 August 1909.

88 Ibid.

89 *Irish Independent*, 27 August 1909.

90 *Irish Independent*, 22 April 1909.

91 Ibid.

92 *Irish Independent*, 22 April 1909.

93 Ibid.

94 *Irish Independent*, 22 April 1909.

95 *Irish Independent*, 19 March 1912.

96 Ibid.

97 *Irish Independent*, 19 March 1912.

98 *Irish Times*, 26 April 1913.

99 *Irish Times*, 13 April 1913.

100 *Irish Times*, 3 May 1913.

101 See Lord & Lady Aberdeen, '*We Twa*', vol. 2, pp. 224–5.

102 Ibid., p. 226.

103 See Lord & Lady Aberdeen, '*We Twa*', vol. 2, p. 230.

104 Ibid., p. 231.

105 See Lord & Lady Aberdeen, '*We Twa*', vol. 2, p. 232.

106 Ibid., p. 234.

107 See Lord & Lady Aberdeen, '*We Twa*', vol. 2, p. 234.

108 Ibid., p. 236.

109 See Lord & Lady Aberdeen, '*We Twa*', vol. 2, p. 238.

110 M. Keane, *Ishbel: Lady Aberdeen in Ireland*, (Newtownards: Colourpoint Books, 1999), p. 219.

111 Ibid.

112 See Keane, *Ishbel*, p. 220.

113 Ibid.

114 See Aberdeen & Temair, *More Cracks*, p. 235.

115 Ibid., p. 230.

116 See Pentland, *A Bonnie Fechter*, p. 104.

THRONE ROOM, DUBLIN CASTLE.

Fig. 09.01.
The Throne Room, Dublin Castle, 1900–2, detail.
Private collection.

Nine

(Re)making Majesty

The Throne Room at Dublin Castle
1911–2011

William Derham

It could be said that the Throne Room at Dublin Castle, as it appeared in 1911, was a symmetrical construct, both figuratively and literally. Ceremonially it accommodated the similar court functions that those other throne rooms of the British Empire did, whether they were located as close as England or as far away as India. Architecturally it sat behind a symmetrical façade, situated at the centre of a loosely symmetrical floor plan and was itself symmetrically decorated, taking as its cue the main central axis of the room on which sat the throne, its canopy and the Irish Sword of State. One hundred years, later its position could be described as decidedly asymmetrical. A throne room in a republic, a presence chamber without a royal presence, a reminder of a long relationship between two countries that have 'experienced more than their fair share of heartache, turbulence and loss'.[1] Architecturally altered, its authoritative axis skewed, it has somehow managed to survive. This essay aims to chart that survival, describing the history of the room from the visit of King George V to Dublin Castle, in 1911, to that of his granddaughter Queen Elizabeth II, in 2011.

Many Happy Days in Ireland

A good description of the Throne Room, or the Presence Chamber, as it stood and was used by 1911, can be garnered from a surviving 1908 inventory of its contents; several images; and various written and printed accounts that survive from the first part of the twentieth century. The walls of the room were covered simply with painted paper on canvas, which persisted into the middle of the century. As per the inventory mentioned above, among the room's contents were: seven suits of figured crimson silk brocade window curtains, with carved and gilt wood cornices; two large mirrors in richly carved and gilt wood frames, surmounted with the royal arms; a throne in carved and gilt wood frame covered in ruby velvet; six gilt frame Austrian bentwood chairs; a crimson Wilton carpet, 40'0" x 38'9"; two oval and four circular paintings attributed to 'A. Kauffman'.[2] The inventory is silent on two features: the carved and gilt frames around the paintings, and the chandeliers. One can only guess that these were considered fixtures as opposed to furnishings and so were not a liability in terms of being moved or stolen and, as such, they were not being checked on a yearly basis.

A postcard image of the room, which was published in 1902, tallies with the inventory mentioned above and shows that the carved and gilt frames were still in situ, but that the lighting had been changed. Instead of the suite of five ornate chandeliers commissioned from Higginbotham, Thomas and Company in 1839 (see Fig. 04.02), the room appeared to be lit with electricity (Fig. 09.01). A central light fitting with twelve glass globes and a run of evenly distributed 'spotlights' along the top of the cornice seem to have taken the place of the more stately fittings. A pair

Fig. 09.02.
'Festivities at Dublin Castle: The Lord Lieutenant's Levee on Tuesday'.
Black & White, 8 February 1902.

of crystal chandeliers between the columns of the Throne Room are visible in a view of a viceregal levee held by George Cadogan, 5th Earl Cadogan (1840–1915), which was published along with the postcard image, on 8 February 1902 (Fig. 09.02). The exact point at which electricity arrived in the room is unclear. Certainly, by 1892 St Patrick's Hall was lit 'by electric lights placed along the cornice'.[3] In March 1897, the Hall was being 'splendidly illuminated by electric lights' mixed with 'rows of silver candelabra, with wax lights'.[4] The introduction of electric light, into St Patrick's Hall at least, occurred just twelve years after the first public electric light had appeared in Dublin, outside the office of *The Freeman's Journal*, on Prince's Street, in 1880.[5] As the first recorded appearance of electricity in the State Apartments was in 1892, and the Throne Room featured new electric lighting by 1902, the Higginbotham chandeliers must have been removed in the ten years between these dates. They appear to have been redistributed throughout the State Apartments, and one is visible among the wreckage of the burnt-out old Presence Chamber in 1941 (see Fig. 02.17).

The room as presented at this time compared well with other throne rooms within the British Empire, chiefly in London and Calcutta (now Kolkata). While

Fig. 09.03.
The Throne Room, Government House, Calcutta, 1922.
Library of Congress, Prints and Photographs Division, LC-B2-71-8 [P&P] LOT 7225.

not as large as those at Buckingham Palace, the official residence of the monarch, and Government House, the official home of the Viceroy of India, it was still a substantial space (see Fig. 04.03). Unlike those in London, including that at St James's, the official home of the English court, it was not lined with rich fabric and presented a more delicate and less overwrought picture.[6] However, like the Calcutta room, the clarity of the space was lost in the encroachment of less formal furnishings; in the Dublin room, these chiefly took the form of Austrian bentwood chairs, in Calcutta, the buttoned upholstery of Victoriana (Fig. 09.03).

The particulars of the Castle season, and of how the Throne Room at Dublin Castle was being used on the eve of Irish independence, are worth noting. The only known surviving photograph of the room in use during the season illustrates the standard arrangement of the viceroy and his household, in front of the canopy and throne, facing a so-called 'pen' opposite them, which was reserved for selected spectators (Fig. 09.04). It must not be forgotten that, in addition to the deputations, levees, presentations and drawing rooms, the room also offered a much more public platform for the projection of viceregal majesty in the form of its balcony, which was placed centrally on the façade of the south range of the Upper Castle Yard. The balcony communicated directly with the Throne Room through a pair of French doors, and was used to best effect for the Trooping of the Colour on St Patrick's Day. Typically, the viceregal couple would arrive into the Upper Castle Yard from the Viceregal Lodge, the viceroy

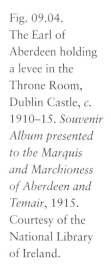

Fig. 09.04. The Earl of Aberdeen holding a levee in the Throne Room, Dublin Castle, *c.* 1910–15. *Souvenir Album presented to the Marquis and Marchioness of Aberdeen and Temair*, 1915. Courtesy of the National Library of Ireland.

would inspect the troops and shortly afterwards the couple would appear on the balcony accompanied by their guests and household staff, where it could be seen that 'One and all wore shamrocks'.[7] A rarer, but much more imposing use of the balcony can be seen during the proclamation of George V as King of Great Britain and Ireland in May 1910 (Fig. 09.05). Following the death of King Edward VII on 6 May 1910, letters patent were delivered to the Privy Council at Dublin Castle proclaiming the succession of King George V:

> The Proclamation proper in the Upper Castle Yard was accompanied by a very imposing display, somewhat similar but vastly more elaborate than the ceremony of trooping the colours ... After the meeting the Lord Lieutenant and the members of the Privy Council appeared on the balcony ... The Dublin Herald then commanded silence, and the Ulster King of Arms proclaimed his Majesty from the Courtyard of the Castle.[8]

The accession of King George V, and his coronation visit to Ireland the following year, provided the viceregal court at Dublin Castle with a worthy apotheosis. In preparation for the visit, 'an extensive scheme of redecoration and renovation'

Fig. 09.05. The proclamation of King George V at Dublin Castle, 1910. *Souvenir Album presented to the Marquis and Marchioness of Aberdeen and Temair*, 1915. Courtesy of the National Library of Ireland.

had been 'decided on in the State apartments of the Castle', overseen by Sir Aston Webb (1849–1930).[9] The recollection of Elizabeth Burke-Plunkett, Countess of Fingall (1866–1944) that 'there was only one bathroom in the whole of Dublin Castle ... until King George's visit in 1911', while fanciful, suggests a need for modernization and upgrading.[10] While no record of specific work to the Throne Room in advance of this visit has come to light, it has been suggested that the Irish Sword of State, around which the symbolism of the room was articulated, may have been re-covered in velvet in advance of the King's arrival.[11] The typical Castle season was postponed and 'No Levees or Drawing Rooms were held, in view of the Levee and Court to be held by their Majesties in person during the summer'.[12]

The decision of the King and Queen to reside at Dublin Castle during their stay, rather than at the Viceregal Lodge as previous royal visitors had done, served to reinforce the Castle's status as Ireland's royal palace. They arrived on Saturday, 8 July, left on Wednesday, 12 July, and in between carried out a packed programme of official events. Among these were the receiving of deputations, followed by a levee, in the Throne Room on the Monday, and the holding of a court on the Tuesday. These events largely followed the same pattern as those of their viceregal counterparts, albeit imbued with more weight in the presence of the sovereign rather than of his surrogate. There were 131 addresses presented to the King in the Throne Room from a quarter past ten in the morning.[13] These came from 'Corporations, local Councils, University bodies, ecclesiastical authorities, public institutions and societies of various kinds from all parts of the Kingdom', each represented by two delegates (with the exception of the corporations of Belfast and Cork, which had more, including mace-bearers and sword-bearer).[14] It was reported that:

> The function took place in the Throne Room at the Castle, and was invested with ceremonial of a very elaborate character ... the scene was a brilliant and an impressive one ... The address[es] on behalf of the citizens of Dublin and the National University of Ireland were read, and all the others were handed to the King by the first member of the deputation who bent the right knee and remained in this position until his Majesty presented a copy of the reply and afterwards extended his hand which the members of the deputation kissed. The second members also made similar obeissances.[15]

The presentations were followed immediately by a levee, which was very largely attended and lasted from eleven o'clock to half past twelve. Despite the large attendance and added ceremonial gravitas due to the presence of the King himself, the report of the scene in *The Irish Independent* captures both the pomp and the sense of pomposity that the occasion represented:

> The men who attended yesterday were young and old, and middle-aged, they were solemn, suave, serene, superb. Some were horrently bearded; others were never bearded. There were dignitaries of the Church and captains of industry. There were generals with explosive plumes and admirals with be-medalled breasts. There were honest plain people in Court dress who carried swords and looked very un-heroic. There were landlords who looked like butlers, and amazingly great men who looked amazingly ordinary. There were heralds, pursuivants, beefeaters, garter knights, gentlemen of the guard. They were all smothered with sartorial glory – so riotous and so gorgeous as to suggest an earthquake in a dye factory.[16]

On Tuesday evening, 11 July, the King and Queen held a 'Court' at the Castle, *The Freeman's Journal* reporting that they entered the 'Throne Room' at half past nine, accompanied by the Prince of Wales and Princess Mary.[17] However, according to *The Irish Times*, 'Their Majesties entered St Patrick's Hall at 9.30', which appears to have taken on the functions of the Throne Room for the event.[18] A drawing survives in the library of the Office of Public Works (OPW), dated 26 May 1911, showing St Patrick's Hall laid out for such an event (Fig. 09.06). The construction of a new supper room for the royal visit early in 1911, known since as George's Hall, to accommodate the large events attendant on such royal visits, had freed up St Patrick's Hall for uses other than dining. The large attendances at the events of the coronation tour in Dublin had also, to an extent, outgrown the confines of the Throne Room. We see St Patrick's Hall, with seating for 294 guests, taking on that function, the King and Queen being accommodated on a pair of smaller, secondary thrones that had been made during the reign of Queen Victoria.

The morning after the 'Court', before the royal couple departed Ireland, the 'King held an Investiture in the Throne Room of the Castle at half-past ten o'clock'.[19] Among those bestowed with honours were Sir George Holmes, 'Chairman of Public Works, Ireland', and Mr C.A. Stevenson, 'Commissioner

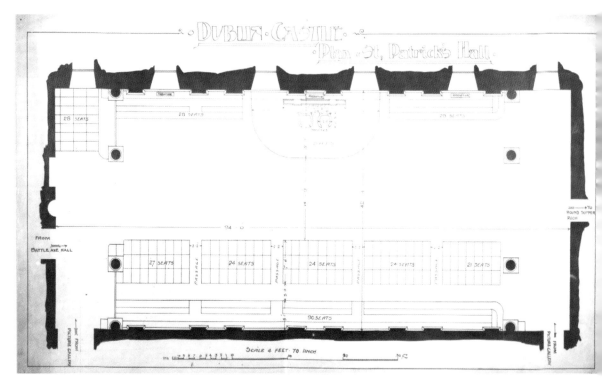

of Public Works'.[20] Evidently, the arrangements for the royal visit, which were overseen and carried out by the OPW, including the improvements made to the Castle, had pleased the King and Queen. Following their departure, the State Apartments, so recently imbued with the majesty and mystery of the royal presence, were opened to the public over the course of five days, the money raised from admission going to charity.[21]

It is recorded that the King had replied to the deputations he received in the Throne Room at the beginning of his visit by stating that: 'During past years I have spent many happy days in Ireland, and I hope to enjoy many more in the years that lie before us'.[22] It was not to be. The visit of King George V and Queen Mary marked the beginning of the end of the viceregal court at Dublin Castle. In an ominous way, the seasons of the following three years were disrupted by tragedy. The death of the 1st Duke of Fife (husband of the Princess Royal, sister of George V) in January 1912 resulted in 'five weeks court mourning' and the announcement that part of the season would be 'postponed to dates after Easter'.[23] In 1913, Easter itself disrupted the usual calendar of events, as did the death of the King of Greece and the accompanying period of court mourning.[24] In 1914, political tensions had led to a boycotting of the viceregal court and its social functions by many who held Unionist views.[25] In June of that year the Austro-Hungarian Archduke, Franz Ferdinand, was shot in Sarajevo. Political tensions across Europe steadily increased. On 4 August 1914, Britain declared war on Germany. On 7 August, the British Expeditionary Force arrived in France and on 12 August, Britain declared war on Austria-Hungary.

Broken-Bone Room

As Europe lurched headlong into war with itself, Ishbel Hamilton-Gordon, Countess of Aberdeen, later Marchioness of Aberdeen and Temair (1857–1939), wife of the viceroy, busied herself in Dublin. She established a Dublin branch of the British Red Cross Society, into which she threw almost all of her considerable energy. Having learned from the military that hospital accommodation would be the most useful assistance the Society could provide, she shared the information with her husband, the viceroy, John Campbell Hamilton-Gordon, 7th Earl of Aberdeen, later 1st Marquess of Aberdeen and Temair (1847–1934). In response, 'He at once telegraphed to the King, who was in France, asking his permission to use and equip the State apartments at Dublin Castle as a Red Cross Hospital. This telegram was dispatched … about 7p.m. and the reply came back by 9 p.m. cordially approving of the proposal, and promising a donation of £100'.[26] The proposal was also welcomed by the press, who described it as 'a purpose more humane and useful than it [Dublin Castle] has ever known in its long grim history'.[27] On 30 November 1914, a large public meeting was held in the Mansion House, Dublin 'for the purpose of promoting the collection of funds'.[28] It was hoped that the hospital might provide 480 beds, at an estimated cost of £10 to equip each bed, meaning that '£5,000 (roughly) would be the total sum required'.[29] Thus, fundraising began in earnest.

The proposed conversion of the State Apartments, even with the blessing of the King, did not come to fruition easily. The OPW appears to have been considerably put out, and demanded that the Red Cross Society insure the State Apartments for £100,000, plus £5,000 for 'the furniture left … in the building'.[30] This almost scuppered the whole idea. Lord Aberdeen departed Dublin without forcing the issue, leaving his successor to reach the inevitable conclusion that the OPW would have to back down, as the hospital was now a necessity.[31] A letter from Sir Matthew Nathan (1862–1939), Under-Secretary for Ireland, described the likely outcome of pressuring the Red Cross Society too much: 'either the hospital which is much needed ... will have to be closed or the full cost of maintaining it will fall on the Exchequer'.[32] After much back and forth, an agreement was eventually reached whereby the OPW would be allowed to keep 'the baths, lavatory basins, water closets and piping' that had been installed by the Red Cross Committee in preparing the Castle, and demands for insurance were dropped.[33] Inspectors from the War Office came to Dublin, and the scheme for conversion was approved. After much battling, fundraising and preparation, the Dublin Castle Red Cross Hospital was formally opened on 27 January 1915.[34]

No detailed plan of the layout of the hospital has yet emerged, but from newspaper accounts and other sources it is possible to infer that it occupied the whole of the south range of the Upper Castle Yard, over all three floors, as well as extending into the whole of the west and part of the north-west ranges. The Drawing Room, Ante-Drawing Room (old Presence Chamber), Throne Room, Portrait Gallery and George's Hall became hospital wards. The viceregal quarters overlooking the garden were also fitted out as such, and were reserved for officers. St Patrick's Hall 'had not been acquired as part of the hospital, but it would be used during the time of the hospital as a recreation hall', as it, 'was never better used than when it provided for the solace and recreation of ... brave wounded soldiers'. [35] It was here that many concerts and entertainments were held – both to entertain the patients and also to raise much-needed funds. These fundraising concerts took place quite regularly, and showcased a range of talent. At one, which took the form of a variety performance, the prologue to the proceedings was authored by the Irish writer Oliver St John Gogarty (1878–1957). In it, he pointedly made reference to that room which, above all others, symbolized the viceregal court, writing:

> And that is why we find the Throne Room,
> Transformed into a broken-bone room,
> But, judged by retrospective tests,
> 'Twas never filled by worthier guests.[36]

The prominence of the Throne Room as a leitmotif for the viceregal court may have been reinforced in the mind of Gogarty by the Aberdeens themselves. A scheme of sponsoring beds had been instigated. In exchange for the £10 needed to equip a bed, a small plaque would be erected above it in recognition of the

Fig. 09.07.
The Throne Room,
Dublin Castle, as
a hospital ward,
1915. *Weekly Irish
Times*, 30 January
1915. Courtesy
of the National
Library of Ireland.

benefactor. Lord and Lady Aberdeen had set an example by sponsoring a bed themselves – the one they chose being that which sat beneath the canopy in the Throne Room (Fig. 09.07). Lady Aberdeen herself remarked:

> There was ... much competition for the bed under the canopy over the Throne, which we endowed especially in remembrance of our dear and gallant Captain Hope, the first of our staff to fall in the war.[37]

Despite the changed circumstances of the State Apartments, the Throne Room's position at the top of the spatial hierarchy within the Castle was recognized by this small mark of distinction (see Fig. 08.08). The throne itself was likely moved into storage in the area below George's Hall, with most of the Castle's remaining furnishings.[38]

One of the most interesting periods in the history of the Red Cross Hospital at Dublin Castle came just over a year after it was officially inaugurated. The events of Easter Week, 1916, have also left us with one of the best descriptions of the layout and workings of the hospital, by a Voluntary Aid Detachment (VAD) nurse, as well as giving us an atypical view of the Rising itself, witnessed from within the Castle.[39] The atmosphere was one of unrest. After dinner in the afternoon of Monday, 24 April, all the windows of the Picture Gallery and Throne Room were thronged with spectators. The windows of the State Apartments provided the ideal vantage point for the patients to amuse themselves by watching these events unfold, and spotting snipers on the nearby rooftops. By mid-afternoon, a 'Tommy' had joined the throng in the Throne Room. Shortly afterwards, 'They soon began firing through the window – probably at the sniper … seen earlier in the afternoon'.[40] It eventually occurred to the soldiers that the rebel snipers would likely begin to return their fire and 'they turned everyone out of the ward, and locked the doors'.[41] The firing continued for the whole afternoon. By evening time, the beds from the Throne Room and other wards facing onto the Upper Castle Yard had been moved to the State Corridor, the landing of the staircase and St Patrick's Hall to shield them from rebel fire. By the end of the first day, 'City Hall had been stormed and taken; but the "Evening Mail" office, opposite the Front Gate [directly in sight of the Throne Room], was still in the hands of the Rebels'.[42] The sound of the fighting had re-awoken in many of the patients their memories of the war in Europe: 'their faces were white, with horror and repulsion … They saw again their friends being killed, and all the horrors they had tried to obliterate from their minds'.[43]

On the evening of the following day, the hospital occupants 'watched the men in the Yard bombing the office of the "Evening Mail". The noise was terrific, but eventually the building was successfully stormed'.[44] By Wednesday, the Throne Room had been re-occupied as a ward. Since the *Evening Mail* offices had been retaken, the room 'was in no greater danger than any other ward, so the beds had been moved back in'.[45] There were now 'eight or nine' patients recuperating, who had arrived to the hospital the previous day.[46] They included several soldiers from different regiments and a 'Sinn Feiner' who reminded the VAD nurse of a 'picture-house villain'.[47] Whether the 'Sinn Feiner' in question occupied Lady Aberdeen's coveted spot beneath the throne canopy is not recorded. Among the patients brought into the Throne Room ward on Thursday were two more 'Sinn Feiners'.

The VAD nurse clearly remembered the 'fifteen or sixteen respectable-looking men, brought from the Four Courts the Tuesday morning after the Surrender' and one wonders if any of them were admitted to the Throne Room ward.[48] Those who had occupied the Four Courts had fashioned a pair of makeshift thrones, complete with 'canopy' from the furniture within. It was described by *The Illustrated War News* as the 'The "Throne Room" of the "Irish Republic"' (Fig. 09.08).[49] Presumably, the arrangement had been contrived in mockery of the King and his viceroy, against whom they were rebelling. Even with its transformation over a year previously, the Throne Room seems still to have been a prominent representation of majesty to those fighting against it – and, one

Fig. 09.08. The 'Throne Room' of the Irish Republic, the Four Courts, Dublin, 1916. *The Illustrated War News*, 10 May 1916. Courtesy of Dr Sylvie Kleinman.

assumes, to those fighting in support of it. On Saturday, 29 April, the rebels surrendered. From the window, presumably of the Throne Room where she was on duty, the VAD nurse observed James Connolly (1868–1916) 'lying on the stretcher, his hands crossed, his head hidden from view by the archway'.[50] He was placed in 'a small ward in the Officers' Quarters, where he could be carefully guarded'.[51] By this time:

> The Hospital itself presented an unusual appearance. Sentries, with fixed bayonets, sat or stood at the top and bottom of every staircase, and outside every ward in which was a Sinn Feiner … Those who were not on duty sat round the fire at the top of the main staircase, and some turned the "baths," used in peace times for palms and plants, into beds. There are two of these tanks, and about six men fitted into each, three at either end, their feet overlapping in the middle.[52]

On Wednesday, 2 May, our VAD nurse was finally able to leave the Castle Hospital in safety and it soon returned to the 'normality' it had known before April 1916. It continued to provide a much-needed service at the heart of the second city of the Empire, up until it was handed back to the OPW on 19 June 1919.[53] The OPW got to keep the bathroom fittings it had agreed upon with the

Red Cross Society. As things worked out they also got a 'Roasting Oven and Vegetable Steamer' for £30.[54] However successful the tenure of the Red Cross Hospital, and however happy the OPW, the events of Easter Week, brief though they had been in the life of the Castle, boded ill for its future as a viceregal palace. After the events of 1916, Ireland sank back into an uneasy peace, while in the background the prospect of more violent agitation simmered.

Tudor's Typists

The return of the State Apartments to the government, and to the care of the OPW, did not see a return to their former viceregal circumstances. Ireland was sliding into a state of war. On the same day that the First Dáil (Irish Parliament) met, on 21 January 1919, two members of the Royal Irish Constabulary (RIC) were shot dead. This unofficially marked the start of the War of Independence between Ireland and Britain. The opening months saw the Irish Republican Army (IRA), led by Michael Collins (1890–1922), primarily involve themselves in capturing weapons and freeing prisoners. By September, however, the government had declared both the Dáil and Sinn Féin (the political party associated with the IRA) to be illegal, following which violence began to escalate. As the situation intensified, those parts of Dublin Castle that had in former times been reserved for the retainers of the viceregal court (including the Comptroller, the State Steward, the Master of the Horse), and indeed the court itself (the State Apartments), were requisitioned.

A good description of the Castle at this time, locked down and under siege, was penned by the civil servant G.C. Duggan, writing anonymously as 'Periscope'. He describes how:

> Owing to the murders of November [1919] … those more closely connected with the defence of the Dublin District were quartered in the Castle. Increased numbers of English civil servants had taken up their quarters there, and the rapidly-growing Intelligence Staff of the Chief of Police also sought cover. The premises were indeed becoming almost uncomfortably crowded …[55]

The exact date of the occupation of the Throne Room is not known. It was likely late 1919 or early 1920, at the same time as other buildings and spaces in the Castle were being taken over.[56] On 27 April 1921 Edmund Bernard FitzAlan-Howard, 1st Viscount FitzAlan of Derwent (1855–1947) was appointed Viceroy of Ireland.

He was sworn into office at Dublin Castle on 2 May. 'The ceremony, though following upon historic precedent in detail, was of a semi-private nature'.[57] The newspapers did report that he was escorted to the Presence Chamber, or Throne Room, where he met the Lord Justices 'sitting covered as Chief Governors'.[58] He presented them with his letters patent and royal warrant of appointment, following which 'a procession was made from the Presence Chamber to the Council Chamber', where the rest of the ceremony was conducted.[59] Whether the Throne Room was at this point vacant, whether it had simply been cleared of its new furnishings for the day, or whether the ceremony was conducted around them is not known. As with the swearing-in of the previous two viceroys, Ivor Churchill Guest, 2nd Baron Wimborne, later 1st Viscount Wimborne (1873–1939) in 1915, and John Denton Pinkstone French, 1st Viscount French of Ypres and High Lake, later 1st Earl of Ypres (1852–1925) in 1918, the exact logistics of using the room for ceremony, while it was already in use for something else, remain a mystery at present. It is possible that it was not used at all, but that the same formula of ceremony was issued to the press by the office of Ulster King of Arms to keep up appearances.

The requisitioned Throne Room appears to have been occupied by a 'normal staff' of twenty-two ladies, whose work meant that they 'must necessarily sit near the windows'.[60] These were likely the ladies known as 'Tudor's typists'.[61] Henry Hugh Tudor (1871–1965) had been promoted to Lieutenant General and simultaneously appointed 'Police Advisor' to Dublin Castle in May 1920, thereafter assuming the title 'Chief of Police'. As 'Periscope' described, the measure of the importance of a government department was not the number of charwomen it had, but the number of 'typists and women clerks' and that by that test General Tudor's office assumed 'its rightful place'.[62] These ladies were recruited from England; Irish typists being considered 'suspect'.[63] A 'spice of adventure' seems to have been an inducement, though the 'pressure of economy' was probably the main factor in their willingness to travel to war-torn Ireland for work.[64] The authorities were probably right to consider Irish typists to be 'suspect'. Michael Collins had several typists feeding him information from within the Castle, including Elizabeth 'Lily' Mernin (1886–1957), and it is possible that, from what had once been the symbolic heart of British rule in Ireland, information that would prove vital to its undoing was leaking its way out, underneath the watchful eyes of the lion and unicorn perched on top of the throne canopy.

Tudor's typists 'became all the rage, and the sight of large numbers … trooping to the balcony when anything novel appeared in the Castle Yard, lent a new flavour of romance to the scene'.[65] They presented an exotic sight, in 'summery attire, more suited perhaps for tea at the Shelbourne or the Bonne Bouche than for office routine'.[66] These ladies were witness to the varied comings and goings in the Upper Castle Yard, from their perch on the room's balcony, including the occasional 'score of Sinn Fein prisoners' exercising there before being moved to an internment camp; a different sight indeed from the Trooping of the Colour, which was once witnessed from the same spot every St Patrick's Day.[67]

Despite the claim that administrative importance was measured in typists, it appears that they were expected to make do with their makeshift workplace and meagre rations, just like everybody else. The grates of the Throne Room, either side of the throne, had 'been bricked up to limit the consumption of coal' to the ration allowed 'per grate per day'.[68] Under these circumstances, the Throne Room proved itself particularly unsuitable as an office space. By 18 November 1921, one of the ladies was 'suffering from a severe attack of Jaundice' the cause of which was 'due to her having worked in too cold a room'.[69] By the beginning of December, eight of the staff were 'absent on sick leave', which the Medical Officer attributed 'to these adverse conditions'.[70] It was decided to remedy this chilly environment with a new heating system, in the form of two '8 double loop gas radiators fixed near the windows, at a cost of £30' or 'four steam radiators … at a cost of about £70', but just before either system was installed events took a turn.[71] 'In view of recent political developments', it was noted, it was 'unnecessary to proceed with arrangements for additional heating of … the Throne Room'.[72]

On 6 December 1921, the Anglo-Irish Treaty was signed in London between Ireland and Britain, and on 16 January 1922, Dublin Castle was handed over to the forces of the Provisional Government of Ireland, led by Michael Collins. The transition period that followed, overseen by this new government, would result in the establishment of the Irish Free State on 6 December 1922. By August 1922 it had been noted that in the Castle's

> … all but deserted rooms the dust is beginning to gather; the silence becomes oppressive. One feels that in spite of all the curses that were heaped upon it by a nation, in spite of all the wrongs that it did, the evils that it condoned, here was something which lived, and now the life has gone from it.[73]

While this was true of the Castle as a whole, it was particularly so of the State Apartments. Of those apartments, the Throne Room was the most obviously redundant under the new political order. The attitude of the old guard who remained at the Castle, to its change of circumstances, was captured by Sir Nevill Wilkinson (1869–1940), Ulster King of Arms:

> A brass band in dull green uniforms, under the bâton of a Prussian bandmaster, plays the rebel tune known as the 'Soldiers' Song,' while the tricolour emblem of Sinn Fein droops dejectedly in the drizzle over the old Throne Room.[74]

The King's Bench

As the new Irish state began to find its feet in 1922, circumstances dictated that it was only a matter of time until attention again turned to the 'all but deserted rooms' of Dublin Castle. The mechanics of government were of pressing concern. Much had been lost in the preceding years: the General Post Office had been all but destroyed in 1916; the Custom House had been gutted by fire following its brief capture by the IRA in 1921. The architectural infrastructure of government was much diminished and Dublin Castle lay unoccupied. By 23 May 1922, the Provisional Government, chaired by Michael Collins, was requesting 'a detailed report on the accommodation available for office purposes in Dublin Castle'.[75] In the report that the OPW produced, it was suggested that:

> If questions of sentiment can be left out of consideration, there is little doubt that the most economical and satisfactory use for the Castle is as a Parliament House and for the offices of the Cabinet and Finance Ministry. It is eminently adapted for these purposes both by its situation and construction.[76]

Shortly after, in a letter to Sir Philip Hanson (1871–1955), Chairman of the OPW, dated 16 June 1922, it was observed that:

> Mr Collins is taking a personal interest in the disposition of the accommodation available in the Castle, and the recent Office of Works' report to the Secretary to the Provisional Government is being brought up for his personal decision. He has, however, told O'Brien that under no circumstances whatever is any Department to be placed into the Castle until he has given his decision and O'Brien wishes me to communicate this to you.[77]

It is not surprising that Michael Collins might have had strong feelings about the Castle. On the day that he had received custody of it from the last viceroy, 16 January, he wrote to Kitty Kiernan: 'I am as happy a man as there is in Ireland today … Have just taken over Dublin Castle'.[78] The building can be seen to have represented everything he had fought against and, its surrender, his greatest achievement.

The suggestion of accommodating a new parliament at the Castle does not appear to have been dismissed out of hand. However, on 27 June 1922 the forces of the Provisional Government opened fire on the Four Courts, the seat of the judiciary in Ireland, which had been occupied by forces opposed to the Treaty signed with Britain in December of 1921. The building was reduced to rubble and immediately the question of a new home for the courts arose. As early as mid-July, *The Irish Times* was reporting that 'Opinion has now become centred on the Viceregal apartments in Dublin Castle as the most suitable place available'.[79] By 4 September, the Provisional Government had reached a decision to that effect.[80]

The layout of the courts within the Castle complex seems to have been decided upon principally by Hugh Kennedy (1879–1936), 'Law Officer' to the Provisional Government at the time; Sir Philip Hanson, Chairman of the OPW; and Thomas Francis Molony, later 1st Baronet of the City of Dublin (1865–1949), Lord Chief Justice of Ireland. A report prepared by an OPW architect, Mr Allberry, which was 'by no means an arbitrary allocation', suggested the placing of 'Court No. 4' in the 'Presence Chamber'.[81] Numbers had replaced the traditional court names. The Lord Chief Justice visited the site and submitted his views on 23 October. He observed that 'The Presence Chamber will make a distinguished King's Bench I. and the portion of the State Drawing room adjoining … will do for a King's Bench 2'.[82] One imagines that the Lord Chief Justice had a sense of humour. Work on the conversion proceeded with haste. On 2 February 1923, another OPW Architect, H.G. Leask (1882–1964), reported to the chairman:

> As directed I have taken down on 31st inst [31 January] the two carved + gilt coats of arms, the lion + unicorn + crown from canopy in the Throne Room + for safe keeping – as we have no proper storage for such fragile things – I conveyed them to the Office of Arms + placed them in Mr Sadlier's custody. I understand that the coats are, in any case, the property of that office.[83]

The courts took up residence at Dublin Castle in time for the Easter Sittings, on Wednesday, 11 April 1923.[84] It was noted that 'a good deal of interest in the occasion was taken by the public'.[85] In an effort to mitigate the confusion that would likely be attendant on those navigating the new premises for the first time, *The Freeman's Journal* published a plan of the new courts the day before.[86] On Saturday, 21 April 1923, *The Irish Law Times and Solicitors' Journal* reported that 'The first jury case was held in the Courts at Dublin Castle on Tuesday'.[87] Mr Justice Samuels, 'summing up evidence to the jury, recalled the fact that this was the first jury trial that had taken place in the Castle for the last 270 years, or, perhaps, a little more, so that they were making history'.[88] The courts had once been held in the medieval Great Hall of the Castle before moving to a dedicated home next to Christ Church Cathedral and eventually to their purpose-built home on Inns Quay (see Fig. 01.01).

The Throne Room, Court No. 4, had undergone a less invasive transformation than one might imagine. *The Irish Law Times and Solicitors' Journal* reported that:

> The internal arrangements of the Courts have been constructed on simple lines. The Judge's Bench, though cut off from the main body of the court, is, unlike the arrangement in the Four Courts, only raised slightly above the general level. In front of the bench is the desk for the Registrar and other officials. In front of this is the accommodation for the members of the inner Bar and the Press, and next are the places for the Junior Bar.[89]

This arrangement of Court No. 4 in the Throne Room is illustrated in a surviving plan in the OPW Library (Fig. 09.09), as well as by a photograph that appeared in the press at the time (Fig. 09.10). From these it can be gathered that in addition to the royal symbols on the throne canopy, including the embroidered royal arms, the throne itself had been removed. Apart from this, the room seems only to have had an array of benches, desks and other temporary spatial partitions inserted, leaving the architecture and decoration of the space largely unaltered and 'attractive and artistic in appearance'.[90]

Human drama replaced viceregal ceremony, and the courts continued at Dublin Castle until early 1931. By this time, Hugh Kennedy had become Chief Justice, and he was made aware in late May 1931 of the proposed return to the Four Courts on Inns Quay.[91] They were officially re-opened on 12 October

Fig. 09.09.
Plan of the State
Apartments,
Dublin Castle,
as courtrooms
of the Irish Free
State, detail of the
Throne Room,
c. 1923.
Courtesy of the
Office of Public
Works Library.

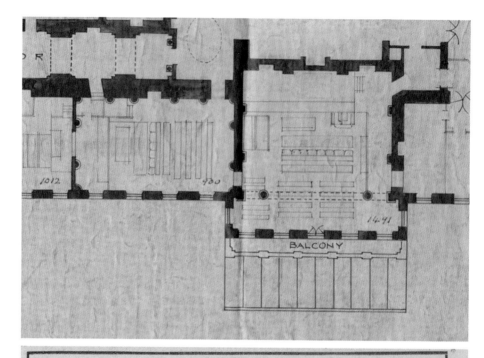

Fig. 09.10.
Court No. 4, the
Throne Room,
Dublin Castle,
1923. *The
Freeman's Journal,*
5 April 1923.

THRONE ROOM'S NEW USE

1931. Shortly before, *The Irish Law Times and Solicitors' Journal* reported 'that the portion of the Castle occupied for the last seven or eight years and now being vacated will be utilised next year for the accommodation of visitors for the Eucharistic Congress'.[92] The State Apartments were to be re-appropriated and re-invigorated to bolster the majesty and dignity of the young Irish state, with the driving force being the most unlikely of persons.

A New 'Court'

On 9 March 1932, the Fianna Fáil party of Éamon de Valera (1882–1975) came to power. The question of the State Apartments came to the fore almost immediately, as it was intended that they be pressed into use for part of the forthcoming Eucharistic Congress in June. It has been stated that de Valera was 'obsessed with ridding the Irish Free State of any sign of monarchical authority'.[93] However, his actions once he assumed a position of direct political control indicate a more nuanced attitude to such things. It has also been noted that 'Between 1932 and 1936, the provisions of the 1922 Treaty, in so far as they allowed the Crown a role in the government of the Irish Free State, were systemically abolished'.[94] Yet de Valera himself stopped short of breaking all ties with the Crown. He recognized that to do so would completely jeopardize any chance of rapprochement with Northern Ireland. Although the *role* of the monarch was removed from the constitution, the *presence* of the monarch was kept – however tenuously and however slightly – as a possible card to play in any future negotiations with the Unionist-controlled north of the island.

The Eucharistic Congress went ahead as planned, and a state reception was held in the State Apartments at Dublin Castle. Guests arrived into St Patrick's Hall, where they were greeted and then directed into the other state rooms, including the Throne Room, where screens had been erected for the assembled company to watch the formalities unfold. As the focus of the reception, St Patrick's Hall was intended to look its best and, to that end, 'de Valera asked Wilkinson to re-hang the banners of the Knights [of St Patrick]' in the room.[95] Among these banners was the royal standard. Such a move is important for two reasons. It shows the extent of de Valera's authority and control as regards the State Apartments. More importantly, it illustrates a much more complex attitude to such things as symbols of monarchy, and Ireland's place under it.

Less than a year later, in April 1933, de Valera was quite emphatic in his denunciation of such symbols:

Let it be made clear that we yield no willing assent to any form or symbol that is out of keeping with Ireland's right as a sovereign nation. Let us remove these forms one by one, so that the state we control may become a republic in fact: and that, when the time comes, the proclaiming of the Republic may involve no more than a ceremony, the formal confirmation of a status already attained.[96]

In this light, it is perhaps even more surprising to see de Valera appropriate the Throne Room as a stage for his own brand of 'majesty'. In 1934, in what *The Irish Times* described as 'the first time the Throne Room ... has been used for a state function since the establishment of the Free State', de Valera held an evening banquet in the room, which may have looked similar to an undated twentieth-century photograph of the room set for dinner (Fig. 09.11).[97] The banquet, which took place on the night of 9 April, was in honour of the Minister Plenipotentiary of the United States of America to the Irish Free State, W.W. McDowell (1867–1934). It was described by *The Irish Times*, in the same article, as 'a private function' that 'had all the brilliance of a State Reception'.[98] The dinner ended in tragedy when the new envoy, seated between President de Valera and his wife, got up to speak. He had been speaking for about five minutes when, shortly

Fig. 09.11.
The Throne Room, Dublin Castle, arranged for a dinner, 1932–59. Courtesy of the Office of Public Works Library.

before 11 o'clock, he 'collapsed on the ground, to the consternation of his fellow-guests'.[99] Attended to by the German Minister and the Minister for Agriculture, both of whom were doctors, as well as the Papal Nuncio, he did not survive the massive heart attack he had just suffered.

The tragic circumstances of this occasion did not prevent de Valera from using the room again. Almost thirty years later, in the same space, he received another distinguished American guest. In June 1963, President John F. Kennedy (1917–1963) visited Ireland. The State Apartments were again employed as the backdrop to 'a smooth, neat package of pageantry, dispatched in the space of an hour', during which President Kennedy was awarded honorary doctorates from the National University of Ireland (NUI) and the University of Dublin (Trinity College).[100] The ceremony was carried out in St Patrick's Hall, but the 'purple, bottle-green and scarlet robes' of the NUI 'had been presented to him in the Throne Room by the [University's] Chancellor, President de Valera'.[101] Again, we see de Valera using the Throne Room as a backdrop to semi-private diplomatic moments. We can only guess at what was going through de Valera's mind as he engaged to use the Throne Room in this way. Given how attuned he was to symbolism, he could not have been ignorant of the history and symbolism that surrounded him there. Some insight into his thoughts on Dublin Castle came to the surface when he visited on 16 March 1952, to inspect building work then in progress. In a memo in an OPW file it is recorded that:

> On the general question of the State Apartments the Taoiseach [Irish Prime Minister] said the aim should be to keep them in good condition. While some people held the view that emblems of British rule should be removed there was a case for preserving them for their historical significance and for the emphasis which they placed on the change over to national independence. This applied particularly to places like St. Patrick's Hall and the State Apartments generally where there is so much of value and artistic merit as well as of historical significance ...[102]

It is worth considering the history of two other thrones at this point, which may contribute to our understanding of de Valera's attitude – that of King Edward I in Westminster and that of Tipu Sultan of Mysore (1750–1799) in Calcutta. The Coronation Chair of Edward I was made in 1300 to fit around and enclose the Stone of Scone, which he had taken from Scotland in 1296, and on which

Scottish (and Irish) kings had previously been crowned. It was very much the creation of a trophy, one that marked the subjugation of the Scots. Similarly, when Tipu Sultan was vanquished by the East India Company in 1799, parts of his throne made their way to the house of the Governor General of the East India Company in Calcutta. When control of India passed from Company to Crown, these trophies remained in what became the Throne Room of the house, where the newly appointed Viceroy of India held court (see Fig. 09.03).[103] They were the ultimate symbols of a deposed regime, kept on display in the room that most symbolized the new, victorious one, a justification and reminder to those received in the room of the might of the current occupant.

Was de Valera taking a similar approach? Was the Throne Room at Dublin Castle his Stone of Scone, or his Sultan's Throne, writ large? His view that such symbols in Ireland, and particularly those at Dublin Castle, *emphasised* the 'change over to national independence' would seem to suggest so. Thus, we find the arch-republican of Irish politics, and to an extent its arch-enigma, quite comfortable in the former viceregal surroundings of the Throne Room at Dublin Castle. But as with so much of de Valera's thinking, the semantics were key; he had not appropriated the room – he had captured it.

A Question of Axis

In between the two episodes recounted above, in 1934 and 1963, the Throne Room at Dublin Castle underwent a protracted and dynamic re-ordering. On a visit to the Castle on 12 February 1939, de Valera (who, on foot of the 1937 Constitution, was now known as Taoiseach instead of President) had remarked that 'there was a lot which could be done to improve the apartments', criticizing in particular the 'general condition of the rooms owing to the fading + discolouration of the decoration'.[104] On foot of these comments, there was much activity within the OPW, and a schedule of proposed improvements was drawn up by March. It included 'Partial redecoration' of the Throne Room, noting that the 'canvas wall coverings' were 'in bad condition'.[105] It also included a proposal for the improvement of the electric lighting in the room, it being noted that the Taoiseach, de Valera, had 'commented on the lighting ... at the last function'.[106] This proposal took the form of 'flood lighting the ceiling from the cornice' of the room.[107] These changes were halted dramatically when, in the early hours of 24 January 1941, a fire broke out in the State Apartments.[108] Immediately next to the Throne Room, the old Presence Chamber was completely gutted and the

State Drawing Room next to that was badly damaged (see Figs 02.14 & 02.17). This disastrous blaze provided the impetus for a wholesale restoration and re-ordering of the State Apartments over the following twenty-eight years, which left a more considerable mark on the Throne Room than the preceding proposals intended.

To begin with, the shells of the old Presence Chamber and State Drawing Room were boarded up and life continued in the rest of the rooms around them much as it had done before. A collection of photographs of the State Apartments as they were arranged for the 1952 presidential inauguration has recently come to light in the OPW's furniture division.[109] Following the ratification of a new constitution in 1937, St Patrick's Hall had been chosen for the inauguration of the new Irish President in 1938. One of the viceregal thrones that had once furnished the room, had its crown and 'VR' monogram removed; was reupholstered; and, like the Hall itself and the rest of the State Apartments, was pressed into the service of the new Irish state (Figs 09.12 & 09.13).[110] Most of these photographs have handwritten notes on the reverse and two depict the Throne Room. One of these notes reads: 'Lay-out of Throne Room used as viewpoint [to the proceedings in the Upper Castle Yard] for Ministers wives etc during Installation ceremonies and as Buffet for Reception. The Buffet tables – not shown in photograph were placed between the columns in front of windows'.[111] The adjacent Portrait Gallery was filled with tables and chairs for the diners. The second image (Fig. 09.14) is inscribed as follows:

> Layout of Throne Room showing circular desk in corner used during Reception as dispense bar and portion of Gable Wall (next to Burnt-Out Drawing Rooms) which was rebuilt in 1952. The central table is that made in Debtor's Prison + presented to Queen Victoria. Original chandelier was re-burnished in conjunction with general re-decoration of the State Apartments – original gilding cleaned only. The murals previously ascribed to Angelica Kauffman are now believed to be the work of a Venetian painter.[112]

These images provide an important record of the room on the eve of its major twentieth-century re-ordering. Several things are worth noting. The brackets either side of the large mirrors (see Fig. 04.18) had by this time been removed, as had the candelabra (see Fig. 04.19) that sat on them.[113] This was possibly done when the east wall was being rebuilt, but more than likely dates from the conversion

of the room into a hospital. The lintels of each of the chimneypieces had been replaced, and lacked the three laurel wreaths they previously displayed (see Fig. 04.11). The lion, unicorn and crown were still absent from the canopy of the throne, and the throne itself lacked its small wooden dais. Both of the fireplaces had been blocked up. The painted decoration of the room was much more crude than earlier images show; the pilasters were monochrome and the detail of the canopy and throne was no longer picked out in gold on a white background. The oval wreaths over each of the chimneypieces were still in their original positions and, in addition to the throne, the room had retained its original set of small stools and its original flooring. A pleasant surprise was the return of one of its original chandeliers. These were dispersed throughout the State Apartments in the early twentieth century and the main central chandelier returned to the room at some point between 1933 and 1952.[114] Of the four smaller chandeliers, one is at the Irish Embassy in London, one is at Áras an Uachtaráin (formerly the Viceregal Lodge) and one is still at Dublin Castle. Of the fourth, half of its arms were removed to create three, three-light sconces to accompany the chandelier at Áras an Uachtaráin and what remains, deprived of every second arm, is still at Dublin Castle.

The works undertaken following the fire of 1941 were overseen by Raymond McGrath (1903–1977),

From top: Fig. 09.12. Viceregal throne in St Patrick's Hall, Dublin Castle, *c.* 1911. Courtesy of the National Library of Ireland.
Fig. 09.13. Irish Presidential Chair, used from 1938–2011 (formerly viceregal throne), *c.* 1849. Photograph by Davison & Associates, courtesy of the Office of Public Works, Dublin Castle.

Fig. 09.14. The Throne Room, Dublin Castle, June 1952. Courtesy of the Office of Public Works, Dublin Castle.

principal architect of the OPW from 1948 to 1968. Oscar Richardson (1922–2014) and J.B. Maguire were two of the architects on site who directed a significant amount of the work, which can be divided into several distinct phases. The first of these was the 'taking down' and rebuilding of the wall between the Throne Room and old Presence Chamber, between 23 March and 15 May 1958.[115] This had already been done once in 1952, and seems to have been quite straightforward. With the old Presence Chamber and State Drawing Room boarded up following the fire, the next problem was that the Throne Room proved a particularly 'inconvenient and unsuitable' space to enter.[116] Proper access could only be gained from St Patrick's Hall, via the Portrait Gallery. On 21 July 1958, workmen were instructed to strip plaster from some of the walls of the Battle Axe Landing in order to inspect the condition of the brickwork behind it.[117] On Tuesday, 9 September, it was discovered that 'on the Main Landing, where the fireplace stands, there was an arched opening, which it is proposed to reopen' (Fig. 09.15).[118] This was the outline of the door leading to the old Battle Axe Hall or Guard Chamber (see Fig. 02.04) that had been blocked up in the 1780s when George Nugent-Temple-Grenville, 1st Marquess of Buckingham (1753–1813) remodelled that room as his Presence Chamber. In reopening this doorway, the circulation problems attendant on the room were alleviated. A drawing for the design of the new doors and their surround in the south wall of the room survives in the OPW Library. The drawing (Fig. 09.16), dated February 1959, shows the provision of a pair of new 'wallnut or other selected hardwood' doors. Unfortunately, the doorway that had been blocked up in the 1780s lay immediately behind the throne and its canopy, necessitating their removal. On 27 January 1959, the architects recorded in their works diary: 'At the Throne Room to see removal of the throne, and to see it offered up in its new position. All satisfactory'.[119] On 30 January they recorded that 'The throne is now being fixed in its new position, and the ope to the Battleaxe Landing is in hand'.[120]

The result of this work has created a certain sense of confusion in the space, albeit not immediately apparent. The re-opened door calls attention to itself, not just through its position, but also through its materials and scale. Its polished hardwood contrasts with every other surface in the room, while the size of the opening defers much more to the architecture and scale of the Battle Axe Landing than to the Throne Room. What is perhaps most interesting about this project, however, is that the throne and its canopy, charged symbols of Ireland's past, were kept and the room dramatically re-ordered to accommodate them. The

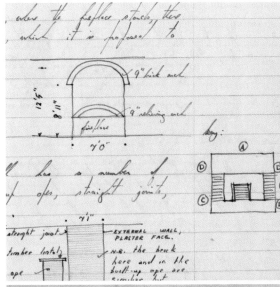

Left:
Fig. 09.15.
Job diary of works to the State Apartments, Dublin Castle, 1957–64, detail showing blocked up eighteenth-century doorway to Throne Room. Courtesy of the Office of Public Works Library.

Below:
Fig. 09.16.
Drawing of new door to Throne Room, Dublin Castle, 1959. Courtesy of the Office of Public Works Library.

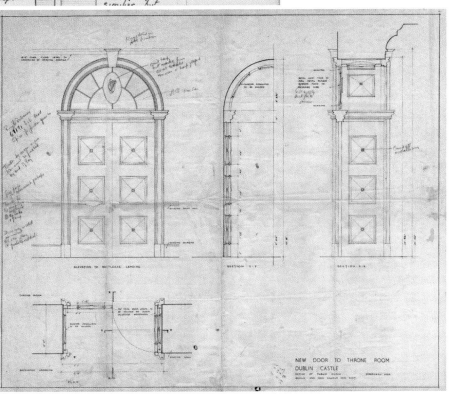

large mirror with the royal arms on the east wall was taken down and the throne and canopy moved into its position.[121] It is perhaps worth noting that de Valera was again in office at the time this work was undertaken. Given the sentiments that he had previously expressed, it is not implausible to detect his hand in the preservation of the two things that gave the room its name and lent it so much of its meaning. While the new arrangement can be considered partially successful when used on formal occasions, approached from the Battle Axe Landing, it is somewhat disorientating for those who enter the space by its intended route, from the east door.

The next of the interventions, although more structurally invasive, left a much less visible mark on the room. Reconstruction of the adjoining old Presence Chamber (Ante-Drawing Room) and State Drawing Room block had been postponed 'for a long period for reasons of economy'.[122] On 21 November 1962, it was recorded that the Department of An Taoiseach, Seán Lemass (1899–1971), was:

> ... anxious that the project should be completed as soon as possible, the State Apartments being the only suitable premises available for major State functions. In particular, it is desired that the new Block should be completed by Spring 1966, when, in the normal way a Presidential inauguration is due; also, 1966 will be the 50th anniversary of the 1916 Rising.[123]

In March 1963, it was suggested that the proposed contract for rebuilding the State Drawing Room Block also be extended to 'include any strengthening or improvement of the Main Entrance'.[124] It was noted that 'The Throne Room floor requires strengthening; and it is self-evident that the lower part of the entrance facade is out-of-true'.[125] Indeed, it was additionally noted that 'The adjoining walls of the old Drawingroom Block were left standing to first floor level partly because of the support they gave to the entrance' (Fig. 09.17).[126] All furniture was removed from the rooms, presumably including the throne and its canopy, the mirrors and several, if not all, of the room's six paintings, which have since been identified as the work of Gaetano Gandolfi (1734–1802). These, as well as many of the salvaged architectural features from the rest of the State Drawing Room Block, were stored in George's Hall and St Patrick's Hall for the duration of the project.[127] By 26 November, the work had been 'completed satisfactorily'.[128] The scope of the rebuilding work was evidently still being fine-tuned, however, and a structural survey of the Entrance Block, containing the Throne Room, had revealed much larger problems. It recommended:

> The whole of the facade to the Upper Yard and its returns to the main building must be taken down and re-built in toto ... the east wall of the Throne Room section must be taken down and re-built [this had already been done in 1952 and 1958] ... All the floors with the possible exception of the Battleaxe landing itself, are unsafe, and must be replaced.[129]

A letter from the Department of An Taoiseach to the OPW, dated 14 February 1964, approved the permanent removal of 'the existing balcony and [its lean-to] canopy' (Fig. 09.18).[130] The ambitious completion date for all of this work, Drawing Room Block and Entrance Block, was set as 11 March 1966.[131] After a nine-week delay, due to a building strike, work on the reconstruction proper began on 19 October 1964.[132] The political will and urgency behind the project is illustrated by a letter from the secretary of the Department of An Taoiseach to the OPW, dated 5 February 1965. The secretary states: 'The Taoiseach has asked me to impress upon everybody concerned his view that it is necessary to have the State Apartments available for the celebration of the 50th anniversary of Easter Week, 1916'.[133] By July 1965, work was well advanced, on the Entrance Block at least. However, delays were now mounting up. The provision of new Portland Stone capitals for the rebuilding of the entrance portico had stopped the progression of work for three weeks.[134] The installation of a new ventilation system for the Throne Room had also not been provided for in the

Fig. 09.17.
The east wall of the Throne Room, Dublin Castle, during rebuilding work, 1963.
Courtesy of the Office of Public Works Library.

Fig. 09.18.
Entrance to the
State Apartments,
Dublin Castle,
during rebuilding
work, 1963.
Courtesy of the
Office of Public
Works Library.

original contract.[135] Neither had the 'extensive replacement of stonework in the Entrance facade'; the 'new ventilation ductwork in roof space of Throne Room, including cutting through existing coved ceiling'; nor the 'provision of "Minerva" fire detection system'.[136] The delays meant that the entirety of the works were not finished on time for the 1916 anniversary, but that the reconstruction and consolidation of the Entrance Block and Throne Room were.[137]

The contract drawing for the 1960s works gives some indication of their extent (Fig. 09.19). They had included 'the complete rebuilding of the flank wall from foundation to roof … the replacement in reinforced concrete of two timber floors … the removal of the balcony in the front and replacement of defective stonework … the installation of up-to-date heating, and electrical services, including facilities for television and sound broadcasts … and fire detection; replacement of sundry joinery & ornamental plasterwork, redecoration & regilding'.[138] Two photographs survive showing the extent of the building work. The first comes from an engineer's report dated November 1963, and shows the condition of the existing floor, distinctly out of level (Fig. 09.20). From this, it is possible to see

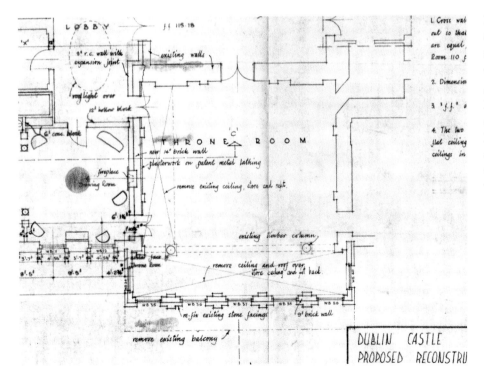

Fig. 09.19. Contract drawing for rebuilding works, State Apartments, Dublin Castle, detail of Throne Room, 1964. Courtesy of the Office of Public Works Library.

that by the time building work began, the lion, unicorn and crown had returned to the canopy of the throne. The second image shows the room with its floor removed, illustrating the extent of the renewal and consolidation. The paintings, their roundels and the door frames had been removed while the floor was taken out (Fig. 09.21). The floor was replaced with a reinforced concrete structure and finished with '11in. x 3in. x 1in. oak ... woodblock in interwoven basket pattern with 3in. x 3in. mahogany inset dot'.[139] It would appear that the south wall, adjoining the Battle Axe Landing, was re-plastered and in the process, the two oval paintings appear to have moved upwards. Much of the joinery was

renewed. What had once been a false door in the east wall was opened up, giving access to the rebuilt lobby behind it (see Fig 09.19). The original single-leaf doors (designed to appear as double-leaf) were replaced with actual double-leaf doors to the same design. The Victorian plate glass windows made way for Georgian-style sash windows, with glazing bars. The dado rail was renewed completely, and the decision taken to gild it, in order to discourage future over-painting. A section of the original was kept by J.B Maguire, and shows the loss of detail suffered by much of the joinery from almost two centuries of paint renewal (Fig. 09.22).

Fig. 09.22.
Section of chair
rail, Throne Room,
Dublin Castle,
removed 1964–6.
Private collection,
courtesy of
Graham Hickey.

Despite the drastic and invasive nature of the work undertaken between October 1964 and April 1966, its impact on the Throne Room was less severe than that of the re-opening of the door to the Battle Axe Landing in 1959. It conserved, restored or renewed most of the existing elements of the room at that time, and where new interventions were made (such as heating), they were done quite sensitively. The finished room also reflected the emerging 'state style' of the OPW's principal architect Raymond McGrath, or what Nicholas Sheaff described as the 'recognizable "look" [he gave] to Ireland's state buildings'.[140] This 'look' included 'specially-designed woollen carpets, Waterford glass chandeliers, Irish silk poplin hangings and, in terms of fittings, 18th-century chimneypieces and ornamental plasterwork, the latter often salvaged'.[141] While the rest of the State Apartments, in particular the restored State Drawing Room, reflected this style more fully, the most arresting evidence of the 1964–6 restoration of the Throne Room was its new carpet (Fig. 09.23). It was one of a series of carpets, which McGrath began utilizing in the early 1950s, and which were 'the particular hallmark of his government work'.[142] They were made by hand at the factory of

Fig. 09.23.
The Throne Room, Dublin Castle, *c.* 1999.
Courtesy of the Office of Public Works, Dublin Castle.

Fig. 09.24.
The Throne Room, Dublin Castle.
Photograph by Davison & Associates,
courtesy of the Office of Public Works, Dublin Castle.

Donegal Carpets Ltd in Killybegs, Co. Donegal. In supporting this native Irish industry, one wonders if McGrath was aware that 'Donegal Carpets' had been among those chosen for the refurbishment of the State Apartments in advance of the royal visit in 1911.[143] The carpet designed by McGrath for the Throne Room was based on the designs of the eighteenth-century Savonnerie Factory in France. It was a source he employed repeatedly – in the Drawing Room, again at Dublin Castle, and in the Grand Salon of the Irish Embassy in Paris. The consolidation and rebuilding works of 1964–6 left the room almost exactly as we see it today. The project was awarded the RIAI's silver medal for conservation for the years 1946–76.

The Past as a Repository of Sources

Following the completion of the State Apartments project in 1969, the Throne Room settled into a new pattern of life, employed as the backdrop to state entertaining and ceremonial, and open to the visiting public when not being used by government. It would appear that, in addition to serving as an appropriately stately backdrop, the Throne Room still proved itself an attractive political tool to Irish politicians, as Stephen Kelly recounts in his description of the visit of Margaret Thatcher (1925–2013), the British Prime Minister, to Dublin Castle in 1980:

> Figg [the British Ambassador to Ireland] recalled with fondness that following the conclusion of private talks between the two premiers, Haughey showed Thatcher the throne in the main Throne Room. He then, somewhat surprisingly, invited her to sit on it. Thatcher declined, instead suggesting that he should do so if he wished. They both laughed and made their way to lunch. The story, however, did not end there. Figg noted that after the press conference, Haughey returned to the Throne Room, where officials were relaxing and drinking. Suddenly Haughey ascended the throne and sat on it, his feet not quite touching the floor and informed his entourage that they would have to kneel before him! In view of the successful summit meeting, Pádraig Ó hAnnracháin jocosely remarked to Haughey: 'Sure after today aren't you the King of Ireland?'[144]

This incident displays something of Charles Haughey's regard for the props of diplomacy and the trappings of power. His invitation to Thatcher can been seen as playful but, as with de Valera before him, it is possible that the throne was being deployed as a reminder of Ireland's success in its long struggle for independence from its island neighbour. His own ascension to the throne, in more informal circumstances, after Thatcher had left, speaks volumes of his regard for his own position. In a strange way, he was appropriating it for its intended use, as a signifier of position and status – albeit in a somewhat relaxed and insouciant way that recalls Daniel O'Connell's holding of a 'National Levee' at the Rotunda in 1845 (see Fig. 06.09).

Since the work of the 1960s, the room, along with the rest of the State Apartments, has been subject to the ongoing work of maintenance and repair. At some point in its intervening history, this involved the injudicious repair of the room's gilded surfaces with the application of gold paint, in particular to the carved foliate frames around the paintings by Gaetano Gandolfi, and to the canopy itself. More recently, the decision has been taken to reverse this work: the throne was re-gilded and both it and its canopy re-upholstered in 1992; the overmantel mirrors were re-gilded in 2014; the large mirror with the royal arms was re-gilded in 2015; and the foliate roundels were stripped of their dulled gold paint and re-gilded, also in 2015. This work was carried out by Susan Mulhall, and has gone some way to counteracting less sensitive, earlier interventions (Fig. 09.24). Among these earlier interventions was the incorrect re-arrangement of the carved figures of the lion and unicorn on the throne canopy, which had their positions swapped sometime after November 1963. Redecoration had also been undertaken in advance of the state visit to Ireland of Her Majesty Queen Elizabeth II, in 2011. The visit came 100 years after that of her grandfather, King George V, in 1911, and to many it marked an important milestone in the relationship and shared history of Britain and Ireland, as well as 'a culmination of the success of the Peace Process' in Northern Ireland.[145] As President Mary McAleese remarked of that shared history in her speech, 'Inevitably where there are the colonisers and the colonised, the past is a repository of sources of bitter division'.[146] It was perhaps for this reason that although the invited guests passed through the Throne Room prior to the official State Dinner in St Patrick's Hall, Queen Elizabeth and President McAleese did not. This may suggest, despite the words of President McAleese, that 'with time and generosity, interpretations and perspectives can soften', that the Throne Room at Dublin Castle still retains more than a trace of its former potency, as a symbol of majesty.

Conclusion

The century covered by this essay illustrates the varied history and surprising survival of the Throne Room at Dublin Castle. Already by 1911, its use was beginning to outgrow its elegant and symbolically charged confines. The use by King George V of St Patrick's Hall for the court of 1911 illustrates the necessity for a bigger space for the largest of court functions. However, while St Patrick's Hall was architecturally more commodious, the Throne Room was the more regally emphatic of the two rooms, and was still employed as much as possible for court functions such as deputations, presentations and levees. This ceased after the outbreak of the First World War, and its conversion into a hospital ward, during which it offered a vantage point on the unfolding of the 1916 Rising. Later, its use as an office for typists during the War of Independence, while the viceroy retreated to the confines of the Viceregal Lodge, marked a decided shift away from any possible return to its former use.

Following Irish independence in 1922, the functions of the room, insofar as they remained, were divorced from the space. While the new government of the Irish Free State eschewed any form of ceremonial redolent of Ireland's days under the Crown, the home of the new Governor of Northern Ireland, Hillsborough Castle, Co. Down, was equipped with a throne room where similar, if scaled-down, functions were staged. The room was appropriated as a courtroom for almost ten years, following which it found a saviour in a most unlikely person. That Éamon de Valera, who had fought so long against everything the room represented, should appropriate it for his own use, and encourage the preservation of its royal symbols, indicates the power of its majestic trappings. The symbolism of the room came to represent not the royal presence but the removal of that presence from Irish affairs. It is perhaps something that could only have been achieved by de Valera, and the survival of the Throne Room can largely be ascribed to his sensitivity to history, even when an ideal opportunity for its destruction arose in 1958. As he himself recognized, its symbolism would not have endeared it to many and it seems only to have been used for smaller, more intimate meetings rather than larger ceremonies of state. Following the trend of the royal visit of 1911, St Patrick's Hall lent itself as a more suitable space for larger events, helped by the fact that it was a less obviously contentious room. Thus it, and one of its two thrones, was appropriated for the inaugurations of the Irish Presidents while the Throne Room remained a secondary space.

The reconfiguration of the Throne Room in 1959, and the distortion of its powerful symmetry, appears to have been effected largely for practical reasons of access rather than to diffuse the formal axis, centred on the throne and canopy, which reinforced its symbolism. This raises the question of whether it should be returned to its original arrangement in any future scheme of work on the State Apartments. While four of the original suite of chandeliers could be returned to the room from their current locations, as could the second large mirror with the royal arms, the question of re-instating the canopy and throne in their pre-1959 positions throws up several complex questions about history; conservation versus restoration; use; and integrity. Despite the reorganization of the room, its impact has not been diffused entirely, as can be seen from attitudes to its use in 1963 and 2011. Whatever the future holds for the Throne Room, it can only be hoped that the often surprising motivations that shaped its recent past, will encourage people to explore more fully the multifaceted, and at times contradictory, attitudes that shaped the building of modern Ireland.

For their help, advice and many kindnesses as I prepared this essay, I wish to thank Nuala Byrne, Caroline Costello, Sylvie Kleinman, Kelly Mackey, J.B. Maguire, Michael McDowell, Susan Mulhall, Ludovica Neglie and Turlough O'Donnell.

Endnotes

1   Speech by Queen Elizabeth II at Dublin Castle on the occasion of her state visit to Ireland, 18 May 2011; see *Irish Times*, 19 May 2011.

2   Inventory of State Apartments, Dublin Castle, 1908, OPW Library, book 1.

3   *Supplemental Guide to the Irish International Exhibition* (Dublin, 1907), p. 37.

4   *Freeman's Journal*, 15 March 1897.

5   'The pre-history of the Shannon scheme', *History Ireland*, 12, 4 (Winter 2004), viewable online: http://www.historyireland.com/20th-century-contemporary-history/the-pre-history-of-the-shannon-scheme/ (accessed 19 April 2017).

6   D. Souden, *The Royal Palaces of London* (London and New York: Merrell Publishers Limited, 2008), pp. 139, 146, 151.

7   *Freeman's Journal*, 18 March 1910.

8   *Freeman's Journal*, 10 May 1910.

9   *Freemans Journal*, 23 January 1911; The Marquis & Marchioness of Aberdeen & Temair, *More Cracks with 'We Twa'* (London: Methuen & Co. Ltd, 1929), p. 144.

10 The Countess of Fingall and T. West, *Seventy Years Young: Memories of Elizabeth, Countess of Fingall* (Dublin: The Lilliput Press, 1991), pp. 115–16.

11 'The Irish Sword of State', in C. Blair (ed.), *The Crown Jewels: The History of the Coronation Regalia in the Jewel House of the Tower of London* (London: The Stationery Office, 1998), vol. 2, p. 354.

12 *Irish Independent*, 23 February 1912.

13 *Donegal News*, 15 July 1911.

14 *Irish Examiner*, 11 July 1911. See also *Visit to Ireland of Their Most Gracious Majesties King George V and Queen Mary 8th to 12th July 1911: Programme of the Royal Progress* (Dublin: printed by Alex. Thom & Co. Ltd., 1911).

15 *Irish Examiner*, 11 July 1911.

16 *Irish Independent*, 11 July 1911.

17 *Freeman's Journal*, 12 July 1911.

18 *Irish Times*, 12 July 1911.

19 *Irish Independent*, 13 July 1911.

20 Ibid.

21 *Irish Independent*, 17 July 1911; *Freeman's Journal*, 15 August 1911.

22 *Sunday Independent*, 16 July 1911.

23 *Irish Independent*, 2 February 1912.

24 *Freeman's Journal*, 4 November 1912; *Belfast Newsletter*, 21 March 1913; *Irish Examiner*, 21 March 1913.

25 *Irish Independent*, 7 February 1914; *Freeman's Journal*, 15 April 1914.

26 Lord and Lady Aberdeen, *'We Twa': Reminiscences of Lord and Lady Aberdeen* (London: W. Collins Sons & Co. Ltd), vol. 2, p. 284.

27 *Freeman's Journal*, 28 November 1914.

28 *Freeman's Journal*, 1 December 1914.

29 *Irish Independent*, 1 December 1914.

30 Letter to the Secretary of the City of Dublin branch of the British Red Cross Society from Sir E. O'Farrell, Secretary to the Treasury, 9 March 1915, OPW file: Dublin Castle Red Cross Hospital, OPW Papers, National Archives of Ireland, OPW[5]5969/19.

31 Letter to the Secretary to the Treasury from H. Williams, Secretary to the Board of the OPW, 30 March 1915, OPW file: Dublin Castle Red Cross Hospital, OPW Papers, National Archives of Ireland, OPW[5]5969/19.

32 Letter to the Secretary to the Treasury from

Sir Matthew Nathan, 11 May 1915, OPW file: Dublin Castle Red Cross Hospital, OPW Papers, National Archives of Ireland, OPW[5]5969/19.

33 Letter to Sir Matthew Nathan from Constance Heppel Marr, Honorary Secretary to the City of Dublin branch, British Red Cross Society, 23 June 1915, OPW file: Dublin Castle Red Cross Hospital, OPW Papers, National Archives of Ireland, OPW[5]5969/19.

34 See Lord and Lady Aberdeen, 'We Twa', p. 238.

35 *Irish Examiner*, 28 January 1915.

36 *Irish Times*, 23 April 1915.

37 See Lord and Lady Aberdeen, 'We Twa', p. 238.

38 Draft of a letter to the Under-Secretary for Ireland from the Secretary of the Board of the OPW, 15 January 1915, OPW file: Dublin Castle Red Cross Hospital, OPW Papers, National Archives of Ireland, OPW[5]5969/19.

39 I am very grateful to Dr Sylvie Kleinman for bringing this source to my attention.

40 Anon., 'Experiences of a V.A.D. at Dublin Castle during the Rebellion', *Blackwood's Magazine*, 200 (July–December 1916), p. 816.

41 Ibid.

42 See Anon., 'Experiences of a V.A.D.', p. 820.

43 Ibid., p. 817.

44 See Anon., 'Experiences of a V.A.D.', p. 824.

45 Ibid., p. 826.

46 See Anon., 'Experiences of a V.A.D.', p. 826.

47 Ibid.

48 See Anon., 'Experiences of a V.A.D.', p. 830.

49 *Illustrated War News*, 10 May 1916.

50 See Anon., 'Experiences of a V.A.D.', pp. 832–3.

51 Ibid., p. 833.

52 See Anon., 'Experiences of a V.A.D.', p. 839.

53 Letter to the Secretary of the Dublin Castle Red Cross Hospital Committee from J.J.

Healy, Secretary to the Board of the OPW, 3 July 1919, OPW file: Dublin Castle Red Cross Hospital, OPW Papers, National Archives of Ireland, OPW[5]5969/19.

54 Letter to the Secretary of the Board of the OPW from the Secretary of the City of Dublin branch of the British Red Cross Society, 29 May 1919, OPW file: Dublin Castle Red Cross Hospital, OPW Papers, National Archives of Ireland, OPW[5]5969/19.

55 'Periscope' [G.C. Duggan], 'The Last Days of Dublin Castle', *Blackwood's Magazine*, 212 (August 1922), pp. 165–6.

56 Letter to the Under-Secretary for Ireland from J.J. Hanson, Secretary to the Board of the OPW, 8 January 1920, OPW file: Dublin Castle Residences - General Arrangements, OPW Papers, National Archives of Ireland, OPW[5]15026/20.

57 *Belfast Newsletter*, 3 May 1921.

58 Ibid.

59 *Belfast Newsletter*, 3 May 1921.

60 Memorandum, 1 December 1921, OPW file: Heating of George's Hall & Throne Room, Dublin Castle, OPW Papers, National Archives of Ireland, OPW[5]14991/21.

61 See 'Periscope', 'The Last Days', p. 169.

62 Ibid.

63 See 'Periscope', 'The Last Days', p. 169.

64 Ibid.

65 See 'Periscope', 'The Last Days', pp. 169–70.

66 Ibid., p. 169.

67 See 'Periscope', 'The Last Days', p. 168.

68 Memorandum, 1 December 1921, OPW file: Heating of George's Hall & Throne Room, Dublin Castle, OPW Papers, National Archives of Ireland, OPW[5]14991/21.

69 Letter to the Administrative Officer, Chief of Police from the Captain, R.A.M.C., 18 November 1921, OPW file: Heating of George's Hall & Throne Room, Dublin Castle, OPW Papers, National Archives of

Ireland, OPW[5]14991/21.

70 Memorandum, 1 December 1921, OPW file: Heating of George's Hall & Throne Room, Dublin Castle, OPW Papers, National Archives of Ireland, OPW[5]14991/21.

71 Ibid.

72 Memorandum, 12 December 1921, OPW file: Heating of George's Hall & Throne Room, Dublin Castle, OPW Papers, National Archives of Ireland, OPW[5]14991/21.

73 See 'Periscope', 'The Last Days', p. 190.

74 N. Wilkinson, *To All and Singular* (London: Nisbet & Co. Ltd, n.d.), p. 272.

75 Letter to the Secretary of the Office of Public Works from Diarmuid Ó h-Éigceartuigh, Secretary to the Provisional Government, 23 May 1922, OPW file: Utilization of Dublin Castle for Government Offices, OPW Papers, National Archives of Ireland, OPW[5]25374/25.

76 Report, 8 June 1922, OPW file: Utilization of Dublin Castle for Government Offices, OPW Papers, National Archives of Ireland, OPW[5]25374/25, p. 3.

77 Letter to Sir Philip Hanson, Chairman of the Office of Public Works from the Secretary, Ministry of Finance of the Provisional Government, 16 June 1922, OPW file: Utilization of Dublin Castle for Government Offices, OPW Papers, National Archives of Ireland, OPW[5]25374/25.

78 M. Ryan, *Michael Collins and the Women who Spied for Ireland* (Cork: Mercier Press, 1996), p. 145.

79 *Irish Times*, 15 July 1922.

80 Letter to the Law Officer of the Provisional Government from the Secretary, Commissioners of Public Works, 18 September 1922, OPW file: Law Courts Dublin Castle, OPW Papers, National Archives of Ireland, OPW[5]20375/23.

81 Report on the Proposed Transfer of Law Courts to the Castle, 5 October 1922, OPW file: Law Courts Dublin Castle, OPW Papers, National Archives of Ireland, OPW[5]20375/23, p. 2.

82 Letter to Sir Philip Hanson from T.F. Molony, 23 October 1922, OPW file: Law Courts Dublin Castle, OPW Papers, National Archives of Ireland, OPW[5]20375/23.

83 Memorandum to Chairman of the OPW from H.G. Leask, 2 February 1923, OPW file: Law Courts Dublin Castle, OPW Papers, National Archives of Ireland, OPW[5]20375/23.

84 *Irish Law Times and Solicitors' Journal*, 14 April 1923.

85 Ibid., p. 95.

86 *Freeman's Journal*, 10 April 1923.

87 *Irish Law Times and Solicitors' Journal*, 21 April 1923.

88 *Irish Law Times and Solicitors' Journal*, 14 April 1923.

89 Ibid.

90 *Irish Law Times and Solicitors' Journal*, 14 April 1923.

91 G. Horgan, 'Hugh Kennedy, The Childers Habeas Corpus Application and the Return to the Four Courts', in C. Costello (ed.), *The Four Courts: 200 Years* (Dublin: Incorporated Council of Law Reporting for Ireland, 1996), p. 207.

92 Ibid., p. 211.

93 P. Galloway, *The Most Illustrious Order: The Order of Saint Patrick and its Knights* (London: Unicorn Press, 1999), p. 201.

94 Ibid.

95 See Galloway, *The Most Illustrious Order*, p. 201.

96 R. Fanning, *A Will to Power: Éamon de Valera* (London: Faber & Faber, 2015), p. 169.

97 *Irish Times*, 10 April 1934.

98 Ibid.

99 *Weekly Irish Times*, 14 April 1934.

100 *Irish Times*, 29 June 1963.

101 Ibid.

102 Extract from Report on A6:1/23/52, 27 March 1952, OPW file: Dublin Castle – State Apartments, Heraldic Insignia in St Patrick's Hall, OPW Papers, National Archives of Ireland, OPW[5]2006/34/00435.

103 J. Morris with S. Winchester, *Stones of Empire: The Buildings of the Raj* (Oxford: Oxford University Press, 2005), p. 67, n.; P. Davies, *Splendours of the Raj: British Architecture in India, 1660 to 1947* (London: John Murray, 1985), p. 67.

104 Memorandum to Mr Osborne from Mr McNicholl, 16 February 1939, OPW file: Dublin Castle – State Apartments: Redecoration, furnishings & improvements, OPW Registry, A6/1/13, p. 2.

105 Memorandum to Div. A [April 1939], OPW file: Dublin Castle – State Apartments: Redecoration, furnishings & improvements, OPW Registry, A6/1/13, p. 21.

106 Ibid., p. 21 v.

107 Memorandum to Div. A [April 1939], OPW file: Dublin Castle – State Apartments: Redecoration, furnishings & improvements, OPW Registry, A6/1/13, p. 22.

108 *Irish Press*, 24 January 1941.

109 My thanks to Jacquie Moore, OPW Art Management, for bringing these to my attention.

110 The other throne is used today by the Cathaoirleach, or Chairman, of Seanad Éireann, the Irish Senate at Leinster House, Dublin.

111 Collection of photographs of State Apartments, Dublin Castle, 1952, Collections and Research Office, Dublin Castle.

112 Ibid.

113 Two of the four original brackets were repaired and conserved by Cresten Doherty in 2016/17. The four original candelabra were repaired and conserved by Church Art Metals in 2017.

114 The chandelier does not appear in an image of the room published on page 11 of *The Weekly Irish Times*, 18 March 1933.

115 Job Diary for demolition of cross-block and drawing rooms, Dublin Castle, 1957–64, OPW Library, pp. 13–14.

116 Copy of letter to J.J. McElligott, Secretary, Department of Finance from Department of External Affairs, 24 October 1941, OPW file: Dublin Castle – State Apartments: Restoration of burnt-out drawingrooms, vol. 1, OPW Registry, A6/33/6, p. 16.

117 Job Diary for demolition of cross-block and drawing rooms, Dublin Castle, 1957–64, OPW Library, p. 18.

118 Ibid., p. 19.

119 Job Diary for demolition of cross-block and drawing rooms, Dublin Castle, 1957–64, OPW Library, p. 23.

120 Ibid.

121 The mirror is still in the care of the OPW and is currently at Áras an Uachtaráin.

122 Supplementary Information [May 1962], OPW file: Dublin Castle – State Apartments: Restoration of burnt-out drawingrooms, vol. 2, OPW Registry, A6/33/6/2, p. 280.

123 Letter to Mr Fanning from Unknown, 21 November 1962, OPW file: Dublin Castle – State Apartments: Demolition of bedroom and drawing rooms sections, OPW Registry, A6/1/43, p. 1.

124 Memorandum to Mr Alcock from Oscar Richardson, 3 April 1963, OPW file: Dublin Castle – State Apartments: Restoration of burnt-out drawingrooms, vol. 2, OPW Registry, A6/33/6/2, p. 325.

125 Ibid.

126 Draft letter to the Secretary, Department of An Taoiseach, May 1963, OPW file: Dublin Castle – State Apartments: Restoration of burnt-out drawingrooms, vol. 2, OPW Registry, A6/33/6/2, p. 328.

127 Memorandum to Div. A from Oscar Richardson, 13 September 1963, OPW file: Dublin Castle – State Apartments: Demolition of bedroom and drawing rooms sections, OPW Registry, A6/1/43, p. 33.

128 Memorandum to [Div.] A from Oscar Richardson, 26 November 1963, OPW file: Dublin Castle – State Apartments: Demolition of bedroom and drawing rooms sections, OPW Registry, A6/1/43, p. 36.

129 Report to Div. A from Oscar Richardson, 3 December 1963, OPW file: Dublin Castle – State Apartments: Restoration of burnt-out drawingrooms, vol. 2, OPW Registry, A6/33/6/2, pp. 357–8.

130 Letter to the Secretary, OPW from the Secretary, Department of An Taoiseach, 14 February 1964, OPW file: Dublin Castle – State Apartments: Restoration of burnt-out drawingrooms, vol. 2, OPW Registry, A6/33/6/2, p. 383.

131 Schedule of works [January 1965], OPW file: Dublin Castle – State Apartments: Restoration of burnt-out drawingrooms, vol. 2, OPW Registry, A6/33/6/2, p. 437.

132 Memorandum to Div. A from Oscar Richardson, 3 November 1964, OPW file: Dublin Castle – State Apartments: Restoration of burnt-out drawingrooms, vol. 2, OPW Registry, A6/33/6/2, p. 422.

133 Letter to the Secretary, OPW from the Secretary, Department of An Taoiseach, 5 February 1965, OPW file: Dublin Castle – State Apartments: Restoration of burnt-out drawingrooms, vol. 2, OPW Registry, A6/33/6/2, p. 459.

134 Letter to Oscar Richardson from W. & J. Bolger, 19 January 1966, OPW file: Dublin Castle – State Apartments: Restoration of burnt-out drawingrooms, vol. 2, OPW Registry, A6/33/6/2, p. 499.

135 Ibid.

136 List of extra work undertaken in the Entrance Block [February 1966], OPW file: Dublin Castle – State Apartments: Restoration of burnt-out drawingrooms, vol. 2, OPW Registry, A6/33/6/2, p. 501.

137 Memorandum re. reconstruction of State Apartments, 26 April 1967, OPW file: Dublin Castle – State Apartments: Restoration of burnt-out drawingrooms, vol. 2, OPW Registry, A6/33/6/2, p. 524.

138 Ibid.

139 Floor schedule for State Apartments, Dublin Castle, 1970s, Collections and Research Office, Dublin Castle.

140 N. Sheaff, 'The Harp Re-Strung', *Irish Arts Review*, 1, 3 (Autumn 1984), p. 40.

141 Ibid.

142 See Sheaff, 'The Harp', p. 40.

143 *London Journal*, 22 July 1911, p. 305.

144 S. Kelly, *A Failed Political Entity: Charles Haughey and the Northern Ireland Question 1945–1992* (Newbridge: Merrion Press, 2006), p. 197.

145 Speech by President Mary McAleese at Dublin Castle on the occasion of the state visit to Ireland of Queen Elizabeth II, 18 May 2011; see *Irish Times*, 19 May 2011.

146 Ibid.

Ten

The Creation and Evolution of Hillsborough Castle's Throne Room

What's in a Name?

Christopher Warleigh-Lack

Hillsborough Castle is the official residence of Her Majesty Queen Elizabeth II in Northern Ireland. Located in Co. Down, some fourteen miles south of Belfast on the historic route to Dublin, it has its roots as a Georgian Irish 'big house' created by the Hill family, later Earls of Hillsborough and Marquesses of Downshire, for whom the adjoining town is named (Fig. 10.01). Historic Royal Palaces (HRP), the independent charity that cares for five other royal palaces in England, including the Tower of London, Hampton Court Palace, Kensington Palace, Kew Palace and the Banqueting House, Whitehall, took over the care of Hillsborough Castle and Gardens in April 2014 from the Northern Ireland Office, a British government department. As a charity, HRP's aim is to open up the site to over 200,000 visitors annually, and to enable those visitors to explore the stories of how Hillsborough Castle's inhabitants have shaped society.

As an official royal residence, Hillsborough Castle includes a throne room as part of its suite of seven State Apartments. As part of HRP's major plans for Hillsborough, which will include a car park, visitor centre and education spaces, the Throne Room is one of the several State Apartments that will undergo

Facing page:
Fig. 10.01.
Entrance front
of Hillsborough
Castle, Co. Down.
© Historic Royal
Palaces.

restoration, redecoration and representation during the winter of 2017/18. While distinct from the Throne Room at Dublin Castle in almost every way, the Throne Room at Hillsborough is nonetheless inextricably linked to it. Were it not for the cessation of the official functions of the Dublin room in 1922, the Throne Room at Hillsborough might never have come into existence. Its creation soon after, and subsequent evolution, offer an interesting counterpoint to the fate of the Dublin room in the twentieth century. After setting out the physical and historical context of Hillsborough Castle, this essay then explores the creation of its Throne Room. It poses several questions about the room's development. What was the status of Hillsborough Castle and therefore the space we now know as the Throne Room? Was a specific perception of majesty or royalty intended for those who experienced it? Did this perception change over time? Who *did* create this space and why? The semantics of the naming of this space are of interest too, as its name changed through time: interchangeably Saloon, Ballroom and Throne Room, it finally came to be known exclusively as the Throne Room in the 1950s. This essay also considers whether this is significant.

History of the House

The central core of Hillsborough Castle was completed by 1788 for Wills Hill, 2nd Earl of Hillsborough and later 1st Marquess of Downshire (1718–1793). The house was of the standard double-pile form, of five bays, drawing on a traditional villa type overlooking the town square.[1] The Throne Room is located outside the footprint of this original eighteenth-century house and within the south range that was added by Robert Furze Brettingham (*c*.1750–1820) for Arthur Hill, 2nd Marquess of Downshire (1753–1801), in 1797. Over the following decades, and at the hands of the 1st Marquess's son and grandson, the house was altered and added to, until the footprint in existence today was created by 1844. During the latter part of the nineteenth century, the family tended to focus their attention on their estates in England and the south of Ireland. By 1900 the house was rented, and by the 1920s the decision was made to sell the estate in its entirety. The contents were sold in 1924 and the British Office of Works purchased the house and demesne in January 1925 for £25,000, in order to provide a residence for the Governor of Northern Ireland.[2] The first holder of this newly created post, from December 1922, was James Hamilton, 3rd Duke of Abercorn (1869–1953). This was mirrored in the Irish Free State, where the Office of Public Works (OPW) established a residence for the Irish

Governor-General, Timothy Healy (1855–1931), in the former Viceregal Lodge in Dublin's Phoenix Park. The overriding involvement of the Office of Works at Hillsborough, immediately after the purchase of the house, can be seen in its correspondence with the OPW in Dublin about the provisions for Healy in the Phoenix Park. The OPW declined to reveal details about his accommodation, but did provide details of the Viceregal Lodge before 1921.[3]

Following alterations to Hillsborough Castle in 1925, the site was presented to the government of Northern Ireland for use as the residence of the governor. This of course changed with the introduction of direct rule to Northern Ireland from Westminster in 1972, and the fifth, and last, governor to live there was Ralph Grey, Baron Grey of Naunton (1910–1999). He vacated the house, which was then returned to the ownership of the British government, and the new post of Secretary of State for Northern Ireland was filled by Willie Whitelaw, later 1st Viscount Whitelaw (1918–1999), who moved in. From 1925, as the residence of the governor, Hillsborough Castle also therefore acted as the residence of the British monarch in Northern Ireland and it is for this reason that it started hosting royal visitors, the first being Mary, Princess Royal and Countess of Harewood in 1928, and her brother, Edward, Prince of Wales, later King Edward VIII, in 1932. The first crowned heads to stay at Hillsborough Castle were King George VI and Queen Elizabeth in 1937. HM Queen Elizabeth II's first visit, as HRH Princess Elizabeth, was in 1945. Other well-known guests have included Eleanor Roosevelt (1884–1962), Dwight D. Eisenhower (1890–1969), George W. Bush (*b.* 1946), Hilary Clinton (*b.* 1947), Akihito, Emperor of Japan (*b.* 1933) while Crown Prince – and Cilla Black (1943–2015). For the governors, who were royal appointees, Hillsborough tended to be a long-term residence, often one of many. For the secretaries of state, however, their appointment was political and they would often only 'live above the shop' for a matter of months. The attachment, and interest, of these residents, could therefore vary. For these reasons then, the continued change of the Throne Room, its meaning and function, is complex.

The Throne Room from 1925
In its present incarnation, the Throne Room is the result of successive adaptations of a nineteenth-century space. The walls are lined from chair rail to ceiling cornice in green silk damask, installed in 1936, with modern bright white paintwork (Fig. 10.02). Modern blue curtains, installed in the 1990s beneath

Fig. 10.02.
The Throne Room,
Hillsborough
Castle, Co. Down.
© Historic Royal
Palaces.

simple gilded pelmet boxes, frame the four windows, which look south over the Jubilee Parterre and the lawns leading to the nineteenth-century picturesque gardens. Three very small chandeliers light the room, highlighting the gilded surfaces of the door mouldings and architrave. A gold fillet, copied from that of Osterley House in west London in the 1990s, frames the walls. At present, an Old Master 'gallery hang' of paintings from the Royal Collection and other, private collections, adorns the walls. As its frequent renaming suggests, the use of the Throne Room for ceremonial events and receptions was somewhat fluid over time: ballroom, saloon, ballroom again, and throne room by the 1950s. This mirrored and continued the activities of what Patrick Maume and James Loughlin have described as the 'welfare monarchy' of nineteenth-century Britain and Ireland.[4] This can still be seen in its current royal use, as a space where a range of functions including investitures, citizenship ceremonies and musical events, attended by members of the royal family or their representatives, the

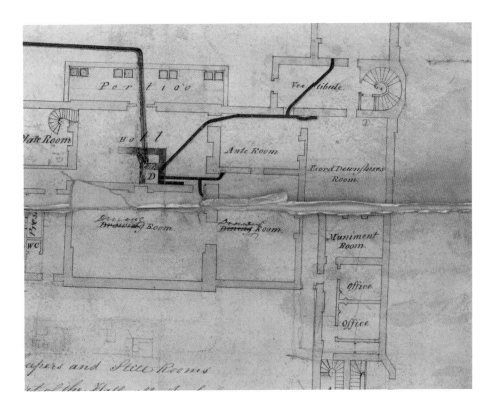

Fig. 10.03. Plan of the ground floor of Hillsborough Castle, Co. Down, 1833, detail. Downshire Papers, D671/P8/17. © Public Record Office of Northern Ireland.

Lords-Lieutenant of the counties of Northern Ireland, take place today.

The first detailed plan of the house, dated 1833, shows that the space now occupied by the Throne Room was subdivided into several smaller rooms including Lord Downshire's Room, a muniment room and an office (Fig. 10.03). The plan of the house made in 1925 as part of the alterations by the Office of Works shows the Throne Room in the form recognizable today. It is described on this plan as the Ballroom (Fig. 10.04). The date of the conversion is not recorded, but the dividing walls were removed before 1868 since an inventory compiled at that date records the whole space as the Ballroom.[5] Later inventories record different names: that of 1878 shows the Ballroom; that of 1909 the Saloon.[6] The continuation of the name 'Ballroom' on official floorplans well into the middle decades of the twentieth century is significant as this is the function for which it was used – entertaining large groups of people at events that included music and dancing.

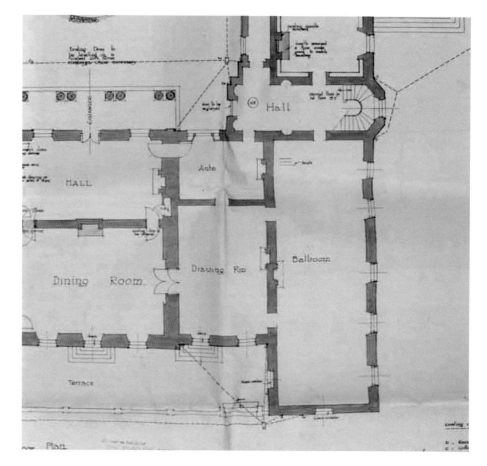

Fig. 10.04. Plan of the ground floor of Hillsborough Castle, Co. Down, 1925, detail. Ministry of Finance Papers, NI FIN/46/2/7. © Public Record Office of Northern Ireland.

What if anything, was influencing the design of this new 'imperial' space from 1925, following the creation of the new state of Northern Ireland? Four years earlier, King George V had opened the new Parliament of Northern Ireland, in June 1921, at Belfast City Hall. The Irish Sword of State, visible to the right of the King in a painting of the occasion, had been brought from its usual position across the throne at Dublin Castle to Belfast for the event (Fig. 10.05). Despite the onset of partition, the sword still represented the King's authority over the whole of the island of Ireland, and continued to do so until the establishment of the Irish Free State in December 1922. As far as we know, the sword never came to Hillsborough Castle, but its inclusion in the opening ceremony of the

new Belfast Parliament reinforced the all-island references in the King's inaugural speech, in which he had been ambivalent about the future of partition in Ireland.[7] As James Loughlin has noted:

> ... the national identity the King's speech encouraged was primarily Irish, not British, and was even ambiguous about whether a separate northern state would endure: "May this historic gathering be the prelude of a day in which the Irish people, North and South, under one Parliament or two, as those Parliaments may themselves decide, should work together in common love for Ireland".[8]

Coupled with this was the King's insistence on removing from his coronation oath, when he was crowned in June 1911, the declaration of non-belief in the Roman Catholic faith that had been part of the oath since 1688.[9] Naturally, many of those from the Loyalist and Unionist communities in Northern Ireland

Fig. 10.05. William Conor, *State Opening of Parliament*, 1921. Courtesy of the Northern Ireland Assembly.

may have felt insecure, but there is little evidence, so far, that this influenced the creation of the spaces at Hillsborough Castle in general, or the Throne Room in particular.

Following its purchase in 1925, it was necessary to alter the house to create a suitable government residence. The change of use was also reflected in the change of name to Government House, which persisted until direct rule was introduced. The physical changes required not only the creation of private domestic space for the governor, his family and household, as well as reception rooms required for large-scale entertaining, but also the unusual requirement of space for a secretariat; a requirement found in ambassadorial residences throughout the world. While alterations to the Throne Room occurred in 1936, 1953, 1989 and 2010, and are planned for 2017/18, it was the interventions of 1925 that established a pattern for those that were to follow. Responsibility for the upkeep of the new Government House was quickly brought into question after its purchase. As stated in correspondence between the Office of Works in London and the Northern Ireland Ministry of Finance in Belfast, neither of which wanted responsibility, the maintenance and running costs of a governor's residence were in the hands of the dominion or colony in which it was located; but, as part of the United Kingdom, how was Northern Ireland to be dealt with?[10] The decision was made to transfer ownership of the house to the government of Northern Ireland, and this took place in January 1927.[11] This was, in part, due to the fact that annual budgets for Hillsborough Castle would have to be approved by the House of Commons at Westminster if it remained in 'home' government ownership.

A series of detailed bills outline the alterations and repairs carried out. Of note, the biggest alteration was the creation of the Governor's Stairs, an imperial style staircase rising from the ground floor to a set of new cloakrooms, which were now required following the change of use from a private family mansion to a government residence hosting large-scale events. The cost of this was £902.3.9, including £69 for Portland Stone, the installation of a new Wyatt window, and the Honduras mahogany used for the cloakrooms.[12] This practical requirement was seen as more important than the enhancement of the space we now know as the Throne Room, which was merely redecorated.[13] Discussions regarding the general decor of the Castle concluded that neutral tints, such as greys and creams with white detail, would be most appropriate.[14] It was felt that this would allow the walls to harmonize with any form of furniture or fabric that might be installed by future governors.[15] The intended overall effect was to be dignified, with little

Fig. 10.06.
The Ballroom
(Throne Room),
Hillsborough
Castle, Co. Down,
1926.
© Historic Royal
Palaces.

furniture.[16] It was suggested that Rosalind Hamilton, Duchess of Abercorn (1869–1958), wife of the first governor, should discuss colour schemes directly with Sir Lionel Earle of the Office of Works, as anything passing through the Governor's Office in Belfast was, in any case, forwarded to the Office of Works and to Sir Lionel.[17] Moving in similar circles, Earle was an occasional weekend guest at the Abercorns' country estate, Baronscourt, Co. Tyrone, and the Duchess would occasionally 'harry' him on her trips to London to move things along.[18] Thus, the simple colour scheme agreed upon also applied to the Throne Room. As shown in the 1926 photograph of the Throne Room, it was lit by the three glass-bowl light fittings that are extant today (Fig. 10.06). Apocryphally, it is claimed that these came from Sandringham House, Norfolk, as a gift from King George V; however, no evidence supports this. Stylistically they would appear to date from the period in which the house was redecorated in 1925, so it is more likely that they were purchased new by the Office of Works. To supplement these three ceiling lights, two gilt wall lights were brought from Baronscourt, which were then repaired and installed in the Throne Room, and remain there to this day.[19]

Discussion around the need to create a space used as a throne room, if not referred to as such, is evident from changes in proposals made during this period. Initially a throne was not intended. The original plan was to procure two Louis XIV parade sofas, which would be more appropriate for a space used primarily for music and entertaining.[20] However, very quickly it was felt that these should be substituted for a single throne chair.[21] The reason for this change is unknown at present. Some time later, it was felt that two throne chairs would be more appropriate and the decision was made to procure a second, which arrived from London in October 1925; together, the two were felt to look 'extremely well'.[22] The archives are yet to reveal who instigated this change and for what reason, but it likely anticipated the need for a seat for the spouse of the governor.

The need for a canopy of state above the thrones was also discussed, albeit briefly. Canopies can be seen in the Throne Room at Buckingham Palace, at St James's Palace, and at Dublin Castle. Nineteenth-century photographs show the same canopies in position. Research carried out by the Northern Ireland Ministry of Finance claimed that none of the British throne rooms, including that at Buckingham Palace, had a canopy, so the idea was dropped for Hillsborough, although it would later resurface again in 1991.[23] Why the staff of the Ministry of Finance made this claim is a mystery; the Palace of Holyroodhouse, Edinburgh, is the only British royal palace not to have a canopy above its thrones. Perhaps as a constituent part of the United Kingdom but not the centre of imperial power, Hillsborough Castle was seen as being on a par with it. Cost, and the proportions of the space, which is very long and low, may have dictated the decision not to include a canopy. It is also important to recognize that the throne chairs were representative of the monarch, 319 miles away in London, and were not *used* by the monarch. This may have negated the need for a canopy that, in accordance with standard ceremonial precedent, was typically required to cover the monarch's head while they were seated. While there is evidence of the monarch's representative, the governor, sitting on one of the throne chairs, there is no evidence that any of the monarchs who have stayed at Hillsborough Castle have done so.

Anxious to do away with 'the hotel look', the Duke of Abercorn provided a number of paintings from his Scottish house, Duddingston, Edinburgh and from Baronscourt, for Hillsborough Castle, in addition to approximately fifty of his own engravings and a number of mirrors.[24] This supplemented the few paintings provided by the Office of Works. However, the Office of Works raised the possibility of borrowing further pieces from the National Gallery in Dublin. The Duke, however, felt it was better not to approach the Gallery unless there were very specific paintings of 'decided historical value to Northern Ireland'.[25] This could suggest a certain reluctance on his part, rather than on the part of the London administration, to engage with the institutions of the new Irish Free State, but other motivations may have been at work – the Duke also declined an offer of paintings from the Tate in London, as he felt the responsibility for their care to be too great.[26]

Fig. 10.07. James Holland & Sons, design for the redecoration of the Throne Room, Hillsborough Castle, Co. Down, 1936. Ministry of Finance Papers, NI FIN/14/2/14. © Public Record Office of Northern Ireland.

The Throne Room after the Fire

In 1934, a major fire destroyed most of the central block of the house, including the Throne Room. In the wake of this calamity, responsibility for the site returned immediately to the Office of Works in London and the governor, the Duke of Abercorn, and his staff moved out for a period of two years.[27] Discussions regarding the decorative schemes started almost immediately, and it was stated within the Office of Works that 'their graces do not wish too much alteration but they would like the house to be more dignified'.[28] In order to contribute to this effect, the Abercorns requested that decorative schemes be introduced into the overdoors and architraves and that the entrances to state rooms, including the Throne Room, be widened and fitted with double doors, as we see them today.[29] The footprint of the Throne Room remained the same. The chandeliers, somehow, survived the fire. One concern raised about the new decorative scheme, which included a green silk wall lining, was the reduced freedom in the arrangement of pictures.[30] This would imply to a modern reader that the intention was not to hang many pictures or mirrors in this room; indeed, the sketch by designer Mr James of Holland & Sons, Mount Street, London, shows a very small number of mirrors, but a space that we would recognize as the Throne Room today (Fig. 10.07). The colour scheme of the newly created Ballroom (Throne Room) was to be a soft green, using textured damask.[31] This wall damask survives, in a rather ruinous state, and is to be replaced in late 2017.

No evidence survives to indicate how the government paintings were re-hung in the Throne Room, although the portraits of King George V and Queen Mary had been moved into the room from the State Entrance Hall some time between 1924 and 1936 and, like the chandeliers, had survived the fire.[32] This move is indicative of the evolution of the space from ballroom to throne room, which was then underway. In 2014 these royal portraits were hanging in an upstairs office and were relocated to the State Apartments by HRP. A portrait of each of the five governors was commissioned on their retirement; the artists including Derek Hill (1916–2000). It is unclear where they hung, as they do not appear in photographs of the Throne Room until 1991, and only then intermingled with other portraits, including that of the builder of Hillsborough, Wills Hill. In April 2014, HRP was told, apocryphally, that the governors' portraits always hung in the Throne Room and must be re-instated, but it would appear they did so for less than twenty years, from 1991.

After the retirement of the Duke of Abercorn in 1945, William Leveson-Gower, 4th Earl Granville (1880–1953), became governor and moved into Government House. Wartime shortage meant that no change was made upon his appointment, and domestic arrangements were the responsibility of the incumbent and not the state. This appointment was significant, however, in that Lady Granville, as Rose Bowes-Lyon, was the elder sister of HM Queen Elizabeth The Queen Mother, and therefore aunt to HM The Queen. As young princesses, Their Royal Highnesses Princess Elizabeth (as she then was) and Princess Margaret Rose (named for her aunt) carried out their first official lone engagements away from home in Northern Ireland, discretely supported by their aunt and uncle.

Alterations to the Throne Room from 1953

Following the arrival of John de Vere Loder, 2nd Baron Wakehurst (1895–1970) as the third governor in 1953, just ahead of HM The Queen's coronation tour of Northern Ireland, changes took place at Hillsborough Castle. Within the Throne Room, these concerned the need for more chairs for functions, and, for the first time, a carpet. It would appear that Margaret 'Peggy' de Vere Loder, Baroness Wakehurst (1899–1994) raised the question of the need for a carpet, and proposed obtaining a section of that used in Westminster Abbey as part of the coronation of HM The Queen on 2 June 1953, less than a month before her visit to Hillsborough. In response, David Eccles from the Ministry of Works wrote to Lady Wakehurst:

> Dear Peggy … A long time ago a statement was made that carpets from the Abbey would be sold and that churches would have priority … at this late stage [it] would mean redoing the whole thing.[33]

The response, then, was to commission the same carpet from the same supplier as that used for the coronation.[34] However, with no historical association and considering the cost, the idea was abandoned by the governor and Lady Wakehurst.[35] So for the coronation visit of HM The Queen in 1953, there was no carpet, and in February 1954 one was ordered from the Ulster Carpet Mills Ltd, chosen by Lady Wakehurst.[36]

The Throne Room today is also the setting for the tapestry, or more correctly, the applique banner, of the Royal Arms. The circumstances surrounding the creation of this banner are confusing. The banner was reputed to have been created in 1953 by the Royal School of Needlework for the coronation of HM The Queen, and some members of the school had commented on their involvement in producing it.[37] However, the small crown, known as the Tudor crown, at the top, technically a coronet, became popular with Queen Victoria after she became a widow in 1861 as it was easier to wear and it was subsequently used by monarchs in armorials from then until the death of George VI in 1952. It is therefore not used by Queen Elizabeth II.

A planned visit to Hillsborough Castle by Edward, Prince of Wales in 1926 forced the issue of the need for a banner, as at that point the west wall of the Throne Room was bare. In March 1926, the question of a piece of tapestry to hang in the 'Ball Room' in Government House behind the thrones was still being addressed, along with the suggestion that some 'prosperous person' be approached to fund it.[38] Professor Earls at the Belfast Technical College was approached, with a view to such a banner being made in one of his classes, free of charge.[39] Whether or not it was actually started at this stage is again unclear, as by 1935, the Office of Works was checking progress, only to be told: 'the Principal has not gone very far with the work of making the Banner'.[40] The delay was probably due to the fact that the banner was being worked up during a two-hour needlework class on Friday afternoons. It is understandable that the Office of Works was checking progress, as it was some months after the fire and rebuilding plans were underway. Concern was expressed that the lion and unicorn on the banner would appear to be sitting on the heads of the Duke and Duchess of Abercorn when they were seated on the thrones.[41] Following the death of King George V in January 1936, it was not until September that the question of whether the banner should retain the initials 'GR', or whether these should be changed to 'ER' in reference to the accession of King Edward VIII, was resolved.[42] As Hillsborough was an official royal residence, 'ER' was, of course, chosen. With the abdication of Edward VIII in December 1936, the banner was rapidly removed and stored, to be returned in 1953 following the coronation of his niece, Elizabeth Regina, and some alterations were made by the ladies of the school of needlework, some of whom recall this.[43]

The Throne Room under Direct Rule
Prior to the introduction of direct rule to Northern Ireland, in 1972, few changes are known to have been made by John Erskine, 1st Baron Erskine of Rerrick (1893–1980), who succeeded Wakehurst as governor, or by the last governor,

Baron Grey of Naunton. By 1987, the Secretary of State for Northern Ireland, Tom King, later Baron King of Bridgwater (*b.* 1933), had established an advisory committee for Hillsborough Castle. The remit of this new group was to advise on the structure, decoration, furnishing and maintenance of the Castle, and the planting and maintenance of the grounds.[44] This new committee was tasked with improving the aesthetic of the Hillsborough Castle rooms. In 1988, the chair of the committee reported on the condition of the rooms at that point:

> ... they have received no consistent oversite [*sic*] as distinct from piecemeal repair, since the last Governor of Northern Ireland left sixteen years ago. Though not dilapidated, they are a jumble of inconsistent styles with an anonymous, improvised, somewhat forlorn, un-lived in look.[45]

As funds were limited, the committee decided to focus on the state rooms in which the simple lines of the 1936 rebuild had remained. The committee's minutes show that they agreed to appoint the Dublin-based designer John O'Connell (of John J. O'Connell Architects) to carry out a survey and make recommendations, acknowledging him as one of the best people in Ireland to advise on Irish country houses.[46] O'Connell's stated influences included Castle Coole, Co. Fermanagh, and Fota House, Co. Cork, both late-Georgian Irish country houses from which it was felt that Hillsborough should derive inspiration.[47] In the Throne Room, as late as 2006, the committee had commissioned research into the wall fabric, installed in 1936, with a view to finding a sensible and financially viable solution for its replacement.[48] Additional proposals made, but not carried out, included three new ceiling chandeliers, larger than those installed in 1925. It was intended that these should hang level with a proposed canopy, which was intended to hang above the thrones.[49] As before, the canopy proposal was rejected, still on account of the cost, but this time by a committee consisting of, among others, senior ex-National Trust and Christie's auctioneers' employees.[50]

Conclusion

Despite the position of Hillsborough Castle as the official residence of the monarch in Northern Ireland since 1925, its Throne Room, as we have seen, differs from its counterparts in London and Edinburgh, as well as in Dublin, in several respects. While there can be no doubt about the status of the room, that status is not reflected to the same extent as it is elsewhere, particularly given the absence of a canopy of state. We have already seen that the scheme for this space, still referred to as the 'Ballroom' in 1925, was based on a need to ensure that the furniture of different governors would sit comfortably in neutral surroundings. This, coupled with the provision of minimal royal trappings, would suggest that the intended aim was not to create a specific perception of majesty but rather to achieve an overall effect that was adaptable and dignified, allowing for a variety of events, with a range of guest numbers. Attempts at enhancing that perception of majesty appear to have been conceived at different times, in particular with reference to the provision of a canopy over the throne chairs. However, whether for financial reasons, due to the low proportions of the room, or due to a lack of resolve, nothing came to pass. Who, then, was influencing the creation of the Throne Room at Hillsborough Castle? It is evident from the papers that survive, and more evidence may always surface, that the creation of what we now know as the Throne Room at Hillsborough Castle in 1925, which at the time was the ballroom of Government House, was firmly in the hands of the Office of Works in London, with the final say, where possible and practical, lying with the governor and his wife. The new, Unionist government of Northern Ireland was not involved in any way, until ownership was handed over to it after completion of the works. This continued following the fire of 1934, where the practical aspects of the reconstruction again returned to the care of the Office of Works in London, but with the governor and his wife once again having substantial input. The Imperial Office within the Office of Works dealt with embassies and governors' residences throughout the world and, as such, there was no involvement of the possibly insecure Unionist government of Northern Ireland. It is more the case that, rather than being seen as part of establishing a new Northern Irish identity within the United Kingdom, the creation of the Throne Room is best understood in the context of a centralized administration in London. It was steered by an overworked and underfunded government department in Whitehall, more used to dealing with lodges in Ascension Island, Nova Scotia or Queensland, and being directed by the personal ideas of various governors and their wives.

Endnotes

1   Most secondary sources describe the house within its wider setting and include Hillsborough Fort, the Market House, the Parish Church of St Malachy and the wider townscape, which was planned as a whole. See, for example, J. Barry, *Hillsborough: A Parish in the Ulster Plantation* (Belfast: W. Mullan, 1962). Barry claimed to have access to the family papers but his text has no referencing, and so modern historians have therefore no means of corroboration. He does not discuss the work carried out in 1925 when the Throne Room was created. See also J. Cornforth, 'Hillsborough Castle, Co. Down – I', *Country Life*, 188, 30 (28 July 1994), pp. 64–7; J. Cornforth, 'Hillsborough Castle, Co. Down – II', *Country Life*, 188, 31 (4 August 1994), pp. 48–51; C.E.B. Brett, *Buildings of North County Down* (Belfast: Ulster Architectural Heritage Society, 2002); P. Rankin, *Hillsborough Castle* (Belfast: Ulster Architectural Heritage Society, 1993). Rankin's book acts as a contributory chapter to the current and only Hillsborough Castle guidebook. A new guidebook, created by Historic Royal Palaces, is planned for 2019.

2   Letters between Sir Lionel Earle, Office of Works and the Secretary, HM Treasury, November–December 1923, Home Office Papers, National Archives of the United Kingdom, HO 45/13010.

3   Letter to Mr Martin-Jones from T.P. Lefanu, 20 January 1925, Home Office Papers, National Archives of the United Kingdom, HO 45/13010.

4   P. Maume, 'Lady Microbe and the Kailyard Viceroy: The Aberdeen viceroyalty, welfare monarchy, and the politics of philanthropy', in P. Gray and O. Purdue (eds), *The Irish Lord Lieutenancy c. 1541–1922* (Dublin: University College Dublin Press, 2012), p. 199; J. Loughlin, *The British Monarchy and Ireland: 1800 to the Present* (Cambridge: Cambridge University Press, 2007), p. 10.

5   Inventory, 1868, Downshire Papers, Public Record Office of Northern Ireland, D671/A/38/12.

6   Inventories, 1878 & 1909, Downshire Papers, Public Record Office of Northern Ireland, D671/A/38/4 & D671/A/38/14.

7   K. Rose, *King George V* (London: Weidenfeld and Nicolson, 1983) p. 240.

8   See Loughlin, *The British Monarchy and Ireland*, p. 318.

9   J. Wolffe, 'Protestantism, Monarchy and the Defence of Christian Britain 1835–2005', in C.G. Brown and M. Snape (eds), *Secularisation in the Christian World: Essays in Honour of Hugh McLeod* (Surrey and Vermont: Ashgate, 2010), p. 63.

10 Memorandum to Secretary of Ministry of Finance for Northern Ireland from Sir Lionel Earle, Office of Works, undated, Office of Works Papers, National Archives of the United Kingdom, WORK 27/17.

11 Conveyance Papers, Treasury Solicitor Papers, National Archives of the United Kingdom, TS 18-393.

12 Internal Alterations and Repairs Schedule Bill 2, Ministry of Finance Papers, Public Record Office of Northern Ireland, FIN/46/2.

13 Letter to the Duchess of Abercorn from Sir Lionel Earle, Office of Works, 18 November 1924, Governor of Northern Ireland Papers,

Public Record Office of Northern Ireland, GOV/3/8/3.

14 Letter to the Duchess of Abercorn from Commander Henderson, Private Secretary of the Governor, 18 November 1924, Governor of Northern Ireland Papers, Public Record Office of Northern Ireland, GOV/3/8/3.

15 Memorandum headed 'Colour Scheme of Decoration for Hillsborough Castle', 26 February 1925, Governor of Northern Ireland Papers, Public Record Office of Northern Ireland, GOV/3/8/74, folder 5.

16 Memorandum headed 'Decoration of Castle', 26 February 1925, Governor of Northern Ireland Papers, Public Record Office of Northern Ireland, GOV/3/8/74.

17 Letter to the Duchess of Abercorn from Commander Henderson, Private Secretary of the Governor, 18 November 1924, Governor of Northern Ireland Papers, Public Record Office of Northern Ireland, GOV/3/8/3.

18 Letter to the Duchess of Abercorn from Commander Henderson, Private Secretary of the Governor, 18 November 1924, Governor of Northern Ireland Papers, Public Record Office of Northern Ireland, GOV/3/8/3.

19 Letter to Commander Henderson, Private Secretary of the Governor from Robert Bell, Demesne Office, Baronscourt, 13 March 1925, Governor of Northern Ireland Papers, Public Record Office of Northern Ireland, GOV/3/8/74.

20 Memorandum headed 'Proposed Alterations in the Schedule – Ball Room', 1925, Governor of Northern Ireland Papers, Public Record Office of Northern Ireland, GOV/3/8/5.

21 Letter to Mr Powell, Office of Works from Commander Henderson, Private Secretary of the Governor, 15 October 1925, Governor of Northern Ireland Papers, Public Record Office of Northern Ireland, GOV/3/8/5.

22 Letter to Mr Powell, Office of Works from Commander Henderson, Private Secretary of the Governor, 15 October 1925, Governor of Northern Ireland Papers, Public Record Office of Northern Ireland, GOV/3/8/5.

23 Telephone message from Mr Thompson, Ministry of Finance, 17 July 1925, Governor of Northern Ireland Papers, Public Record Office of Northern Ireland, GOV/3/8/74.

24 Letter to S.G. Tallents, Ministry of Finance from Commander Henderson, Private Secretary of the Governor, 6 October 1925, Governor of Northern Ireland Papers, Public Record Office of Northern Ireland, GOV/3/8/5.

25 Letter to S.G. Tallents, Ministry of Finance from Commander Henderson, Private Secretary of the Governor, 4 October 1925, Governor of Northern Ireland Papers, Public Record Office of Northern Ireland, GOV/3/8/5.

26 Ibid.

27 Letter to Mr Blackmore, Cabinet Secretary from Oscar Henderson, Private Secretary of the Governor, 9 August 1934, Cabinet of Northern Ireland Papers, Public Record Office of Northern Ireland, CAB-9T-2-1.

28 Memorandum headed 'Notes on Plans for discussion with Mr Rippingham', undated, Governor of Northern Ireland Papers, Public Record Office of Northern Ireland, GOV/3/84, folder 9.

29 Ibid.

30 Letter to Commander Henderson, Private Secretary of the Governor from Anon., Ministry of Finance, 26 October 1936, Governor of Northern Ireland Papers, Public Record Office of Northern Ireland, GOV/3/8/85.

31 Memorandum headed 'Colour Scheme', undated, Governor of Northern Ireland Papers, Public Record Office of Northern Ireland, GOV/3/8/79.

32 Uncatalogued photograph albums, commissioned in autumn 1926 and July 1936, Historic Royal Palaces Collection.

33 Letter to Lady Wakehurst from David Eccles, 24 November 1953, Governor of Northern Ireland Papers, Public Record Office of Northern Ireland, GOV/3/8/83, folder 2.

34 Letter to Mrs Haslett, Assistant Private Secretary to the Governor from Anon., Ministry of Finance, 23 February 1954, Governor of Northern Ireland Papers, Public Record Office of Northern Ireland, GOV/3/8/83, folder 2.

35 Memorandum to Governor and Lady Wakehurst, 24 November 1953, Governor of Northern Ireland Papers, Public Record Office of Northern Ireland, GOV/3/8/83, folder 2.

36 Letter to Mrs Haslett, Assistant Private Secretary to the Governor from Anon., Ministry of Finance, 23 February 1954, Governor of Northern Ireland Papers, Public Record Office of Northern Ireland, GOV/3/8/83, folder 2.

37 Conversation between author and David Anderson, former House Manager, who had hosted the students to afternoon tea at Hillsborough Castle.

38 Letter to Mr Thompson, Ministry of Finance from Commander Henderson, Private Secretary of the Governor, 20 March 1926, Governor of Northern Ireland Papers, Public Record Office of Northern Ireland, GOV/3/8/44.

39 Letter to Mr Thompson, Ministry of Finance from Commander Henderson, Private Secretary of the Governor, 23 July 1928, Governor of Northern Ireland Papers, Public Record Office of Northern Ireland, GOV/3/8/44.

40 Letter to Commander Henderson, Private Secretary of the Governor from Mr Ingelby-Smith, Ministry of Finance, 13 March 1935, Governor of Northern Ireland Papers, Public Record Office of Northern Ireland, GOV/3/8/44.

41 Letter to Mr Rippingham, Architect at Ministry of Finance from Commander Henderson, Private Secretary of the Governor, 29 September 1936, Governor of Northern Ireland Papers, Public Record Office of Northern Ireland, GOV/3/8/84, folder 10.

42 Ibid.

43 Conversation between author and David Anderson, former House Manager, who had hosted the students to afternoon tea at Hillsborough Castle.

44 Letter to Katy Barron, Loans Officer of Royal Collection Trust from Dese McCall, 14 September 2001, uncatalogued papers of the Northern Ireland Office, at Stormont House.

45 Letter to Mr Pease, Principal Finance Officer at the Northern Ireland Office from John Lewis-Crosby, Chair of Advisory Committee, 25 July 1988, uncatalogued papers of the Northern Ireland Office, at Stormont House.

46 Minutes of the Advisory Committee, 22 December 1987, uncatalogued papers of the Northern Ireland Office, at Stormont House.

47 Conversation between author and Commander Maxwell, Secretary of Advisory Committee, 19 August 2016.

48 Minutes of the Advisory Committee, 23 January 2006, uncatalogued papers of the Northern Ireland Office, at Stormont House.

49 Public Services Agency Works Schedule, Annex A, 1988, uncatalogued papers of the Northern Ireland Office, at Stormont House.

50 Discussions between author and former committee members Commander Maxwell, Mark Donnelly, Tom King and Lady O'Neill, summer 2016.

Index

Note: Figures are indicated by '*f*' following a page number.